MIDPASSAGE

MID-PASSAGE

Alexander Herzen
and European Revolution,
1847–1852

JUDITH E. ZIMMERMAN

UNIVERSITY OF PITTSBURGH PRESS

Series in Russian and East European Studies No. 10

Published by the University of Pittsburgh Press, Pittsburgh, Pa., 15260
Copyright © 1989, University of Pittsburgh Press
All rights reserved
Feffer and Simons, Inc., London
Manufactured in the United States of America

Library of Congress Cataloging-in-Publication Data

Zimmerman, Judith E.
  Midpassage : Alexander Herzen and European revolution, 1847–1852 / Judith E. Zimmerman.
    p. cm. — (Russian and East European studies ; 10)
  Bibliography: p. 283.
  Includes index.
  ISBN 0-8229-3827-8
  1. Herzen, Aleksandr, 1812–1870—Political and social views.
2. Herzen, Aleksandr, 1812–1870—Biography—Exile—Europe.
3. Europe—History—1848–1849. 4. Revolutionists—Soviet Union—Biography. 5. Authors, Russian—19th century—Biography.
I. Title. II. Title: Midpassage. III. Series: Russian and East European studies (Pittsburgh, Pa.) ; 10.
DK209.6.H4Z56 1989
947'.073'0924—dc19
                                        88-23610
                                            CIP

Portions of this book appeared in somewhat different form in "Herzen, Proudhon and *La Voix du Peuple:* A Reconsideration," *Russian History* 2, no. 4 (Winter 1984) and in "Herzen, Herwegh, Marx," in *Imperial Russia, 1900–1917: State, Society, Opposition. Essays in Honor of Marc Raeff,* ed. Ezra Mendelsohn and Marshall S. Shatz (DeKalb, Ill.: Northern Illinois University Press, 1988).

CONTENTS

	Acknowledgments	*vii*
	Preface	ix
1.	The Background	3
2.	The Traveler	29
3.	Paris: The First Months	50
4.	Herzen and the Paris Revolution	76
5.	Geneva and Proudhon	107
6.	The Uncensored Voice	135
7.	The Crisis	166
8.	The Revolutionary Community	194
	Conclusion	221
	Notes	231
	Bibliography	283
	Index	295

ACKNOWLEDGMENTS

MATURITY has become one of our most elusive goals. As the waistline thickens and the hair turns gray, we still feel that we have not yet quite grown up, but one day it will indeed happen. Each milestone seems to mark the transition, until another looms on the horizon. For me, this book marks one such milestone, for it completes the transition from research undertaken as a graduate student to independent unsupervised work. I was fortunate, however, in being able to recapture at least some of the atmosphere of student life when working on *Midpassage*. A sabbatical leave from the University of Pittsburgh at Greensburg allowed me to spend a semester in New York, back at Columbia University. It was different, to be sure. The great iron gates around the Morningside Heights Campus, that we thought were there only for decoration and to commemorate one or another ancient graduating class, now serve their intended purposes and usually are firmly locked. Library access is through a single door, and security is tight. The Russian Institute, now the W. Averell Harriman Institute for Advanced Study of the Soviet Union, has moved from an old brownstone to a highrise. And, of course, the undergraduates are ever younger.

But for all the change in appearance, I was fortunate to find continuity in substance. My graduate school mentors, Marc Raeff and Leopold Haimson, now friends and colleagues, provided guidance and support as before. For all its high-tech splendor, there was a touch of the familiar about the Institute. And the library resources, behind the locked gates, were superb as ever. My first thanks, then, to Columbia University and its people, then and now.

Research for this book carried me from Columbia to archive collections in a number of European cities. While grateful to all of them, a special thanks to the smaller ones. Stephen Corrsin, then at the

ACKNOWLEDGMENTS

Bakhmetev Archive, Columbia, not only, provided a helpful introduction to the materials I knew were there, but also directed me to a number of gems that I would never have found otherwise. In Liestal, despite a severe language barrier, the staff of the Dichtermuseum put the Herwegh materials at my disposal with exceptional graciousness. At the Manchester Cooperative Union, I was looking for needles in a haystack; the staff was most accommodating, and I even found some.

Pittsburgh is a difficult place to do Russian history; at times the isolation seemed overwhelming. Special thanks are due Jonathan Harris, who breached that isolation. He read and criticized the entire document, first as a friend, and then to encourage its submission to the University of Pittsburgh Press.

Library resources are a particularly difficult problem here. I wish to thank Eleanor Milton, librarian at the University of Pittsburgh, Greensburg, whose mastery of the OCLC system brought materials to me with incredible efficiency; without her help, it would have taken far longer to complete this work. My colleagues at UPG, Colette Levin, Joanne Viano, and Guy Rossetti helped with translations from French and Italian.

PREFACE

RUSSIA'S modern revolutionary movement really begins with Alexander Herzen. He is often considered the first of the émigré revolutionaries. This is not strictly true—from the time of the Decembrists Western Europe had hosted a sprinkling of disenchanted Russians, some of them guilty of criminal opposition to the government. It is possible, however, to see in him the beginning of the "emigration," as a force for revolutionary change. Herzen's uniqueness came from his using the West as a haven while continuing to direct his energies toward Russia. "Here," he wrote his friends, "I am your uncensored voice, your free press, your chance representative."[1] Moreover, he would attempt to be more than an isolated, individual voice; he would establish institutional mechanisms for struggle (the Free Russian Press and his journals), and would gather about him other émigrés in a concerted effort to change conditions at home.[2]

The present work traces the origins of Herzen's vocation during his first years abroad. Between 1847, when he came to Western Europe, and 1852, when he settled in London, Herzen chose a life of permanent emigration, while at the same time making Russia his battleground. He also accumulated the personal and financial capital he would need to carry out his mission. This preparatory work is the subject of this book.

The first mechanism by which Herzen would serve as his friends' "uncensored voice" was the Free Russian Press, which he established in 1853 in London. His plan was to provide a forum where different views could be freely expressed, different programs and ideologies tested against public opinion. Eventually the press did indeed serve that function, although Herzen had to struggle for several years before he awakened a response in Russia. In the interim, he published his own works through the press, and thus publicized his own views, perhaps to a greater extent than he had originally anticipated.

The views he propagated, like the pattern of his career, were balanced between Russian and Western values and themes. His theory of "Russian socialism" was developed during his first years in the West and was originally presented to a Western audience. Essentially, it consisted of a belief that the Russian peasantry's communal tradition might become the source of an advanced socialism, if it could be infused with the individual liberty sought by Western radicals (see chapter 6). A stratum of educated, revolutionary, upper-class Russians would provide the link between the Russian peasants and European ideology.

The combination of Russian traditions and European ideals in his program, as well as in his political activity, is emblematic of Herzen's lifetime pattern of dividing his loyalties between Russia and Western Europe. He began, in Russia, as the leader of the "Westernizer" circle, which insisted that the path of development for Russia must be the adoption of Western values and institutions, as well as Western technology. When he arrived in Western Europe in 1847, he became acquainted with Western revolutionaries, and witnessed Western revolutions. But by 1849, he had turned his attention to the revolutionary potential of his native land.

In part, the ideological and emotional return to Russia was the result of disillusionment Herzen suffered in the West, but it also reflected a new literary role. By the time he founded the Free Russian Press, he had made significant contributions to Western radical literature, as historian of the revolution of 1848, as independent theorist, and—in the position that gave him special status in the West—as interpreter of Russia to European radical opinion. "Russian socialism" was part of the new image of the Russian people he presented to his Western colleagues. He saw the Russians as temporarily passive opponents, rather than willing abettors, of the repressive policies of the Russian sovereigns; one day his people too would join the international struggle for freedom. This image retained its vitality until the revolution of 1917, and has still by no means completely disappeared.[3] By the early 1850s Herzen had established himself in the eyes of Western radicals as the chief spokesman for the Russian left.

With the founding of the press, Herzen's position between Russia and the West had crystallized. He was self-consciously and vehemently Russian, and his primary energies were directed toward bringing about change in Russia. However, that was a task to be accomplished only in the freedom offered by the West, specifically by Great Britain. Moreover, the role he had adopted—revolutionary journalist—was one he discovered in the West.

In Russia, there was not as yet a milieu in which revolutionary ideals could be propagated and nurtured. Eventually, to be sure, there would be a flourishing radical subculture, but during the height of Herzen's activity, he could find such a supportive community only among Western radicals, who provided him not only with moral support, but with the tools of his trade as well—everything from type and typesetters to networks of smugglers to carry his publications across the Russian border. Furthermore, at home his prestige and that of his publications were enhanced by his role within the international revolutionary movement. His readers might have been hard pressed to differentiate between Pierre-Joseph Proudhon and Louis Blanc, but both were famous radicals, and Herzen's personal relations with both of them legitimized his claim to speak in the name of the revolutionary movement. The first issues of *Poliarnaia zvezda* [Polar Star] contained greetings and testimonials by many of the leading lights of European radicalism. Herzen actively solicited these letters, used his lesser-known contacts to get them from their more famous comrades, and—as his correspondence testifies—spent a great deal of energy on them.[4] They were, he believed, an important source of legitimation for his journal: these strong men, he wrote, realize that their place is with the enemies of Russian autocracy, not with the enemies of the Russian people: "V. Hugo, G. Mazzini, J. Michelet, Louis Blanc, Proudhon are with us! Nicholas used to conclude his manifestoes, saying 'God is with us.' We do not need the aid of the tsarist God; *the revolution is with us, socialism is with us!*"[5]

This book is, then, about Herzen's physical movement from East to West and his intellectual search, which culminated in the balance between Europe and Russia that characterized his maturity. But these years of transition involved still more. Almost like a character from mythology, Herzen underwent a series of ordeals during this period in which his old life was destroyed and from which he emerged tempered and sobered, ready for his vocation. Almost everything that he brought with him from home was lost: his circle of friends, and his homeland; his faith in the West, his faith in revolution, and his faith in the revolutionaries. He also lost much of his family—his mother, a young son, and his wife did not survive these years. Finally, the terrible family crisis of 1849–1852 shattered his youthful faith in the redemptive power of love and friendship.

Herzen regularly used metaphors of sea travel and its hazards. The intellectual passage he was undertaking he described in *S togo berega* [From the Other Shore]. Images of storms at sea and shipwrecks are scattered through his writing, and then they found terrifying reflection in his life—in the shipwreck that killed his son. Even after the tragedy, the metaphor does not disappear entirely from his work. The title of this work—*Midpassage*—expresses my sense of Herzen's political, intellectual, and emotional movement, and also reflects Herzen's own imagery.

By 1852 Herzen had emerged from the ordeal to make a new life and a new career for himself. The present work ends at the brink of this new life, with Herzen in England, and with the materials prepared that he would need for his future activity. With the exception of the first chapter on background, and the last, which deals with the revolutionary milieu during Herzen's London life, *Midpassage* is limited to the years of transition. It is intended to be self-contained, but I hope to follow it with another volume devoted to the London period.

The major concern of this work is to explore the process by which Herzen became an effective political actor. I believe that an essential element in this development was for him to become a part of an established revolutionary community. Thus, I explore in detail the manner in which he built up a network of contacts among the European radicals active in the various revolutionary movements of 1848 and show how these contacts determined his position within the radical community.

There are two foci to this discussion of Herzen and European revolution. Once he had made the decision to remain an exile, he first sought a political movement in which he could take a major part. This demanded defining the revolutionary process so as to provide a role for a Russian, who had no immediate hope of revolution in his native land, and no movement of his own to head. Herzen responded by stressing the internationalism of revolution. This was a strand of radical thought that long predated Herzen's arrival in Europe, and one he sought to develop. Up through the collaboration with Proudhon on *La Voix du peuple*, described in chapter 5, this effort was paramount in his activity. The attempt failed; revolutionary internationalism had a long and fascinating history of its own, but not in a form in which an Alexander Herzen could participate. And so he turned his energies to Russia and its special concerns.

But, as indicated above, even Herzen's Russian orientation would not have been possible without a supportive milieu in which he could function. The other focus to this work is Herzen's gradual integration into the revolutionary community. The Herzen who returned to his countrymen through the printed word was not the same isolated *littérateur* who had left Russia six years earlier. He lived now within a new community, was accepted by other radicals as a compatriot in the new fatherland of exile. Thus, he was able to present himself to his Russian readers as a participant in a viable tradition, a person who spoke the language of European revolution even as he provided a special Russian color to European doctrines.

Herzen's intellectual growth and the formation of his contacts with the European left took place in a constantly changing environment in which yesterday's harried oppositionists first had a chance to snatch at real power, then subsided again into illegal, often émigré coteries. With each change in political conditions, the nature and scope of Herzen's contacts shifted, until finally the exile community, where he eventually found his home, was established.

The process was complex, and chance encounters played as great a role as conscious choice in determining Herzen's final position. As any casual reader of biographies of Karl Marx knows, there was no unified, homogeneous radical community; instead, radical thinkers and politicians from many different countries were torn between their desire to unite their efforts in a common cause, and centrifugal forces created by mutual antipathies and power rivalries within the radical camp. Therefore, an exploration of Herzen's contacts involves considerable concentration on the revolutionary coteries and an analysis of just which groups Herzen ended up working with, and why.

The revolutionary milieu was a nascent social environment as well as an arena of political conflict. Midcentury socialists looked beyond the seizure of political power to the creation of a more rational, harmonious social order in which human instincts and passions would be guided by reason, rather than being repressed by an obsolete religious and moral code. While waiting for revolution to transform society as a whole, they attempted in their own lives to redefine various aspects of personal mores in order to create a little society of their own, a model for the future.[6]

In addition to capturing the fullness of the revolutionary milieu, I have attempted to keep in focus the fullness of Herzen himself. Intellectually, he was a skilled writer, a sensitive and perceptive literary critic, and an acute and highly intelligent observer of the contemporary political world with a flair for historical generalization. But he was also a man profoundly involved with and influenced by personal relationships: a family man with a wife and three young children and with a great need for friendship.

The son of a landlord who was a member of one of Russia's most prominent families, Herzen was born to great wealth. He succeeded in preserving most of his property, even as he became an exile socialist revolutionary. Perhaps as a carryover from his artistocratic heritage, he always lived in the midst of an extended domestic group. He left Russia in a party of eight; and even at his most isolated, in London in 1852, he lived with a son, a friend and hanger-on, and domestic servants. Moreover, his home was open to a series of tutors for his son who were also political allies of the father. His was a world of property to be managed, which meant regular dealing with bankers and their agents; the Russian revolutionary had good relations with his Rothschild financial advisers. It was also a world of mid-nineteenth-century sociability and extensive social contacts. Indeed, part of the fascination of Herzen's life is how he transformed the institutions of the rich—at-homes and calling cards, tutors and governesses—into instruments of radical politics.

The single most important source for Herzen's life is his own account, *Byloe i dumy* [My Past and Thoughts]. Although it is a magnificent work of literature, and surprisingly accurate in detail, it is still necessary for the scholar to stand at a certain distance from Herzen's masterpiece. It was not conceived as a unified work, but was, rather, written in segments and published separately over a sixteen-year period (1852–1868).[7] While the sections dealing with Herzen's youth in Russia constitute a coherent chronological account, this is not the case for the period after his departure. (Even the early sections are not complete; Herzen rarely mentioned people who were still alive and living in Russia at the time he wrote; thus, his brother and Natalie's family disappear almost entirely, the circle shrinks to its most crucial members, and generally for all its apparent fullness the account is pared down.) In the European segments, Herzen dealt with individuals and episodes in a series of vignettes that stressed his own responses to surrounding events. He made no attempt to give a complete account either of his own life or of the lives and politics of his subjects. Precision was unnecessary in any case, since his Russian readers were in no position to follow the complexities of émigré politics; they wanted a good story, and that is what Herzen gave them.

Because the period under investigation, 1847–1852, is one of transition, and moreover one for which documentation is relatively sparse, it has received little attention in the secondary literature. The standard Soviet work, El'sberg's biography of Herzen, largely limits itself to using Herzen's own writing, published and unpublished, and adds little to *Byloe i dumy*.[8] More substantial work has been done in the West, but it still does not address the issues raised in this work.

The single most important biographical study is Martin Malia's *Alexander Herzen and the Birth of Russian Socialism*.[9] Malia focuses on Herzen's psychological makeup and intellectual development. The content of the ideas that influenced Herzen and the way these ideas functioned in the Russian milieu are analyzed very closely, but Malia has little interest in the mature Herzen. Although he extended the work to 1852, in order to argue that it was his Russian ideology, and not his Western experiences, that determined Herzen's reactions to the West and revolution, the section dealing with Herzen in the West is truncated and inaccurate in detail.

There is no similarly substantial study of the mature Herzen. The only full-scale work, E. H. Carr's *The Romantic Exiles*, concentrates almost exclusively on the personal relationships of Herzen and his entourage.[10] Carr did not concern himself with the milieu within which the extended Herzen family functioned, and he paid little attention to Herzen's ideological development because he did not take his views seriously.

In contrast to Carr, other scholars have explored specific works by Herzen, or his views on specific subjects, almost in isolation from his personal, social, and political life.[11] The monographic literature has also tended to concentrate on episodes from Herzen's later life, when his political influence was at its height. I feel that for all the value of such studies, they present a somewhat one-sided view, for Herzen was not an isolated intellect surveying the political and social scene *sub specie aeternitatis*, but a person who quickly adopted the attitudes of a defined segment of public opinion—while, of course, adding his own Russian and individual traits. One historian who has managed to convey the fullness of his subject is N. Ia. Eidel'man, who has

PREFACE

written splendid studies of Herzen's Russian contacts during his London years, but I know of no similar works on the earlier period, or that deal with Herzen's European life.[12]

I hope that this study can convey something of the richness of Herzen as a human being, and can also integrate his story with that of the European revolutionary movement more thoroughly than has been done before. By analyzing the origins of his Western career, it will provide new perspective on the manner in which he functioned during the great years to follow.

MIDPASSAGE

1
THE BACKGROUND

Well, having found myself in Pokorsky's group . . . I was completely reborn. I curbed my conceit, began asking questions, learned, rejoiced, worshiped—in short, it was like entering some kind of church. Yes indeed, when I think about our meetings, well, my God, there was much that was uplifting and affecting in them! Imagine a gathering of half-a-dozen boys, our only light one tallow candle, tea like slops and dry biscuits as old as Adam—but if only you'd heard our speeches and looked at our faces! Excitement in everyone's eyes, cheeks on fire, our hearts beating fast, we'd talk about God, about truth, about the future of humanity, about poetry, sometimes talking nonsense, carried away by empty words, but what did that matter! . . . And the night would fly away calmly and smoothly as if on wings. And then grey dawn would break and we'd go our separate ways, brimful of feelings, happy, honourable, sober (we never even thought of having strong drink), with a kind of pleasant drowsiness in our souls. . . . I'd even gaze in a sort of trustful way at the stars as if they'd grown closer to me and easier to understand. . . . Oh, it was a marvelous time then, and I don't want to believe that it's all gone in vain! And indeed it hasn't gone in vain—not even for those whom life may have trivialized later.[1]

WITH this fictional account of the Stankevich circle, Turgenev introduced the Russian reading public to one of the distinctive institutions of nineteenth-century Moscow. While certain of the characteristics Turgenev provides are unique to one circle, or are even entirely fictional—primarily the poverty and sobriety—others could be found in a number of groups. The passionate intensity, the involvement with philosophical and moral issues rather than mundane reality, and the belief that belonging to the circle had been a transfiguring experience in the members' lives were generally true of these groups.

The fictional Rudin and Lezhnev were not more enthusiastic about their circle memories than was Alexander Herzen, for whom circle membership (and leadership) in the 1830s and 1840s constituted one of the high points of his life.[2]

Participation in the circle gave Herzen a model of what life in a humanely organized society would be like; it helped to form his views and his intellectual approach to solving problems, and the circle members remained his imagined audience long after he had lost face-to-face contact with them.[3] When this little model universe lost its cohesion, the bereavement Herzen suffered was one of the major factors impelling him to leave Russia for Western Europe.

Herzen actually belonged to two successive circles. The first, made up of students and recent graduates of Moscow University, was a less philosophical (and more alcoholic) counterpart to Rudin's "Pokorsky circle." It broke up when most of its members were arrested in 1834. The second coalesced in the mid-1840s from remnants of the old Herzen and Stankevich circles. The new group took on an ideological and propagandistic character, becoming the "Westernizers," in opposition to the rival, conservative Slavophiles. It was this second circle that ultimately launched Herzen into the West.

The Westernizers differed in some important respects from the student circles. For one thing, the group was older and involved women as well as men, since it included some wives, one or two widows of circle members, and at least one sister.[4] Thanks primarily to Herzen, it was decidedly prosperous; the group's activities were centered around comfortable Moscow salons and an estate rented by the Herzens for two successive summers (1845 and 1846). It was necessarily in a closer, if uneasy, relationship to the workaday world than were the student groups. The general tone is less that of an ascetic student commune than of Bloomsbury.

The most fundamental continuity in function between the two Herzen circles lay in the fact that both served to insulate their members from the reigning values of Nicholaevan Russia. It was difficult for circle members to accept wealth that was based on the ownership of serfs, and unquestioning enrollment in the corrupt bureaucracy that ruled their country was equally painful for them. In accord with the circle ethos, the wealthiest landowner, Nikolai Ogarev, freed most of his serfs and further legitimized his role by attempting (unsuccessfully) to turn his remaining property into an example of progressive and cooperative industrial development. Less wealthy members had to earn their living within the oppressive system, but they too avoided the service, looking instead for careers in the professions. They thereby managed to maintain a certain distance from the government's values.

Members of the circles also rejected prevailing sexual mores. They condemned both the crude depravity and the loveless marriages of convenience of their parents, and they believed that relations between the sexes should be based on mutual respect, esteem, and affection. By and large, they married. They knew only too well how exploitative free unions were in a society based on male power and privilege, for Herzen himself, his wife, Natalie, and her closest friend Tatiana Astrakova all were bastards. On the other hand, they did not believe that the bonds of marriage were absolute, and they tolerated irregularities in cases, such as Ogarev's, where a marriage had gone sour and divorce was unobtainable. (The degree of tolerance varied, however, and some circle members found Ogarev's emotional involvements after his marriage irresponsible and unacceptable.)[5]

While the circle rejected prevailing social values, it believed in and tried to live by its own. Informality, tolerance, honesty, intellectual examination of accepted values, and the cultivation of sensibility— values that were in very short supply in the society about them—were all part of the circle's ethos. Thus the circle was implicitly subversive. It also rejected the Slavophiles' idealization of the Russian past and present; circle members could see only too clearly that the people of their country were not merely poor and submissive, but also ignorant, dirty and violent, and kept that way through the unlimited arbitrary power of landowners and bureaucrats. Through teaching and example, members hoped to help enlighten and humanize their country and to lead it away from its brutal, benighted condition to a more humane future. The philosophic justification for their views of social and political change came from Hegel, whom they interpreted in a progressive, "leftist," manner.

After his arrest in 1834, Herzen had spent five years in exile, first in Viatka, on the eastern border of European Russia, and then in more comfortable Vladimir, which was close enough to Moscow to enable him to elope with Natalie. He was allowed to return to Moscow in 1839. In *Byloe i dumy*, he describes how he discovered on his return that the members of the Stankevich circle had become fascinated by Hegel and were vigorously promoting a conservative interpretation of his views. (Stankevich himself was in Germany at this time, and would not survive to return to Russia.) Since the real, they argued, was the rational, the Russian state by its very existence demonstrated its rationality and legitimacy. In self-defense, the rebellious Herzen was forced to take up the study of Hegel himself to try to refute the new doctrine.[6] There is no reason to doubt the essential accuracy of Herzen's account, although it is certainly somewhat overdrawn for humorous effect. But the impression it gives of a monolithic devotion to Hegel among the *intelligenty* is exaggerated. By and large, it was men fundamentally more conservative than Herzen who were swept up by the enthusiasm for Hegel. Herzen mentions only two Hegelians from the circles by name, Vissarion Belinskii and Mikhail Bakunin, and they were indeed two of the most visible and influential members of the Moscow intelligentsia. Bakunin led the Stankevich circle at this period and proseletyzed enthusiastically, and Belinskii's "conversion" had special force because he was so obviously sacrificing his rebellious attitude to the demands of the new doctrine.[7] The sudden surge of conservatism does not seem to have influenced the former members of Herzen's own circle. In all probability, conservative Hegelianism looked so powerful to Herzen because it was the only coherent politico-philosophical system current at the time.

Herzen himself did not stay around for the combat, but left Moscow almost at once for St. Petersburg, and in a few months he was exiled again, this time to Novgorod. It was only in the summer of 1842 that he was able to return to Moscow and reestablish the circle. He used the interim to study Hegel on his own, with the help of books and (no doubt) advice from his Moscow friends, and he arrived at a leftist, revolutionary interpretation of Hegel's dialectic of development. The dialectic, he argued, implied that every social form would be succeeded by its opposite; this included the existing autocratic state. Once a system had become outmoded, it was no longer rational, and therefore no longer had any legitimate claim to continued reality; thus revolutionary replacement of an "irrational" system was justified. This interpretation was made public, in very aesopian language, in Herzen's "Diletantizm v nauke" [Dilettantism in Science], published in *Otechestvennyia zapiski* [Notes of the Fatherland] in 1843.[8]

While Herzen was undertaking his study of Hegel, Bakunin, the loudest spokesman for the conservative, romantic interpretation of the dialectic, left Russia. Once in Germany he began his own evolution to a leftist position not unlike Herzen's own. Belinskii, partly under Herzen's influence, repudiated his own infatuation with the status quo and emerged from the period of "reconciliation with reality" determined not to let his commonsense understanding of the world about him again be clouded by lofty and abstruse philosophical explanations. Thus, by 1842, the fad for conservative Hegelianism had lost its spokesmen, and we hear no more of it in the groups in which Herzen moved.

Herzen's interpretation of Hegel was radical, as were his political views. By the time the Westernizer circle formed, he had become thoroughly alienated from the political and social reality surrounding him. His second, utterly unjustified, exile, despite its relatively mild nature, enraged him. His experience as a bureaucrat in provincial towns had given him first-hand knowledge of the corruption, incompetence, and ignorance of government and society outside the capitals. He even managed to blame the government for his wife's ill health and the couple's personal difficulties. His philosophy corresponded to his mood. Herzen was particularly pleased by an article he read in 1842 in Arnold Ruge's *Deutsche Jahrbücher*. Entitled "The Reaction in Germany," it was one of the few he saw that matched his own extremism, which it expressed in the phrase, "The passion for destruction is also a creative passion." He was even more pleased when he learned, a few days after reading the article, that the author was the Russian, former romantic conservative Bakunin.[9]

But at home, in the circle, Herzen was at the extreme pole right from the start. More representative was Timofei Granovskii, a young historian at the University of Moscow with whom Herzen became friendly after his own return to the city. Granovskii had studied for several years at the University of Berlin, and there he imbibed the prevailing academic liberal-left Hegelianism. For people who took this approach, Hegel promised progress toward freedom, and philosophy was to be a means to bring about enlightenment and change.[10] The difference between this view and Herzen's was one of tone. Granovskii was no radical—he had a deep love for the civilization of Western Europe, hoped to inspire his students with an appreciation of Western history, and believed Russia would one day become a part of this civilization.

Herzen was far more critical of the West. As the forties passed, he turned his attention from German philosophy to French social thought, which provided content for his long-held romantic socialism. In addition to writers like Charles Fourier and Pierre Leroux, who offered beautiful visions of how life ought to be organized, Herzen now read Pierre-Joseph Proudhon and Louis Blanc, who supplied acid criticism of the corruption, exploitation, and oppression of the France of Louis Philippe and of the bourgeoisie that played a leading role in it. It became clear to Herzen that Russia was not the only country that needed a profound revolutionary transformation, and he came to doubt that contemporary Western Europe could serve as a model for Russia.

Religion as well as political philosophy divided Herzen and Granovskii. Granovskii was unwilling to give up some belief in religious verities, and his Hegel, in fact, justified religion. Herzen, on the other hand, rejected all religion. It was a difficult subject for them to handle. Granovskii felt that Herzen simply could not comprehend his own need for comfort in the bereavements he had suffered; in 1844 he complained of this to his wife: "I am never comforted for my spiritual losses. I carry every grief with me for my lifetime. Stankevich, my sisters—they die for me anew every day. . . . I never spoke with Herzen about my sisters. He somehow has little understanding of such relationships. But he did not know such sisters."[11]

For the first several years of the Westernizer circle, these differences were not important. Deep friendship between the Granovskii and Herzen families formed the axis around which the entire group revolved. (Ogarev, Herzen's closest friend, was in Western Europe for most of this period, and played little direct role in the circle until its final year.) Within the context of fellowship provided by the circle, political differences could be interpreted in temperamental terms. As in his friendship with Ogarev, the strong-minded, volatile, active Herzen was paired with the gentler, more passive Granovskii, and Herzen's greater violence and radicalism was merely one aspect of this attraction of opposites. Their mutual desire to transform the Russian political and social system overrode differences with regard to pace and degree, especially since practical politics were out of the question in any case. Moreover, the Slavophiles provided a common enemy to help keep the Westernizers united.

The circle was the seed bed for ideas about philosophy, religion, and politics, Russia's past and its potential. But for left Hegelians it was not enough to develop ideas and theories. The ultimate aim of philosophy was social and political change, and Herzen and his friends had to find ways to aid this process. They could begin the task of undermining the existing order and preparing the way for something new by making public their criticisms of the present and their ideals for the future. The professorial members of the group had a ready-made platform, and through them the Westernizers' ideas eventually had some impact on the progressive public officials of the 1860s who had been their students. More exciting, in the 1843–1844 season, Granovskii received permission to give a series of public lectures on the medieval history of the West. He used the occasion to publicize his admiration for Western culture, his view of progress, and his use of Hegel to provide a philosophical framework for his historical views. The Westernizers were delighted at the success of the series, and Herzen undertook to make a truly public event of it by writing an article reporting on each of the first two lectures. Only the first of these got past the censor.[12]

Journalism was the logical activity for the nonprofessors, but, as this experience showed, publication presented serious difficulties. For one thing, there was the problem of an outlet. As a general rule, the Westernizers could publish their material in the St. Petersburg "thick journal," *Otechestvennyia zapiski*, through the influence of Belinskii, strategically located on the journal's editorial staff. But they could not control the general tone of the magazine, which was published by an apolitical editor looking primarily to increased circulation.[13] And so they attempted to found their own journal that could make a clear statement of the Westernizers' position and need not worry about clearing a profit. Permission, however, could not be obtained.[14] The Westernizers would have to go on sending their message through pseudonymous articles published in a journal they did not entirely trust.

But even if they had received permission to publish their own Moscow journal, the Westernizers would still have been faced with the problem of censorship. They could and did write and publish, but they had to use such convoluted or allusive aesopian language that only the initiated could truly understand what they were trying to say. Herzen published a good deal in these years; his Hegelian rationalism was embedded in his series, "Dilentantizm v nauke," and his view of the development of rationalist philosophy in his "Pis'ma ob izuchenii prirody" [Letters on the Study of Nature].[15] Social evils were mooted in his fiction, and his essays publicized some of the issues in the debate with the Slavophiles. All these works were either pseudonymous or unsigned, and only after his emigration did Herzen publicly identify himself as the "Iskandr" of *Otechestvennyia zapiski*. Nowhere did he clearly set forth his political and social views, for there was no way these could be published. The soul of Westernism, like that of Slavophilism, could be found only in the living conversations within the circle and in controversy in other salons, and it cannot be fully recaptured by later historians.[16]

The summer of 1845 was the high point of the Westernizer circle. The Herzens rented a country estate, and other members of the group lived either with them or in dachas nearby. Study and discussion, drink and high spirits made this summer a feast of friendship. For both Herzens it was one of the best periods in their lives.[17]

In the expectation of repeating this experience of friendship and community, the Herzens went back to the same estate the following summer. The same friends lived either with them or nearby, and this year Ogarev and another long-absent friend, Nikolai Satin, would be there and add the one element that had been lacking the year before. But instead of finding perfect harmony and friendship, the friends discovered to their horror that the circle was breaking up. Neither at the time nor later have the reasons the bonds of friendship unraveled that summer been clear; Herzen in *Byloe i dumy* spoke of ideological quarrels, primarily between himself and Granovskii. These began with religion and then spread to a whole range of issues that divided the two men. However, all of these differences had been present for several years, and it seems likely that other factors, primarily personal, turned what had been points of intellectual disagreement into questions of principle that outweighed friendship.

There had, in fact, been a number of changes in the group in the preceding year which, taken together, may well have produced some alteration in its chemistry. It had been a difficult year, and the friends were eager to get away from Moscow's cares. Granovskii had given a second series of public lectures that had not enjoyed nearly the success of the first, and this no doubt rankled with him. Herzen's father had died in the early part of 1846, and this meant that Herzen had additional business concerns to preoccupy him. It is also quite possible that his new wealth and the end of dependence on his father made him somewhat lordly and overbearing—or that, in the hypersensitive atmosphere that had been created, he would be so perceived by his friends.[18] The return of Ogarev, Herzen's most intimate friend, probably upset the balance in the circle. In the years he had spent in Western Europe, Ogarev had become considerably more radical than most of the other Westernizers. The special personal relationship that linked him to Herzen had now become a political alliance as well. Before his return there had been a delicate tension in the circle between Granovskii and Herzen. This was now transformed into a cruder factionalism, with the more belligerent, unanimous team of Herzen and Ogarev standing against their generally more moderate friends.

Finally, one of the members of the group, Nikolai Ketcher, had become involved in an awkward mésalliance with a working woman that entered a new, domestic, and official stage in 1846. Belligerent by character and perhaps defensive about his own poverty and relatively undistinguished background, Ketcher was extremely sensitive to any real or imagined slights to Serafima, as he attempted unsuccessfully to integrate her into the group. Natalie Herzen tried to make contact with her, but found herself accused of snobbery, a charge this illegitimate daughter of a serf found unjust and cruel. Ketcher had served as the group's master of ceremonies for high spirits—he was the one who brought the vast quantities of wine, told the jokes, led the pranks. He was also bound by a tender friendship with Natalie Herzen that dated from his collusion in her elopement with Herzen years before. A physician, he had also been closely involved with the physical and emotional difficulties that she had suffered in the aftermath of the deaths of three of her infant children. Ketcher was the pole around which the nonintellectual activities of the group revolved, and his angry withdrawal left it badly unbalanced.[19]

In the arguments that replaced the old camaraderie, one issue was almost certainly Herzen's hostility to the existing social system in the West. Drawing on Blanc and Proudhon, Herzen denounced the bourgeoisie as selfish, vulgar, and no solution to Russia's problems. No doubt the other members of the circle, all of whom had spent considerable time in the West, felt that Herzen's attacks on contemporary European society were out of place in someone who had never been farther west than St. Petersburg and had only a sectarian, bookish knowledge of what he was talking about. If Herzen were to regain credibility with them, one thing he would have to do was learn about Western Europe for himself.

The family's decision to go abroad was triggered by a number of events. Natalie and Herzen had long wished to travel—in the days of their long epistolary courtship, "Italy" and "the South" had become symbols for them of the blissful life they were seeking. But Herzen's status as a former prisoner still under surveillance had made it impossible for him to receive a foreign passport, and his father, moreover, had opposed his departure. By the end of 1846, these two external hindrances had been removed. His father was dead, and in the fall, perhaps impelled by his need to leave the country after the quarrels of the summer, Herzen renewed his solicitations in St. Petersburg and finally received the long-awaited passport. The ostensible reason for the journey was to consult physicians about Natalie's health, and this too was a genuine concern—the first few months the Herzens spent abroad included doctors' visits and seaside cures, as well as consultations about the condition and prognosis of their deaf son Nikolai.

The urgency of the trip, however, seems to have been a result of the Herzens' dismay at the breakup of the circle and their need to get away and collect themselves. And Herzen was also going to go and get a good look at the West, and thereby regain his authority. It is also likely that he intended to become an expert in his own right, by concentrating his attention on European radicalism. Like other Russian travelers, from Karamzin in 1789 to his friend Botkin recently returned from Spain, Herzen intended to publish an account of his travels. To avoid repeating commonplaces, this latecomer would have to dwell on something other than the tourist attractions that everyone else had already "done." The left, particularly the French left, would be the source of his own special insight into Western life.[20]

Although the circle's collapse impelled the Herzens to go abroad, they had no idea in 1847 that they were leaving for good, or that they were seeing most of their friends for the last time. They wrote to their friends whenever they had a chance to send a letter back with a returning traveler, and sometimes they even entrusted correspondence to the mail. A comparison of Herzen's letters to his Moscow friends with his "Pis'ma iz Avenue Marigny" [Letters from the Avenue Marigny], written for publication in *Sovremennik* [The Contemporary], shows that the journalism did in fact grow out of genuine letters to real friends.[21] Moreover, for the first year and a half of their sojourn abroad, they were accompanied by a circle member, Mariia Fedorovna Korsh, sister of Evgenyi Korsh, who traveled with the family and helped care for their daughter, Natalie (Tata). After her return to Moscow, Mariia Korsh remained one of Herzen's most valuable Russian contacts, an important link in transferring materials from Russia to his press for publication.[22]

Even after regular communication had broken down once Mariia

Korsh returned to Russia in the winter of 1848, Herzen continued to envision the circle as his imaginary audience; he wrote for them, he explained himself to them, and he longed for their approbation for his activities in the West. To his sorrow, this did not come—in fact, the breach became wider, as reaction closed in in Russia and any resistance seemed futile and even counter-productive. Yet Herzen would continue to try to reach his old friends, and ultimately would immortalize them with the reminiscences of "our people" in *Byloe i dumy*.

The European Setting

When Herzen journeyed to Western Europe, there was no single radical movement that he might hope to come to know and to use, both for copy and for inspiration. Familiarization with the left would require a Cook's tour, for there was activity, both practical and theoretical, in many different centers, and everywhere its character was different, the result of varied traditions and external circumstances.

The goal of Herzen's journey, the center of leftist theory and journalism, was Paris. The government of Louis Philippe, the so-called Bourgeois Monarchy, granted political rights only to the wealthy few. Attempts to use violent means to open up the system were severely punished; many revolutionary martyrs, of whom Auguste Blanqui and Armand Barbès became the most famous, languished in fortress prisons under harsh conditions. But intellectual radicals who limited their activity to journalism and theoretical explorations of current political and social evils and their solutions enjoyed considerable latitude. The heady works of Fourier, the disciples of Saint-Simonism, and younger writers had penetrated as far as Moscow and Novgorod, and there, as we have seen, had helped push Herzen beyond liberalism to a belief that the rule of the bourgeoisie was as despotic and corrupt as absolutism. During the 1840s the major contributions of the second generation of French social thinkers were produced—these included Blanc's *Organization du travail* and his histories of the French Revolution and the July Monarchy, and some of Proudhon's most important works.[23]

Among the intellectual radicals, there was no organized movement; nonetheless, a certain informal structure enabled them to exchange ideas, interact with one another, and reach the broader public. Some individuals and institutions assumed a coordinating role among the competing theories and theorists. One person who served effectively as an "influence broker" was the novelist George Sand. The enormous success of her fiction gave her a stature few writers possessed, as well as useful contacts in the artistic and publishing world. Around 1840 she came under the influence of the utopian socialist Pierre Leroux, and from then on her novels became vehicles for expounding socialist ideas.[24] Her sense of herself as a countrywoman with deep roots in the everyday world of Berry enabled her to cross class lines and encourage the socialist ideas that grew out of the artisan milieu. Thus, she provided moral support for the worker-poet Charles Poncy and the would-be reformer of traditional workingmen's organizations, Agricol Perdiguer.[25] Her estate at Nohant provided a milieu where thinkers of all kinds could meet, and her influence enabled her to publicize the work of men she admired.[26]

The press was the most important institution in developing and propagating radical ideas. The restricted political life in Louis Philippe's France gave quite extraordinary importance to the newspaper, which served as a forum for those excluded from direct participation. The interlocking roles of artist, journalist, and political figure must have looked most attractive to Herzen, who had been attempting the same combination of functions in Moscow. Journalism was a career open to talent, perseverance, and luck, and it could open the doors of the intellectual elite.[27]

The two decades from the end of the Restoration to the outbreak of revolution in 1848 saw the formation of a cadre of oppositional journalists who served on a whole series of papers. As men from the conservative end of this oppositional spectrum were drawn into the government and the establishment—men like Thiers of *Le National,* for example—new recruits were added. These men knew each other, regularly shared the same columns, and sometimes worked together on editorial boards; their political views differed widely, however, and ranged from moderate liberalism through Jacobinism to various forms of socialism. Many were involved in political action groups as well, and these ranged from the legal radical societies of the early days of the July Monarchy to secret, insurrectional organizations.[28]

Two among these journals deserve special mention. In 1841 Sand, Leroux, and the liberal journalist Louis Viardot (husband of Turgenev's love, Pauline Viardot) established *La Revue indépendante.* Among its collaborators was Louis Blanc, who was just coming into his own as historian and socialist theorist.[29] A year later, *La Revue indépendante* was sold, and Sand herself did not directly participate in

The Background

Korsh returned to Russia in the winter of 1848, Herzen continued to envision the circle as his imaginary audience; he wrote for them, he explained himself to them, and he longed for their approbation for his activities in the West. To his sorrow, this did not come—in fact, the breach became wider, as reaction closed in in Russia and any resistance seemed futile and even counter-productive. Yet Herzen would continue to try to reach his old friends, and ultimately would immortalize them with the reminiscences of "our people" in *Byloe i dumy*.

The European Setting

When Herzen journeyed to Western Europe, there was no single radical movement that he might hope to come to know and to use, both for copy and for inspiration. Familiarization with the left would require a Cook's tour, for there was activity, both practical and theoretical, in many different centers, and everywhere its character was different, the result of varied traditions and external circumstances.

The goal of Herzen's journey, the center of leftist theory and journalism, was Paris. The government of Louis Philippe, the so-called Bourgeois Monarchy, granted political rights only to the wealthy few. Attempts to use violent means to open up the system were severely punished; many revolutionary martyrs, of whom Auguste Blanqui and Armand Barbès became the most famous, languished in fortress prisons under harsh conditions. But intellectual radicals who limited their activity to journalism and theoretical explorations of current political and social evils and their solutions enjoyed considerable latitude. The heady works of Fourier, the disciples of Saint-Simonism, and younger writers had penetrated as far as Moscow and Novgorod, and there, as we have seen, had helped push Herzen beyond liberalism to a belief that the rule of the bourgeoisie was as despotic and corrupt as absolutism. During the 1840s the major contributions of the second generation of French social thinkers were produced— these included Blanc's *Organization du travail* and his histories of the French Revolution and the July Monarchy, and some of Proudhon's most important works.[23]

Among the intellectual radicals, there was no organized movement; nonetheless, a certain informal structure enabled them to exchange ideas, interact with one another, and reach the broader public. Some individuals and institutions assumed a coordinating role among the competing theories and theorists. One person who served

13

effectively as an "influence broker" was the novelist George Sand. The enormous success of her fiction gave her a stature few writers possessed, as well as useful contacts in the artistic and publishing world. Around 1840 she came under the influence of the utopian socialist Pierre Leroux, and from then on her novels became vehicles for expounding socialist ideas.[24] Her sense of herself as a countrywoman with deep roots in the everyday world of Berry enabled her to cross class lines and encourage the socialist ideas that grew out of the artisan milieu. Thus, she provided moral support for the worker-poet Charles Poncy and the would-be reformer of traditional workingmen's organizations, Agricol Perdiguer.[25] Her estate at Nohant provided a milieu where thinkers of all kinds could meet, and her influence enabled her to publicize the work of men she admired.[26]

The press was the most important institution in developing and propagating radical ideas. The restricted political life in Louis Philippe's France gave quite extraordinary importance to the newspaper, which served as a forum for those excluded from direct participation. The interlocking roles of artist, journalist, and political figure must have looked most attractive to Herzen, who had been attempting the same combination of functions in Moscow. Journalism was a career open to talent, perseverance, and luck, and it could open the doors of the intellectual elite.[27]

The two decades from the end of the Restoration to the outbreak of revolution in 1848 saw the formation of a cadre of oppositional journalists who served on a whole series of papers. As men from the conservative end of this oppositional spectrum were drawn into the government and the establishment—men like Thiers of *Le National*, for example—new recruits were added. These men knew each other, regularly shared the same columns, and sometimes worked together on editorial boards; their political views differed widely, however, and ranged from moderate liberalism through Jacobinism to various forms of socialism. Many were involved in political action groups as well, and these ranged from the legal radical societies of the early days of the July Monarchy to secret, insurrectional organizations.[28]

Two among these journals deserve special mention. In 1841 Sand, Leroux, and the liberal journalist Louis Viardot (husband of Turgenev's love, Pauline Viardot) established *La Revue indépendante*. Among its collaborators was Louis Blanc, who was just coming into his own as historian and socialist theorist.[29] A year later, *La Revue indépendante* was sold, and Sand herself did not directly participate in another newspaper until 1848. Others, however, did achieve the establishment of a paper that would provide a single, influential voice for the left. *La Réforme*, founded in 1843, was edited by Ferdinand Flocon, who would later be a minister in the Provisional Government. Blanc wrote the paper's program, and another future cabinet minister, Alexandre Ledru-Rollin, provided much of the money to keep the low-circulation daily afloat.[30] *La Réforme* succeeded. Its leadership was too diverse for it to develop a consistent ideological position, it made compromises, and it even flirted with the legitimists for the sake of short-term political benefits; but its broad-based radicalism answered a real need of the left. Even its critics found themselves forced to support it.[31] In 1848, as the government lost control of the capital, *La Réforme* became a major locus of political decision making.

As the 1840s wore on, the mood in Paris heightened. "In these years . . . when the end of a regime hastened, when popular effervescence, scandals and catastrophes made a revolution seem as inevitable as it was near, all political, philosophical, economic and social problems were on the agenda. France never saw such a blossoming of concepts, systems, and vast ideological constructions for renewing the world. The doctrines of Saint-Simon, Fourier, Louis Blanc, Proudhon and Pierre Leroux were asserted, were propagated, interacted with each other." Sand was not the only artist whose work assumed an ideological tone under the influence of this ebullience; the popular composer of songs Béranger, the novelist Eugène Sue, and the playwright Félix Pyat were others who employed the ideas of the radical theorists and made them part of the intellectual currency.[32]

In all the intellectual excitement, ideological and political lines were not tightly drawn. The staff of *La Réforme* could easily include socialists like Blanc and liberals like Ledru-Rollin; Sand could be a friendly supporter of Blanc, a good friend of her ex-lover Michel de Bourges, the liberal leader, a supporter of Mazzini, a patroness of worker-socialists, and a respectful acquaintance of Mikhail Bakunin, without feeling any ideological strain. There was no unified opposition that encompassed all these people, but contacts and friendships linked each group to its ideological neighbors and created a "chain of friendship." This made a sense of solidarity possible and, when the time for action came, led to involvement by many different groups who put pressure on the government at many different points.[33] Only when revolution actually came in 1848, when immediate, practical decisions became necessary, would the inherent contradictions among the groups and individuals on the left become crippling. For the moment, the fact that they were all in opposition to the complacency and selfishness of the Bourgeois Monarchy, and were almost all drawn from the educated upper and middle class and could converse in the same salons, allowed them to work together and to think of each other as friends and allies. Moreover, programmatic differences within the French opposition were not very significant at the time, for almost all espoused democracy and rejected Manchester liberalism in favor of some form of collectivism.[34] The differences that would fatally divide the left in 1848 were less over social policy than over the nature and control of political power.

There was another radicalism in the France of the 1840s, but it had little influence on the intellectual leftists who made France the Mecca for an Alexander Herzen. There was the tradition of secret societies and conspiracy, which ran from Babeuf in the 1790s to 1848. The leaders of this orientation were in prison or exile; the rank and file remained secret and out of the ken of the bourgeois radicals. Intersecting with the secret societies were the clandestine working-class radical associations that developed their own forms of organization and class consciousness during the Bourgeois Monarchy.[35] Men of the conspiratorial tradition would emerge in 1848; whether Jacobin or socialist, they were characterized by an intensity and toughness not often found among the radical journalists.

GERMAN ÉMIGRÉS

France's relative freedom and the attractions offered by Paris as both an economic and a cultural center drew refugees from other countries who made their own contribution to the Parisian spirit.[36] Many German radicals, both intellectuals and workers, found they were unable to function in the narrow, enclosed world of their own little principality. Exile became their fate, and its stages might include sojourns in other German states, Switzerland, Belgium, and England. Most spent at least some time in Paris, and there connections were knitted that would influence the entire history of the European left. There too organizational activity began, with the establishment in the 1830s of the League of Proscripts, a secret, republican society of German émigrés.

German artisans and communist intellectuals in Paris soon split away from the Proscripts and formed the League of the Just, a secret society dominated by a self-educated tailor, Wilhelm Weitling. For years German artisans had traveled widely looking for work, and they had established colonies in many European cities. Contacts between these scattered colonies were maintained by the workers' frequent moves. As they followed the availability of work from one place to another, they carried the league's organization with them; soon there were branches in France, England, Holland, Sweden, and the United States, as well as Germany and Switzerland.[37] The league espoused a moralizing communism, its members believing that capitalist productive relations were evil and that workers' solidarity in the struggle for change was a moral imperative. In mood it was insurrectional, and it was associated with Blanqui's Society of the Seasons. The Paris branch played a major role in the uprising led by the society in 1839.[38]

The leaders of the group fled Paris after the failure of the uprising and went to London. There, in the next decade, they made contacts with English and Polish radicals. They also formed the nucleus of the Communist League, the first working-class organization affiliated with Marx, and the group for whom the *Communist Manifesto* was written.[39] Meanwhile, in Paris, the League of the Just continued to exist, in a weakened state, under the guidance of Hermann Ewerbeck and other, less well-known figures. The communism of Weitling and of the French theorist Etienne Cabet (whose *Voyage en Icarie* was translated into German by Ewerbeck) defined the prevailing mood in the league. The moralizing strand of Hegelian socialism, which was presented to its members by the Berlin "True Socialist" Karl Grün, also met a sympathetic response. This large group of radical German artisans would provide the constituency for German émigré politics in 1848.

German leftist intellectuals followed a different trajectory from that of the artisans, but they too found it increasingly difficult to function in Germany as the 1840s wore on. Tolerant, German-speaking Switzerland provided a convenient haven for moderates whose interests were less political than academic. Their colonies, in turn, provided stops for the more doctrinaire radicals, when the latter were forced to leave Germany and needed a chance to regroup. The theoretical basis for German radicalism, meanwhile, was being developed in the German universities, where Hegel's legacy was dissected by a younger generation that refused to see the Prussian state as the crowning triumph of historical development.

One of the left Hegelians, Arnold Ruge, wished to establish a forum where this left-Hegelian tendency could be expressed and developed. Although he failed in his efforts, Ruge did succeed in establishing connections among a number of advanced thinkers, and also helped transfer a segment of German radicalism to Paris. In 1838 he founded a left-Hegelian journal, the *Hallische Jahrbücher für Wissenschaft und Kunst*, which lasted until 1840, when the Prussian authorities closed it. Ruge left Halle for Dresden, where he reestablished the journal as the *Deutsche Jahrbücher*. The Halle journal had criticized the Prussian political system in cautious, aesopian form; its successor, however, made the political implications of its philosophy explicit, defining itself as constitutional, democratic, and republican.[40] If that were not enough, in 1842 it published Bakunin's revolutionary article, "The Reaction in Germany." In January 1843, the Saxon authorities closed the journal, and Ruge was on the move again. Having decided to go to Paris, he asked one of the leading Young Hegelian radicals, Karl Marx, to accompany him and co-edit the next form of the journal, the *Deutsch-Französische Jahrbücher*. Marx soon would come to represent something entirely new in the radical movement. His path never crossed Herzen's, for the mutual antipathy of the two men was such that they consciously avoided each other.[41] Nonetheless, Marx played a significant role in Herzen's life, if only as a negative influence; and Herzen's response to Marx reflects a more general response to him among the radical intellectuals. The qualities that would eventually set Marx so sharply apart from the other revolutionaries became manifest with his move to Paris with Arnold Ruge.

Marx was known at this time as a leading left-Hegelian philosopher, more acute, and perhaps more rebellious, than others of the group, but not cut from a different mold altogether. He had come to Cologne in 1842, to participate in the vigorous intellectual life there, and shortly to become editor of a new liberal newspaper, the *Rheinische Zeitung*. Cologne was a major center of Germany's early industrialization, and was one of the few German cities with a vigorous, self-confident bourgeoisie; the *Rheinische Zeitung* had been founded by this group of businessmen, who intended it to reflect their views. The city also had a flourishing group of radical intellectuals; at the center of this group was the longtime Cologne resident Moses Hess, who worked on the *Rheinische Zeitung* himself and to whom Marx owed his position on the paper.

The Marx who came to Cologne was a rebel in the manner of the German left-Hegelian intellectuals; that is, he was an atheist and a democrat. However, it was only after his move to Cologne, and under the influence of Hess, that he arrived at the view that economic injustice lay at the source of all the other ills of mankind, and that only the abolition of private capital could end that injustice. Despite these new communist views, Marx knew he must answer to the bourgeois liberal owners of the *Rheinische Zeitung,* and therefore he attempted to steer the paper on a relatively moderate course and to curb the radicalism of his editorial staff. Nonetheless, he and the paper still became too outspoken for the Prussian authorities, and the paper was banned early in 1843, leaving Marx without a job. He was, thus, eager to accept Ruge's offer to join the *Deutsch-Französische Jahrbücher.*

Two other new associates accompanied Ruge to Paris, both from outside his own German university milieu. Each would have a major impact on Herzen's future. One was Bakunin, who had left Russia in 1840 to study philosophy in Berlin. There he became friendly with Turgenev and established contacts with the men and women who constituted intellectual society in the Prussian capital. Bakunin's Hegelian conservatism soon gave way to a violent repudiation of all existing society. In 1842, after his meeting with Ruge, Bakunin moved to Dresden and established a friendship with his editor. Another of Bakunin's Dresden friends was a musician named Adolf Reichel, who would later play an important part in his and Herzen's lives. But it was Georg Herwegh, the poet whom Heinrich Heine somewhat ironically called the "iron lark," whom Bakunin also met in Dresden, who would have the greatest impact on Herzen.[42]

Herwegh brought star quality and popularity to German radicalism, hitherto concealed behind the academic demeanor and Hegelian jargon of the university men. He had dropped out of university and then fled his military service. He went to Zurich, where the liberal German exiles welcomed him. One of them, Julius Fröbel, established a printing press primarily for the purpose of publishing Herwegh's poetry and channeling it across the border.[43] Herwegh's first collection, *Gedichte eines Lebendigen,* was an immediate sensation, and the poet suddenly found himself a much-courted spokesman for the German left. This successful use of a foreign-based press to provide a voice for material unable to pass the censors may have inspired Herzen a decade later. Fröbel followed up this first success with other books that were smuggled from Zurich into the German states.

Encouraged by the success of the press, the Zurich group drew up plans for a journal and appointed Herwegh editor. Herwegh hoped to use the journal to create a forum for opinion from all over Germany (another idea that recurs in Herzen's career), and in 1842 he traveled extensively through the German states to contact potential contributors. The journey became a triumphal procession; in every university town where he stopped there were banquets and speeches in his honor, as well as meetings with intellectual leaders. In Berlin he had a well-publicized interview with the king of Prussia, and also met and courted his future bride, Emma Siegmund, whose wealthy family was at the center of the city's cultural life.[44] In Cologne, Herwegh met Marx, and in Dresden Ruge and Bakunin. The last, who was bored in Dresden and pursued by creditors, was greatly attracted to Herwegh and followed the poet back to Switzerland.

The journal, in the end, could not be published. But Bakunin and Herwegh continued to build a network of radical friends. Herwegh in Geneva had some contact with the artisan-communists of the League of the Just.[45] He and Bakunin also knitted a friendship with the Vogt family, which was connected by marriage to leading academic liberals of the Zurich group. One of the Vogt brothers, Karl, was a well-known physiologist who would be a major participant in the revolutionary events in Germany in 1848. Later he became a close friend of the Herzen family and ultimately the mentor of Herzen's son Sasha (Aleksandr Aleksandrovich). He was also the subject of a bitter polemic by Marx.

While Herwegh and Bakunin were still in Switzerland, Ruge went to Paris, where he hoped to establish contact with the French left and create an international journal. He was joined by Fröbel, who hoped to open a Paris office for his press as well as to collaborate with Ruge. Between them, they entered into contact with the men of *La Réforme*—Blanc, Flocon, and Etienne Arago, the communist Cabet, the socialist Victor Considerant, the romantic poet Lamartine, and the Christian rebel Lammenais.[46] But although personal links were established, the attempt at collaboration failed.

Undaunted, Ruge, along with Marx and a group of collaborators that included Moses Hess, Herwegh, and Bakunin, all of whom came to Paris, undertook to issue a purely German *Deutsch-Französische Jahrbücher*. The venture was not a success, and only one issue appeared. The reaction of Marie d'Agoult, one of the journal's few French readers, may help explain the *Jahrbücher*'s failure: "I have read Ruge and Marx. I am too French to understand *what good this can be*. They are correct on certain points, but they betray a great lack of understanding of Christianity and, consequently, of the Middle Ages. And then, once again, what are political publications that can have only one reader per two thousand individuals? Produce either philosophy *books* or *clear, lively, gripping* polemics; this middle way is absurd."[47]

The group of German intellectuals associated with the project was in any case far from agreement on political and social issues, and was further divided by Ruge's condemnation, and Marx's defense, of Herwegh's sexual conduct. Marx and Ruge soon separated completely, Marx appalled by Ruge's conservatism, and Ruge by Marx's arrogance.[48] Despite their own conflict, though, both men turned to another German magazine published in Paris, the *Vorwärts*, whose staff included the poet Heinrich Heine, the "true socialist" Karl Grün, and Hermann Ewerbeck, who was associated with the League of the Just.[49] The *Vorwärts* in its turn was closed by the police early in 1845, and Marx and Ruge both expelled from France. Marx fled to Brussels, where he was to spend most of the time remaining before the outbreak of revolution in 1848.[50]

For Marx, the Paris episode was most important: it marked the beginning of his collaboration with Friedrich Engels and his break with moderate left Hegelianism. Strongly influenced by the French socialists he encountered at this period, he now began the evolution which would lead to his mature, post-1848 position.[51] He also moved toward a dogmatism and insistence on intellectual domination that would bar any later collaboration with men like Grün, whom he would soon attack violently in his *Holy Family*.

Of the members of Ruge's group who remained in Paris, Herwegh and Bakunin became the most involved in French political and social life. Herwegh became the friend, and probably the lover, of the comtesse d'Agoult, former mistress of Liszt and former friend of Sand.[52] She wrote novels and journalism under the pseudonym Daniel Stern, and later produced the authoritative history of 1848 from the point of view of a liberal supporter of Lamartine. In her salon, Herwegh and Bakunin met leaders of liberal opinion as well as cultural lions. They made contact there with members of the editorial staff of *La Réforme*, to which Bakunin contributed in 1845 and again in 1848–1849. Turgenev was another useful contact; through him, Bakunin became friendly with the Viardots and acquainted with Sand. He also engaged in intense discussions with Proudhon, whom he attempted to instruct in the subtleties of the Hegelian dialectic.[53]

For the Germans, far more than for the French, these years saw differentiation and quarrels, as well as the formation of personal and political networks. The divisions among them would have considerable impact in directing Herzen's course a few years later. Between 1844 and 1848 the mature Marx emerged; on the one hand, he worked his way theoretically to the historical materialism of the *Communist Manifesto*. On the other, his special style also manifested itself at this time. He sought domination of the intellectual movement of which he was a part through his aggressive and brilliant theoretical and polemical articles, and at the same time he sought a mass basis for socialism.[54] From Brussels he began to build a working-class base in England and Germany.[55] He also maintained contact with some of his former *Vorwärts* collaborators in Paris and tried to use them to exert influence on the German workers' community there. Engels remained in the city in the winter of 1846–1847 and used his presence to assure that one segment of radical opinion in Paris would respond to Marx's directives.

The splintering process also affected Herwegh. The quarrel with Ruge was never healed, and Herwegh was repelled by the sectarian dogmatism and practical futility he saw developing within the German left: "Do you read the ... *Vorwärts*? Truly, this whole world gives me the impression it is devouring itself. The Germans, a friend writes me, guillotine every one *before* the revolution, wishing to accomplish this redoubtable process only in theory. At Berlin, the Hébertistes sit; at Paris, the Gironde, with Ruge's features, the Mountain, with those of Marx—Robespierre will find his representative in some philistine German, and we shall lack only a Napoleon."[56]

At the same time, Herwegh himself was perceived by his erstwhile comrades as vacillating, unstable, and utterly unable to take a position and hold to it. German associates also expressed considerable hostility to Herwegh's companion Bakunin, who was seen as irresponsible, tactless, and unreliable.[57] The pattern of power politics and personal animosities dividing the radical left was being set in these prerevolutionary years.

POLISH ÉMIGRÉS IN PARIS

Another important exile colony in the Paris of the 1840s, one that was much larger and even more diverse than the Germans, was made up of Polish émigrés. The flood of refugees who had left their homeland after the unsuccessful insurrection of 1831 provided the basis for Polish colonies in many Western cities. Once in Western Europe, they immediately began to develop the techniques of émigré politics: a National Committee was formed to provide for the welfare needs of the exiles and to coordinate propaganda; attempts were made to organize support among the politically most active members of the host countries, which resulted in parliamentary expressions of support for the Polish cause; in France, an effort was made to form a Polish legion within the army; and everywhere the exiles busily plotted conspiracies aimed at raising a new revolution in Poland.[58] Soon the embarrassed French government banned the National Committee and expelled the leading émigrés.

Scattered geographically, especially after their expulsion from Paris, the Poles were also bitterly split politically, with the rival factions blaming each other for the failure of 1831. The most fundamental division was between the conservative faction, led by Prince Adam Czartoryski, and the radicals who hoped that Poland would be resurrected as a democratic republic. The radicals formed the Polish Democratic Society, which eventually had branches in Paris, London, and the island of Jersey. The Poles' taste for conspiracy and revolutionary action brought the Democratic Society into alliance with the oldest form of revolutionary activism in Europe, the Carbonari.[59] But Carbonarism itself was dealt a mortal blow in 1833, when a planned conspiracy failed completely.

Some of the mystique and methods of the Carbonari were taken over by a former member, Giuseppe Mazzini. Mazzini founded the Young Italy movement to fight for Italian liberation, and he encouraged the formation of other branches of Young Europe to carry on the struggle in other areas. Like the Carbonari, Young Europe advocated international solidarity. Tactically, however, it shifted emphasis; where Carbonarism had projected a single international conspiracy, Mazzini's plans called for coordinated popular revolutions by the individual nationalities of Europe.

The failure of the 1833 conspiracy led to a split within the Polish left. The Democratic Society remained affiliated with Carbonarism, while the historian Joachim Lelewel, the single most prestigious spokesman for the radical wing of the Polish emigration, organized Young Poland as a branch of Young Europe.[60] A year later, a Polish legion provided much of the striking force when Mazzini attempted unsuccessfully to invade Savoy and thereby liberate Italy.[61] Henceforth, the Polish cause would be associated with that of Italy, and the Poles would benefit from Mazzini's superb propagandistic talents.

Moreover, the Poles had established that their primary orientation was toward action, and many of them achieved self-definition through participation in uprisings. From this point on, Poles would be present whenever there was a national revolt against the international system imposed by the Congress of Vienna.

The split in the Polish left was not healed until 1845, when Lelewel joined the Democratic Society. In the intervening years, amid the flood of discussion and recrimination within the emigration, both factions came to the conclusion that the political democracy they advocated was not a strong enough program to attract a broad popular base for their movement. Concerned that ultimately they could achieve victory only if they had the Polish peasantry behind them, and influenced by the socialist theories bubbling out of the French intellectual effervescence, the Polish democrats during these years of exile began to work out a program of agrarian socialism to supplement their political democracy.[62]

In addition to establishing their own organization, Poles participated in political movements in their host states—they could be found in virtually every secret society in France, and in England one group played a major role in prodding the Chartists into international involvement.[63] In France, Poles with access to the press helped to crystallize anti-Russian opinion, and in at least one case to familiarize the French public with nonofficial Russian views. Charles Edmond Chojecki in 1847 published articles in *La Revue indépendante,* thanks to which, "Belinskii's name was spoken [in France], associated with Iskandr [Herzen], Kol'tsov, Goncharov, and also with Kavelin and Granovskii."[64]

The Polish radicals also had contacts with Bakunin and the German leftists. Bakunin met Lelewel in Brussels in 1844, and in 1845 brought himself to the favorable notice of the Democratic Society by means of an article that appeared in *La Réforme.*[65] Herwegh too had Polish contacts—he also knew Lelewel, and his house in Paris was a regular meeting place for Poles as well as Germans.[66] In 1846 yet another Polish conspiracy was hatched. A group in Poznan, one of whose leaders was a member of the Paris Polish Democratic Society, Ludwik Mieroslawski, was planning a general Polish uprising, but was arrested before the revolt broke out. Then an uprising did occur in Cracow, which was ruthlessly suppressed by the Austrians, who encouraged the Polish peasants to rise in their turn against their rebellious landlords. These events, however dismal, had the effect of noticeably quickening revolutionary excitement in Europe and of centering the attention of revolutionaries of all nationalities on the Polish struggle.[67] Bakunin defended the uprising in *Le Constitutionnel*, and entered into formal relations with the Polish Democratic Society, despite his personality clashes with the Polish leadership. The Herweghs, who knew Mieroslawski's sister, seem to have been more deeply concerned by the uprising. Emma Herwegh was visiting Berlin in the autumn of 1847, when the Poznan conspirators were tried. She sent news about them to her husband, and after the Poles' conviction managed to see Mieroslawksi and the others in prison and to bring them gifts.[68] In this way, the ground was being prepared for Herzen's later cooperation with the Polish exiles in London.

Paris, with its openness and the intellectual excitement of the 1840s, provided an arena for debate on social issues and set the framework in which alliances and enmities could develop—thus setting the stage for the emergence of leaders in the various camps once the revolution broke out. But Paris was by no means the only place in Europe where there were people who felt oppressed by the social and political order and longed for change. Much less visible because of real or potential repression, these concealed radicals would emerge into public view with the revolutions. After the failure of the movements with which they had been associated, they too would join the exile community. The experiences and cast of mind of each new wave of radicals would make its own contribution to the characteristic tone of international radicalism.

RADICALISM IN GERMANY

Germany had long been the source of the Russian intellectuals' cultural sustenance. They had perceived the world through the eyes of German idealist philosophy, and many of them had studied at German universities, especially Berlin. As late as 1840, Bakunin made Berlin his goal when he went to the West, and it was through the influence of left Hegelianism, itself a university product, that he became an advocate of the violent destruction of the existing order. But by the time Herzen arrived in Berlin in February 1847, this current had largely dried up; the radical professors had been driven from their chairs, and the theoreticians who derived programs of change from philosophical foundations were scattered—Bakunin and his friends were in Paris and Marx in Brussels. Herzen reported to his Moscow companions:

> I was at Berlin University today. The building itself is excellent, now that it has been finished by Schinkel, and involuntarily something stirred in my soul when I looked at the corridors along which passed Fichte and Hegel—but the time of its great glory has passed. In Königsburg a merchant said to me of Berlin University: "Das ist so ein Herculaneum der Wissenschaft." I looked at the board—a mass of theology courses, many philosophy courses, with little-known names. . . . Each and every person here understands that natural sciences and history are the only real, *kernhafte* occupations, and indeed this awareness has begun to enliven the mass of dry occupations.[69]

There is an element of gloating in this—Herzen was staking his claim to new, up-to-date knowledge about Europe by telling his friends that the experiences that had formed their understanding were obsolete, and he was also justifying his own penchant for the natural sciences. But it is also clear that Herzen, who found that throughout Germany "there is a sort of character of sensible mediocrity and conscientious order that is extremely antipathetic,"[70] did not know where to look for political and intellectual vitality in the German lands. He was basing himself on his Moscow connections; these would serve him in good stead in Paris, where he would make contact with the slightly older group of émigré German intellectual radicals, but they were of little help in Germany itself. And so Herzen hastened through the German states, not accompanying his mother when she went to visit her relatives in Stuttgart and making no important stops between Berlin and Cologne.

After 1848 Herzen would have many contacts among German activists who were not visible in 1847. They came into view in response to revolution: during 1848 a democratic-left group would emerge in the major representative bodies—the Pre-Parliament and the Frankfurt Parliament and some of the assemblies in the individual German states. Farther to the left, there would be an attempt to form a democratic party that would include both socialists and radical democrats. The veterans of these movements would become Herzen's associates after their flight from Germany in late 1848 or early 1849.

German radicalism is amorphous and difficult to define. Intellectually, the radicals were left-Hegelian followers of Ruge and his friends. They operated out of those institutions within Germany which allowed a certain amount of political freedom. The Landtags of the German states offered in varying degrees the kind of freedom of speech necessary for the radicals. Southwestern Germany—Baden, Württemburg, and Hesse-Darmstadt—had the best-developed constitutional systems, and there after 1846 radicalism emerged as a separate political tendency. By the fall of 1847, radicalism had defined itself to the extent that a conference was held in Oppenheim which published a democratic program. In other parts of Germany, where political life was more constricted, oppositional circles grew up around outspoken Landtag deputies whose forthright stands lent them great moral authority in the eyes of the young. Such a person was the Königsburger Johann Jacoby, a nonsocialist radical who resolutely stood up to the establishment, despite prosecution.[71] After the revolution, Jacoby would become a friend of Herzen.

The other institution that fostered German radicalism was the university. There was no intellectual movement in the 1840s comparable to the ebullience that had marked the debate over Hegel's legacy—the left-Hegelian resolution was still accepted by the students, but their primary concern lay elsewhere. "Most students were less interested in the specific ideas advanced by Ruge, Bauer, Feuerbach, and others than in what these men represented, namely a very vocal, sometimes heroic, and increasingly persecuted opposition."[72] The organizational focus of the new radicalism was a revived *Burschenschaft* movement, both nationalist and democratic, which tried to instill in its members the qualities necessary for leadership in a modernized, reformed Germany.[73] Links were established between the organizations at the various universities, and also with sympathetic liberal faculty members. Other links connected the student organizations and radical politicians. In East Prussia, Jacoby and others enjoyed the support of student organizations, while at the other end of Germany the Baden Landtag radical Gustav Struve edited the student movement's most important journal, the *Zeitschrift für Deutschlands Hochschulen*.[74]

There were also religious manifestations of German radicalism in the German Catholic movement and the Protestant Lichtfreunde, but these are not relevant for our purposes, since they appear to have had no contact with Herzen. (Herwegh, however, was briefly intrigued by German Catholicism in 1846.)[75] To an even greater extent than in France, ideological positions in Germany were not hard and fast. Party outlines were still very fluid, and far more a question of personality and temperament than of ideological rigor. Even Marx, at this period, is to be distinguished far more by his efforts to organize and work with a working-class constituency, both on the continent and in England, than by efforts to enforce his own theories on his followers.

RADICALISM IN ITALY

If Germany was the land where revolution emerged from the university and was weighted with a heavy load of philosophic theory, Italy was the classic arena of revolutionary action. The tradition of conspiracy dating back to the resistance against Napoleon survived, transformed by Mazzini and Young Italy in the 1830s. Mazzini was the acknowledged leader of Italian revolutionary, democratic nationalism. Based usually in England, he used his massive correspondence to spin a web of conspiracy, with collaborators scattered in cities throughout Italy. Periodically, an attempted uprising or the discovery of a revolutionary band would provide the nationalist mythology with new martyrs and keep it in public view. Mazzini, sensitive, intelligent, delicate, and romantic, dressed always in black in mourning for his country, and resorting to violence without compunction, was the archetype of the nineteenth-century romantic revolutionary. With his enormously attractive personality, he created an international public opinion favorable to his cause. In England he had an influential circle of supporters. Rivalry with Buonarotti and the remnants of the old Carbonarist organization, plus the inability to spend a great deal of time in the country for security reasons, kept him from exerting as powerful an influence in France. Nonetheless, his star quality was widely acknowledged. He met George Sand in 1847 and was an instant success with her. She translated his "Open Letter to the Pope" herself, wrote an article supporting it, and worked to get it published in a newspaper with a large and influential audience.[76]

While Mazzini was active abroad, the pace of political life within Italy markedly quickened. In 1846 Pope Gregory XVI died and was replaced by Pius IX, who inaugurated his reign with a series of actions that served as the prologue to the revolutions of 1848. He amnestied political as well as ordinary prisoners and established commissions to begin working out reforms to modernize the political and economic system in the Papal States. Inadvertently, and to his ultimate great regret, the pope had started a revolution. It would burst out in full flame a little over a year later, and Alexander Herzen would be there to observe and describe it.

2
THE TRAVELER

HERZEN'S experiences in 1847 and early 1848, before the outbreak of the French revolution of 1848, laid the groundwork for his later political activity. A wealthy, upper-class, cosmopolitan gentleman, he traveled armed with the names of friends and friends of friends whom he would seek out for companionship and enlightenment. Unlike most of his own companions from the circle, Herzen was going to the West as an unattached tourist, not as a student or in some other capacity that would provide him with his own entrée into a specific milieu. Thus, socially he was quite dependent on these contacts. As a result, the people he met, and who in turn introduced him to others, were a fairly random lot, and they were not necessarily those with whom he was politically congenial. Indeed, throughout Herzen's life he was considerably more radical than most of his friends, and he had very few personal contacts with men whose views were in the same general position on the political spectrum as his own.

Herzen's first year in the West was one of rich intellectual development. He went abroad in the hope of gaining a new understanding of politics and society. In this regard, he was more abundantly rewarded than he had dreamed possible. From the very first stages of the journey, the contrasts between European ways and the Russia he was familiar with stimulated his creative processes. Soon he experienced revolution and its failure, and these stupendous events, along with his earlier observations, provided the raw material for much of his theoretical work. This chapter will examine Herzen's initial personal contacts with European society and his early intellectual response to the West. While not dealing systematically with Herzen's ideology, I will attempt to integrate his experiences with his developing social thought.

The adventure began in January 1847. The circle gathered for one last party, and then the friends accompanied the travelers as far as the first posting stage. Toasts were drunk, goodbyes were said, and the party set off, unaware that they would never see Moscow or most of their friends again.

It was a large party. In addition to Herzen, Natalie, and their three children, Aleksandr (Sasha), age seven, three-year-old Nikolai (Kolia), and two-year-old Nataliia (Tata), they were accompanied by Herzen's mother, Luisa Haag, and two other women who helped care for the children: Mariia Korsh, and Mariia Ern. Ern, a young woman who had been befriended by Herzen while he was in exile in Viatka, had virtually grown up in the Iakovlev household.[1] Natalie took sole charge of Sasha; the deaf boy, Kolia, was in the care of Luisa Haag and Mariia Ern; and Mariia Korsh had primary responsibility for Tata. This arrangement not only made it possible for the frail Natalie to undertake the rigors of travels with her children, but also enabled the party to break up periodically while still guaranteeing adequate supervision for them.

They traveled overland, through Pskov and across Livonia, and first encountered the "West" in East Prussia.[2] From Königsberg they went on to Berlin, where they remained about two weeks, visiting theaters, seeing the sights, meeting people, and consulting physicians for Natalie and Kolia. It was then that the Herzens learned that their son's deafness was incurable. From Berlin the main party went by way of Brunswick to Cologne and Brussels, with a side trip to Bruges and Ostend. Late in March they traveled from Brussels to Paris, where they took up residence near the Champs-Elysées at Number 9, Avenue Marigny.[3] The impressions from these two months of travel were important enough that the first of Herzen's "Pis'ma iz Avenue Marigny" was devoted to them.

This "Letter" may be closer to the Herzen of the circle than anything else he wrote. It is witty and high-spirited, decidedly argumentative, but in so good-humored a fashion that his friends in Moscow, despite their reservations about its content, were delighted with it. The "Letter" makes two points, one looking back to the quarrels in the circle, the other forward to much of Herzen's later work. The first is a criticism of German culture and, by extension, the views of his friends, steeped as they were in German university attitudes. Herzen makes his point through an extended metaphor attacking German cooking, to which Herzen ascribed all the weaknesses of the national character.

> You laugh, you are still such idealists that you all need incorporeal, immaterial causes—and not boiling and broiling. You have scorned the flesh enough, joked about it enough! It oppresses your entire bold mind with a corn, and jeeringly shows your proud spirit how it is in thrall to a tight shoe. . . .
>
> I did not idly say that Europe's comfortable way of life begins at the Rhine, for it is precisely there that German cuisine approaches *the one and indivisible* cuisine. There is nothing bad without some good; in the sad period from 1793 to 1814 Rhenish cuisine was subjected to the strong influence of French cooks, who in many ways subverted the morally tasteless and domestically insipid character of German viands.[4]

But it was Herzen's perception of the contrasts between East and West, treated with less humor in the "Letter," that prefigures his later thought. On the one hand, there was Russia, not yet arrived at historical life—Herzen recalled the peasants of Pskov, among whom they had passed on their way West:

> The Pskov peasant is more savage than the Muscovite; he seems to have put neither his left nor his right foot onto the road that leads from patriarchalism to civil development—the road which is called progress, education, the story of which is called history. He stands beside half-ruined fortifications and knows nothing of them. . . . After two or three generations the *muzhik* will rebuild his wooden huts, which have rotted without a trace, will grow old in them, will transmit his meadow into his sons' and grandsons' hands, will lie on a warm stove for two or three years, and then will pass imperceptibly into the frozen earth. . . . At the first [census] revision they will exclude his name from the number of the living, then his children too will grow gray. . . . A life which leaves no solid traces is obliterated with each step forward and stubbornly stays in one and the same position.[5]

The Europeans, on the other hand, had a past and a civilization, but their future was problematic. The European counterpart to the primitive Pskovian was the Livonian cultural backwater—a world of clean linen, flowers in windows, education, but no future, a cultural dead end. And in contrast to the still formless Muscovite culture was the rich heritage of Western Europe, exemplified in Cologne:

> What isn't here: unshattered walls, heavy romanesque churches, the colossal example of the gothic cathedral, the house of the Templars—gloomy warrior monks standing sullenly on the border

of feudalism and centralization; the college of the Jesuits, gloomy monk-warriors, sullenly standing on the border of papism and the Reformation; churches from the Renaissance, offices built during the domination by the one and indivisible republic; new fortifications, recalling the Napoleonic era, and finally, forests near the church which testify to the Germany of today, with its slow production of medieval work by contemporary hands. Memories everywhere, legends everywhere; glance above—from a fourth story two horses' heads of white marble gaze out—there was a miracle here; look down—there is the place where Christ appeared to a lad at prayer several centuries ago and took an apple from him.[6]

But if Russia was poor and unformed by comparison, lacking this rich and visible heritage, which nonetheless involved "slow production of medieval work by contemporary hands," Russia had succeeded in grafting Western achievements onto its own stock. The result was a culture with all the potentiality of the West, but not so burdened by the weight of the past that future development had become impossible: "Our past is poor; we do not wish to invent heraldic tales; we have few memories—but what is poverty, when Europe's memories, her past, has become our past? Moreover, under the influence of his past the European cannot separate from it. For him the present is the roof of a many-storied building, for us and for North America, it is a high terrace, a foundation; his terrace is our ground floor. We begin from his end."[7]

The contrast between the Livonian and Pskovian peasants, and the attendant notion of a distinction between people with a historical and those with merely a cultural life, was repeated and developed a few years later in a work Herzen wrote to acquaint Western readers with Russia, *Du Développement des idées révolutionnaires en Russie*.[8] The view of Russia as both historically destitute and able to develop more freely by selectively adopting Western culture underlay much of his mature political thought, including the notion of "Russian socialism."

The journey was far more successful intellectually than politically. A closer examination of Herzen's activities and contacts during the first stage of his travels shows how he made his entrée into radical life, and just how limited these initial contacts were.

In Berlin his Russian acquaintances included the novelist Ivan Turgenev, who was there in Pauline Viardot's train. Herzen had never known the younger man well, and he shared his friends' scorn for Turgenev's idolatry of Viardot; nonetheless, the two men established relatively friendly relations at this time which persisted throughout Herzen's life. In this period Turgenev was a close friend of Bakunin and linked to other survivors of the Stankevich circle, and so had shared interests with Herzen. Herzen also spent time with Dmitrii Mikhailovich Shchepkin, son of his friend the actor Mikhail Shchepkin, who was pursuing his studies in Berlin. He was a pleasant, scholarly young man who provided the Herzen family with companionship and introduced them to the places frequented by Berlin University people.[9]

Herzen's most important German acquaintance in Berlin was Hermann Müller-Strübing, a friend of all the former Berlin students in the circle.[10] In *Byloe i dumy* Herzen gives an ironic portrait of Müller as the eternal cicerone of visiting wealthy Russians, an amiable parasite and hard-working idler, who years later in London became an ardent German nationalist moved by his patriotic passion to break relations with Herzen. This picture conceals as much as it reveals. In 1847 Müller must have looked quite impressive to Herzen, as his first link to the European left and a survivor of autocratic repression. In 1833 Müller had been condemned to death for participation in student secret societies. His sentence was commuted, but he remained in prison until 1840, when he was finally amnestied. Even then he had to scrounge a living as a journalist, since his academic career was ruined.[11] What later seemed parasitism to Herzen was a consequence of Müller's victimization. Müller was in touch with Ruge's *Deutsche Jahrbücher* group of left Hegelians, among whom Bakunin was a special friend. He thus reinforced Turgenev as a contact with Bakunin, and the rapidity with which Bakunin and Herzen joined company once the latter had arrived in Paris suggests that Herzen had received his address in Berlin and arrived knowing where to find him.[12]

Since Herzen depended socially on the contacts provided by his friends and their friends, and in Germany these were restricted to Berlin, he appears to have been on his own between Berlin and Paris, a tourist and nothing more. His interest in modern scientific achievements was manifest; he was most excited and enthusiastic about his first train ride, and especially by railroad tunnels. A new hospital in Brussels with its exploitation of steam power was worth a special trip. He spent one night in Elbersfeld and was impressed by the factories in this center of early German industrialization, but he seems not to have visited them.[13] The fascination with technological marvels was also reflected in the first "Letter" from the Avenue Marigny:

> It is already difficult, indeed almost impossible, to see Europe, but in a few years it will be completely effaced from human memory; it was for just this reason that railroads were established. Europe for the traveler will turn into several points illuminated by lanterns, several buffets decorated with glasses. Only new Cooks and Dumon-d'Urvilles will leave the cars . . . and go into the interior of Europe, and they will tell us about the life and customs of people who do not live along the railroad. How often I dreamed of how splendid and useful it will be to travel when they finish the Königsberg road. You will drag yourself to Königsberg, sit in the car, and very likely not emerge—the machine will whistle and start to clatter; Berlin—four minutes for a drink of water; Köln—three minutes to grease the wheels; Brussels—five minutes to grab a ham sandwich; Valenciennes—four minutes to prove to the French government that it cannot find hidden cigars; Paris—fifteen minutes to cross by omnibus from one platform to another; Havre—three minutes to transfer to the ship . . . and then in New York, and, in a word, before you come to your senses, you will be back in Sitka, in Siberia, i.e., home again.[14]

From the political point of view, Herzen's travels were as superficial as this paragraph suggests. In Cologne, available evidence indicates that he had absolutely no notion of the active working-class movement with which Marx was still involved, and he did not look up the remmants of the staff of the *Rheinische Zeitung*, which Marx had edited there a few years earlier; this city was merely the symbol of a glorious past. In Brussels, too, he was impressed only by ancient and modern tourist attractions—he did not meet either Lelewel or Marx, both of whom were then living in the Belgian capital and developing their own radical organizations. Herzen had to go to Paris and meet the people to whom he had entrée before he would even know where to look for other representatives of the radical left.

Herzen in Paris

Paris, city of revolutions and center of contemporary radicalism, had long been Herzen's goal. He had finally arrived and, as it turned out, this was indeed the beginning of a new phase in his life. But as with all milestones, this one brought disillusionment as well as fulfill-

The Traveler

ment. After experiencing French life, first under the July Monarchy and then during the revolution, Herzen would never again be able to believe in political or social panaceas, or in the men who claimed to be able to produce them. But once he had ceased to idolize the revolutionaries and had brought them down to human size, he was able to take his own place among them.

Part of Herzen's difficulty with life in Paris before the revolution was social. At home he had become accustomed to the intense conviviality of the circle, and he would never again feel comfortable in the absence of at least one intimate friend. He was also a star of some magnitude in Russia, whose articles and fiction gave him a renown well beyond the limited sphere of his personal friends. In France there was not a great deal of interest in a writer whose works could not be read. Herzen was thus forced to make his own way socially, and Natalie worried that he went out so little, and she threatened to bring him back a domesticated homebody.[15]

It was only in comparison with the constant social effervescence of Moscow, however, that Herzen could be considered isolated. Not only was he traveling with a party that included up to five adults, all of them more or less compatible, he did have a number of Russian contacts as well. There was Ivan Galakhov, a peripheral member of the circle who had fallen gently in love with Ogarev's wife, Mariia L'vovna, and followed the unhappy couple to the West. The Herzens, who attended Galakhov's marriage to an English woman,[16] were very fond of this kindly, idealistic man, although Alexander apparently found him too simple and naive; Galakhov served as the model for the idealistic interlocutor of the first segment of *S togo berega*, which was based on actual conversations between the men.

Other contacts included Turgenev, who returned to Paris in August, and Pavel Annenkov, a sightseer of the left like Herzen himself. The Herzens also frequently saw Nikolai Petrovich and Ekaterina Nikolaevna Botkin, brother and sister-in-law of their Moscow friend Vasilii. Late in the summer Belinskii stopped briefly in Paris, on the way home from his unsuccessful cure for tuberculosis; despite his grave illness, the Herzen salon once again rang with impassioned debate, especially on the role of the bourgeoisie in French and Russian development, echoes of which reached all the way back to Moscow.[17] Finally, there were two sisters, Mariia Ivanovna Poludenskaia, widow of one of Herzen's professorial friends and herself a peripheral member of the circle, and Elizaveta Sazonova. Sazonova returned to

Russia in July; Poludenskaia remained abroad for some time and in 1849 suffered a psychotic episode while staying with the Herzens.[18]

The sisters had come to France, at least in part, to look after the affairs of their brother, Herzen's old school and circle friend, Nikolai Sazonov. He had managed to leave Russia on an extended tour to Italy at the time the rest of the circle was arrested; from then on, with only a short return, he lived in the West, mixed with various radical politicians and institutions, and ran through his once-impressive fortune. Sazonov had written for *La Réforme;* he knew Marx and periodically offered to collaborate with him;[19] he appears to have made it his practice to establish as broad a network of contacts as possible, ranging from moderate-left to radical-revolutionary, and to have brokered relations among his associates. Herzen and Sazonov spent much time together in 1847, and in the summer of 1848 Sazonov became Herzen's most important Russian companion. Nonetheless, neither Herzen nor Natalie was quite comfortable with this brilliant, yet arrogant and not altogether trustworthy man. They also sympathized with Mariia Poludenskaia, who was gravely distressed by her brother's irregular personal and financial life.[20]

Although an émigré, Sazonov was still loosely associated with the old Moscow group; the friends looked him up when they came to Paris and carried letters back and forth between him and his sisters. The Herzens freely discussed him and his problems in their letters back to the group (most of which were not, however, entrusted to the post).[21] Herzen's other, and more important, Russian contact in Paris, Mikhail Bakunin, was much further beyond the pale of respectability. The Russian government considered him a criminal and after 1847, actively pursued him because of his advocacy of the cause of an independent, democratic Poland. Former Moscow friends were almost as hostile toward Bakunin. His departure in 1840 had come when he was barely on speaking terms with his old comrades of the Stankevich circle; relations with both Belinskii and Botkin were embittered when the two men became unsuccessful suitors of Bakunin's sisters. Other members of the group were appalled by his financial irresponsibility and his general habit of manipulating and exploiting his friends. Ogarev, from the rival circle, was also hostile, apparently because Bakunin had suggested to him that his wife, Mariia L'vovna, was involved in a flirtation with Mikhail Katkov, a former friend who was already perceived by the circle members as a renegade.[22] When Ogarev ran into Bakunin in Berlin in 1842, he refused to speak to him.[23] Like Herzen, Bakunin left Russia as much because of tattered relations with his friends as for political and intellectual reasons.

But to journey abroad one needed money, and Bakunin was habitually short. Herzen, despite scarcely knowing him, had helped subsidize his trip, and he and Natalie had befriended him in St. Petersburg before his departure, when none of his old friends wished to see him. It was at this time that the two men first became relatively friendly.[24] Despite this moderate warmth, there seems to have been no direct contact between them after Bakunin's departure. Herzen must have been eager to renew the acquaintance after the appearance of Bakunin's "The Reaction in Germany," which established him as an intellectual and political comrade-in-arms. Once the two men met in Paris, they were close companions until Herzen left France at the end of the summer.

This contact was Herzen's most important entrée into the world of the French and émigré left. The star quality that Herzen had exercised in Russia was Bakunin's asset in Paris, and to some extent Herzen remained in his friend's shadow. As Cadot summarizes: "But if he [Herzen] contributed powerfully in making certain aspects of Russia known to his friends, it seems that his personal influence in the democratic camp was less than that of Bakunin. It might have been different if Herzen, like Bakunin, had been present in Paris from 1844 to 1847, in those years of enthusiasm and faith that preceded the great shipwreck of generous dreams."[25]

Through Bakunin and Sazonov, Herzen was launched into the world of Parisian radicalism. He did not get very far in this first venture, finding himself unhappily relegated to the sidelines. Developing friendships with established radicals was difficult for him; he was used to dominating the scene in Moscow and was unwilling to pay court to anyone.[26] He was aware only of the middle-class, journalist radicals—as he acknowledged later, he had no notion of the underground political life that seethed in clubs and secret societies.[27] The evidence is scanty as to whom he did meet. His memoirs mention Proudhon, who was on rather close terms with Bakunin at this time. An 1848 letter from Rome mentions Jean-Baptiste Bocquet, a young radical who would be active during the revolution, was arrested after the June days, and later became Sasha's tutor as well as Herzen's friend.[28] Positive evidence regarding other French political figures is simply lacking, although it is likely that through Bakunin and Sazonov he met some at least of the *La Réforme* staff.

Herzen was more successful with other marginal figures, the other foreigners in the French capital. The most fateful of his early acquaintances was Georg Herwegh; the friendship that developed at once between the two families not only had a profound impact on the Herzens' (and the Herweghs') personal lives, but also played an important part in determining Alexander Herzen's political course over the next several years. The meeting with Herwegh was a certainty; it was Bakunin who introduced them, but had he not done so, Herzen had contacts with the German poet from a number of his Moscow friends, and most especially Ogarev and Satin.[29] Herwegh was a star in radical circles, so Herzen would probably have looked him up if Bakunin had not conveniently brought them together. The affinity that developed between them could not have been foreseen, however.

Another of Bakunin's friends would indirectly have a major impact on Herzen's career. This was the composer and music teacher Adolph Reichel, who briefly shared an apartment with Bakunin. Herzen mentioned Reichel only in passing in *Byloe i dumy*, and primarily in connection with other people: "Bakunin then lived with A. Reichel, in an extremely modest apartment on the other side of the Seine in the Rue de Bourgogne. Proudhon often came there to hear Reichel's Beethoven and Bakunin's Hegel—the philosophic arguments lasted longer than the symphonies."[30]

Reichel's wife died in the cholera epidemic of 1849, and a year later he married Mariia Ern, the young woman who had accompanied the Herzens abroad and remained with them after Mariia Korsh returned home. Mariia Reichel spent the rest of her life in the West and was always a faithful friend of Herzen and his family. She was also his European contact through whom correspondence for *Poliarnaia zvezda* and *Kolokol* [The Bell] passed. Her service did not end with the journals. She also saved all of Herzen's letters to her, and these provide one of the best sources for his biography in the period after 1850. Unfortunately, her letters to him probably were not preserved.[31]

Herzen's network of acquaintances almost certainly spread out beyond Bakunin and Herwegh and their immediate friends, but there is no evidence available to confirm this. The Herweghs at this period were being subsidized by Emma's wealthy parents and lived comfortably. Their salon was a meeting spot for Polish and German exiles alike.[32] Herzen made contact with the Polish Democrats this summer, probably through his new friends, who were themselves excited by the recent events in Poland.³³ There is also some indication that Herzen accompanied Herwegh to the political salon presided over by the comtesse d'Agoult, but Herzen himself left no account either of any reaction to the countess, or of any people he may have met there.³⁴ It is possible that Herzen, habituated as he was to the intensity and intimacy of the circle, was not fully able to appreciate or utilize the kinds of social contacts available to him in the far more impersonal world of French society and politics.

One indication that Herzen did meet political sophisticates and learn from them, as well as from the press, is the change in his views over the course of that first summer. The bleak view of France and the West generally that appears in the "Pis'ma iz Avenue Marigny" has evoked a great deal of discussion. The issue has been posed in terms of the extent to which Herzen's views were formed before he left Russia, or were they the result of disillusionment with the society he encountered before, during, and in the wake of the 1848 revolutions. In *Byloe i dumy* Herzen himself laid the foundation for the traditional view, that life in the West destroyed his illusions. Malia, on the other hand, has taken the extreme contrasting view, arguing that "all through his first years in the West Herzen was talking about the constructs of his own mind much more than about European events. . . . Herzen would have reacted much the way he did even if the Revolution had succeeded in establishing good liberal republics everywhere west of Russia, or if there had been no Revolution at all."³⁵

An examination of Herzen's early Western works shows both negative preconceptions and subsequent disillusionment. But these works also show that Herzen was reflecting the views expressed by French radicals and learning to orient himself among the competing cliques and doctrines.

There is no doubt that he came to the West ready to criticize; he was a socialist, an opponent of the bourgeois society which he had never seen, but which his reading of Proudhon and Blanc had taught him to despise. He had already quarreled with his friends over it, and was surely seeking evidence to support his side of the dispute. But there is little evidence that he was impassioned or enraged. He had also come to Europe intending to translate his impressions into articles for *Sovremennik*. The first "Pis'mo iz Avenue Marigny," with its combination of wit, high spirits, and criticism, shows the direction he intended to take.

But once in Paris, Herzen was genuinely shocked by his new environment; the articles got out of hand, ran into censorship problems, and also distressed his friends. He first tried to express his dismay at the mores and attitudes of French bourgeois society in aesopian language. The first salvo was a letter to the actor Mikhail Shchepkin (which would, of course, be passed around the circle), in which he described his and Natalie's reactions to the French theater, their disgust at the interminable (six-hour) series of off-color jokes in the theaters that catered to the bourgeoisie, and the positive impressions they received from working-class theaters and their audiences.[36] He drew on the same impressions for the second published "Pis'mo iz Avenue Marigny," where he traced the evolution of the bourgeoisie from Figaro to the characters of Scribe, using these characters to analyze the bourgeoisie's history, social role, and philistine way of life. Again, in contrast to his reactions to the middle class, Herzen had high praise for the Parisian working class, both in and outside the theater.[37] At this early stage of his travels, Herzen still appears to be drawing primarily on the ideological baggage he brought with him and on his spontaneous responses to new experiences.

At the end of the letter to Shchepkin, Herzen had promised to comment in a second one about the great vaudevillian Frédéric Lemaître, who was about to open a new play. The Herzens saw this production not long after its May debut,[38] but Shchepkin did not receive another letter. Instead, Herzen devoted the whole of his third "Pis'mo iz Avenue Marigny" to this work, *Le Chiffonier de Paris*, by Félix Pyat. He retained this strange disproportion in the revised form of the "Pis'ma," the *Pis'ma iz Frantsii i Italii* [Letters from France and Italy] of 1854.[39] He did this because *Le Chiffonier* was the first political event he had to report, and he had learned enough in his six weeks in France to recognize it as such; he could not waste it on a private letter.

The work is a dreadful melodrama about a poor Paris ragpicker and the young girl he loves as a daughter, and how they are framed for murder, infanticide, and robbery by the criminally inclined rich. It was a resounding success, and the triumph of Lemaître's career. Moreover, "contemporaries [were] unanimous in attributing to the play an influence on the revolution which it preceded by only a few months."[40] Herzen knew that the Belgian revolution of 1830 was supposed to have been sparked by a theatrical production, Auber's opera, *La Muette de Portici*,[41] and *Le Chiffonier* seemed about to do the same thing for

France. Unfortunately, his perception and account of this prologue to revolution appears to have been a wasted effort, for there is no evidence that his readers were able to see the hidden political meaning of the play or of the letter that described it.

The final "Pis'mo iz Avenue Marigny" is marked by extreme pessimism and a sense that French government and society were approaching a crisis—views that Herzen probably learned from his new contacts. Scandals involving vast government corruption and a duke's murder of his wife and subsequent suicide, both alluded to in this "Letter," had created shock waves in Paris. Herzen could not have known that a radical journalist had predicted the imminent collapse of the regime in a private letter to his mother, but the comtesse d'Agoult's similar reflections, made to Herwegh, may well have been familiar to him and formed the basis of his own assessment.[42] In the "Letter," he expressed the view that French politics had run into a blind alley in which the party in power could only offer more of the prevailing rampant corruption and hypocrisy, the opposition had nothing but palliatives, and the socialist opposition was too far out of contact with the real feelings of the working people to be a viable force. The "Letter" also includes a recognition of the primacy of economic problems in determining social and political conditions, and in very general terms it discusses the emergence and weaknesses of socialist and liberal economic doctrines. None of these themes, nor the others in the "Letter," is fully developed or well related to the others, and the entire article lacks a sense of direction and focus. It gives the impression that Herzen was not interested in merely describing the events he was witnessing, and he needed time for reflection before he could fully assimilate all that he had experienced since his arrival. The knowledge he had already gained would help him quickly orient himself on the left when revolution opened up the political system in France a few months later. But for now Herzen had had enough of Paris, and at the end of the summer of 1847 he went in search of new people and new experiences.

The Italian Adventure

Toward autumn it became unbearably gloomy in Paris. I could not come to terms with the grotesque moral collapse which surrounded me. I felt my soul was being infected by that self-renunciation, that coldness and that "it's all the same" attitude

> which comes from losses, estrangement from reality, and scorn for the present. I was aging, and only occasionally, in anger, did I still feel the youth of my forces. Death in literature, death in the theater, death in politics, death on the tribune, the walking corpse Guizot on the one side, and the childish babble of the gray-headed opposition on the other.... "To Italy, to Italy!" Away with stone walls, with dreary nature. I wanted to rest, I wanted the sea—the sea, warm air, luxurious green, and people not so dissolute, so afflicted with moral senility. I decided to leave.[43]

And so Herzen and his family left France for the warmth of Italy. In the first instance, this was a retreat; they hoped the climate would be better for Natalie's and Sasha's health, they were not greatly enjoying life in Paris, and in times of stress Herzen and Natalie had long dreamed of finding a haven in Italy.[44] Nonetheless, the idea of leaving the splendors of Paris for the quiet life, without newspapers or agitation, seemed mad—so much so, that Herzen commented ruefully on the coach's first stop at Charenton.[45]

The journey turned out to be one of the high points of Herzen's life. The family was happy and relatively healthy; at each stop they encountered good friends, and they found the Italian people extremely sympathetic. But most important, Herzen now found the excitement and new life he had missed in Paris; from Genoa to Vesuvius, the country was in a state of volcanic excitement. Revolutions were taking place everywhere, and in the exceedingly attractive form of street theater.

The Italian peninsula, with its crazy quilt of sovereignties, was still, in Metternich's words, just a "geographical expression." In this early stage of political action, the call for national unification was less strong than the progress of domestic reform moving from state to state, seemingly almost at random. The reformist impulse had begun in Rome, with the election of Pope Pius IX in 1846. The people of Rome had responded to his first timid measures of liberalization with a great outpouring of devotion and with political organization. Moderate and democratic clubs formed, and these organized huge demonstrations, which pressured the pope, "by acclamation," to introduce more changes.[46] By the spring of 1847, Rome's example in relaxing censorship and forming a civic guard were spreading to other states of the peninsula. Herzen claimed that he became aware of these Italian developments only in Nice, but this seems unlikely.⁴⁷ He certainly knew of the pope's popularity and progressive reputation during the summer in Paris, even if his own attitude was skeptical,⁴⁸ and he appears to have gone to Italy armed with introductions to opposition journalists. It seems reasonable to assume that once again he was a tourist, but one whose special area of interest was politics.

The entire Herzen party traveled from Paris, by way of Lyons and Avignon, to Nice, which was then still part of Savoy and thus was their first introduction to Italy.⁴⁹ Although far from enchanted with the town, they remained there several weeks; Natalie recuperated from an illness, and Herzen spent time with Ivan Galakhov, recently married and now living in Nice with his bride, and sadly afflicted with tuberculosis.⁵⁰ From Nice, by a combination of sea and overland travel, they made their way down the west coast of the peninsula, with stops in Genoa, Livorno, back to Pisa, and then to Civitavecchia, the port for Rome, and to Rome itself. They arrived in Rome in November, took an apartment on the Via del Corso, and planned to remain there for the winter.

On the way they had been spectators of exciting events, which Herzen described in the first of three "Pis'ma s Via del Corso" [Letters from the Via del Corso].⁵¹ This "Letter" shows a familiarity with the immediate background that suggests that Herzen had informants who were able to fill him in on the meaning of the events taking place, but there is no evidence as to who they were. The "Letters" portray the party merely as tourists, watching and being revitalized from the outside:

> I left France, seeking peace, the sun, works of art—and some sort
> of human situation, and I expected none of this in Piedmont.
> And what happened—as soon as I set foot on Italian soil, another
> milieu embraced me—living and energetic. I am obliged to Italy
> for the resurrection of my best hopes, a renewed faith in my
> forces and those of others. Here I saw animated faces and tears,
> and I saw that I too had not forgotten how to feel strongly. Infinite gratitude to fate that I happened into Italy at such a great
> moment of her life—at this peaceful, noble *Risorgimento,* full of
> force, consciousness, and that civility which is a quality of everything Italian.⁵²

In Nice, news arrived that King Charles Albert of Savoy had granted increased communal autonomy and judicial reforms. The Herzens witnessed the celebrations in this French-speaking corner of

Charles Albert's state. They arrived in Genoa, their first stop in ethnic Italy, just as the city was providing a tumultuous welcome for the king. Then they crossed the border into Tuscany where, in Livorno, they witnessed the enactment of another set of reforms, of which the newly created civil guard was the most important.

All these new experiences, along with reflections on the France he had just left, stimulated Herzen's imagination. Two works that described and reflected them were written shortly after the party arrived in Rome. One was the first "Pis'mo s Via del Corso," already cited; the other was a more philosophical reflection on ideology and reality, "Pered grozei" [Before the Storm], which was destined to become the introductory chapter of *S togo berega*, Herzen's single most evocative and popular work.[53]

The "Letter," in addition to describing sights and events, contains expressions of Herzen's most socially conscious radicalism to date. It also shows his first search for alternative forms of social organization that would be more convincing than the prescriptions of the French doctrines he had considered and dismissed in the last "Letter" of the Avenue Marigny series. His description of Lyons and its role in the French Revolution of 1789, and then again in 1832, demonstrated his new awareness of class conflict lying behind political change. In discussing the suppression of the 1832 uprising, he wrote:

> The ministers [of the government of Louis Philippe] were for the most part philanthropists, liberals, political economists, historians, journalists—what must it have cost their tender hearts, their sentimentality, to give such orders [for the bloody pacification]—but there was nothing to be done, it was necessary to calm the bourgeoisie, it was necessary to give a guarantee, to remove any doubt, to strengthen the bond between the new order and the bourgeoisie. The Lyons pacification and the fighting in Clôtre St.-Merry loudly proclaimed how the questions of wages, of hunger, and of other disorders would be decided by the ministry . . . these were the September days of the second Restoration; on the one hand, they cut off all hopes, and on the other they burnt all bridges.[54]

Two alternatives to France's regime of centralized government and the dominance of bourgeois private property suggested themselves to him. In this "Letter," Herzen for the first time expressed admiration for the Russian village, which was not afflicted with the stone walls he found in the West and with the passion for private property they symbolized.⁵⁵ On the other hand, travel through Italy introduced him to the possibilities of autonomous municipal development. From his observations of Italian towns in revolt and reorganization, he developed a notion of municipal anarchism, an ideal of free cities capable not only of governing themselves, but also of preserving a value system based on local culture and autonomy against the leveling tendencies of centralization.⁵⁶

In counterpoise to Herzen's assimilation of new experiences and his awareness of new potentialities went his rejection of old theoretical analyses of historical development and old codes of demands and obligations. This ground-clearing was expressed in "Pered grozei." The sense of impending crisis, of the bankruptcy of the old order, is manifest in the work's title, with its suggestion of approaching thunder. This is a dialogue in which the voice that approximates Herzen's own position insists that development, historical and natural, is not constrained by human intellectual constructs and cannot legitimately be judged by them; the malaise of the intellectuals is a consequence not of real evils, but of their own ideological straitjacket. Continuing the arguments that had begun in Moscow long before, he called for the jettisoning of romanticism, which he saw as an ideology no less repressive than the medieval Catholicism it had replaced. Herzen demanded that every conscious individual orient himself in an indifferent universe and make his own decisions, neither constrained nor supported by abstract, arbitrary systems.⁵⁷

While Herzen was completing these two essays, the family had settled in, to see the sights of Rome, to visit the galleries, and to watch the storm clouds gather. They were joined there by the family of Aleksei Tuchkov, Ogarev's friend and neighbor in Penza *guberniia* and an old acquaintance of Herzen's. Politically, the Tuchkovs were sympathetic—Aleksei had been peripherally associated with the Decembrists and had suffered for it. In Penza he had been marshal of nobility, and his use of that office to support peasant needs estranged him from his neighbors.⁵⁸ Together he and Herzen watched the political atmosphere darken and exchanged speculations on the possibilities of revolution breaking out in France.

The arrival of the Tuchkovs was even more important for Natalie than for her husband. She found in the daughters of the family, and particularly the younger, also named Natalie, the emotionally satisfying intimate friendship which she had missed ever since the breakup of the circle more than a year earlier. Natalie Tuchkova become one of the emotional poles in Natalie Herzen's's life, and this in turn helped define the younger woman's relationship both with Ogarev and with Herzen himself in later years.[59]

Herzen did not limit his contacts to the Tuchkovs, who had followed Ogarev's advice and looked him up; he also actively sought people out. Among the scant surviving correspondence from this period is a letter to the artist A. A. Ivanov, resident in Rome, to whom Herzen introduced himself, using Galakov as a reference.[60] Although the two men quarreled, primarily over Gogol's *Selected Passages from Correspondence with Friends*, a tenuous friendship was established.[61] Herzen also used names provided by Herwegh to attempt to make contact with spokesmen of the Risorgimento. Although not all these leads could be tracked down, Herzen did become friendly with the editors of a moderate liberal paper, *Epoca*, which he even attempted to push toward republicanism. One board member, Leopoldo Spini, became a close friend. It was probably Spini who familiarized Herzen with Italian developments and introduced him to other political figures.[62] Another journalist whom Herzen met at this time, Michelangelo Pinto, would soon play a diplomatic role for the Roman Republic of 1848, and later would be a friend to Herzen in his personal crises.

The Herzen party remained in Rome for slightly over two months, from the end of November 1847 to February 1848. They were able to watch the reform process, but during this period they also became aware that there were limits to change granted from above by an essentially conservative ruler. In the year and a half since the election of Pius IX and the first reforms, public opinion had become organized through popular clubs. The more democratic of these, the Circolo Popolare, had been established by a wine carrier, Angelo Brunetti, also known as Cicerouacchio, with whom Herzen became acquainted. By greeting each reform with massive demonstrations of thanksgiving, accompanied by requests for further change, Cicerouacchio and his followers had pressured the pope, "by acclamation," into liberalizing still further. But by the end of 1847 the limits had been reached. The moderate consultative government Pius was setting up satisfied neither the conservative cardinals nor the crowds. First measures of repression—especially the censorship of the popular press—evoked hostility. Continuing news of radical activity, in Switzerland, Tuscany, and the Kingdom of the Two Sicilies, aroused enthusiasm in the crowds, fear in the pope. The popular movement became more militant and began to demand a genuine constitution; the pope withdrew behind the Vatican walls in confused silence.[63]

Dismal weather and political stalemate lowered the spirits of Herzen and his friends. Then news came of revolution in Palermo, followed two weeks later by an uprising in Naples. (The two cities were the major urban centers of the Kingdom of the Two Sicilies.) On January 30, Rome heard that the king of the Two Sicilies, having promised a constitution and amnesty, asked ten days to fulfill his promise. The Herzens decided to go to Naples to watch. On February 5 they left Rome. Mariia Korsh remained behind with the two younger children, while the Tuchkov family and Leopoldo Spini accompanied the travelers.[64]

On the personal level, the trip south was all the Herzens could have asked. They were delighted by the climate, scenery, and people; they had adventures, to provide spice, and happy endings; and the political events they had come to see were indeed stirring. They were present at great demonstrations in Naples in which political prisoners were freed and feted, and the constitution, briefly delayed, was granted amid jubilant celebration. Herzen continued to expand his network of radical contacts. Through Spini he became acquainted with the staff of *Italico*, a Neapolitan paper, and he probably owed his understanding of southern events to the background provided by these men.[65] The three weeks the Herzens spent on this side trip did not exhaust their interest; once back in Rome they made abortive plans to return to the excitement of the south.[66]

Politically, Naples was much less satisfying. Beneath the surface of demonstration, celebration, and solemn promise was the reality of concessions extorted from a reluctant monarch who remained on his throne and waited for an opportunity to reassert his control. Four months earlier Herzen had been enthusiastic about reforms granted from above by the king of Sardinia; Rome, and now Naples, undermined his confidence in peaceful change brought about by the cooperation of the crowds and the monarch. It was splendid to see Ferdinand II and his retinue take the oath of loyalty to the new constitution, but clearly this was not the end of the story.

New developments in the north drew the party back to Rome— constitutions in Tuscany and Piedmont, as well as in Denmark, and a new ministry in Rome.[67] Almost immediately after their arrival, at the end of Carnival, they learned the most overwhelming news of all— revolution had broken out in Paris itself, and Louis Philippe had fled, leaving a republic behind him. The storm Herzen had sensed ever since his arrival in France had finally burst out, and seemed to be washing away the entire political system.

Despite this spectacular news, Herzen, connoisseur of revolutions though he was becoming, did not hasten off to Paris.[68] Events in Italy were still very exciting; it seemed quite possible that there would be a republic on the peninsula as well, and their Italian contacts put his party in a better position to observe events than they would have in Paris.[69] Moreover, the family was happier and healthier in Italy than they had been in the north, and so they remained in Rome until the end of April.

The Roman people were demanding a constitution by the time the Herzens returned to the city, and this was granted on March 15. The Russians were present for the celebrations. Natalie wrote her friends about them, adding, "We wanted you to know that everything that happened here, but we *cannot write.*"[70] This rather heavy-handed discretion may have concealed the fact that she and her family had not only observed, but also participated in the demonstration.

Their participation in others is documented. Herzen said later that he lived "in the street" that winter in Rome.[71] In *Byloe i dumy* he described the demonstration that expressed Roman support to the Piedmontese ambassador in the war between Piedmont and Austria. The ambassador and Cicerouacchio shared the limelight with four Russian women—Natalie Herzen, Mariia Ern, and Natalie and Elena Tuchkova—who stood with them on the balcony of the embassy.[72] Another description of Herzen's involvement in political events was provided many years later by Natalie Tuchkova:

> Al[exander] marched at the head with the men, and we three in the middle—almost the only representatives of our sex. The men pointed us out to the Italian women standing on the balconies. "Look at your sisters," they said, "throw aside your harps [sic] and share their tireless energy.[73]

Soon, however, the carnival period of the revolution had passed. With the outbreak of unrest in the parts of the peninsula controlled by Austria, the policy of concessions ended; the Hapsburg monarchy reinforced its garrison and undertook the suppression of rebellion in Venice and Milan. Charles Albert of Savoy responded with a war intended to drive the Austrians out of Italy and bring about unification under his own leadership. The war undermined political consensus in Rome, for the pope refused to intervene on the Piedmontese side. He did provide moral and military support for the volunteers, however, and in a great torchlit ceremony in the Forum the young men of Rome were signed up. The next day they marched off.[74] Politically, this was really the beginning of the end of Italy's 1848 adventure; the war was a disaster for Piedmont that soon forced Charles Albert to abdicate. The pope now ceased his hesitation and gave his allegiance to Austria and the reassertion of order; henceforth further change would come not from reform, but only through the overthrow of existing regimes.

Herzen's second and third "Pis'ma s Via del Corso" describe Italian events up to the departure of the volunteers. The autonomous Italian story was played out, and the future now would be determined by the fate of revolution in the great powers. The outburst in Vienna, which forced the resignation and flight of Metternich, was a hopeful sign. But the Hapsburg dynasty itself was still in place, if feeble. Only in Paris had the monarchy been routed altogether, and so Paris had once again become the pivot of European political and social change. The Herzens and their friends headed back, to see the new republic in action.

3

PARIS: THE FIRST MONTHS

NO matter how many the portents of imminent collapse visible to observers, the actual outbreak of revolution and the sudden disappearance of established structures of authority always comes as a shock. So it was in France in 1848.[1] The symptoms of governmental dysfunction and public alienation had multiplied throughout 1847, but Guizot's cabinet had strong enough control over the levers of power to respond by silencing opposition, rather than changing policy. Censorship was tightened, and enough pressure was exerted in the 1847 elections to the Chamber of Deputies to increase the proministry majority. As it turned out, this policy was distinctly shortsighted; it made change within the system virtually impossible, and thereby forced the opposition to use extraparliamentary methods. Resistance to Guizot was conducted in the first instance by the extremely moderate dynastic opposition, but its members' recourse to unconventional methods to bring about reform soon led to an attempt to force the prime minister away from controls, and then, suddenly, to change the system altogether.

The prelude and provocation came in a series of public banquets convened by the dynastic opposition in towns across the country, which were held between the summer of 1847 and February 1848. After the speeches, the banquet participants adopted resolutions calling for change. Some of these gatherings took a more radical line, giving a platform to republican spokesmen like Ledru-Rollin and passing resolutions that, by not mentioning the monarchy, were implicitly republican. The crisis came when the government, supported by the Chamber of Deputies, banned a banquet scheduled by the moderate opposition to take place in Paris's twelfth arrondissement.[2] The banquet, its ban, and possible compromises were discussed at length in the chamber, the press, and the streets; the issue became inflated to one of political morality, the right of resistance, and the government's challenge to fundamental civil rights. Ultimately, the sponsors backed down and canceled, but by the time they did so the stakes had been forced up. At a meeting hosted by the republican opposition and attended by professional journalists and working people at the *La Réforme* offices, it was decided to turn the affair into an antimonarchical manifestation.[3]

The demonstrations that broke out on February 22 to protest the ban soon surpassed the republicans' expectations and got out of hand, for the National Guard, the armed force of the Paris bourgeoisie, would not or could not suppress demonstrators whose demand for reform they found sympathetic. The following day, the king yielded to the call for reform and dismissed Guizot and his cabinet, charging the moderate Molé to form a new government. Molé entered into negotiations with the leaders of the dynastic opposition, Odilon Barrot and Adolphe Thiers, and the issue of reform appeared to have been resolved. The king and the establishment relaxed, while the demonstrators paraded victoriously from the swarming popular districts of St. Martin and St. Denis across the luxurious enclaves of the section just north of the Tuileries and the Palais Royal, on their way to a thanksgiving service at the Madeleine.

In the course of the celebration there were some confrontations between demonstrators and troops; shots were fired and, in one incident, a large number of demonstrators—between forty and one hundred—fell dead or wounded. All accounts agree that at this point the entire movement changed tone; the demonstrations again became militant, only this time the Paris workers demanded not reform, but a republic. By midday on February 24, the Tuileries and Palais Royal threatened to become battlegrounds, and the king abdicated in favor of his grandson and fled. An attempt by the child's widowed mother, the duchesse d'Orléans, to have the succession acknowledged and herself recognized as regent by the Chamber or Deputies failed when a crowd stormed the chamber and made clear their demand for a republic. Rule by the Orleans family, and with it the entire hereditary line of the Bourbons, was ended.

The precise dynamics of the crowd actions that pulled down the monarchy will never be known. Still, it seems clear that to a considerable extent these were not spontaneous, undirected mobs. The terrible economic conditions of the preceding two years undoubtedly increased the number of recruits for revolutionary violence, but the demands of the crowd were for political change, not for the alleviation of economic distress.[4] They appear to have been called out by the republican secret societies, which provided leadership in building barricades and storming buildings, and also provided the slogans—for reform, when that appeared to be the limit of the possible, and then for a republic, once the events of the night of February 23 had further radicalized the Parisian people.

By February 24, the republican politicians and journalists recognized that the monarchy might well fall and began to put together a provisional government. The list was drawn up by a committee composed of men from *Le National* and *La Réforme*. A somewhat revised list, which most importantly omitted the name of socialist Louis Blanc, was presented to the Chamber of Deputies in the confusion following the invasion of the Chamber and the withdrawal of the duchesse d'Orleans. The cowed deputies approved, and the new ministers marched in procession from the Palais Bourbon, along the Left Bank quays to the Pont Neuf, across the river and over to the Hôtel de Ville, where they found a very active revolutionary crowd demanding the declaration of a republic. In the middle of some of the most stormy activity of the entire revolutionary process, the members of the government managed to enter the building and present themselves from a balcony for the approbation of the crowd. Under popular pressure, and at his own insistence, Blanc was again included in the government, but merely as a secretary with no portfolio. Again on Blanc's insistence, a worker known as Albert, who had fought actively on the barricades and had long been involved in the secret societies, including Blanqui's Societé des Saisons, was added to the government.[5]

The cabinet that now attempted to take control of the governmental mechanism and perhaps reshape the country was severely divided regarding aims, methods, and constituencies. A simple dichotomy between men from *Le National* and those from *La Réforme*, or between "political republicans" and "social republicans" will not adequately explain the conflicts and crossed purposes that characterized the republican government from its very first hours.

To paper over the differences and serve as a symbol of republican virtue and continuity, the list makers chose as president of the Council of Ministers the octogenarian Jacques Dupont de l'Eure, an irreproachable veteran republican whose career had spanned more than fifty years. His role was to personify the republic, while real political decisions were made elsewhere; in the event, however, this role was largely taken over by Lamartine.

Alphonse de Lamartine, aristocrat, poet, diplomat, and natural conservative, had been a late convert to reform.[6] His move into the opposition was all the more impressive because it came late—if Lamartine had decided that the Guizot goverment must be resisted, then who could disagree? At the time the revolution broke out, he enjoyed great authority among the educated and prosperous. He came into the Provisional Government apparently believing in "the people" as an undifferentiated, fraternal body politic; he did not appeal to class interests and did not attempt to develop a specific constituency of his own. Characteristically, he took the post of minister of foreign affairs, which offered him great prestige but no administrative power domestically.[7] As "persuader in chief" (and for all their vast differences, one can see some significant parallels between Lamartine in 1848 and Kerenskii, who originally won that ironic title in 1917 Russia), he did not develop a genuine power base; instead he used his sincerity and his oratorical talent to replace power politics. For the first two weeks, he succeeded with his oratory and the flattery implied by his assumption that all citizens were equally a part of the great nation. Soon, however, these wore thin, and eventually the poet was left isolated.[8]

The other members of the government were far more aware that government was a matter of power, both personal and for one's constituents. The more conservative ministers, the men from *Le National*, largely succeeded in winning for themselves (or being handed) administrative posts. Garnier-Pages became mayor of Paris; soon he took over the Ministry of Finance from the equally conservative Goudchaux, and the mayoralty went to Marrast, editor of *Le National*. The Ministry of Justice went to Cremieux. In the first days of the revolution, the conservatism of these men was expressed less is specific policy questions (usually, the government was close to unanimity on policy decisions) than in their effort to use the traditional tools of administration to carry on business as usual without interference from Paris crowds, popular pressure groups, or any other manifestations of revolutionary organization. This approach was conservative in substance as well as form, however, for the usual way of conducting business in the July Monarchy had been to the advantage of the wealthy and the established. The conservative ministers saw no reason to change that.

The Ministry of the Interior was held by Alexandre Ledru-Rollin, a democratic republican of *La Réforme*, who had led the republican opposition in the Chamber of Deputies. Herzen saw Ledru-Rollin as the sole genuine revolutionary in the cabinet, and with reason.[9] It was not his ideology—Ledru was a nonsocialist, and he had little sympathy for the popular movement, now that republicans controlled the machinery of government—that set him apart, but his vigorous use of the instruments of power that came with his vital ministry. He attempted to undermine the old political establishment and to republicanize the still conservative countryside. To these ends he sent commissars out to the provinces to administer them in a republican spirit—outside the chain of command established by the constitution of the monarchy—and to rally and organize whatever republican sentiment was already present. His ministry also provided a barrage of propaganda, some of which favored republicanizing the French people before turning over the government of the people to them.[10]

The other major figure in the government was Louis Blanc. He had built up a considerable working-class audience in his ten years of journalism and theoretical work, and was probably the most genuinely popular member of the new government. The Paris workingmen were grateful to him for his advocacy of their cause, and at the same time protective of a man so small that he often had to be carried through difficult situations and who had to stand on tables to make himself seen and heard. Blanc tried and failed to turn this popularity into administrative power. He strenuously fought for the creation and the leadership of a Ministry of Progress that would have the authority and the means to enact measures concerning labor relations and other economic problems. He was overruled by his colleagues, who insisted that to establish such a ministry would be to encroach upon the rights of the constituent assembly, and the nation itself, to determine its future form of government. Blanc threatened to resign over this issue. To keep him in the government, his colleagues offered him instead the opportunity to chair an investigating commission charged with studying the conditions of labor in the country. This body, which met in the Palais de Luxembourg and hence was known as the Luxembourg Commission, drew delegates from the various craft-organized working people's associations in the capital. It was not only the first serious involvement of workers in government activity; it also gave Blanc an opportunity to organize his constituency through the associations, and also to alleviate some problems by means of negotiations with employers.[11] While the Luxembourg Commission did not have enough influence and organizational potential to affect the outcome of the revolution in 1848, it was a major step in workers' organization and politicization.

The other radicals in the cabinet were the worker, Albert, and the editor of *La Réforme*, Ferdinand Flocon. Albert seconded Blanc at the Luxembourg Commission. Neither he nor Flocon had his own ministerial appointment, and neither had very much influence on the workings of the government.

An important conquest for the radicals was the Paris police. Marc Caussidière was a jacobin veteran of the secret societies with some contacts with the *La Réforme* group. Showing a lively instinct for power so often lacking in the other republicans, Caussidière transformed the police and turned it into an instrument of the revolution rather than of the old order. Political prisoners were freed, and they and secret society members were enrolled in a new People's Guard. Further assuring radical republican control of the municipal police, the department was transferred from the jurisdiction of the city of Paris, with its conservative mayor, to Ledru-Rollin's Ministry of the Interior. As a conservative counterforce to Caussidière's men, the government then established a Garde Mobile, made up of paid volunteers. But despite distrust for Caussidière's radicalism and unconventionality, contemporaries agreed that in fact his men did a good job of restoring order in the capital.

Revolutionary politics consisted of a complex interplay of actions by constituted authorities and crowd interventions into decision making. The volatility, militancy, discipline, and political views of the crowds would shape the great *journées* of the revolution and have a major impact on the outcome of events. There were, in fact, two sources of street action, one conservative and the other radical.

Conservative street action centered around the National Guard, supplemented by the Garde Mobile. The guard was drawn from middle-class men; it had supported the movement of February in the belief that to do so would bring about parliamentary reform and the fall of Guizot. It was by no means enthusiastic about the republic that resulted. It was still less enthusiastic about the opening of the guard to all citizens and the loss of special privileges for the elite units, which were among the first acts of the Provisional Government. By mid-

March, the guard was established as a force that would resist democratization or proletarian pressure on the government. It might be used against the government if it disliked its policies, or it might be used by the government, in a potential conflict with the radically minded Paris crowd.

This crowd was organized by the clubs. In the immediate aftermath of revolution, clubs were established in support of every conceivable social and political theory; there were three hundred of them within a few days. The main ones, however, were popular, democratic, and socialist in orientation. The veterans of the struggle against the July Monarchy returned to Paris upon release from prison where many had been incarcerated since the failed uprising of 1839, and soon were at the center of a large, loose movement whose nuclei were probably the secret societies. Two clubs were especially large and important: the Societé Centrale Républicaine, headed by Auguste Blanqui, and the Club de la Révolution, headed by Armand Barbès.[12]

The differences between the two clubs were matters of style, tactics, and personality, rather than ideology. Barbès and Blanqui had been comrades in arms in 1839, but then had quarreled and broken with each other. Barbès became the hero and favorite of politicicans and journalists of the republic. Wealthy, self-sacrificing, courageous, charming—the contemporary accounts are unanimous in their praise of him.[13] Blanqui, on the other hand, was caustic, embittered, and tough. He did not attempt to charm the bourgeoisie, and he did not; rather, from the first day he attacked the Provisional Government from the left, hoping to see it overturned by a genuinely revolutionary and democratic movement. He became the focus of middle-class fears of violence and conspiracy; every act by popular revolutionary groups that threatened the Provisional Government's authority was blamed on him. A document published in a new journal, founded specifically for the purpose of printing it, indicated that Blanqui had turned informer after his 1839 arrest. He refused to appear before a revolutionary "court of honor" to answer and rebut the charges. The document was probably a forgery, but Blanqui appeared more malignant than ever.[14]

On the theoretical level, however, both Barbès and Blanqui espoused a nondoctrinaire democratic socialism. Their radicalism lay less in their programs than in their assertion that the legitimacy of the revolution came from the crowd action, and that the demands of the popular movement should be compelling for the government. The "people" whose will they thought supreme was the Parisian populace; rural folk were dominated by priests and landlords, and so were unable to know or express their own will. Barbès was more inclined that his rival to utilize the crowd in support of the Provisional Government; Blanqui was more likely to threaten to overthrow it with a new surge of revolutionary violence. The difference, however, was one of degree.

The issues confronting France in 1848, then, were primarily about the sources of sovereignty and the proper uses of power, rather than about specific policies. On major programmatic points, there was fundamental agreement not only within the government, but also between the government and organized public opinion. Thus, the republic promptly instituted broad civil liberties—the incredible expansion of the press, with most of the new voices shrill and critical, and the seething activity of the nightly meetings of clubs in public buildings all over the city were possible only because censorship had been removed and the right of association had been established. With an eye on the fearsome example of the great French Revolution of 1789, the new government also abolished the death penalty for political offenses, a measure generally applauded.

For the clubs and the governmental left, the idea of the republic included a nondoctrinaire socialism. The newspaper that came closest to expressing this republican left mood was *La Vraie République,* edited by Théophile Thoré. It defined its socialism in this fashion:

> [Despite the vagueness of socialist ideas], the idea of republican justice has nonetheless found some formulas that only immorality could oppose. For example, is it not true that everyone has the right to live and the duty to work; that each person who brings to society the tribute of all his strength, all his intelligence, all his sentiments, has the right to ask in exchange the satisfaction of all his legitimate needs; that strength, capacity and virtue impose duties; finally, that the destiny of each and every person is the complete development of all his faculties. This is even in society's interest as much as it is in the individual's.
>
> The aim of a well-organized republic will thus be to give all citizens the means to perfect their spirit, heart and activity. Education, the family, the fatherland, labor and property are at present truly established only for a restricted minority. What the socialists demand is precisely that everyone enjoy the advantage of these essential elements of human life.[15]

Once again, the conservative republicans were disturbed less by the content of these demands than by their source, in the popular movement. Indeed, the government unanimously acknowledged the right to work, and it was the conservative group within it that established the ill-fated national workshops, which at the very least provided some relief to some of the unemployed.[16]

The conflicting aims and anxieties of the different groups involved in revolutionary politics led to a series of confrontations on the streets of Paris, each of which marked a stage in the progress of the revolution. The first took place in mid-March. The national guardsmen, who were disturbed by the prospect of democratization of their ranks, were encouraged in their opposition to the imposition of these measures by conservatives, who disliked the direction in which Ledru-Rollin was taking the Ministry of the Interior. Instructions to his commissars to undermine the old elite, organize elections in favor of new men, and act in favor of the workers against the "respectable interests" provided a pretext for opposition.[17] These two strands of conservative resistance resulted in an angry National Guard demonstration on March 16; apparently, the guard expected to receive support from the conservative members of the government for its complaints against Ledru-Rollin and the "communists," but this was not forthcoming. On this occasion, the government presented a united front against outside pressure and set the guard units home cowed.

A massive counterdemonstration took place the next day. The timing turned it into a response to the guard, but in fact it had been planned for some time. Two issues agitated the Paris clubs and workers' associations, whose members turned out in the hundreds of thousands on March 17. One was concern that regular troops were still stationed in Paris; the fear that these units could ultimately be used to smash the revolution turned out in the event to be all too valid. The other was the demand that elections to the National Assembly be postponed.

The timing of the elections involved questions of political power and differing views on the nature of democracy. All groups on the left considered democracy their fundamental goal; nonetheless, they were afraid that their own form of urban, popular, socialist democracy would be swamped in nationwide elections based on universal suffrage. The peasants, they thought, were so dominated by priests and landowners, so backward politically in comparison to their urban compatriots, that they could neither perceive nor act in accord with their true interests.

The answer to this problem for many on the left was for the government not to hold the elections until substantial democratization of institutions and attitudes had taken place. Ledru-Rollin's reorganization of local government had been designed to achieve this end, but time was short. Initially, April 9 had been set for the elections. The socialist left—from George Sand to Blanc to Thoré and the Blanqui and Barbès clubs—were unanimous that they should be postponed.[18] Herzen, writing after the June Days, argued that the Provisional Government should have acted as a temporary dictatorship and used its power to prepare the people for democracy.[19] In this he was not far from the views attributed to Blanc by Caussidière.[20] Herzen too argued that universal suffrage could not produce truly revolutionary results under existing conditions:

> And what result *could* universal suffrage give; voting for the first time, without preparation, without education, under the influence of the clergy, the wealthy landowners and urban bourgeoisie, who could the peasants elect? What could the army, which was unaccustomed to discussion, give? What could the bourgeoisie, which was too accustomed to intrigues and plotting, and whose [social] position made it hostile to democracy, give?[21]

Herzen differed from the prevailing view of the democratic left only in a greater skepticism about democratic forms in general. "An arithmetic count of votes, *faute de mieux* might express something in a country where education was universal—but in France?"[22]

The government responded to the demonstrators' demand by postponing the elections, but only by two weeks, to April 23. Virtually all commentators agree that this weakened the republic—an election held in the first flush of victory might have capitalized on enthusiasm for the revolution; one held later might have benefited from the successful operation of republican institutions. By late April, new institutions were not yet in place and, as we have seen, the government majority was reluctant to establish them. On the other hand, the government had had time to make itself thoroughly unpopular in the countryside, through the imposition of a forty-five centime surcharge on major taxes.[23]

The second great *journée* of 1848 intervened before the elections took place. April 16 was important because it showed the government majority retreating from the relatively benevolent view of the popular movement it had taken a month earlier. It also marked the beginning of a split among the radical republicans, with Ledru-Rollin making a decisive move toward the conservative majority, leaving Blanc almost completely isolated. The occasion was the mustering of the new, popular units of the National Guard to elect their officers. The elections turned into a massive demonstration, apparently aimed at showing support for the government. Rumor and panic interpreted the events differently, however, and it was believed that the worker-guardsmen were marching toward the Hôtel de Ville with the intention of carrying out a Blanqui-inspired coup d'état. Ledru-Rollin responded by sounding the alarm to call out the older, conservative units of the guard. The demonstration took place, with the Garde Mobile herding the workers' units through streets lined by prerevolutionary guardsmen shouting hostile slogans. The workers dispersed after a cold welcome by representatives of the government, their confidence severely shaken. Blanc never forgave Ledru-Rollin for sounding the alarm, and the breach between the men would only grow wider in the future. It would make concerted republican action extremely difficult, if not impossible.

On April 23 the elections took place, and outside of Paris they sent conservative local notables to the National Assembly. The outcome evoked the first scattered confrontations between the forces of the new order and the revolutionary movement. There was a riot in Limoges, and in Rouen a postelection protest by the left resulted in a bloody clash with the National Guard in which thirty-nine people were killed.[24] Thus, the assembly that convened on May 4 operated from the start in an atmosphere of potential conflict between the forces of "order," which it represented, and continued unrest from the Paris populace, representing, as they thought, the genuine spirit of the revolution. The assembly's primary function was to write a new constitution for France. Until this great task was completed, it held sovereign power and took over the responsibility of appointing the ministry, approving or reversing its measures, and making sure it maintained order in the capital. Once it was in office, the revolution moved into a new phase. Just at this time, on May 6, Alexander Herzen and his family arrived back in Paris. They would be eyewitnesses to the tragic dénouement of the revolution and the election of

Louis Napoleon Bonaparte to the office of president of the Second French Republic.

Revolutionary Internationalism in the Paris Revolution

On May 15, 1848, *La Vraie República* declared:

> The French revolution and the European revolution are scarcely commenced. The people of '92 have not resigned. No, it is impossible that our internal Revolution should stop at a simulacrum of democracy, that the Revolution of Europe should be indefinitely adjourned. Let us resume our glorious initiative and declare that France is still the inspired Joan of Arc who, with the aid of God, will proclaim the deliverance of all people.[25]

There was an international dimension to the revolution of 1848 from the start. It combined ideology and power politics, and within France it involved interrelationships between the government, the popular movement, and the foreign nationals. For the émigrés in France, it also renewed and complicated their links with their sympathizers at home. For Alexander Herzen, a stranger himself, revolutionary internationalism justified involvement in revolutionary activity; and the contacts he had established with the exile community in 1847 made it possible for him to participate in events, at least on a limited basis. The ethos of revolutionary solidarity and the legacy of 1848 would help define the attitude of the refugee world in which he was to live for the remainder of his life.

The notion that a community of interests linked revolutionaries everywhere, that in fact there was a single struggle for progress and freedom against the united forces of the reactionary governments of all the European states, went back to the first French Republic and its promise to "accord fraternity and aid to all peoples who wish to recover their liberty."[26] The Congress of Vienna and its resulting Quadruple and Holy Alliances confirmed the idea, for the victorious monarchical powers did indeed perceive the revolution as a single threat to all of them, and cooperated to suppress it. The fact that Poles, Italians, liberal Germans, Hungarians, and South Slavs hald a single enemy in the Hapsburg monarchy, and that the Hapsburgs were the conductors of the reactionary concert of Europe, reinforced the belief that radicals everywhere were natural allies.

The personal relationships established among the members of the foreign communities in Paris under the July Monarchy supported this sense of alliance. On a more institutional basis, both the Carbonari and Mazzini's Young Europe movement had involved international cooperation, at least by the leaders. Thus, both tradition and personal experience fostered sentiments of international solidarity among the educated, cosmopolitan émigrés.

Working-class radicals made their own contribution to internationalism, and by 1848 revolutionary solidarity across national lines had become a part of their program. Proletarian internationalism appears to have derived particularly from England, where the Chartists made alliances with the German workers of the League of the Just, Polish refugees from the 1831 uprising, and Italian supporters of Mazzini. Chartism itself soon divided into two wings. The radical, "physical force" Chartists were fundamentally alienated from the establishment and inclined to revolutionary violence. The more moderate "moral force" Chartists, dominated by the skilled workmen of the London Workingmen's Association, on the other hand, were able and eager eventually to move into a tributary, if not the mainstream, of English politics, forming an alliance with the left fringe of the middle-class parliamentary radicals. Both groups continued to have important international concerns and contacts. The physical force Chartists linked up with the Germans and the radical faction of the Poles. The more moderate group found that a major bridge linking them to the middle class was Mazzini and the organizations he inspired to promote sympathy for the Italian cause.[27] One of the Polish democratic factions was also involved in this branch of English internationalism.

The British workers extended their sense of solidarity beyond the foreign émigrés in their own country. As early as 1836, the prosecution of labor organizers in Belgium inspired the moderate London Workingmen's Association to issue a manifesto that called for the formation of a federation of working-class organizations of Holland, the Rhineland, Belgium, and England to fight against their common enemy.[28] By the early 1840s, the idea has been picked up in France by the group of workers who published *l'Atelier* in Paris (and who were in touch with the Chartists), and by Flora Tristan in her book *l'Union ouvrière* (1843).[29]

By 1848, several groups had taken the first steps beyond mutual sympathy toward international organization. The English moderates in 1847 established a People's International League, whose goals were:

> To enlighten the British public as to the political conditions and relations of foreign countries; to disseminate the principles of national freedom and progress; to embody and manifest an efficient public opinion in favour of the right of every people to self-government and the maintenance of their own nationality; to promote a good understanding between the peoples of all countries.

To further these aims, the league distributed Mazzinian propaganda to the members of Parliament and the press and also established communications with oppositional groups on the continent, with the aim of "obtaining correct and ready information on all important questions."[30] Shortly after the February Revolution broke out, a deputation from the London Workingmen's Association, consisting of William Linton and J. D. Collett, accompanied Mazzini to Paris, carrying greetings from the association to the Provisional Government.[31]

The internationalism of the more radical groups was institutionalized in the Fraternal Democrats, which was established by the Chartists Ernest Jones and Julian Harney and the German radicals. The organization also included representatives of other national groups. On March 5, a delegation from the Fraternal Democrats, consisting of Harney, Jones, and Philip McGrath, and accompanied by Karl Schapper, Joseph Moll, and Heinrich Bauer—all veterans of the League of the Just and now members of the Communist League—presented their own congratulatory address to the Provisional Government.[32]

Another center of international organization was Brussels, and there the major figure was Karl Marx. During his stay in Belgium, Marx, in collaboration with Engels, developed his mature style. Theoretically, he moved from the 1844 *Economic and Philosophical Manuscripts* to the *Communist Manifesto*. His intellectual development was not an independent phenomenon; it was inextricably linked to his other roles as organizer and polemicist. All were part of Marx's effort to politicize and then dominate his movement. He attempted to win control of existing working-class radical organizations, while his theoretical work fueled his remarkably bitter polemics, which served to undermine the sense of socialist solidarity and to drive real or potential middle-class rivals out of the movement.

Marx's working-class base was the League of the Just, and his special style was displayed in his efforts to control the workers organized in the league's scattered branches and to impose on them his own brand of socialism. In 1846 he and Engels were among the founders of a Communist Correspondence Committee, and the following year this became a branch of a new organization, the Communist League. Soon after, Marx and Engels gained control of the Correspondence Committee by forcing Weitling out, charging him with theoretical vacuity and thoughtless leadership. It was the first time that socialist ranks had been purged, and Weitling was not the only one stunned by it. Moses Hess, appalled, wrote to Marx, dissociating himself from his former comrade's "party."[33] The Correspondence Committee was, thus, the first socialist group solely under the control of Marx and Engels; it was also the first to purge deviators and heretics, and to establish the principle that disagreement with the organization's leaders was unacceptable.[34]

Marx apparently hoped to dominate theoretical discussion not only within the league, but among the intellectual radicals in the various European capitals as well. In this vein, he explained to Proudhon, whom he was trying to recruit for his organization, that the major aim of the committee's correspondence would be "to put German socialists in touch with English and French socialists, to keep foreigners informed of the socialist movement that will develop in Germany and to inform the Germans in Germany of the progress of socialism in France and England. In this way differences of opinion will be brought to light and we shall obtain an exchange of ideas and impartial criticism."[35]

Once they were in control of the committee, Marx and Engels attempted to transform other existing branches of the League of the Just into Communist League affiliates, that would be under the committee's control. Upon the outbreak of revolution, the central committee of the Communist League, in London, formally transferred its authority to Marx.[36]

Marx and Engels also succeeded in taking over another organization, the International Democratic Association, founded in September 1847 by a group of Germans in Brussels who were opposed to Marx. Despite this, Engels managed to get himself elected vice-president of the new body and then to turn this post over to the temporarily absent Marx. Carrying a mandate from the association, Engels then returned to Paris, where he proceeded to propagandize Marx's views in the Paris branch of the Communist League. In that forum, however, he was opposed by workers loyal to the older artisan communism of Weitling, and who found Karl Grün more compatible than Engels.[37]

However insignificant and peripheral these organizations may have appeared, they played their part in the complex of ideology and power politics of 1848. Quarrels among them helped establish the fault lines along which movements would later split, while all of them, joined together in a rather cacophonous chorus, helped to make the international issue one that could not be avoided by French politicians.

The unpopularity of the July Monarchy had derived in part from its illiberal foreign policy. It had supported the conservative, Catholic side in recent civil conflict in Switzerland; it had been friendly with reactionary Austria; and lately had even attempted, with some success, to improve relations with the intransigently legitimist Nicholas I.[38] Moreover, international relations were still technically governed by the treaties which had emerged from France's defeat in 1815, and thus were a continuing humiliation. Some change was clearly expected from the new government.

In his official manifesto, the foreign minister, Lamartine, hedged. On the one hand, he did assert that France was repudiating the 1815 treaties. On the other hand, he promised a peaceful policy, thus bitterly disappointing all those who hoped to see a renewal of the activism of the First French Republic. The foreign radicals were also disappointed, and the new government made it easier for them to articulate and voice their complaints. Freedom of association and freedom of the press were major benefits for them. The new government also removed the expulsion orders that had driven some of the most prominent of the radicals out of the country. Mazzini arrived from England and rallied the Italians; Marx was expelled from Brussels almost simultaneously with the cancellation of his 1845 French expulsion and at once returned to Paris; and Bakunin, who had been forced to leave the previous autumn, simply came back without permission.[39] Each would do his best to stir up the foreign colonies in Paris further.

The émigrés greeted the revolution with a spate of organizational activity of their own. Their essential aim was to spread the revolutionary flame to their own homelands; the methods they envisaged, and the remoteness of this ultimate aim, varied from group to group. Poles, Belgians, and many Germans wished to use Paris as a base for organized armed resistance to their home government, and attempted to obtain the Provisional Government's support for their projects. The Italians, whose peninsula was already in a state of revolution, appear to have been more concerned with propaganda, organizing their own nationals for action and the French public for sympathy. To achieve the support they sought, the émigrés dealt directly with the government, and they also used the popular movement, the clubs especially, to exert pressure on the government in their behalf.

The mechanisms used for these purposes were their own clubs, which generally grew out of the older, more conspiratorial organizations. Thus, the Polish Democratic Society served as the nucleus of a Polish club (variously known as the Club des Polonais and the Club de l'Émigration Polonaise).[40] The German Communist League formed two rival organizations, the Club Démocratique Allemand, controlled by Herwegh, and the Club des Ouvriers Allemands, which, as we shall discuss later, was strongly influenced by Marx. Mazzini assumed leadership of an Italian group (Assemblée Nationale Italienne or Club des Émigrés Italiens).[41] Finally, there was also a Swiss club.

The notion of revolutionary solidarity was reflected in clubs with an international clientele or orientation. In the early days of the revolution, two were established: the Emancipation des Peuples and the Fraternité des Peuples. The former appears to have been primarily French, with a program of French radicalism, to which was appended a second section on "the duties of the republican toward humanity." These included the abolition of slavery, the reestablishment of Polish nationality, the constitution of an Italian federation, and the development and application of democratic principles in Germany. The foreigners who turned up at the club's aborted first meeting seemed themselves to be interested primarily in raising the issue of naturalization.[42]

The other group, the Fraternité des Peuples, has evoked a good deal of speculation among biographers of Herzen because he and/or his friends may have been involved in it. In the first edition of his *Du Développement des idées révolutionnaires en Russie*, Herzen stressed the role of Russians in the French revolutionary process. Among those he mentioned was Ivan Golovin, an émigré who had been consorting with oppositional groups since the mid-1840s.[43] According to Herzen, Golovin had presided over the Fraternité des Peuples, a statement that Golovin himself corroborated.[44] In *Byloe i dumy*, Herzen mentioned that Sazonov had led an international club during the summer of 1848, and described the proceedings with great irony. These accounts raise several questions: were the two men involved in the same organization? Was Herzen himself involved, and how important was Russian participation in 1848 France? Since Golovin stated that Herwegh and Sazonov were members of his club, it seemed reasonable to suppose that Sazonov too was involved with the Fraternité des Peuples. All the

French sources, however, indicate that the Fraternité des Peuples, founded in March, was headed by a German named Rebstock. Since different members presided over the club meetings, it is quite possible that upon occasion Golovin did "preside" over meetings of the Fraternité des Peuples. There may, however, have been a second Fraternité des Peuples which Golovin did lead; an invitation to radical journalists of all nations to join the club was extended by an unnamed president in April, one month after the papers carried the original Fraternité des Peuples announcment. This new body had formerly been the Club de la Naturalisation Française, and naturalization of foreigners resident in France was still, it seemed, its primary concern.[45] This sounds cranky enough, and insignificant enough, to suggest that it might have been a club founded by Golovin.

Neither Rebstock's organization, nor a second club with the same name, was likely to have survived the closing of the clubs that took place after the May 15 demonstration.[46] Hence it would not have been possible for Herzen, who arrived in Paris only on May 6, to take part in it; and indeed Golovin did not claim Herzen as a member. The Sazonov club, which did include Herzen, was established in the summer; it appears to have been a different organization altogether, one that remains an undocumented mystery.

If the clubs dedicated to internationalism remained ephemeral, the better-documented, national groups pressed the idea of solidarity on their own. Charles Edmond Chojecki visited the Club des Émigrés Italiens and gave a "brilliant discourse," in which he expressed Polish solidarity with the Italian movement; his speech was "heard with emotion and covered with applause."[47] Similarly, at a meeting of the German democrats, "there was special applause for an eloquent Englishman [probably a member of the Fraternal Democrats delegation] who had come from London to attend this meeting in order to assure the German patriots of the lively sympathies in England for the reconstitution of their nationality." At the same session, *La Voix des Clubs* reported:

> An Italian, a member of the patriotic association recently established, seized the occasion to give proof of fraternity with the Germans, as the Poles had done with the Italians, and to dissipate a fatal error that the government does its best to propagate in Germany, . . . which consists of a supposed hatred of the Italians for the Germans without distinctions. . . . Repeated cries of "Vive la liberté italienne" greeted this declaration.[48]

To complete the circle, Herwegh wrote an "Address to the Poles," in which he argued that the idea of free Germany was inextricably linked to a free Poland, and foresaw an alliance of Germany, Poland, and France against Russian despotism. The Central Committee of the Polish Democratic Society—which included the future leaders of the London emigration, Worcell and Albert Darasz, among others—replied on March 24 in a statement that in its turn called for a united, democratic Germany.[49]

Beyond these expressions of mutual sympathy, an alliance, a *Schutz und Trutzbundniss*, was established between the Polish and German organizations in their approach to French politicians. It made political sense; the Poles wished to arouse the sympathy of the German people, through whose country they would have to march if they were to launch a campaign in their own land, while the Germans hoped to share the sympathy of the French, which the Polish cause had enjoyed for so long.[50]

The exile organizations appealed to the French clubs for political and financial aid, but with only limited success:

> A steady stream of emissaries from the Polish Central Committee passed through the clubs to plead, appeal and beg. . . . The organizers of the German democratic legion under the poet Herwegh and of the Italian revolutionaries under Mazzini's inspiration were only slightly less ubiquitous and equally strapped for funds. A passionate appeal by Pole, German or Italian, followed by the tinkle of copper into the collection plate, became routine at club meetings. Club members were unfailingly sympathetic, polite and patient. Yet when all is said and done, European solidarity occupied a small niche in a dimly lit background. French revolutionary politics was never crowded from the stage.[51]

The clubs might set the mood of sympathy, and some money might be raised in them, but the refugees could hope for military support for campaigns in their own country only from the Provisional Government. Lamartine was stoutly opposed to involving France in any adventures of this type—in talks with émigrés and through warnings to foreign courts he tried to establish the principle that France would not intervene in other countries' political conflicts. He directly rebuffed requests for aid from Irish and Polish exiles.

Ledru-Rollin and his Interior Ministry were less sure. Caussidière was eager to support exile offensives, especially by groups with large numbers of workers in Paris. By sending large numbers of foreign workingmen back home, he hoped to ease French unemployment at the same time he encouraged foreign democracy. Ledru-Rollin himself was hesitant. Ultimately, the French government did give a small subsidy to a group of Belgian émigrés, who marched back home and were defeated by the Belgian army as soon as they crossed the border.[52]

Herzen's own future was to be influenced by the conflicts within the German colony and the subsequent actions of the German Legion.[53] Marx's and Engel's efforts during the winter of 1847–1848 to establish their control over the Communist League initiated the political controversy that culminated in a direct confrontation between Marx on the one side, and Herwegh and Bakunin on the other. The reverberations from this dispute alienated Herzen from Marx and his followers; they became political enemies, despite never meeting and never engaging in direct polemical controversy.

Immediately after the February revolution, a German Democratic Association was established. The initiator was apparently Adalbert von Bornstedt, a former officer and spy for several governments, a member of the Communist League, a former editor of the Paris *Vorwärts*, and now editor of a Brussels journal with which Marx was associated. The first meeting of the Democratic Association, which consisted of about four hundred members of the German colony, elected a committee, with Herwegh president and Bornstedt one of the two vice-presidents.[54]

On March 6, the Democratic Association held a large public meeting, with 4,000 in attendance, most of them probably workers and many with some connection to one or another of the radical organizations of the previous decade. Herwegh and Bornstedt, vigorously supported by Bakunin, proposed that the Democratic Association form a legion to carry revolutionary democracy back to Germany by force of arms. Marx strongly opposed them, sensibly pointing out the thorough futility of such a course of action. He proposed instead that the Germans in Paris return to their homes individually and work from there for internal revolution. Despite his realism in opposing the legion, Marx's scheme was, of course, no more practical than Herwegh's.

Herwegh and Bornstedt carried the day; Marx pulled out of the association and seems to have succeeded in pulling the titular faction of the Communist League with him. On March 8 he held a meeting with his own followers, including the London delegation mentioned above, to reorganize the league, reorient it toward work in Germany, and plan to expel Bornstedt.[55] Soon after, his followers organized their own club, the Ouvriers Allemands, with the London leader Heinrich Bauer as president. (The club's committee included Marx, Engels, and their faithful follower Wilhelm Wolff, and the other London leaders Karl Schapper and Joseph Moll.) The club publicly dissociated itself from the adventure of Herwegh's legion.[56] It seems likely that the Communist League split, for the working-class majority of the legion appears to have been drawn from the same political background as Marx's followers. Possibly those workers who found the traditional communism of the League of the Just more compatible than Marx's brand of socialism seized this opportunity to act on their resentment at the recent transformation of their organization.

Marx was not the only one to disapprove of the legion on either practical or ideological grounds. Its assertive republicanism was a problem; backward, divided Germany, with its memories of imperial glory and the need for some overriding force to hold the parts together, did not seem a good candidate for republicanism. Conservative nationalists were offended and refused to participate.[57] But on the left as well there was criticism: Andreas Gottschalk, a communist, the leader of the Cologne working-class organization, and a man who admired Herwegh,[58] nonetheless felt the legion was a mistake. He warned Moses Hess to dissociate himself from it; since German public opinion was ready for nothing more than a constitutional monarchy, the adventure was doomed from the outset.[59]

Despite this criticism, Herwegh's group proceeded to organize the legion under the military leadership of a former Prussian officer, Otto von Corvin–Wiersbitzki. While the volunteers were drilled, an appeal was circulated to all the Paris clubs, and negotiations were undertaken with the Provisional Government to provide support.[60] The German Democratic Association's leadership had conversations with Ledru-Rollin and Flocon, who was, according to Corvin, the legion's warmest supporter within the government. The Germans wished to be supplied with arms, ammunition, and expense money. The government, however, was not very receptive—confused, according to Corvin, by Herwegh's vague ideas and sanguine hopes. Corvin also told a rather unlikely story of a conversation that Flocon held with Herwegh and others. Flocon waved around a pile of bills and asked Herwegh how much money he needed. To the horror of the other Germans, Herwegh, who was reluctant to accept money from the

French government, replied that he needed a mere 2,000 francs (later increased to 2,500), whereupon Flocon counted them out and handed the money to him in a patronizing manner. Corvin himself later went back to the minister, explained that Herwegh was an impractical poet who did not understand money, and got another 5,000 francs.[61] This is the only account of negotiations with the government that I have found.

When Marie d'Agoult was planning her history of the revolution, she requested information from Herwegh about his contacts with the Provisional Government, but either he provided none or she chose not to use it. Her account of the German Legion in the history of the revolution is extremely brief and uninformative.[62] Ultimately, the legion received an allowance of fifty centimes per day per legionnaire and some support while it marched on French territory. Even this pittance was probably granted more for internal political reasons than from any altruistic desire to aid German democracy. There was discontent among French workers regarding foreign competition, and the legion was one way of moving some 500 foreign workmen out of the city. The legion's spokesmen made the same point in their arguments to the government, and in their propaganda: "A secondary point, but one which deserves to be taken into consideration in present circumstances must also fix your attention. The greater part of our legion is being recruited among the class of workers who, in leaving Paris, will cede their places to the same number of their French brothers, in order to seek, along with liberty, their bread in their own country."[63]

The legion set off on March 21, amid celebrations of revolutionary solidarity. Poles, Hungarians, and the Garde Mobile demonstrated their support before the departure. "An immense crowd made the air resound with cries of 'Long live the universal republic!' "[64] The plan was for the legion to cross into Germany and link up with a group of insurgent Baden republicans, led by Gustav Struve and Friedrich Hecker.

Revolutions had already broken out in many of the German states, forcing rulers to appoint liberals to cabinet office, grant civil liberties, and allow preparations for a national constituent assembly to take place. Early in March a group of public figures, mostly from liberal southwestern Germany, met at Heidelberg to discuss how to achieve national unification. Struve and Hecker were soundly defeated when they proposed that a republic be proclaimed at once. Because the liberal German nationalists perceived them as impractical hotheads, they were also excluded from the group that was chosen to organize the convocation of the Pre-Parliament at the end of the month. (The Pre-Parliament, in its turn, would be responsible for organizing the Frankfurt Parliament.) Angered by the treatment they had received, the Baden republicans raised a rebellion. They gathered an armed force that was led by August Willich, a former artillery officer who had become a socialist and an artisan.[65] Herzen eventually came to know and admire Willich, who briefly joined the London emigration and there served as a leader of the anti-Marxian faction among the Germans. In 1853, he emigrated to the United States, where he enjoyed a distinguished career.

Hecker, one of the two political leaders of the Baden republicans, was not enthusiastic about Herwegh's legion. Despite his resistance, the plan called for the legion to join up with the Baden force.[66] The actual campaign was a tragicomedy of missed connections, futile marches and countermarches, changed plans, and a single disastrous encounter with the Prussian army.[67] A defeated and humiliated Herwegh escaped capture and made his way back to Paris, where he would renew his friendship with Herzen. Although he remained active as a journalist, henceforth he was increasingly seen as a spent force.[68] The poet assuaged his bruised feelings by concentrating on personal relations.

Bakunin: A Digression

On the eve of his departure for Italy in October 1847, Herzen held a farewell party. Among the guests were Georg Herwegh and Bakunin.[69] Herzen would not see his compatriot again until 1860. Nonetheless, Bakunin's contacts and reputation would continue to affect Herzen; Bakunin made contacts that Herzen developed, and Bakunin's "martyrdom" enhanced Herzen's status as the spokesman for a Russian revolutionary tradition that Bakunin embodied. A brief summary of Bakunin's adventures from the fall of 1847 until his imprisonment in the Peter and Paul Fortress by the Russians in 1851 will, therefore, help illuminate Herzen's career.

Bakunin's contacts with the Polish Democratic Society led to his being invited in 1847 to give a speech at the annual meeting commemorating the uprising of 1831. The invitation, and Bakunin's response, marked an important stage in the process of linking the causes of Polish liberation and Russian revolution. In his speech,

Paris: The First Months

Bakunin strongly asserted this linkage, using Lelewel's phrase, "For your and our freedom," to make his point. The Russian government was disturbed by the speech and prevailed upon the French government to expel Bakunin from the country.

This action became part of the liberal indictment of the Guizot regime. Bakunin publicized it as well as he could; he told George Sand all about it in the postscript to a letter originally written to accompany a copy of his speech. Sand responded by agreeing with his sentiments on Poland and with personal sympathy for him.[70] By late December the expulsion was already the subject of gossip in Berlin, for Varnhagen von Ense, who knew Bakunin from the latter's Berlin years, expressed indignation in his diary.[71]

Bakunin went from Paris to Brussels, where he reestablished contact with Lelewel and with Marx. Relations with the latter seem to have been testy; in a letter to Annenkov, Bakunin expressed admiration for the German's brilliance, but deplored his intolerance and dictatorial tendencies.[72] He returned to Paris right after the February days and immediately threw himself into a continuous round of demonstrations and meetings, while still finding time to write for *La Réforme*. Caussidière is reported to have said about him: "On the first day of a revolution, he is a perfect treasure; on the second he ought to be shot." His involvement in Herwegh's conflict with Marx has already been mentioned. On March 31 he set out for Germany and Poland, hoping to foment revolution among the Slavs, and also apparently acting as an emissary for the German Legion.[73]

In Frankfurt he made contact with the left wing of the Pre-Parliament. He told Annenkov of three men with whom he had become particularly friendly: Johann Jacoby, the Königsburg liberal deputy; Count Oscar Reichenbach, whose political involvement began with religious reform; and August Willich, whose role in the Baden campaign was mentioned above.[74] All three would later be part of Herzen's web of contacts. From Frankfurt Bakunin made his way to Berlin, where he arrived on April 21, only to be sent off almost immediately by the authorities. From Berlin, his trajectory took him to Leipzig and Breslau, and then on to Prague and the Slav Congress, where he was the only Russian in attendance. By July he was back in Berlin. There he socialized and politicked with Müller-Strübing, Varnhagen von Ense, Bettina von Arnim, Fröbel, and Arago, of the French government—a mixed, and on the whole, very moderate group. Fröbel later went to Vienna carrying letters of recommendation, including one to the Czech nationalist Frantisek Palacky, from Bakunin.[75]

While Bakunin was in Breslau, following the Prague Conference, Marx's *Neue Rheinissche Zeitung* reported that George Sand had received information that Bakunin was a spy for the Russian government. Bakunin, appalled, wrote to Sand himself and also sent a message to her through Adolph Reichel requesting that she refute the statement. This Sand did in a letter written on July 20. In was published by the *Neue Rheinische Zeitung* along with an extremely cold retraction: "We communicated the rumor that Sand had such evidence as it came to us from two independent sources—in so doing, we fulfilled the duty of the press, which is to keep a sharp eye on personages in public view, and we invited M. Bakunin to refute a suspicion, which was in any case widespread in many Paris circles. Thus, we have printed his declaration and Sand's letter."[76]

E. H. Carr argues that the incident was not handled inappropriately by Marx, and Bakunin did not perceive it to be; the two men met later in the summer and renewed their friendly relations. In a letter published in the London *Morning Advertiser* five years later, when the rumor cropped up again, Marx repeated the substance of his 1848 statement. In that letter, Marx asserted that he had received the information from two sources, the Havas-Bureau and "a Polish refugee." The latter was actually the German exile living in Paris, Hermann Ewerbeck, who was a member of the League of the Just and the Communist League. Although Ewerbeck was a communist of the French style, he was, nonetheless, a close friend of Moses Hess and on good terms with Marx and Engels; in 1848–1849, he was the Paris correspondent of the *Neue Rheinische Zeitung*.[77] It may be that friendly relations were reestablished between Marx and Bakunin, but Herzen, who did not know Marx and had no direct contact with Bakunin for another decade, did not know it; his own animus against Marx does owe a good deal to the episode.[78]

Bakunin, meanwhile continuing his peregrinations about Germany, was in Dresden, Saxony, when insurrection broke out in May 1849. Along with Richard Wagner, Bakunin took part in the fighting. He was captured and eventually condemned to death. However, instead of executing him, the Saxon authorities turned him over to the Austrian government, which also had brought charges against him. In Austria, he was condemned to death once again, and finally turned over to the Russians in May 1851. Herzen was kept informed of

Bakunin's whereabouts while he was in the West, and Luisa Haag sent him money in 1850.[79] But once in Russia he disappeared from view for some time. It was rumored he had been tortured, and in the autumn of 1851 a Polish newspaper and the Paris *Le National* carried reports of his death.[80] Only in November 1853 was Herzen able to report to Jules Michelet that their friend was alive in the Peter and Paul Fortress.[81] Bakunin had become a genuine revolutionary martyr, Russia's first since the Decembrists, and Herzen made use of it to establish his own credentials. He wrote an article about Bakunin for Michelet, gave him prominent notice in his other writings of the period, and in 1851 used the Bakunin connection to cement his relationship with the French historian.[82] In effect, Herzen helped legitimate himself as a revolutionary by dramatizing his friendship with Bakunin.

4

HERZEN and the PARIS REVOLUTION

HERZEN remained in Paris from early May 1848 until June 1849. These months saw the decline of the French Republic into authoritarianism and the election of Louis Napoleon Bonaparte as president. Outside France, the revolutionary movements that had seemed so universal and invincible in the spring were defeated by the forces of the old governments. Popular protest was met with repression, and the radical leaders, after their brief moment of power, feared for their safety; some were arrested, a few executed, and many took the road to exile.

These thirteen months marked a decisive change in Herzen's life. It was at this time that he chose to devote himself to the radical cause, and in so doing was forced to break most of his personal ties with his country. Paradoxically, at the same time his views about the "rottenness" of Western culture and the youthful potential of the Russian people also took shape. His decision meant that he would use the hopeless, but still freer, West as a haven from whence he would work to develop the revolutionary potentialities of his own people.

Herzen's Paris stay can be divided into two relatively distinct periods. During the summer of 1848, he remained essentially a bystander, observing the most dramatic and, for one of Herzen's convictions, the most terrible events of the revolutionary process. Although he had some contacts with French radicals, he functioned primarily within a small Russian colony of friends and friends of friends; together they saw the revolutionary sights and reacted to events. The first period drew to a gradual close at the end of the summer, when the Russians returned home. The Herzens had decided it was not yet time for their family to go back, and over the next few months came to the decision to remain indefinitely in the West as expatriates. As the Russians departed, refugees from the rest of Europe arrived in Paris, their first step on what would become, for many, a long journey of exile. They came bearing the scars of a year of bitter struggle, not only with the old regime, but with other radicals as well. Among the new arrivals, Herzen was less an outsider than he was in the world of French politics; his activity and stature increased commensurately. As he worked with them, he adopted some of their attitudes and factional positions. Unfortunately, this period is poorly documented, so large gaps remain in our understanding of Herzen's activity and contacts.

Upon their return to the French capital, the Herzens took an apartment on the Champs-Elysées. The family, which had tended to go off in different directions during the first year in the West, was now reunited (although Luisa Haag, Kolia, and Mariia Ern may have had a separate apartment), and still included the two woman friends from Russia, as well as the three children and Herzen's mother. They were joined now by the Tuchkovs, who traveled from Italy at about the same time and took an apartment in the same building. The friendship between Natalie Herzen and Natalie Tuchkova continued to flourish and to add a new emotional dimension to the older woman's life. The other Russians who orbited around the center formed by the two families included Nikolai Sazonov, about whom Herzen's opinion continued to fluctuate, Pavel Annenkov, and Ivan Turgenev, who became a habitué of the Herzen household when he was not in attendance on Pauline Viardot. (Turgenev's constant presence rather distressed Natalie Herzen, who was uneasy around the writer.) In the spring the Herzens were to nurse him through a bout of what may have been cholera.[1] Another of Ogarev's neighbors from Penza, I. V. Selivanov, became a part of Herzen's circle; while never a close friend, he accompanied Herzen to banquets and political meetings, and carried home souvenirs of his experiences and of Herzen himself. He was to suffer severely for this friendship after his return to Russia.[2]

The friendship with the Herwegh family was resumed once the latter had returned from the humiliating defeat of the German Legion. Herwegh appears to have been Herzen's most important contact for an entrée into French, German, and Polish political circles. To some extent, this involved renewing acquaintances from the previous year. One witness to Herzen's activity was his cousin, Sergei Levitskii (son of "the Senator" of *Byloe i dumy*), who was a fashionable photographer. Within a few weeks of Herzen's return, Levitskii lamented that his kinsman was to be seen consorting with democrats.³ The only "democrats" specifically mentioned in Herzen's correspondence as friends are Jean-Baptiste Bocquet and his brother Camille, both of whom were involved in the middle-level politics and fighting of 1848. The former, Sasha's old tutor, was arrested in the aftermath of the May 15 demonstration and was released only in September.⁴ Herzen's journalism indicates, however, that he did attend the remaining clubs with some regularity (and took Selivanov with him), and it is probable that he made additional contacts at them.⁵

The Paris to which Herzen returned had lost the sense of revolutionary enthusiasm and unity that many had perceived in the first weeks after the overthrow of the monarchy. This was now a polarized society, the "people" had lost the election, and the struggle for genuine democratization would have to continue. In the words of an editorial of April 1848,

> It is certain that the bourgeoisie will be mistress of the National Assemby. . . . The role of the popular republicans is thus fatally delineated. After having made the revolution two months ago, now, as before, we are condemned to struggle. . . . We shall be active and devoted combatants who shall call all the friends of the social republic to the fore, to march toward the ideal shown us by tradition, the sentiment of the living generation, history, philosophy, politics, and that irresistible enthusiasm of the people.⁶

Herzen had nothing but disdain for the new National Assembly, which had convened just before his own arrival. It was, he said, "a stupid, limited crowd of provincials and retrograde people, without initiative and for the most part hostile to the revolution of February 24 and the Republic. Of 860 representatives, there were perhaps 100 ardent patriots, 200 republicans, and the rest came to defend the bourgeoisie, privilege, monopoly."⁷

The Assembly did, indeed, soon make its conservative political intentions clear. It dismissed the Provisional Government, which had attempted to strike a balance between the demands of middle-class liberals and those of the urban democratic-socialist populace, and it reappointed none of the more radical members except Ledru-Rollin to the five-man Directory which for the next six weeks would serve as the assembly's executive arm.⁸ (By his actions at the April 16 demonstration, Ledru-Rollin had distanced himself from popular radicalism.

Even so, Lamartine had to use all his persuasive powers to win him a seat on the Directory.) Thus the assembly served notice that as far as it was concerned the period of popular revolution was over, and there would be no more flirtation with socialist notions.

Forewarned by its own spokesmen, the politicized sector of the Paris populace lost no time moving into opposition to the assembly. The occasion was the one time that revolutionary internationalism played a vital role in the internal political battles of the French republic. The ostensible issue in the demonstration of May 15, 1848, was a demand that France support Polish claims to independence; in actuality, in the tangle of motives of the last of the revolutionary *journées,* the Polish issue was rivaled in importance by questions of internal power.

The initial impetus behind the May 15 demonstration does indeed appear to have been a desire to express support for the Polish cause; it is not clear, however, precisely what measures the organizers thought the government should take to encourage the achievement of Polish independence. The announcement of the demonstration merely stated that there would be a "democratic manifestation of the French people in favor of Poland." It was to be peaceful and limited in aims: "No drums, no music, no arms! No other slogans than 'Vive the Republic! Vive Poland!'"[9] In conjunction with the planned demonstration, Théophile Thoré, who represented the views of Barbès and his Club de la Révolution, the major bastion of popular action, wrote an editorial in support of the Polish cause. Asserting that the Poles had been "betrayed" by the French Revolution, he recounted the contributions of Poles to France's revolutionary tradition and the tribulations they had suffered in their efforts to free their own country. France, the Joan of Arc of nations, should proclaim the deliverance of all people, Thoré wrote, but he did not spell out what this meant with any specificity.[10]

Some time between the planning and the execution of the demonstration, the issue got complicated by political intrigues, and tempers were heated by the assembly's treatment of Louis Blanc. The socialist former cabinet member lost his government posts and also heard his proposal for the creation of a Ministry of Labor contemptuously rejected. Some among the clubmen, and most importantly Blanqui, apparently hoped to use the demonstration to channel popular protest into a revolutionary action aimed at abolishing the assembly and returning power to the popular crowds that had overthrown the monarchy in the first place. Fearing the outcome of revolutionary action, and also apprehensive that the effort to revolutionize the demonstration might have been provoked by counterrevolutionary groups looking for a chance to suppress the popular movement by force, Barbès and his allies drew back. The night of the fourteenth, the Club de la Révolution, influenced by Barbès and Thoré, and the Club of the Rights of Man decided not to support the movement.[11] Regardless of this loss of leadership, the Paris clubmen marched on May 15 in the tens of thousands, while Blanc attempted to restrain them from rash action. Despite his efforts, the National Assembly was invaded by the crowd, amid much tumult. Ledru-Rollin called out the National Guard, which cleared the assembly and the streets with considerable violence. If indeed the demonstration had aimed at insurrection, it had—as Barbès had feared—merely served to justify repression.

That followed at once. The club leaders—Barbès, Blanqui, and a number of others—were arrested immediately. Blanc managed to avoid arrest and indictment at this time, but this episode meant the end of any active political role for him. Within days the major clubs were closed and restrictions placed on the right of popular assembly.[12] The revolution of 1848 as a popular movement was dead; henceforth the new rulers would be concerned with establishing a stable, conservative republic and would react to crowd action and organization with fear and repression.

Responses to the *journée* were as various as the conflicting motives of the participants. Interpretations differed as to whether it was an innocent demonstration viciously repressed, an attempted insurrection, or an effort to manipulate the mass movement for the private political ends of one or another leader. Blanc was perceived by some as aiming at an insurrection, then refusing in a cowardly manner to take responsibility for his actions. He insisted that he had opposed insurrection; moreover, once he realized that the demonstration (which he knew about only by hearsay) might get out of control, he had urged Barbès to cancel.[13] Blanqui was suspected by some of playing the part of *agent provocateur*. The fact that there had been secret negotiations between him and Lamartine only further undermined his credibility, already weakened by the accusation that he had been an informer. George Sand, who had already retired from active participation in Ledru-Rollin's ministry, criticized the movement; she felt that manipulation of a non-revolutionary mass action for the revolutionary aims of the leaders was wrong and would, if successful, only have led to a new dictatorship.[14] Other commentators, however, justified revolutionary action by claiming that the conservative vote for the National Assembly had not truly represented the opinion of the people.

Herzen, who was an eyewitness to the storming of the assembly, took a radical view. His account altogether omits mention of the Polish issue in explaining the demonstration. For him, it was a justified insurrectionary attempt, an effort to restore sovereignty to the people. As such, the appropriate response by the democratic members of the government should have been to support it; their failure to do so was Herzen's proof of their incapacity or bad faith:

> If Lamartine were a political man, if Ledru-Rollin were not a braggart, they would have done what Caussidière did negatively . . . and Barbès, Courtais, Raspail, Louis Blanc did positively. They should have stood at the head of the movement; they should have organized it, and then the loud proclamation of the *dissoute* [dissolution] would have been the first day of the true republic. They wanted this, but dared not. . . . I was at the door of the Assembly when Huber pronounced: *Au nom du p[euple] fr[ançais] l'Assemblée est dissoute* [In the name of the French People, the Assembly is dissolved]. This news spread to the people at once. What rapture there was.[15]

The "rapturous" tumult in the assembly, however, was followed by the invasion of the National Guard, and Herzen watched in horror as the guardsmen manhandled various of the radical spokesmen. No very great atrocities took place at this time—but he perceived a malice and brutality that he attributed to bourgeois class hatred, when it was probably no more than the violence to be expected when untrained troops are used to suppress civil disorder:

> These janissaries tore Lous Blanc's coat, one of them seized him by the hair, and pulled so hard that a tuft of hair remained in his hand. Others grabbed old Courtais, tore off his epaulets, beat him in the face, spit on him—these are the methods of the bourgeoisie. I saw myself the cannibalistic joy of these pretorians, when they took the Hôtel de Ville—took it without a shot, for there were no armed people there. The mocker [Clement] Thomas [National Guard Commander] tore up the Montagnard banner and threw the scraps out the window. And pitiful Lamartine and Ledru rode in triumph, surrounded by petit bourgeois [*meshchane*].

Herzen's first bitter commentary dates from August; since his views between May and the end of June are not recorded, the impact of the June Days on his perceptions of class antagonism in May cannot be determined. Natalie did write one letter to her friend Tatiana Astrakova during the period between the May events and the June Days. It was sent by post, so she was very circumspect. Nonetheless, she expressed a feeling of uneasiness and foreboding, a sense that the story was not yet played out.

> As for what is going on about us, I think you know in part—ferment, and even movement, and sometimes it seems as though something were going to emerge from all this—but so far all this is like a struggle of elemental forces, stifling and heavy, a terrible agitation in the blood—clouds gather and there is a burst of thunder and lightning—but the air is not cleansed, the sun does not appear; you fail to breathe freely, there is another flash of lightning.... I may be mistaken, but I tell you frankly how it affects me.[16]

Two weeks later, Natalie again wrote her friends—a chatty letter about friends at home and domestic concerns in Paris. As she told of her plans to have Sasha learn to ride horseback and her pleasure that unexpectedly he was displaying some musical talent, she commented, "Sometimes I feel that I am reliving my life...." "At the word 'life'," she resumed six days later,

> I was interrupted by cannon fire, which continued—day and night!—*four days*, the city is still *en état de siège* [under martial law], they say there are 8,000 dead. That's all. I haven't the spirit to go into detail. I am surprised that we are alive, but we are alive only physically. Tania, there are moments when I wished to be destroyed *with the whole family*. I do not know if we shall revive enough that anything in life will ever again be able to evoke a sincere smile.[17]

Thus the Herzen family shared with the Paris populace the experience of the bloodiest episode of the revolution.

Underlying the outburst of violence was the inability of the French government to deal with the crisis created by high unemployment. In the early days of the revolution the Provisional Government, inspired by its conservative members, had established the "national workshops" as a stopgap measure to provide for the thousands of men whom the prolonged economic crisis had left unemployed. Basically these were simply camps which provided minimal subsistence to the unemployed, who were then put to unskilled, make-work tasks. The camps were overcrowded, and the men restive; moreover, they were expensive to maintain, and the new government was very short of funds. In the early days, when socialist theories and socialist ideas abounded, they had served as a way of paying lip service to these notions, although it is quite unlikely that there was ever any intent to provide the substance of anything beyond limited emergency welfare.

After May 15, when the new, conservative National Assembly was in control and a large portion of the popular movement had been suppressed, these workshops were increasingly out of place. Talk of social welfare and social progress had become suspect, and action in behalf of these ideas virtually impossible. After some partial steps limiting access to the workshops and the freedom of their residents, the assembly decided to dissolve them altogether. On June 21, the men were given the choice of joining the army, if they were fit, or clearing land in the provinces. The announcement sparked an uprising in the camps that soon spread to the workers' districts of Paris. Barricades went up on June 22, and briefly the workers appeared to have control of the city.

The government of the republic responded to this threat with far greater vigor than had the monarchy. The army, which despite popular demands had never been removed from the capital, was called in, along with the Garde Mobile. A systematic campaign was launched on June 23, and it lasted through the next day. The troops under the command of General Eugène Cavaignac, a professional officer from an old republican family, were thorough and merciless; barricades were broken, the death toll was very high, and in the first days after the insurrection many prisoners were shot after courts martial. The Herzens could hear the firing squads from their apartment. Herzen himself was seized as a suspected Russian agent as he made his way around the city under martial law. Although he was released after a few hours, his house was searched and his papers temporarily confiscated.[18]

The social fabric of France was badly torn. Men of the left, like Herzen and his friends, could see only the greed and ruthlessness of the propertied classes. He had no other explanation of what looked to him like the furious murder of a defenseless population by armed supporters of an "order" that benefited only the bourgeoisie. The quarrels of the circle came back to him now. He wrote back to Moscow, "The savagery of the National Guard and the Assembly exceeded anything you ever heard of. I propose that Vas[ili] Petr[ovich] Bot[kin] cease quarreling about the bourgeoisie."[19]

On the other hand, more moderate elements felt that the insurrection by the propertyless threatened all lawfulness, all civil order. For them, the use of the troops was regrettable, to be sure; however, they felt the insurrection must be stopped by whatever means were necessary. Fear of the renewal of "anarchy," which seemed so terrifying in June, would continue to justify repression of initiatives by the crowd and the political left.[20]

The National Assembly, broadly speaking, represented this "moderate" position. To ensure the maintenance of order, governmental power was now entrusted to a dictatorship by General Cavaignac, and Paris remained under martial law. Arrests of radical leaders continued, and with the departure from France of former Minister Louis Blanc and former Prefect of Police Caussidière, the new political emigration began. In July, the daily newspaper edited by Pierre-Joseph Proudhon, *Le Répresentant du Peuple*, was suppressed; unbridled freedom of the press would no longer be tolerated. Soon the shooting of suspected insurrectionists ended, but it was replaced by the "dry guillotine," the transportation of thousands to prison colonies overseas.

With street action rendered impossible and the clubs that still existed constrained in their activity, the focus of political interest shifted to more traditional leaders and concerns. Once again the newspapers were the major forum for political expression, and the concerns of their editors became once again the traditional political activities of elections and coalition building. For French citizens, the provisions of the constitution, which the National Assembly was still in the process of drafting, were of course of primary importance.

None of this held much interest for Herzen. He recoiled in horror from the entire business of politics and government. The republican government had shown itself to be just as hostile to crowd spontaneity as the old regime, and more ruthless in repression. Democratic forms, not animated by popular involvement, were simply a mechanism by means of which the bourgeoisie could manipulate the political process for its own benefit—the outcome of the elections had made that clear enough. Moreover, a people as a whole could be lacking in the democratic will that might legitimize truly popular government; in France, the peasant majority was bourgeois. Hinting at a class analysis unusual in his thought, Herzen wrote: *"The man without land, without capital,* the worker will save France." Moreover, "In general, the French do not understand respect for the personality, this is an oppressive people, stupid in its respect for formal legality, an inquisitor and spy in the absence of the concept of honor that lies deep in the soul of the proletarian and the aristocrat, but which is altogether absent in the petit bourgeois and the jurist."[21]

Herzen's radicalism had never put major emphasis on political forms; the emergence of the conservative, repressive republic confirmed him in his skepticism and impelled him to define his own views more clearly. He drew on the theory he had absorbed back in Moscow, and on Feuerbach in particular, to derive an anarchism based on the premise that any setting up of an authority over oneself is a form of oppression and a diminution of the human personality. This notion became codified in the works dating from 1849 to about 1854 as the concept of "dualism," which linked religion and the state, regardless of its political form, in a single repressive system.[22] In the aftermath of the June Days, he began to formulate this notion:

> Lamartine . . . says that he and his comrades wished a *constitutional republic,* that is, a monarchy without a king, without hereditary power—and that kind of constitutional or, more frankly, *monarchical* republic was established. In fact, can a republic be distinguished from a monarchy solely by the fact that in it instead of a king a motley crowd of representatives, invested with the same power as the banished king, reigns? There is nothing in the world more opposed and antipathetic than these two governmental forms. In a monarchy they *govern* the people, in a republic the people *governs* its own affairs. The model for monarchy is the master directing his workshop, the father, the guardian managing the property of minors. The model for a republic is the *artel* of workers, which has its managers, but no master. Monarchy is based on authority; it needs hierarchy, religio-political ritual . . . it needs *vestments,* rather than clothing; at every step it must recall that the individual is insignificant before authority; it must demand submission. A republic demands only one thing of people—that they be people; it is based on confidence in the person; it is natural and therefore does not impose bonds, but establishes conditions which issue from the very essence of social life, to such an extent that to escape them is absurd or irrational. If it asks more than this, it is not a republic. . . . Monarchism is based on dualism: the government must never coincide with the people; the government is providence, spirit, holy rank; the people is matter,

laymen, subjects. Monarchism is essentially theocracy, it is solid only by *le droit divin*; . . . without a concept of Jehovah there is no tsar. . . . The inner principle of a republic is immanence and not dualism; it worships nothing; its religion is man, its god is man, "and there is no other god beside him." A republic leads to atheism and anarchy.[23]

The task for a revolutionary was to undermine the conservative institutions and instincts that held the old oppressive system together, while at the same time maintaining faith in the validity and possibility of the goal of a free society and fighting a debilitating despair. The source of conservatism was in people's minds, and so the work of destruction would also have to operate on the level of intellect. The result of this view was that some time during Herzen's stay in Paris, probably in the summer, he finally chose his vocation. He would be a radical journalist, and thereby contribute to the intellectual preparation for revolution.

This was a natural outgrowth of Herzen's earlier activities; while still in Russia he had been a writer, had dreamed of directing a journal, and wished to use his writing to further social and moral change. The difference now was one of commitment—as he well knew, his entire future life would be shaped by this decision. The impulse probably came from seeing that in the West journalism provided more political options than in Russia. The freer press made it possible to express oneself openly, and the radical writers formed a network of influence and support considerably larger than the Moscow coteries Herzen had known before and outgrown. The example of Herwegh, who shared his perceptions of current conditions and who returned to active journalism by contributing to a number of German publications after his return from the campaign in Baden, was important.[24] So was the moral authority achieved by Proudhon, a man Herzen had long admired as a theoretician. As a journalist and member of the National Assembly, Proudhon won great stature as the most courageous spokesman against the excesses of counterrevolution.[25]

There are hints before the June Days that the Herzens were moving toward a decision to remain indefinitely in the West. Natalie informed her friends about the Tuchkovs' tentative plans to return home, but refused to be pinned down about her own.[26] Herzen transferred ownership of his Moscow house to his half-brother, Egor Ivanovich, which may have been a first step toward turning his considerable property into the liquid assets he needed in the West.²⁷ The June Days stunned the family and destroyed any residual faith in the democratic potential of the revolution. All the correspondence in the weeks following tells of their helpless rage and horror. A nostalgia for Russia appears at the same time in Herzen's letters, as does the faith that only the Russian peasants and the Paris workers are true freedom-loving democrats by nature:

> O, *cari miei,* what I would give to be able to rest a little time with you, then I would take up my staff again and return to my place in the desperate struggle, to the place where everything holy, everything human has been defeated. . . . Sometimes I dream of returning, of our poor nature, the village, our peasants, of life at Sokolovo—and I feel like flinging myself at you like the prodigal son, . . . who has lost all hopes.—I desperately love Russia and the Russians—only they have a broad nature, the broad nature which I saw in all its brilliance and greatness in the French worker. These are the two peoples of the future (that is, not the French, but the workers), for the sake of which I cannot tear myself away from Paris.²⁸

Natalie expressed the combination of despair and determination in more extreme terms in a letter written at the same time:

> Our hopes are destroyed. We do nothing. We see nothing. We are living through our death, but I have not arrived at despair. There is still much to be done, and neither Cavaignac nor any force in the world will hinder me or destroy my barricade. Yes, Granovskii, I feel this, and know I could not live without it. Personal happiness is not enough, and there is no personal happiness without this [feeling]. I know I am building a strong barricade—my barricade is—my Sasha! Perhaps it too will be destroyed, but much will be saved behind it. Sometimes I can see prison, chains, the guillotine far away on the path along which I lead him, but my heart neither aches nor trembles. I hold him firmly by the hand and an inner voice keeps saying to me: "Marchons! Marchons!"²⁹

However painful, a decision had been made. For the present, Herzen had no periodical outlets. Nonetheless, he wrote a good deal. Although he knew that he could no longer be published in Russia, he continued his travel letters with the third series, "Opiat' v Parizhe" [Again in Paris],³⁰ writing them, he said, for his friends. The form of the "Letters," which had evolved from the witty essays of the beginning, to social criticism and first-hand descriptions of Italian events, continued to develop. This final series consists of four letters that form a journalist's history of the events of the first months of the revolution.[31] The June Days acted as a natural caesura that greatly altered the form of the last two. The first pair provides a historical narrative of the background of the revolution, the February days, and the formation of the government. In them, Herzen's position was on the far left of the political spectrum, and probably derived from his contacts among the clubmen. His only heroes were the Paris workers who had made the revolution—only, he thought, to have it snatched away from them by the bourgeoisie, fearful for its property and savage in defense of it. He roundly criticized all members of the Provisional Government, denied the socialism of Blanc, and had praise only for the radical journalists Proudhon, Thoré, and Leroux.

The third "Letter," written between August 28 and September 18, reviewed events from the formation of the government to the convening of the National Assembly. While he was highly critical of many of the government's policies and some of its members, the contrast between the early days of the revolution and the martial law under which he now lived mellowed Herzen's view of the former. Less vituperative than before, his account is told more in sorrow than in anger. At the same time, he began to develop his view that constitutional republicanism is a "dualistic" system little different from or superior to the monarchy it replaced.

The final "Letter," dated October 10, 1848, is primarily devoted to Herzen's impressions upon his arrival in France in May. The journalism thus ends at the point where the eye-witness account begins, at the end of the role of the Provisional Government.

As before, the "Letters" were written in conjunction with the essays of *S togo berega;* the latter series, however, continued for almost a year beyond the conclusion of the "Letters" published in the first edition (and in the process became itself somewhat more journalistic). The moods and some of the scenes Herzen witnessed during the June Days dominated the chapter titled "Posle grozy" [After the Storm], dated July 27. For Herzen, the June Days were the ultimate political crisis that changed forever his perception of European society. Initially, he expressed this sense of crisis as a refusal ever again to countenance the least sentimentality or wishful thinking about political and social issues. Sugar-coating reality is part of the ritual of dualistic monarchy, he argued, and so dispassionate awareness became itself a political act.³²

Six weeks later, in the chapter titled "LVII god respubliki, edinoi i nerazdel'noi" [Year LVII of the Republic, one and indivisible], the illusions of the republicans were condemned as obsolete and retrograde. The theme was developed further in "Vixerunt" (dated December 1). So began Herzen's argument that the entire civilization of the West was rotten and would be swept away by the triumph of the proletarian "barbarians" (to whom he later added the Russian peasants).

From his earliest writings, Herzen had been intrigued by the confrontation between the sophisticated Romans and the energetic, if naive and crude, Christians of the declining days of the Roman Empire.³³ He now returned to this theme, identifying himself, civilized and world-weary as he was, with the unjust, corrupt, yet beautiful civilization doomed to destruction. Reformers' dreams and programs, as well as reactionary forms, are all relegated to the old, dying civilization—the 1848 regimes as well as the governments that preceded and followed them. At this point of near-total disillusionment, the Paris workers, with their personality and verve, tend to disappear from Herzen's accounts; the historical process is now furthered by the brute elementality of "the masses."³⁴

The stoic courage of the last Romans, accepting unpalatable reality without delusion and sweetening their isolation with companions and nature, was the only "Consolatio" (dated March 1849) Herzen offered in the concluding essay of the original German edition of *S togo berega*. Herzen here assumed the guise of a disinterested physician who has moved beyond even the disillusionment of the preceding year. The faith in human nature that underlies progressive political activity is rejected in its turn as unsubstantiated and absurd. To Rousseau's plaint, "Man is born free, yet everywhere he is in chains," Herzen's physician responds: "What would you say to a man who, nodding his head sadly, remarked that 'fish are born to fly—but everywhere they swim'?"³⁵

The disenchantment of *S togo berega,* and its stance of uninvolved spectator, defines one aspect of Herzen's attitude at this time. Yet as has been noted, in Herzen's dialogues both characters always have good arguments—they represent a genuine conflict in Herzen's mind, not merely a heuristic device.³⁶ Herzen's own life displays an activist counterpoint to the passivity he appears to advocate. Simultaneously with the later dialogues of *S togo berega,* Herzen began to assume an active role in political and intellectual life for the first time since leaving Russia in 1847.

The Left in the German Revolution

While the destinies of the Republic were being played out in France, events in Germany were even more complex and ultimately more frustrating. Since there was no center to the states of the German lands, the revolutionary process in the heady "March days" was enacted separately in city after city. In the capitals, liberals replaced conservatives in the ministries, while in the provinces local radicals often succeeded in dominating city governments. Cutting across, but never entirely overriding, local struggles were the efforts to unify the nation—as exemplified most importantly in the Frankfurt Parliament, and also in less familiar efforts to forge the political forces that would operate within the prospective unified nation.

It was not unusual for men first to be caught up in the movement in their home town, and then to move on to a larger center—Berlin, Frankfurt, or Vienna, either as an elected deputy to an official or ad hoc assembly, or as a journalist and/or agitator. The men who took a prominent role during that spring of 1848 had often spent years building up local political networks. These now gave them a base from which to operate.

Thus, the radical physician from Königsburg, Johann Jacoby, who had spent years developing political connections that crossed class lines and had established a strong democratic caucus in the ongoing political life of East Prussia, played a major part in the March agitation. He went on to represent his constituency at the Pre-Parliament—his earlier role in embryonic radical networks leading to his invitation. Too radical actually to be elected to the Frankfurt Assembly from Königsburg, he moved instead to Berlin, where he was on the far left flank of the Prussian Constituent Assembly and was active throughout the summer in organizing the left in that body.[37]

In Bonn, the charismatic democratic-socialist art historian Gottfried Kinkel became the chairman of the new democratic club, that institutionalized and probably enlarged the informal group of students who had been politically concerned in the *Vormärz* period. He was seconded by his devoted student, Carl Schurz.[38] In Mainz, a young lawyer, Ludwig Bamberger, found his relatively dormant liberalism awakened by the events he witnessed; he took an active part in the March events and went on to organize a substantial Democratic Association that served as a local nucleus for republican politics. By December he became a delegate to the second Democratic Congress, to be discussed below.[39]

Cologne was the arena chosen by Bamberger's friend from Heidelberg University, Friedrich Kapp, who arrived in the city in January. The Rhenish industrial center was the scene of some of the most interesting developments within the reformist camp. Both the middle and the working class were politically mobilized, and Kapp was impressed to discover a branch of the Communist League, with its links to Brussels and London.[40] In a few months Marx made his headquarters here, and Cologne became the scene of confrontation between traditional working-class communism and the new style, both authoritarian and pragmatic, of the official leader of the international organization of the Communist League. Thus, Herzen's future friend found himself in the middle not just of working-class and leftist politics, but also of radical factionalism.[41]

The style of the Cologne Communist League was similar to that of Paris before Engels took control of the organization in 1847: it had a strong working-class constituency, who espoused traditional communism, and university-educated leaders, who drew support from left Hegelianism for these traditional attitudes. Andreas Gottschalk, a physician and a friend of Moses Hess, was the acknowledged leader of the league; among his lieutenants were Friedrich Anneke and August Willich, both former officers who had sealed their commitment to communism by becoming manual workers. All three were True Socialists, believers in the moral obligation of communism, the view excoriated by Marx in *The Holy Family*.

Once the revolution made open political activity possible in Germany, the conspiratorial league quickly became obsolete. Marx, who arrived in Cologne in April, pushed the league into changes of policy in regard to electoral tactics; Gottschalk's response was to resign from it in May. But Marx himself was apparently convinced that Cologne, with its unsatisfactory traditionalism, was typical of the league branches around the country; in June he used his executive powers to dissolve the organization that had been entrusted to him. (This maneuver foreshadows Marx's virtual destruction of the First International in 1872, when he appeared to be losing control of the organization.)

A month before his resignation from the Cologne Communist League, Gottschalk had established a much larger and more important group, an open Workers' Association (*Arbeiterverein*), with membership in the thousands. The Workers' Association followed a line of cooperation and sympathy with the socialist left, while rejecting worker support of nonsocialist groups. Thus, the association voted funds to aid the remnants of Herwegh's legion, but refused to participate in undemocratic elections or to form alliances with liberal political groups.[42]

Marx found quite a different constituency and took quite a different position. As long as the popular and charismatic Gottschalk was at the head of the Workers' Association, the organized working class was relatively impervious to Marx's efforts to undermine his rival. Instead, Marx worked in alliance with middle-class liberals. The memory of the old *Rheinische Zeitung* enticed both Marx and Hess; in this rivalry, Marx was the victor and became the editor of the *Neue Rheinische Zeitung*. The new paper, like the old, was backed by local businessmen; Marx's editorial line in it was quite consistently democratic, and not communist; he advocated participation in the political process created in the course of the revolution, and rejected workers' demands. Hess and Gottschalk, in sharp contrast, presented themselves as communists, and called for proletarian revolution.[43]

In the late summer Gottschalk, along with Anneke, was arrested "for having preached communism before an assembled multitude of 8,000 citizens."[44] Only now could Marx establish his own influence in the Workers' Association; Gottschalk was replaced by Marx's lieutenant Karl Schapper, who with another of the London Communist League leaders, Joseph Moll, had joined Marx in Cologne. (Moll became vice-president.) When Schapper was arrested and Moll fled after revolutionary disturbances in September, Marx himself took over as president of the association. Despite an understanding that he was serving temporarily, he did not give up the presidency upon Gottschalk's release from prison in December. The incident exacerbated the rivalry between Gottschalk and Marx and undermined unity on the left still more. Gottschalk, angry, left Cologne, and in travels to Bonn, Paris, and Brussels, "he cultivated contacts with the poet Herwegh, Moses Hess, and others whom Marx had offended."[45]

In line with his policy of coalition, Marx, in addition to editing the *Neue Rheinische Zeitung*, became head of the Cologne Democratic Society, an umbrella group of liberals, democrats, and communists that included the Workers' Association as its left wing.[46] He also played a role in early efforts to create a nationwide, relatively broadly based democratic movement. To this end, he convened a Congress of Democratic Associations in Cologne. But having already alienated the communist left by his moderate policy, Marx now proceeded to alienate the middle-class democrats with his arrogant and domineering personality. Carl Schurz described the impression made by the outstanding socialist thinker of the century:

> He already was the recognized head of the advanced socialistic school. The somewhat thick-set man with his broad forehead, his very black hair and beard and his dark sparkling eyes at once attracted general attention. He enjoyed the reputation of having acquired great learning, and as I knew very little of his discoveries and theories, I was all the more eager to gather words of wisdom from the lips of that famous man. This expectation was disappointed in a peculiar way. Marx's utterances were indeed full of meaning, logical and clear, but I have never seen a man whose bearing was so provoking and intolerable. To no opinion, which differed from his, he accorded the honor of even a condescending consideration. Everyone who contradicted him he treated with abject contempt; every argument that he did not like he answered either with biting scorn at the unfathomable ignorance that had prompted it, or with opprobrious aspersions upon the motives of him who had advanced it. I remember most clearly the cutting disdain with which he pronounced the word "bourgeois"; and as a "bourgeois," that is a detestable example of the deepest mental and moral degeneracy he denounced everyone that dared to oppose his opinion. Of course the propositions advanced or advocated by Marx in that meeting were voted down, because everyone whose feelings had been hurt by his conduct was inclined to support everything that Marx did not favor. It was very evident that not only he had not won any adherents, but had repelled many who might otherwise have become his followers.[47]

This Rhenish meeting was only one of several in which German radical democrats attempted to hammer out a political position and organization. The moderate liberalism of the Frankfurt Parliament was far too cautious and hesitant for their tastes. It was, said Kapp, "a ridiculous monster."[48] The left in it was very small, and rather moderate—its leading figures were Carl Vogt, Fröbel, Ruge, and Robert Blum, a socialist of working-class origin from Saxony, whose execution by the Austrian authorities in the autumn would be one of the great reactionary atrocities of the revolutionary year.[49] But alongside the official Parliament, there was a second, unofficial assembly, a Democratic Congress, made up of delegates of democratic associations and workers' organizations, and with a center of gravity considerably to the left of the assembly. Marx, Hess, the poet Ferdinand Freiligrath, Feuerbach, Kapp, and Reinhold Solger were among those in attendance. The congress established a coordinating body, the Central Committee of German Democrats, headed by Fröbel. [50]

A second Democratic Congress met in Berlin in October. It issued a manifesto outlining a semisocialist program that included: nationalization of land and mineral resources, nationalization of banks, nationalization of transport, restrictions on inheritance, direct taxation, separation of church and state, free education, free justice, the dictum that "all must labor, including armies," a state guarantee of "the existence of all who work," state care for those incapable of working, and permission to establish national manufactories.[51] The Congress met during the bloody suppression of revolutionary institutions in Vienna. Ruge's call for support for the Viennese led to popular disturbances that in turn served as the pretext for the proclamation of martial law in Prussia, the dissolution of the Prussian Constituent Assembly, and the reassertion of royal power.[52] The counterrevolution in the two capitals then provoked revolutionary defiance—there were scattered disturbances, and in Baden a second attempt to raise a republican revolution failed as ignominiously as the first. The repression led to the first wave of German emigration, primarily from Vienna.

Despite the reassertion of royal control and the repression of popular action in the major states, some revolutionary institutions continued to function with a momentum of their own. The Frankfurt Assembly finally completed its constitution in the spring of 1849 and offered the crown of democratic Germany to the King of Prussia. After he had scornfully rejected a "crown from the gutter," the assembly declared Germany a republic. The Prussian government responded with an order disbanding the assembly, and troops to back up its demand. While most of the deputies went home, some of the left did attempt to put up an armed resistance. A provisional government was set up, once again in Baden, and the Polish hero Mieroslawski came to lead the republic's forces. The Prussian army easily routed the rebels, and severe reprisals were taken. Among those taken prisoner was Gottfried Kinkel, who was condemned to death, his sentence later commuted to life imprisonment. His young friend Schurz, whose own escape from Rastatt Fortress through the sewers had been spectacular enough, showed his heroism by returning to Germany a year later and rescuing Kinkel.

Schurz, Kinkel, and the others who escaped the Prussian troops could no longer remain in Germany; their flight, to Switzerland in the first instance, and later to France and England, increased the exile colonies. Even some, like Kapp, who had not taken part in military activity, but who had made no secret of their radicalism, found it wise to leave at this time.[53] They traveled West, looking for safety and some comfort amid the defeat of their hopes.

Herzen and the Refugees

When the German forty-eighters arrived in Paris, they sought out Herwegh, whose house had long served as a center for radical émigré life. Now they found the poet discouraged and speaking of withdrawing from political concerns altogether to concentrate on natural science. Through him they met Herzen, whose perceptions of the present were just as bleak, but whose vivacity and humor were less depressing.[54] Soon the Herzens' house became a second haven for the refugees.

Most of the Russians, under some pressure from their government, returned home at the end of the summer. The Tuchkovs left in early August, and Mariia Korsh decided to travel with them. Natalie lamented that she had been "completely orphaned."[55] Annenkov left a month later, and Selivanov in November. Turgenev continued to be a regular visitor, as did Sazonov, but now most of the guests were central Europeans who had made the Herzens' acquaintance through Georg and Emma Herwegh.

In October the family took a new house, which soon became a rallying point for the exiles. Many of them arrived nearly penniless, and Herzen's generosity to them became legendary. Thus, one friend from this period told of twenty extra places laid at each meal, of anonymous contributions to anyone in need, and of providing facilities for two Hungarian women to deliver their babies in the Herzen home.[56] Natalie described their house with its large garden on the Champs-Elysées as "Sokolovo with Paris comforts, only you are not here, friends! Often our circle is large and close, but you give yourself to it only halfway, and often another circle is visible above it—of long familiar, native, dear faces. . . . we have met many new people, who more or less cause sympathetic chords of the soul to sound."[57]

Herzen made a practice of making his own little world as much a microcosm of socialist society as he could, and one of his techniques was to employ members of the radical community whenever possible. In 1847, Jean-Baptist Bocquet had acted as Sasha Herzen's tutor; reflecting the Herzens' new milieu, in late 1848 this task was taken over by the young German forty-eighter, Friedrich Kapp, who also acted as Herzen's secretary and translator.[58]

The filtering process of the past several months helped define who these friends of Herwegh, who became in their turn acquaintances and friends of Herzen, would be. They were on the radical edge of the German political scene, extending from the far left of the official assemblies to the unrepresented socialists and communists. But they also tended to be on the opposite side of a fault line from Karl Marx, who had antagonized so many people of so many different persuasions in the past two years and especially in the summer of 1848.[59] Politically, it was an ill-assorted group, for it ranged from quite moderate democrats to convinced communists; they were by no means a political party, merely a group linked by their disappointed dreams and by their belief that all revolutionaries were part of a fraternity that was obliged to treat its members with a consideration so often lacking among the intellectuals in Cologne. The émigrés' distrust of Marx and desire to avoid falling under his influence was explicit.[60]

Among the men with whom Herzen now became acquainted were Herwegh's former colleagues from the Paris émigré community, Hess and Ewerbeck. Younger men whose political career began with the revolution included Kapp and Gustav Rasch. Gottschalk arrived in Paris after his release from prison, as did one of the leading Baden rebels, Carl Blind, now carrying diplomatic papers from the last German republic.

The members of this new exile colony could no longer act as parliamentary politicians or popular organizers; they had to create (or recreate) an émigré politics of newspapers, ideological self-definition, and, for some, secret societies. In September 1848, Hess, Ewerbeck, Rasch, and others established the first of the postrevolutionary émigré societies, the Deutsche Verein.[61] It was typical of postrevolutionary radicalism in its strong internationalism; it became a truism that only a united front of radical forces from all lands could counter the united front of the monarchical powers. The Verein's first public statement set the tone. It was a response to the charge that there had been a revival of German nationalism and francophobia in their homeland. In denial, the Germans in Paris asserted their own sympathy for the French democrats and the sympathy of the German democratic movement, which was made up of workers and their friends, who were the brothers of the democrats of all countries. "They know that only through the liberation of the Italians and the Poles from the yoke of German and Russian despotism can German and European democracy be secure from attacks by reaction. The slogan of all democrats is 'Long live the French Republic.' "[62] Similar sentiments were expressed by the Central Committee of the German Democrats in Berlin, when it sent its official greeting to the new Verein.[63]

For Herzen, the influx of refugees provided an arena where he could begin to become politically active. In the internationalist climate now prevailing, he defined a role for himself as an emissary of Russian radicalism to the international movement. He would inform the Western radical world about Russia and at the same time work to spread Russian radical propaganda to his homeland.

Although for the moment the German colony provided the largest contingent in the international milieu in which Herzen would move henceforth, they were not his sole contacts. In addition he met Hungarians, Romanians, and Poles. His later cooperation with the Polish Democratic Committee in London may have its source in meetings with Polish radicals in Paris in the winter of 1848–1849.[64]

His new acquaintances certainly deepened Herzen's understanding of European political events, gave him visibility within radical circles, and, as we shall see later, inspired him to participate in the international movement through the periodical press. Did his involvement with the radicals go beyond intellectual exchange and include some kind of conspiratorial action aimed at overthrowing existing governments?

Herzen, in *Byloe i dumy*, denied ever having been a member of a secret society, although he did not reject them in principle.[65] It is more than probable that he was telling the truth. Nonetheless, there is some slight evidence that he took a more active role in the German radical movement than he later acknowledged.

The letter written by Sergei Levitskii back in the summer of 1848, which was intercepted by the Russian authorities, led to an investigation of Herzen's activities. Available evidence indicates that the process of transmitting a request for information to the French police and getting a reply from them was incredibly slow—not until after Herzen had left Paris more than a year after the original letter was seized was any information obtained. In the meantime, the Russian authorities received a denunciation of Herzen that linked him with the German communist Ewerbeck and Carl Tausenau—one of the Viennese radical leaders who had fled to Paris—as well as with Bakunin and Ivan Golovin. On the basis of the denunciation, the Russian consul, V. I. de Shpies, requested that the French police place Herzen under surveillance in order to verify the accuracy of the denunciation. De Shpies also suggested that nothing be put in writing and that a domiciliary search would be useful.[66]

Kiselev, the Russian ambassador, acting on instructions from his government, went to see the prefect of police himself to request information on Polish radicals, Herzen, and the latter's German contacts; this inquiry probably took place shortly after de Shpies's first visit. In requesting cooperation from the French, the ambassador used an argument that was a mirror image of the radical internationalism of the left:

> I told him that knowing with what persistence . . . he . . . was pursuing domestic and foreign revolutionaries and anarchists, I did not hesitate to ask him to inform me of what measures he was taking against these enemies of the order and peace of the entire world and especially against Russian and Polish demagogues, whose evil schemes were of immediate concern to us, since he knows . . . that the reds of all countries extend a hand to each other, and that in their own interests governments must do the same in order to combat them and truly defend the legal order.[67]

It was decided that de Shpies would continue to serve as the contact between the Paris police and the Russian government. De Shpies, on the day following the interview between the prefect and the ambassador, was told of police requests for the expulsion of a number of members of the Polish Democratic Committee and of backers of a journal formerly edited by Adam Mickiewicz, *La Tribune des Peuples*. As for the individuals specifically mentioned by Kiselev, Tausenau had been released from prison, and was being banished to Switzerland, while Ewerbeck remained in custody. (It is likely that both were arrested in the wake of the June 13, 1849, demonstration; Herzen fled to avoid the same fate.) De Shpies was also informed that a search of Herzen's domicile, once its location was discovered, would be a simple matter under current conditions of martial law.[68]

At his next interview, the consul was told that the search had duly taken place, but that Herzen himself had escaped to Geneva and was due to depart shortly for Prussia. Tausenau had been interviewed and had reported his own regular contacts with Bakunin, Golovin, Ewerbeck, and Herzen; he also told about his relations with the German committee in Paris. Further, the prefect reported, "Herzen always attempted to have people take him for a Prussian."[69]

This report seems an odd combination of accurate information, misinformation, and simple confusion. The "German Committee" was probably no more than the Deutsche Verein mentioned above; it was not a secret society, and did not conceal its links with Prussian democrats. (It was, however, a "front organization," in that the communism of its leadership was not expressed in its policy statements.)[70] The fact that the French police did not have information on Herzen available at the time of the Russian request indicates that whatever role he may have played before June 13, it had not been prominent enough to bring him to the attention of the authorities. It is highly unlikely that Herzen ever tried to pass himself off as a Prussian; however, Ruge reported in a letter that he had become acquainted "with a Russian, Herzen, whom, essentially, should rather be called a German than a Russian."[71] It is possible that this reflects a general sense among the German community that Herzen, with his German name, his German mother, his fluency in the language, and his friendship with Herwegh and his circle, was almost a German himself. This sense could have been distorted into the form in which it was reported by the police. As for the indication that he intended to go on to Prussia, presumably with political intentions, there is some very scanty additional evidence pointing in that direction. Back in November 1848, Solger had expected either Herzen or Sazonov to arrive soon in Germany,[72] and Mazzini, in his first contact with Herzen, suggested that the Russian might undertake to organize a German branch of Mazzini's association.[73] The suggestion was bizarre, considering that the two men had had very little personal contact at this time, but slightly less so if one allows for the possibility that Herzen had some reputation for political work among the Germans. The possibility that Herzen was engaged in clandestine activity is lessened by the consideration that there was no political group with which he felt entirely in agreement. He was however, seen as a possible recruit by Mazzini's European Central Democratic Committee (to be discussed later), and speculation about him by the Mazzini people might have filtered into police reports in distorted form.

The information provided the Russian diplomats by the French police was transmitted to St. Petersburg, and at the end of August the vice-minister of foreign affairs, L. G. Seniavin, informed Count Orlov, director of the Third Section, that Herzen had departed for Switzerland, and that "appropriate" instructions had been transmitted to the Russian ambassador there.[74] It is unlikely that Herzen was ever free of at least some observation by Russian authorities from then on.

The French investigation did not end, despite Herzen's departure, and the information provided de Shpies became more dramatic, and less likely. On October 5, the consul was told "At the present time there is a secret society in Paris, called the European Revolutionary Committee, which partially consists of Russians and Germans; the goal of this committee . . . is to establish the universal republic on the ruins of monarchy. . . . One of the main leaders of this anarchistic lodge is the Russian Herzen, who supports its undertakings with his money. He travels often, and his primary assignment is relations between the Geneva demagogues and the Paris committee."[75]

One week later, de Shpies was told that Sazonov was a close collaborator of Herzen's in the work of the Russian-German committee, and that both men worked on the *Tribune des Peuples*, "which is considered the official organ of this party." The prefect had taken measures, he said, for the expulsion of Herzen and Sazonov, which was to take effect as soon as Herzen returned to Paris. Gustav Rasch, one of Herzen's young German acquaintances, was named as another member of the committee; he was in London coordinating the activities of the exiles with those of the Paris Committee, just as Herzen was doing in "Geneva and other places."[76] These reports seem most interesting for the degree of hysteria on the part of the French authorities that they demonstrate and the willingness of the French to cooperate with the Russians, even to the point of carrying out domiciliary searches at their behest. However, the content of the reports does not inspire confidence.

The Russian investigation of Herzen was accurate in one respect; it uncovered a series of documents granting power of attorney to Herzen's agent in Russia, G. I. Kliucharev, for the transfer or sale of his own and his mother's Russian property: these included Herzen's sale of his Moscow house to his brother, the sale of Luisa Haag's

Moscow house, and the mortgage of Herzen's Kostroma property. All these transactions had been stamped at the consulate-general instead of the embassy—a procedure that appeared, correctly, to be an attempt on Herzen's part to be inconspicuous. They show, the consul wrote, that Herzen intended to realize as much of his property as possible in Russia and transfer his capital abroad. The Russians also learned of Herzen's purchase of a house in Paris, but the French police were unable to determine its location and asserted that the transaction had been carried out with great circumspection.[77]

Further evidence of Herzen's intention to emigrate was provided by a letter from Levitskii that was intercepted at the same time as this investigation—that is, just after Herzen's departure from Paris. "They do not wish to return to Russia," he said of Herzen and Luisa Haag, "and say frankly that everything is over between themselves and Russia, and the local embassy knows it."[78]

Herzen's letters show that the decision to liquidate as much of his Russian property as possible was probably made in the winter of 1848–1849, and that the sale of the house in Moscow, initiated months earlier, in March 1848, may well have been a separate issue altogether. In late November he told Kliucharev that he had made a small investment with Rothschild (10,000 rubles), drawing on his capital to do so.[79] The success of this first speculative venture, which he reported to Kliucharev on February 12, 1849, then provided the rationale for removing more capital.[80] By this means he succeeded in transferring all his liquid assets to the West, and in the end the authorities had time to sequester only the Kostroma estate, the planned mortgage of which was dated April 4, 1849. His mother's assets were blocked, but Herzen eventually used the good offices of the Rothschild bank to free them.[81] He had little sympathy for radicals who sacrificed everything to emigrate and join the revolutionary movement, and then lived off charity in the West.[82]

Most of Herzen's funds were invested by Rothschild in American paper of various kinds. The collaboration between the bank and the revolutionary was most successful—Herzen thus supported his generosity to his fellow revolutionaries, paid for the Free Russian Press and subsidized the Polish press in London, as well as keeping himself and his family in comfort. However, at the beginning of the American Civil War he panicked and sold the American paper at a loss, after which his means were reduced, although he remained very comfortably off.[83]

With his bridges burned as far as safely returning to Russia was concerned, his means secured, and some kind of radical community present within which he could function, Herzen was ready to go to work. Work, however, was still to be found.

Herzen was seeking a newspaper in which he could play a role, and, as became clear by mid-1849, he was quite willing to make a major financial contribution to such a venture. Ideally, he sought a journal that would help provide a structure for the inchoate group of international radicals with whom, through Herwegh, he had become affiliated; democracy, socialism, internationalism, and establishing a platform for an exchange of polemics with the Cologne radicals behind Marx were the most important programmatic considerations. The backing of a great star of international democracy would be an additional benefit.

The first paper known to have approached Herzen for support was *La Tribune des Peuples*. The person who inspired this venture was a star of the very greatest magnitude, the Polish poet Adam Mickiewicz, who had attracted a wide following in France just before the revolution through his course on Slavic literature at the Collège de France. Prohibited from resuming his chair, Mickiewicz was able to undertake the newspaper through the generosity of his compatriot, Count Xavier Branicki.[84] Mickiewicz's ideology combined Bonapartism and romantic Polish messianism—views that would make him a strange ally for Herzen, with his atheistic, socialist anarchism. Indeed, in Herzen's account, the attempt to collaborate foundered on this disagreement. As he described the episode in *Byloe i dumy*, Charles Edmond Chojecki approached him and introduced him to Mickiewicz at a banquet. Herzen, however, found the obsequiousness of his followers toward the great poet with his mystical pretensions offensive and the political differences between Herzen and the Poles too great to be surmounted.[85]

A somewhat different picture emerges from piecing together other bits of evidence and examining the pages of *La Tribune des Peuples* itself. Division of opinion seems to have been built into the very structure of the paper. There was a rather shadowy Polish group exercising overall direction, but the paper's historian was unable to define its activity or influence "with any precision."[86] Within the active editorial group, Mickiewicz and his friends controlled the general editorial line, but at the start the correspondents were recruited by a young compatriot of the poet's, Charles Edmond Chojecki. Chojecki was a Polish radical who had left his native country in 1844, fearing arrest for his participation in subversive groups. He came to Paris, where, under the name

Charles Edmond, he became a contributor to opposition journals. In 1848 he fought on the barricades in February and then returned to Poland for several months, hoping to help spread the revolution. He attended the Prague Slav Congress and then in December 1848 returned to Paris. Philosophically, Chojecki was a left Hegelian, and politically he was close to Proudhon.[87] Ladislas Mickiewicz, the poet's son, believed Chojecki was imposed on the paper by Branicki and that his friends constituted the editorial board's left wing, a view not wholly shared by Kieniewicz. Ladislas Mickiewicz further stated that Chojecki did not agree with Mickiewicz's views and would gladly have seen the poet replaced by Herzen.[88]

Chojecki and Mickiewicz did agree, however, on the revolutionary internationalism that was to be the paper's most important ideological position. "Henceforth," Mickiewicz asserted in the first issue, "it will be impossible for one people to march in isolation along the path of progress." The goal of the paper would be to provide an international forum: "we call on all the nations to come to this *Tribune*, each with its free word."[89] Not only was *La Tribune* to be internationalist, but also, in line with Mickiewicz's own position, and in sharp distinction from the rest of the democratic press in France, it was by no means anti-Russian, showing an ability to distinguish the actions of the Russian state from the attitudes of the Russian people that was unique at this time. Among the paper's collaborators was Sazonov, who was at least a peripheral member of Mickiewicz's circle[90] and whose works appeared in the paper under the pseudonym "Iwan Woinof."[91] In an article in the first issue, which by virtue of its position and length looked as though it represented the editorial position, Sazonov clearly distinguished between the Russian state and its people and interpreted the Russian situation in a way that prefigured Herzen's later works:

> Through its diverse oppressions and its successive revolts, under the iron Asiatic yoke, as under the European yoke of formulas, the Russian people knew how to hold intact its communal organization, which it has enjoyed since time immemorial. It allowed a foreign authority, a German administration to be established; it allowed itself to be oppressed and pillaged.
>
> On the other hand, the sentiment of liberty, which is developing ever more strongly in the civilized classes, has had its martyrs as well in the noble insurgents of December 14, 1825.
>
> At the same time, all of Russian literature offers us an uninter-

rupted series of intellectual martyrs in Pouchkine, Gribojedoff, Lermontoff, Polevoi, Belinsky.

The two interests of civilization and of nationality, which hitherto have seemed opposed to each other in Russia, have found in these men a common symbol.

One more effort, and the Russian people will shake off the yoke of a false and obsolete order of things in order to reveal itself to Europe, young, strong, and free. We have complete confidence in the future of this people, and it is because we are persuaded . . . it will justify our confidence, that we ask for its admission into the fraternal circle of European peoples.[92]

Herzen would search in vain for another paper so involved with the international movement, and so willing to hear a revolutionary Russian point of view.

During the brief period that Chojecki served as managing editor, there was considerable overlap between Herzen's circle and the staff of *La Tribune*. Golovin was both a friend of Mickiewicz and an editor.[93] In addition to Sazonov and Golovin, the paper also had at least one other Russian contributor, a correspondent from within the country whose position was oppositional.[94]

Herzen's non-Russian friends were also represented. Chojecki secured the collaboration of the German communist Hermann Ewerbeck, the French Saint-Simonian Lechevalier, and Ramon de la Sagra, a Spanish former deputy whom Herzen admired and who also was in contact with Proudhon.[95] Ernst Haug, a former officer in the Austrian army who had joined the revolutionary forces and who later became one of Herzen's staunchest friends, contributed an article condemning the narrow nationalism of the Hungarian revolutionary government.[96] Herzen's friends must have hoped to control the paper; Gottschalk as late as May hoped that it could be used as a platform for Marx's opponents.[97] This did not happen, however, and instead Chojecki was forced to resign. After his departure, the sense that *La Tribune*'s politics and personnel overlapped with the circle of Herzen's friends disappeared.

Despite this first failure, Herzen continued to plan his new career. His program for his activity in the West was two-fold; not only would he serve as a spokesman of Russia to the West, but also he would speak to Russians of Russian liberty: "Here I am your uncensored voice, your free press, your chance representative," he wrote his friends in explaining his emigration.[98]

Herzen had already chosen his weapon in the fight against autocracy—a foreign-based press that would disseminate censored material to his homeland. The inspiration probably came from Fröbel's success in publishing Herwegh's work in Switzerland. Herzen outlined his intentions in the unpublished introduction to his first planned publications—new editions of his own works. Written in the form of a letter to Granovskii, the introduction stated that censorship in Russia had made it impossible for him to publish at all legally. This was a blessing in disguise, however, for it forced him to remain abroad, where he could say openly what had only been hinted at between the lines of his legal publications. In addition to old works, he planned to issue a new series of articles on Russia. These were probably never written, but judging from the works Herzen published in the Western press in the next two years, he was very likely intending to expound his newly jelled ideas on Russia, the West, and "Russian socialism." That he was not interested merely in seeing his own name in print, but hoped to use the press as a forum for Russian political discussion (as he was later to do with the Free Russian Press), is indicated by his combining his announcement with the solicitation of manuscripts from Russia.[99] Political and personal crises delayed his plans by four years, but the scheme of early 1849 is virtually identical with Herzen's activities from 1853 forward.

For the moment, however, politics intervened. By early 1849 France was well on its way to authoritarianism, while still retaining some of the mythology of revolution. With the left weakened by repression and the emigration of some of its leaders and supporters, efforts were made to overcome the divisions of the past year and to present a united front in the face of the greater danger from the conservatives. The radical democrats, under Ledru-Rollin, had made common cause with some of the remaining moderate socialists, forming a new opposition group called (in memory of 1792) the "Mountain."

Louis Napoleon Bonaparte had become president of the Republic in December 1848. Imperial ambitions were visible from the start,[100] but for the moment the constitution limited presidential powers. At legislative elections in May, the conservatives had won a solid two-thirds majority in the Chamber of Deputies. But on the left, the Mountain, based primarily on the urban electorate, had also done well, greatly improving its voting strength over previous elections. Ledru-Rollin thought there was still revolutionary potential in the Paris populace.[101]

One of the last places in Europe where the revolutionaries were still in control was Rome. There the pope had fled, and a republican government had been set up, run by a triumvirate led by Giuseppe Mazzini. The armed forces of the republic were commanded by Giuseppe Garibaldi. France, in April, joined the forces of order in Europe by dispatching troops to Italy to aid the pope in his attempt to regain his capital. At the end of May the French forces outside Rome opened an attack on the Republic. When news of the French bombardment reached Paris, the French and international left were appalled at this breach of revolutionary solidarity, and also at the defiance of the French constitution. Natalie Herzen, remembering the great moments of the Italian revolution, said it seemed "that the French fire is tearing apart my heart."[102] George Sand apologized to Mazzini for her country.[103] Hoping to capitalize on this mood, Ledru-Rollin introduced a motion of impeachment into the Chamber of Deputies on June 11. After its preordained defeat, he attempted to organize one more revolutionary *journée,* in the guise of a protest demonstration against the government's actions in Italy.

Given the international nature of the provocation, an international response was planned. Ledru-Rollin and his colleagues of the Mountain had already developed contacts with the émigrés. Now on the eve of the demonstration, the émigrés were invited to participate in the protest.[104] With grave misgivings, Herzen took part along with the other exiles.[105] The march was not supported by the Paris populace, and instead of an insurrection there was brutal repression. The presses of the radical papers were smashed by mobs, and the editors were indicted for conspiring to overthrow the republic. Of Herzen's two companions on that day, Carl Blind was arrested and Ruge fled; Herzen decided to do the same. He borrowed a passport and went to Geneva. Though not yet stateless, he had in fact joined the ranks of the refugees.

5
GENEVA and PROUDHON

WITH the move to Geneva, Herzen became part of the exile community. He was not yet technically a refugee—he had been expelled by no government and still held his passport. Soon, however, the Russian government, basing its actions on its own inquiries in regard to Herzen's whereabouts and activities, would begin applying pressure to force him to return home. (These events will be discussed in chapter 7.)

Herzen believed that his participation in the June 13 demonstration had led to French interest in him, and that the French had communicated their concern to Russia. However, as I have indicated in the previous chapter, it was the Russian government that initiated French interference in his life; there is no evidence that the French police even knew of his participation on June 13. Failing to convince him to return home, the tsarist government attempted to sequester his property, and the struggle to save his own and his mother's inheritances would soon occupy a significant portion of Herzen's time. For the moment, however, he found himself involved in the world of the refugees and its special problems.

Also at this time, Herzen succeeded in moving from the sidelines of political life to an active role. In Paris he had begun to find a place in the exile community that functioned in the interstices of domestic political life. But in Geneva, the thousands of refugees made their own politics a major activity, and Herzen found himself a relatively important person in their colony. Here there was a significant number of former politicians who were as cut off from active participation as he was himself. The focus of their activity shifted to journalism, which could still be conducted from safe havens; periodical publication gave them an opportunity to keep alive their own beliefs, to define their theoretical and tactical positions, and to maintain a political presence by smuggling their work back into their home countries. In this milieu Herzen was an outsider like all the rest; he had, however, one great advantage over the others—most of them were almost penniless, and he was very rich. His collaboration was now eagerly sought by a number of radical groups.

For Herzen, however, further disappointment was in store. Surrounded by the heroes of the struggles in several countries, he was impressed only by their futility. Men such as these, he felt, small-minded and self-important, could not lead a revolution. "In Geneva," he wrote later, "I began to understand ever more clearly that the revolution not only had been defeated, but that *it had to be* defeated."[1] To his hatred of the old regimes was now added scorn for those who had sought to overthrow them.

For all his disappointment, the Geneva period was one of substantial growth for Herzen. Politically, he became Proudhon's collaborator on a daily newspaper, *La Voix du Peuple,* an important step in defining his role in the radical community. Intellectually, too, he now staked out his mature position. Beginning with "La Russie," an essay published in *La Voix du Peuple,* a series of important works in Western languages established Herzen as a spokesman for Russian radicalism. Theoretically, these works develop the contrast between the declining West and Russia's potential, and also expound the distinctively Herzenian notion of "Russian socialism." The idea of the West's decrepitude emerged from his bitter disappointment at the failure of the recent revolutions. His views were never more extreme than at this time, when he welcomed the prospect of a new wave of "barbarians" from the East or from Western society's depths that would violently destroy the rotten corpse of Western civilization. The sophisticated, fastidious Herzen now began describing himself as a "barbarian" to his Western contacts, a conceit he maintained in later years.

Herzen arrived in Geneva on June 22, and gradually the rest of the family followed. Ten-year-old Sasha joined him a week later, accompanied by Carl Vogt.[2] Natalie and Tata, along with Georg Herwegh, arrived on July 10.[3] Not without misgivings, Emma remained in Paris with the Herwegh children. Her wealthy family had cut off its aid to the Herweghs after the revolution, leaving the poet with little more than debts. Emma, far more practical than her husband, felt she had to remain in Paris to attempt to bring her family's ruined finances into some kind of order. Shortly thereafter, Luisa

Haag and Mariia Ern brought Kolia Herzen to Zurich, where he was enrolled in a school for the deaf;[4] the women remained in Zurich with the boy.

The Switzerland Herzen encountered was in many respects a new country. The Swiss confederation, established after the Napoleonic Wars, had been the scene of conspiracy, uprising, and civil war since the middle of the 1840s; this unrest eventuated in victory for liberal, reforming forces. A new constitution that greatly strengthened the federal structure and also provided for civil liberties and greater standardization across the cantons, had been ratified only in 1848. In the years before the civil war, a major concern of the reformist radicals had been the treaty right—and the habit—of neighboring powers of intervening in Swiss affairs. The powers, in turn, had justified their intervention by the Swiss tradition of asylum; political refugees regularly fled to the Republic and were there unimpeded, sometimes even aided, by the Swiss as they plotted to overthrow their government at home. The Swiss revolutionaries had aimed at resolving these issues, but the events of 1848 and 1849 brought them close to a crisis.[5]

Revolutionary change had come not just to the confederation as a whole, but to some of the individual cantons as well, among them Geneva. In 1846 a veteran radical politician, James Fazy, had led his faction to power in a successful coup d'état; three years later he controlled the city as cantonal president. Fazy combined the toughness and intransigence of a longtime conspirator with a political moderation that limited reform to political democracy. "He remained attached to the principles of the American school in politics, and in political economy to the scientific facts so well established by the schools of [Adam] Smith and J.-B. Say," he said of himself.[6] Sympathy for revolutionary refugees from all countries seeking asylum in Geneva thus was an instinctive response for Fazy, but at the same time he had no use for the doctrines espoused by many of the guests in his city.[7]

Fazy was not, however, an entirely free agent, despite his commanding position in Geneva itself. The confederation took an equivocal position with regard to the refugees. The central government in Bern feared great-power intervention if the country were used by foreign radicals as a staging area for renewed assaults on the governments of their homelands. Early in 1848 it prohibited the departure of any groups of armed men from the territory of the republic. Despite this policy, Swiss neutrality was violated by the exiles who returned to Germany to take part in the Baden uprising of November 1848. The Baden government protested, and the confederation responded by deporting some revolutionary leaders and interning all other exiles at least six hours away from the border.

When Herzen arrived in late June, the Swiss Republic was again embarrassed by a huge influx of refugees from Baden, numbering this time in the thousands, and perhaps tens of thousands. In response, the government tightened its policy toward them.[8] Swiss fears were not imaginary. The Prussian and Baden governments both considered invasion. The French were concerned by the "more than 15,000" Germans, Poles, and others in Switzerland, who were linked with the French fleeing from the June 13 demonstration and were equipped with fifty six pieces of cannon and "un matériel immense."[9] By September, both the Russians and the Austrians had indicated to the French that unless Switzerland ceased to harbor foreigners who used Swiss territory to endanger its neighbors, Swiss inviolability would not be respected.[10] Finally, the British representative in Bern reported to his government that the French and Germans had arrived at an agreement to destroy that "hotbed of communism."[11]

Fazy's policy in the face of the pressure from Bern, which was itself responding to pressure from the great powers, was to conceal the presence of the refugees to the best of his ability. As long as they remained inconspicuous, Fazy simply pretended they were not there. Conflict arose, however, when they announced their presence and directed revolutionary appeals and proclamations to their homelands.[12] Yet another source of pressure on Fazy were the refugees themselves, who would protest *en bloc* should any of their number be expelled or harassed.

Herzen himself, unarmed, isolated, and wealthy, received a warm greeting. He had met the Genevan leader in December or January,[13] and they had a mutual friend in Sazonov. But while the welcome was cordial and Fazy was helpful both regarding Herzen's papers (he was traveling on someone else's passport) and in getting a passport for Sazonov, he saw no reason to make an issue of the Russian's politics. Thus, when the arrival of the Herzen party was attacked by the conservative *Journal de Genève*, Fazy's own *Revue de Genève* replied: "The *Journal de Genève* speaks of the arrival in Geneva of M. Hertzen and of M. Herwegh. And why shouldn't these gentlemen be here? M. Hertzen, a distinguished Russian writer with a great independence of fortune, a property owner in France, and still owning property in Russia, travels in Switzerland for pleasure, and for this, there he is, accused of being a propagandist."[14]

Other foreigners were less fortunate. The Baden leader Gustav Struve was arrested and unceremoniously taken across the cantonal border while still in his slippers; the police did not even give him a chance to dress properly. The affair became farcical when he was promptly returned by the authorities of neighboring Vaud. Nonetheless, he now left Geneva and the confederation for England, and thence to the United States.[15] At the time, this was an isolated incident, but it did indicate that Fazy had lost patience with the revolutionaries. The political differences that separated him from the radical Herzen also became more marked—Herzen noted to his friends that within a month after his arrival, the Genevan president had cooled toward him.[16] After Herzen's departure, Fazy's attitude hardened further, as the refugee issue was used against him by his domestic opponents on the left. In 1850, despite an earlier promise, he did not respond to requests to grant Herzen Genevan citizenship.[17]

Geneva presented Herzen with a new political and moral world. Republicanism had marked the people's behavior with dignity and simplicity:

> Women in the street avert their eyes; the men dine at one, the artistocrats at five; at ten doors are locked, and by twelve everyone is asleep.... In Switzerland one can survey in practice what a republic is; the mores here are a thousand times more prepared for liberty than in France. The first day I went to Fazy; I rang, he came to the door himself, there was no reception room, no need to wait for a report. In the evening we went to the cafe to drink beer, and there he spoke to some gentleman, sitting in the smoke, about the papers I needed—this was the chief of police. No galloons or uniforms or fierce police officers—nothing of all that is insulting in the Petersburg fashion, and is so at home in Paris.[18]

For now, however, Herzen was more involved with the other foreigners than with the Genevans themselves. His new revolutionary contacts fell into two major groups: the Germans, fleeing from the dissolution of the Frankfurt Parliament and the last of the uprisings in southwestern Germany, and Italians, particularly veterans of Mazzini's Roman Republic. "The shores of Lake Geneva are besieged by the ruins of the Frankfurt Parliament," Herwegh wrote Emma. "The important personages, presidents, regents, etc., however, are in Montreux, the subalterns here in Geneva."[19] The few men whom Herzen and Herwegh found they could respect came from the political side of the German struggle; the military heroes were ridiculous. Thus, the most striking personality among the latter was the former Baden politician, Gustav Struve, too far left for the Pre-Parliament and the Frankfurt Assembly, who had been involved in all three Baden uprisings: "Imagine a senseless fanatic of the middle ages, an ascetic ignoramus and the most limited human being; imagine that he preaches the abolition of animal food . . . and . . . that was the leader of the Baden uprising, along with the swindler Brentano and with the general who is famous only for his defeats [Mieroslawski]."[20] Herzen mocked Struve's vegetarianism and general asceticism; Herwegh his attempt to found a trilingual journal—"he knows how to say nothing in one language—and now in three! that will be a fine Babel."[21] Both found Struve and his followers absurd.

A few of the Germans were worthy of respect, however. Through Herwegh, Herzen met Fröbel, who during the revolutionary period had returned to Germany and edited the republican *Deutsche Volkszeitung* in collaboration with Struve, and had led the Central Committee of German Democrats. Herzen liked Fröbel, unconcerned by his moderation on social issues. Like so many of the German fortyeighters whom Herzen respected, Fröbel soon set off for the United States.[22] Through Friedrich Kapp, who had been his secretary in Paris and had rejoined the family in Geneva, Herzen met many other refugees, including the Baden leaders. Kapp, however, shared his friends' negative view of the exile milieu.[23] One man whom Herzen did find compatible among this group was Kapp's university friend Ludwig Bamberger, who shared Herzen's admiration of Proudhon, although for very different and essentially moderate reasons.[24] Kapp soon went to the United States, and Bamberger to London, where he worked in the family bank. Both drifted to the right and returned to Germany after unification; they also appear to have drifted out of Herzen's orbit after 1850. Of the older men, Herzen met Johann Jacoby, the crusty radical Königsburg physician who was resting in Geneva from the travails of the revolutionary years, and the two men appear to have found each other compatible.

The extent of Herzen's casual contacts among the large German community cannot be determined.[25] It was sufficient to provide entrée to the German émigré press and to the London colony, but these

Geneva friendships did not develop into major ties. The bitter break with Herwegh two years later complicated all his relations with the Germans; the ones he met in Geneva either sided uneasily with the poet (whom in most cases they had known longer and better), or remained in an embarrassed neutrality.[26]

Herzen and Herwegh agreed in their evaluation of the Germans in Geneva, and also in finding the Italians altogether more admirable.[27] In August, Herzen suddenly ran into his old friend from the 1847 Italian journey, Leopoldo Spini. He in turn provided an introduction to Mazzini, through whom Herzen met Aurelio Saffi, another of the triumvirs of the Roman Republic, and the commander of the Roman legionnaires, Giacomo Medici.[28] All three would be Herzen's permanent friends. He was impressed, however, not only with Mazzini's revolutionary intensity and courage, but also with the fact that the Italian refused to go beyond political republicanism, and indeed expressly repudiated socialism. The greatest revolutionary of his time was in danger of becoming a retrograde person.[29]

Other contacts whom Herzen mentioned were "Félix," probably the radical playwright and 1848 politician Félix Pyat, and the Russian Ivan Golovin, whom he described as an unavoidable pest but who also appears to have been a regular companion, at least until Natalie and Herwegh arrived, and whose friendship with Fazy was no doubt useful.[30] Other persons Herzen mentioned in his letters have not been satisfactorily identified.[31] On the whole, French refugees do not seem to have been important to him. Among the native Genevans, he made friendly contacts with Fazy's leftist opposition, as testified to by a warm letter of recommendation from the Proudhonian Albert Galeer to a fellow socialist in Lausanne.[32] This friendship with the local left may have contributed to Fazy's cooling toward him.

The most important activity of all these refugees was journalism. As Herzen put it, "The publication of newspapers was an epidemic disease then: every two or three weeks projects arose, specimen issues appeared, programs were circulated, then two-three issues—and it all disappeared without a trace. People with no qualifications nonetheless considered themselves qualified to publish a paper, scraped up one or two hundred francs and used them on the first and last page."[33]

Struve requested Herzen's aid in publishing his projected trilingual journal; Herzen signed the statement of principles, despite its moderate, purely political character, but sufficient funds could not be raised, and the project never got off the ground.[34] He contributed financially to Mazzini's project for an editorial society that would publish and distribute revolutionary literature, including Mazzini's paper, *L'Italia del Popolo*, to which Herzen contributed an article as well. In the autumn, to Herzen's dismay, his name and Herwegh's were included as contributors to a Genevan socialist paper without their consent.[35] Fazy, for whose paper Golovin wrote, apparently was also courting Herzen, for Sazonov dissuaded him from such a project.[36] He did so in order to tempt Herzen with a far more alluring prospect—collaboration with a man he had long admired, and who had become a hero to him during 1848, Pierre-Joseph Proudhon.

Herzen and Proudhon had met a few times during the summer of 1847 through their mutual friend Bakunin, but this was a most superficial acquaintance.[37] Herzen's admiration of the Frenchman, however, was of some years' standing; he had read and approved *Qu'est-ce que la Propriété?* and *Système des Contradictions économiques* while still in Russia. In France, the notoriety surrounding the first of these, with its infamous question and answer: "What is property? Property is theft," had obscured the argument of this and succeeding works.[38] In his homeland Proudhon was attacked as a firebrand without being read. The German radicals who had spent part of the 1840s in Paris were far more impressed by him; however, one of their number, Karl Marx, launched his own polemical career with a merciless attack on Proudhon's *Système des Contradictions économiques*, his *Poverty of Philosophy*. Thus, like so many of the men whom Herzen considered his comrades in arms, Proudhon was a victim and opponent of Marx, which probably enhanced his appeal to the Russian.

Unlike Marx, the Russians Bakunin and Herzen found their own Hegelianism relatively compatible with the dialectical (and paradoxical) elements in Proudhon's thought. Since, unlike the Germans, they were not absorbed by the Hegelian tradition of Berlin and the sectarian quarrels to which it gave rise, they may have been among Proudhon's most sympathetic readers.[39] But although Herzen certainly knew of and approved Proudhon's theoretical work in the mid-1840s, he was in no sense a disciple. Moreover, among socialist thinkers of the time Proudhon had far less importance than Louis Blanc, Victor Considerant, or Pierre Leroux—to give a few examples. (All of these Proudhon saw as rivals and disliked thoroughly.) He also lacked the social and professional connections, such as collaboration on *La Réforme*, that gave visibility to other radical thinkers. From the mid-

1840s, Proudhon had been dreaming of a newspaper of his own that would remedy his isolation, but his first opportunity came only after the overthrow of the monarchy and the establishment of the Provisional Government.

It is by no means easy to characterize Proudhon's thought and position in the revolutionary period, nor is it possible to be categorical as to why Herzen, after considerable hestitation, chose this collaboration rather than another.[40] Proudhon was a difficult and paradoxical thinker who displayed both radical and conservative qualities, both hard-headed realism and political fantasy. His later stature as one of the major, if least understood, radical thinkers of the nineteenth century obscures the fact that in his own day, and especially at the end of the revolutionary period, he was better known as a political figure than as a theoretician of anarchism.

Despite his rejection of the state in principle, Proudhon had taken an active part in the politics of 1848. He first ran for office as a candidate for the National Assembly. Defeated in the general elections, he won a seat in a by-election and took his place shortly before the June Days. He sat with the Jacobin-socialist left, the Mountain (with whom he disagreed on many issues), and soon won a reputation as the only person who spoke out against the repression of the June insurgents. He was censured twice: for an injudicious remark about the "sublimity of the cannon fire" made during the uprising, and for his proposal that a moratorium be placed on all debts, public and private.[41] His protest against repression had all the greater impact because by this period he was almost the only major spokesman for the left at liberty; in the wake of the May 15 demonstration the club leaders Barbès and Blanqui had been imprisoned, while Blanc and other prominent socialists had begun the emigration, leaving France to avoid prosecution.

In addition to his defense of the defenseless, Proudhon did attempt to influence the structure of the future French constitution; his most important battle was an effort to dissuade the assembly from including a president in the government structure. In the absence of all the other preconditions necessary for a just social order, he was convinced that election of a president by universal suffrage would result in an authoritarian choice.[42]

In the course of his service in the assembly, Proudhon also managed to offend the Jacobin left—even to the point where a duel had to be fought with one of its leading spokesmen, Félix Pyat.[43] On one occasion he refused to vote against a minister of President Louis Napoleon Bonaparte, despite the fact that the man had served under the monarchy; as minister of justice he had chosen not to prosecute Proudhon for an early work, and Proudhon was grateful.

More maddening to the left, Proudhon, who had opposed instituting the office of presidency of the republic altogether, later refused to support the Mountain candidate, Ledru-Rollin. His first choice went to the radical physician Raspail—support for whom, he argued, was synonymous with outright rejection of the office. His second choice, he insisted, was none other than the general who had directed the June offensive against the Paris insurgents, Eugène Cavaignac. Proudhon's reasoning was paradoxical and perverse, and it is difficult to know how seriously to take his arguments—because Cavaignac was the very personification of bourgeois rule, he wrote, there will be no problem knowing where we stand with him, or who is our enemy. An inimical institution will be easier to fight if it is in the hands of an enemy than if it is in the hands of someone who may mean well but who will be a president, with all the authoritarianism and power that implies, nonetheless.[44]

Proudhon's perception of the political and social situation created by the revolution set him at odds with all prevailing shades of opinion and lent an air of perversity to his positions. One superficial, but politically important, paradox was Proudhon's habit of making extreme and provocative statements—"Property is theft" being only the most notorious of these—although in practice he was not only nonviolent, but also felt that attempts to bring about social change prematurely could result only in aborting genuine improvements. But a more fundamental paradox was his rejection of the state—his anarchism—combined with his acceptance of existing popular society.

An unsuccessful printer, the son of an unsuccessful brewer, and of peasant stock, Pierre-Joseph Proudhon knew first-hand that the financial and legal framework created by the state acted to the detriment of the small, independent entrepreneur, whether in town or the countryside. He perceived that the political system served to support the economic system, and his aim was that the entire structure of domination should be superseded. This would happen when the need for credit has been removed, ending the dependence of the ordinary folk on the capitalists—then social and economic life could simply withdraw from the state and capitalist framework, leaving them to wither and atrophy. This process could take place only when the people were prepared to withdraw from the state and had nonexploitative sources for the capital they needed to carry on their activities. The notion that the state itself could bring about a just system was, to his mind, absurd and pernicious. The attempt to legislate socialism would not merely fail, but would also set back the idea of socialism for a generation.

Before the revolution, Proudhon had already determined in his own mind the mechanism for providing the nonexploitative credit that would make a withdrawal from the state possible, but he was able to publicize his notion only in 1848. This was the creation of a People's Bank, to be based on interest-free deposits by the great majority of the population—funds that would then be used to provide interest-free credit for all who needed it. He propagandized this panacea with single-minded determination throughout the revolutionary period and even managed to establish a People's Bank for a short time before his arrest in 1849. (Once it became impossible for him to head the institution, he liquidated it—with no loss to the investors.) Nonetheless, it was clear to him in early 1848 that the propaganda for stateless socialism had not yet made much progress among the French people, and so he greeted the revolution of February with fear and anxiety. He could not see how the new regime could accomplish the goals he felt were vital, and any other action it took would almost certainly prove detrimental.

If Proudhon's criticism of the impact of the state and financial systems on the people was extremely radical, his view of popular society was not. He easily accepted the social mores and attitudes of his own background as normative—his anarchist society would be one in which hard-working men controlled their own economic enterprises and ran their families along traditional patriarchal lines.

There was, however, one major point where Proudhon's views did coincide with more traditional radicalism, and that was his espousal of a broad range of civil liberties. He wished the state to begin withering by not involving itself in its citizens' thoughts and words. Thus, his criticism of the Provisional Government was two-pronged: on the one hand, it did too much when it attempted to legislate social relations, and on the other hand, it did too little to protect the citizens from the state. "It was necessary to abrogate the laws that repressed individual liberty, to bring to an end the scandal of arbitrary arrests, to fix the limits of custody," he argued, but instead the revolutionary politicians "dreamed only of defending the prerogatives of the magistracy, and the liberty of the citizens was more than ever delivered over to the arbitrary action of the prosecutors."[45]

These views set Proudhon apart from all other commentators on the events of 1848, and made of him the Provisional Government's most severe critic from the left. Since his position was not understood, he was seen to be fascinating and unpredictable. Marie d'Agoult described the impression he made: "Each morning M. Proudhon surprised his readers, who had difficulty reconciling the tone and style of his polemic against the revolutionaries with what one knew of his ultra-radical opinions. At each moment he appeared to be in contradiction with himself, because instead of seeking means to organize democracy, his negative radicalism set itself the task of disorganizing all power."[46]

If by mid-1849 Herzen was looking for the opportunity to work on a newspaper, and thus to become a participant in the international radical movement, Proudhon needed money. He had edited two papers in succession since the spring of 1848, first *Le Répresentant du Peuple,* and after it was closed down, *Le Peuple.* He was in prison when the negotiations with Herzen began and would remain there throughout the life of *La Voix du Peuple* and beyond, having been convicted of sedition for articles attacking and ridiculing Louis Napoleon Bonaparte, the president of the new republic. He began serving his sentence on June 5.[47]

Le Peuple was lost a few days later, another victim of the June 13 demonstration. Mobs destroyed the press, and the paper itself was crushed under a load of fines levied for its content. After due consideration, Proudhon and his collaborators decided to float a new journal rather than attempt to pay the accumulated debts of the old. They needed an "angel" for this, however, for by a new law each periodical was required to post a bond of 24,000 francs as security against fines that might be levied against it. Proudhon assumed that his paper would pay for itself in subscriptions, but he needed someone with cash—an Alexander Herzen, for example—to provide the bond.

Among the men who worked with Proudhon on *Le Peuple* and *La Voix du Peuple* were some of the uncomfortable collaborators on Mickiewicz's *La Tribune.* They included Nikolai Sazonov, "Ivan Woinof" of *La Tribune,* whose years in Paris journalism had provided him with contacts both with Mickiewicz and his Polish friends and with Proudhon. Also associated with Proudhon at this time was

Charles Edmond Chojecki, the young Polish left Hegelian who had briefly managed Mickiewicz's paper and had attempted to solicit Herzen's collaboration. He appears to have been the one who suggested Herzen's name for *La Voix du Peuple;* this time he could offer him a more compatible environment. Between them, Sazonov and Chojecki undertook to bring Herzen onto Proudhon's new journal.[48]

What was the extent of agreement between Proudhon and the Russian who wished to use his money to express his own views and to support positions he found acceptable? Clearly, it was by no means complete; and indeed Herzen does not seem to have had illusions in this regard. Still, Herzen did find Proudhon the most attractive actor on the French political stage, and was eager to collaborate with him. (The real source of disagreement, as will be seen below, was not ideology or tactics, but the extent to which genuine collaboration would be possible.

Proudhon, with his criticism of all members of the government and his courage in standing alone against it, won Herzen's admiration. In the aftermath of the June Days, Herzen perceived him as "really the leader of all the socialists," and thought his strength and importance very great.[49] A few months later, he sent his friends portraits of Proudhon and Raspail.[50] And at the beginning of the collaboration, in a letter in which he charged that French radicalism was bankrupt, he made an exception for Proudhon:

> But you have the right to ask: then who is on the same shore with you?—If there were no one, there would be no harm, and the truth would not cease to be true because of it. However, I can add one name, worth hundreds, to the list of *virorum obscurorum*—the name of Proudhon. Proudhon, sitting in prison, does more than the entire refugee Mountain, Proudhon is the real head of the revolutionary principle in France; if they don't kill him in prison (as they hope to do), if he does not die of the cholera . . . then you will still hear about him. There is a circle of Frenchmen around him, not wild men and not fools.[51]

Both men can accurately be called anarchists at this time, but different images underlay their views of society. Proudhon believed that civil society could and should be held together by a system of contracts, a notion quite foreign to Herzen.[52] The distinctively Russian socialism that he was developing would be based instead on the commune and *artel*. Moreover, Herzen, the social radical, always believed that native institutions were oppressive and illiberal; the commune could serve as the germ of an advanced social order only if it were first thoroughly illuminated by the light of reason and Western civilization. In this, he was far different from the conservative and patriarchal Proudhon, for whom the institutions of rural France would provide a good society, if only the oppression of the state and capitalism were removed. (Proudhon's model was, of course, much less primitive than Herzen's, although still far from a free and open social order.) Nonetheless, the Frenchman's notion that civil society, freed of external oppression, was capable of functioning freely and effectively was an important one, and for all the differences between the two men, it probably influenced Herzen's theory.

Herzen and Proudhon were in substantial agreement in perceiving the state as fundamentally oppressive. And while Herzen would never write anything as outrageous as Proudhon's "Universal suffrage is counterrevolution,"[53] he too believed that the vote would be an adequate way of making decisions only in a society far more politically sophisticated than the provincial France of 1848 (to say nothing of Russia).[54]

Proudhon's distrust of government extended to rejection of political action on all levels. Although he later changed his view on this point, early in the revolution he had condemned club activity as a waste of precious time that should much better be spent in productive work.[55] (Throughout Proudhon's criticism of 1848 there runs a concern that productivity was the most essential concern of French society, and it was being hopelessly undermined by continuing revolutionary disorder.) For Herzen, arriving from Russia where all spontaneous public activity was impossible, the spectacle of ordinary men busily involved in politics was exhilarating—in mood he was closer to the club-oriented democratic socialism of Barbès and Thoré than to the bookkeeper's calculations of Proudhon.

Revolutionary internationalism, so fundamental for Herzen's self-definition, was of very minor concern for the Frenchman. Like all on the left, he sympathized with the plight of the nations struggling against foreign domination, especially the Poles and the Italians. However, early in the revolution, his concern with the cost of unrest at home and warfare abroad led him to oppose French involvement in foreign struggles for national independence.[56] He joined with the rest of the left in condemning the French attack on Rome, and he denounced the opposition politicans for not immediately calling for refusal to pay taxes in response. On the other hand, he also condemned the June 13 demonstration, called in protest of the French bombardment, as useless and counterproductive: "June 13 ended like May 15 [1848], and in a still more calamitous manner. The social question defeated."[57] Ultimately, Proudhon felt that the best service France could render other nations was to succeed in creating a free, socialist society to serve as model. His own country was always central in his concerns.

If Proudhon did not share Herzen's interest in popular politics and international revolution, Herzen had no interest at all in Proudhon's economic panacea. The People's Bank was simply irrelevant as far as Herzen was concerned; it is impossible to overstate its importance to Proudhon in these years.

Even more important than these ideological differences was the sharp contrast in mood between the two men. Herzen responded to his disillusionment with rage, and he was certainly hoping for a new upsurge of revolutionary activity; his vocation as revolutionary was to aid and abet such uprisings. Not so Proudhon. He was convinced that the time for political action was over, perhaps for a generation, and he intended to use the interim for serious propaganda to convince people of the validity of his anarchist views. During the course of *La Voix du Peuple*'s existence, his combative temperament struggled with his conservative desire for self-preservation, but at least at the first he was in little doubt that the paper's role was educational, not agitational. For this education to succeed, the first requirement was that the paper survive. He did not wish to take unnecessary risks, and would compromise if necessary.

The two men's hostility was also directed differently; both loathed the government of Louis Napoleon Bonaparte, and feared, correctly, that he would turn his presidential authority into a new empire. But Herzen's social rage, directed against the petite bourgeoisie, the men of the National Guard and the victorious army of Cavaignac, was not shared by Proudhon. It was the large moneyed interests, capitalism, that the Frenchman saw as oppressive, not the little men not too different from himself. But he hoped to win even the capitalists themselves over to his views. Every manifestation of conservative opposition to Bonaparte he greeted as a sign that a great coalition, one that would lead ultimately to the radical solution to the social problem, was in the process of formation.[58] Caution and conciliation thus characterized his approach to the new paper.[59]

La Voix du Peuple

Proudhon's willingness to compromise was manifested even before he began negotiations with Herzen, for he first approached Emile de Girardin, publisher of France's first truly commercial paper, *La Presse*, for the bond.[60] Girardin was combative, and there appears to have been a certain unexpressed sympathy between this paragon of capitalism and the socialist-anarchist Proudhon; still, such a collaboration would have contradicted the latter's expressed principles and alienated his supporters. Moreover, one of Proudhon's collaborators on *La Voix du Peuple*, Chojecki, had pointed up the contradiction when he specifically took the publisher to task for his failure to apply his liberal principles outside France. His policy, Chojecki had written, consisted of

> the most absolute slavery for all citizens; war to the death against all the nationalities as soon as they attempt to reconquer their independence, to all peoples as soon as they prepare to assert their political rights; hatred, calumny and curses for all the fighters for the popular cause in Portugal, Spain, Sicily, Naples, in all of Italy, in Austria, in Hungary, in Wallachia, in Prussia, in Poland; the most ardent sympathy, flattery and benediction for . . . [the commanders of the counterrevolutionary forces], and for the Emperor Nicholas.[61]

How seriously either Proudhon or Girardin took the possibility of their cooperation cannot now be ascertained, but it seems clear that a publication supported by Girardin could not have had the editorial staff that ran Proudhon's other papers.

Simultaneously with Proudhon's bid to Girardin, Sazonov made the approach to Herzen. Despite their long friendship and their close contact in Paris, Sazonov never fully regained the Herzens' trust. His appeal to Herzen to collaborate on *La Voix du Peuple* helps explain why.

Sazonov presented Herzen with a portrait of a Proudhon whose sole interest was furthering the social credit program that Herzen found irrelevant. He would, therefore, be glad to jettison political radicalism as the price of support from Girardin if Herzen failed to come through: "It is all the same to Proudhon, but it is not all the same for us, because instead of 'Voice of the People, a Journal of the Universal Social and Democratic Republic,' there will appear 'Voice of the People, a Journal of the Bourgeois and Social Republic.' "[62]

Geneva and Proudhon

Despite Proudhon's indifference, Sazonov still argued that he should be supported; the paper would be the best in the world, he said, and so worth being connected with; Paris was a far more exciting place to be and to plot than Geneva (and Sazonov urged Herzen to return to France), and he, Sazonov, would like a job on the new paper.[63]

Perhaps the most curious aspect of this appeal was the threat that Girardin would support the paper if Herzen did not. In fact, Girardin had given his definitive refusal while these letters were in progress, but Sazonov never informed Herzen, who never knew about it. It is unclear whether there was a concerted effort on the part of the Proudhon group to deceive Herzen, if Proudhon deceived Sazonov as well as Herzen, or whether Sazonov used this false argument on his own initiative.[64]

There is a gap of nearly two weeks in Sazonov's letters (July 10 to 22). N. E. Zastenker, who discovered and published the Sazonov material, believed that during this interval Sazonov journeyed to Geneva to continue the campaign in person.[65] There is no evidence for this, however; moreover, a long letter from Natalie Herzen in Geneva to her friends at home, in which she described the psychotic episode suffered by Sazonov's sister, Mariia Poludenskaia, before the Herzens' departure from Paris, did not mention Sazonov himself. This provides some slight negative evidence that he had not come to Geneva with news of his sister's progress.[66] Absence of any mention of him in the correspondence between Georg and Emma Herwegh suggests that he simply dropped out of the negotiations. His place was taken by Chojecki.

According to Zastenker, Herzen and Chojecki met during Herzen's first stay in Paris in 1847, but it must have been a very casual acquaintance. In 1849 they still did not know each other well. Herzen's letters to him are extremely formal, as are his third person references to the Pole. Nonetheless, Chojecki had long been familiar with Herzen's work, and was eager to win the Russian's collaboration.

Chojecki and Sazonov assumed different roles in the negotiations with Herzen. Chojecki acted as Proudhon's spokesman and Sazonov as Herzen's friend. The Pole's first approach to Herzen was contained in an enclosure in one of Sazonov's letters: "Proudhon is dissatisfied with all his compatriots and wishes to form an alliance with the socialists of mankind and not of France. In that case, one of the first places belongs to you, Aleksandr Ivanovich, and I should not like that place to remain unoccupied."[67]

Once he had taken an active role in persuading Herzen to participate in the paper, Chojecki wrote not to Herzen himself, but to his friend and near alter ego Herwegh, whom he knew better. Two letters from Chojecki to Herwegh (now in the British Library), dated July 12 and 21, 1849, neatly fit the gap in Sazonov's correspondence.[68]

Apparently Herzen had raised objections and queries to Sazonov, for in his first letter to Herwegh Chojecki promised to respond to them. Herzen's letter to Sazonov has not been recovered, but the entire course of negotiations indicates Herzen's concerns. Most important, he did not wish merely to be a Maecenas to Proudhon. He wished the paper at least in part to be his, as well as Proudhon's—he wanted the right to place articles, either by himself or others, at his own discretion. Second, he hoped the paper would serve as a rallying point for the international revolutionary movement. To do so, it should have a foreign section to serve as a forum for the international left, which Herzen would direct.[69] The program of *La Tribune des Peuples* comes to mind as a possible model for Herzen's idea of the paper's role. Finally, Herzen seems to have objected to recent political statements by Proudhon. In the absence of dated letters, it is impossible to specify the issue that angered Herzen. It might have been the Frenchman's opposition to the June 13 demonstration (although Herzen's views on the episode were very similar), it may have involved his relationship to Girardin, or it may have gone back to the quarrels with the left of the end of 1848.[70]

Despite Chojecki's stated intention to respond to Herzen's concerns, he does not seem to have come to grips with them. Much of his letter is taken up with assurances that the paper would be a financial success. He expressed admiration for Herzen's altruism in being willing to sacrifice the bond, but assured Herwegh that there would be no sacrifice, for Proudhon would be able to steer the journal safely through the hazards of the press laws. Like Sazonov, Chojecki mentioned the possibility of another source of support, but did not dwell on it. Instead, he urged Herzen to decide quickly, for he feared that otherwise a rash of radical papers, scheduled to appear by August 1, would blunt the impact of *La Voix du Peuple*. "While waiting, the peril lies in delay, and if we let this opportunity slip, success in all respects will not knock at our door a second time."

With regard to Herzen's role on the paper, Chojecki offered no new information; however, he assumed that Herzen would be in a position to name some members of the editorial board, for he devoted more than half of his letter to an insistence that he himself not be appointed: "I declare in advance that if the choice were to fall on me, among others, I would be most grateful for your kind thought, but under no pretext would I accept any position in the enterprise. On my part this is a firm and unshakable decision, and I request that you keep this letter, which is an official declaration on my part." It was only proper, Chojecki added, that Herzen think first of all of his compatriots in making appointments to the board.

Herwegh, presumably speaking for Herzen, directed a series of questions to Chojecki; unfortunately, his letter is not known, but evidence for it is provided by a second letter from Chojecki. This is far longer than the first, but still seems only vaguely directed toward Herzen's paramount concerns. In it Chojecki promised to respond to Herwegh's queries: "What guarantee do you have of the vitality of our organ, what course does Proudhon wish to follow, and what will be H's position." In answer to the first query and in part to the second, Chojecki elaborated at some length on Proudhon's honesty and on how rare this quality was among "our co-religionists." The present ethical level was so low, he said, that ideology had become irrelevant.

> For my part I believe neither in dogma nor in promises nor in the dialectic. I believe in a series of actions, and when I see that a man has conscientiously fulfilled his duty, that he has struggled energetically without being driven by any other ambition than causing the truth to triumph, that he has suffered for his cause, and, especially, that he has never sought to line his pockets (something which, believe me, is an immense virtue among the democrats of the nineteenth century), then I accord this man my confidence, and to distinguish him from the great troop, I dispense with the heap of formalities with which I would find it necessary to surround myself if I were dealing with others.

As for Proudhon's policy, he believed it necessary to combat reaction on its own ground. Just because reaction had been victorious, it now had to cope with the reality of the society it governed, and so could not avoid the social problem. Proudhon intended to prove that it could not be resolved within the context of reaction. He hoped to capture a portion of the bourgeoisie, the youth especially, and to convince it that on the eve of universal bankruptcy its sole security lay in active adherence to revolutionary principles.

In regard to the all-important question of the paper's organization, Proudhon proposed that he and Herzen each name three members of the editorial board. He refused, however, to consider a separate foreign section under Herzen's direction: "He wishes that [Herzen's] three associates involve themselves in domestic issues when it seems appropriate, and he reserves the same right relative to the foreign question, for in his mind this distinction does not exist; he merges both into a synthesis of the great universal revolutionary question, interdependent, united, and everywhere identical." Once formed, the editorial board would act as a committee of equals, with no dictator nor absolute authority.

In order to verify his interpretation of the situation, Chojecki would send this letter to Proudhon, so that the latter could indicate on it his agreement with its principles. Proudhon did add a postscript in which he stated quite clearly the cautious line he intended to take; it could not have reassured Herzen: "I entirely share M. Ch. Edmond [Chojecki]'s opinion on the urgency of publishing a new democratic journal. We should not be stopped by the press laws; the problem is no longer to excite the people with pathos, but to explain to the bourgeoisie itself its true interests. It is especially necessary to keep democracy from despair, something which is inevitable if no one explains the situation and the meaning of events to it day by day."[71]

As for internationalism, Chojecki continued to attribute to Proudhon a desire to ally himself with international revolution out of disgust with his compatriots' failure to appreciate him. In this letter, he quoted Proudhon as saying: "I have a horror of my compatriots; they have made use of me as an instrument and rejected me the instant that they believed they would be compromised by associating themselves with my revolutionary principles. I wish to work for the revolution, and not for France; . . . I wish the revolution to become universal, for it will perish if it has adherents only in France."[72]

The remainder of the letter (again about one half of the whole) is devoted to a reiteration of Chojecki's refusal to join the board, which he now explained by a long and impassioned attack on Sazonov, with whom he refused to collaborate. The Russian, Chojecki charged, was vain, petty, false, and malicious.

> You [Herwegh] who have a glorious past in your fatherland, H[erzen], who has acquired so honorable a reputation in his own, you know how much suffering and labor must be expended to claim to believe oneself to be a representative of one's nation or humanity. I do not wish to put myself in the ranks of those who are more worthy than I, but . . . I too labor in a literary career, and thanks to the things I have published—whether good

or bad, I do not know, but numerous in any case—men of good faith in my country have to confess that they know me. I have struggled and labored while M. Sasonoff played at life, and although I have learned much, I still do not know how to explain to myself what right M. Sasonoff has to believe himself chief of the Russian and Slavic democrats, and as such powerful among the democrats of the world.

Chojecki finally remarked that he was being accused by Sazonov of working for his own personal interest in another matter entirely, something which he emphatically denied. The very next day Sazonov did indeed write Herzen again. In the light of Chojecki's remarks, it is clear that this letter is not part of the original negotiations. In it, Sazonov did not renew the request that his friend back Proudhon. Instead, as Chojecki had suspected, he wrote to warn Herzen against allowing his money to fall into the hands of the Pole, "who is carrying on intrigues in all directions," whether or not he decided to support the newspaper.[73]

The continued delay in the negotiations created concern among the Paris collaborators—more than a month had passed without an agreement since Sazonov had first approached Herzen in June. Chojecki came to see Emma Herwegh on the evening of July 25 to ask her advice and to raise the possibility of Proudhon sending an emissary, one Guilllemin, to Geneva to deal directly with Herzen. Emma transmitted a message from Herwegh on tactics;[74] unfortunately, there is no record of an immediate response by the Paris newspapermen.

Guillemin duly journeyed to Geneva on August 13, and his trip marks the next documented phase in the negotiations. He received a draft for 24,000 francs from Herzen, but the agreement was still conditional. Rothschild would release the funds only upon receiving Herzen's authorization.[75]

The final negotiations between Herzen and Proudhon have been illuminated by the research of Michel Mervaud. In the Besançon Archive he discovered six letters from Herzen to Proudhon, of which the first, dated August 19, 1849 (just after Guillemin had received the draft, and possibly carried back by him), shows Herzen's continuing concern with a foreign section for the paper. It also shows the extent to which Herzen perceived himself to be in partnership with Herwegh:

> We [Herzen and Herwegh] wish to know the nature of our moral participation—and it is in regard to our rights to participate in the

editing of the paper that we await a response form you. We thought that we had the right to dispose of one corner of our journal, in order to make it the organ of the European movement— under your direction, certainly, which can only be agreeable, since your convictions and principles are the same as our own. You know better than we do, moreover, that it is not easy to find collaborators for foreign affairs at Paris, since knowledge of other peoples is not your compatriots' strong point. We wish to facilitate your task, to aid you *de jure*. Without this influence on our part of the journal, our cooperation would be reduced to the very humble role of financial backer, and I tell you frankly that this hardly appeals to me.[76]

Apparently Herzen had been able to patch up the quarrel between Chojecki and Sazonov, for in the same letter he suggested that Herwegh would return to France to direct the foreign section, and that both Sazonov and Chojecki had agreed to serve on the board. (Herwegh did not return; during his absence from Paris, he had been expelled, and returning now presented serious legal problems. Both Proudhon and Emma dissuaded him from the step, on the ground it would be dangerous.) He demonstrated that he had developed important contacts within the refugee community by telling Proudhon that he had correspondents for the foreign section lined up from Germany, Italy, and even Russia.

Proudhon's response was implacable, if polite. It appears, in fact, to be a harder position than the one transmitted by Chojecki in July: "Thus, it is understood that you will be part of the editorial board of *La Voix du Peuple*, under my general direction; that your articles will be received there with no other control than that which respect for his principles and fear of the laws imposes on a director of a journal. You feel, Monsieur, that being in agreement on the ideas, we can scarcely differ in our deductions, and as to the appreciation of foreign events, we will always have to rely on you." He made an important gesture toward internationalism, however, when he added, "It is necessary to raise the democratic and social question to the height of a European League."[77]

Herzen accepted defeat. He signed the contract that outlined this situation and released the money. In a long letter to Proudhon, he may have been trying to fire up the older man when he reiterated his own call, in as extreme terms as he ever used, for the destruction of all existing institutions and ideologies. He indicated that he would contact Chojecki regarding further plans for the foreign part of the journal, and demonstrated the success of his revolutionary "networking" by mentioning a string of potential correspondents: "We have the possibility of getting magnificent correspondents: for example, we already have one in sight in Hamburg (Fröbel), one at Berlin (Siegfried), one at Cologne (Dr. Gottschalk). For Germany in general we have engaged Mr. Bamberger; for Italy Mazzini, Spini and Pinto have said they would accept with pleasure the offer to send news on a regular basis."[78]

It was more than two weeks before Proudhon responded, and Herzen interpreted his silence as displeasure. "I wrote to him as a man, and he is a great economist. I did what I promised, and shall insist not so much on Pr[oudhon]'s friendship as on the fulfillment of the concordat—who is the pope here, and who Napoleon?"[79] On September 15, Proudhon did attempt to respond to Herzen's expressed radicalism:

> My sentiments with regard to the democrats of France and Germany and on the pretended republicanism of this variety of doctrinaires, are just the same as yours; I am happy to see that on this chapter we have nothing to say to or learn from each other. . . . I think as you do that the revolution is no longer susceptible to a methodical, pacific direction, to contrived transitions, such as pure economic theory and philosophy of history would like. We will have to make prodigious leaps, terrible bounds. Yet I believe that as journalists we must, while proclaiming social catastrophes, never present them as necessary and just; for each moment we must constantly seek out moderate and very sage temperaments. Otherwise, we will cause ourselves to be hated and persecuted. Now, above all, it is necessary to live.[80]

And so, *La Voix du Peuple* was duly launched. But Herzen was gravely disappointed with it, as Mervaud has documented.[81] The specimen issue of the paper, which appeared on September 25, he found uninspiring. Of Herzen's men in Paris, Herwegh never arrived, and Sazonov left shortly. The Russian had had an article rejected in the specimen issue, and he did not like either Darimon or Proudhon himself. Besides, he got a better position on *La Réforme*.[82] Chojecki was left on his own to represent Herzen and internationalism.[83]

An examination of *La Voix du Peuple* explains Herzen's distress. The specimen issue did acknowledge the international dimension of the revolution in its lead article:

> Without doubt, the treaties of 1815 have been torn up; but a new Holy Alliance is forming. This time it is no longer a case of a league of absolute kings against republican France; it is a case of a coalition of the privileged of all countries against the European proletariat. Nowhere does anyone still deny the problem of misery; but they wish to cut this Gordian knot of hunger with the saber, the last resource of the privileged against the threat of equality.... We must somehow reconquer the scepter for the Revolution; against the Holy Alliance of the men of money we must pose the great European League of workingmen. Come to us, then, friends of liberty of every race and every language! Thanks to the recent victories of the aristocracy, the solidarity of Peoples is no longer based merely on the fraternity of races and the unity of nature; it has its roots in the accord of interests, and in the identity of rights. The Revolution, one like the counterrevolution, henceforth will be durable and legitimate only to the extent that it takes possession of all Europe.[84]

This initial expression of revolutionary solidarity did not, however, have much effect on the paper's content. Its four daily pages were concerned primarily with political analysis of the changing situation within France, and with Proudhon's disputes with other leftist groups. In the autumn the trial at Versailles of the persons implicated in the June 13 demonstration absorbed the paper's space and its staff's time and energy.[85]

As in most contemporary newspapers, foreign news was largely limited to a culling of facts from newspapers and wires around Europe; articles discussing events outside France in a sustained, analytic manner are missing, and so is information about the international revolutionary movement. A single exception in the paper's first two weeks was an unsigned "Revue de l'étranger," that appeared in the weekly supplement of October 15. It asserted that despite the superficial victory of counterrevolution, the "democratic idea" was gathering strength and preparing for "social regeneration" in society's depths. But for the moment, reaction was in command, and the article lamented that so many of the defeated revolutionaries, "Struve, Heinzen, Willich, the German champions; Mieroslawski, the knight-errant of democracy; Garibaldi, Klapka and so many other heroes of the Revolution," unable to find refuge anywhere, were leaving Europe altogether.[86] This sentimental martyrology of men, several of whom Herzen found absurd and futile, was not the kind of internationalism he was espousing.

Chojecki apparently found the going difficult. In mid-October he resigned from the foreign section of the paper; Herzen wrote to oppose the move, and the resignation seems never to have gone into effect.[87] Some of Chojecki's frustration can be seen in the short notes he wrote Emma Herwegh, with whom he had become quite friendly. Through her he attempted to convince Herzen to return to Paris because his presence "was indispensable for his affairs, and I believe that without him everything will go to the devil."[88] Emma also appears to have had some informal role as Herzen's and Herwegh's voice on the paper. Chojecki planned to have her accompany Darimon to see Proudhon in prison, something that would be "not unuseful," and to have dinner with the paper's editorial board.[89] She also served as editorial go-between in the publication of Herzen's "La Russie."[90]

By the end of October, the paper's coverage of foreign affairs had increased somewhat, though it remained far behind the level achieved by *La Tribune des Peuples*. From October 30 to mid-December, most issues had a section titled "Chronicle of the European Counter-Revolution," which cited instances of repression across the continent. The paper's weekly supplement carried a regular "Revue de l'étranger," which gave slightly fuller coverage to foreign events than had been the case at the start. On November 2 an extract from an article by Mazzini on the establishment of a "Holy Alliance of Peoples" appeared. The November 5 "Revue de l'étranger" evoked the Russian menace in a manner familiar to the left—the feudal coalition in its struggle against the revolution would open the cities of Europe to the Eastern barbarians.[91] Much of Herzen's writing on the vivifying nature of barbarism and the need for a thorough shaking up of the Western cities and civilization was produced in response to this view. (This will be discussed in chapter 6.)

The November 12 issue showed some signs of becoming the journal Herzen had longed for. It published an article by Mazzini, "La Papauté," and a "Lettre première: Politique universelle: Solidarité des Peuples" by Chojecki. This "First Letter" was intended to introduce a series of studies of the various states of Europe; Herzen's first Western publication, "La Russie," would be the "Second Letter." Chojecki asserted the essentially international nature of the revolution, attempted to reconcile socialist universality with strivings for national liberation, and looked to *La Voix du Peuple* as an organizing nucleus for international revolution. In the series to follow, the various nationalities would be examined one by one; to the extent possible, this would be done by opening the paper's columns to representatives of the European peoples:

> This association of intellectual workers from all over Europe that we have the task of establishing will be, we hope, the germ of a democratic and social association of all the peoples.... *La Voix du Peuple* thus will be a ministry of foreign affairs of French socialism, a tribune where the Peoples of Europe will come in succession to expose their situation and to conclude fraternity with the French republicans and alliance against the coalition of cabinets, diplomacies, and police forces of the Counter-Revolution.[92]

The next week's issue of the supplement printed Herzen's article,[93] under the same general title, as well as Kossuth's farewell to Hungary. At about the same time, the general reporting of foreign news became far more complete and coherent.

The attempt to serve as an international tribune soon petered out, however. The next in the series of "Letters" was also the last, Chojecki's three-part article on the Austrian Empire, which began in the December 17 issue. This article is striking as a clear statement of Herzen's view of Russia's potentialities, one of the few such published by anyone other than Herzen himself. In comparing the two autocratic empires, Chojecki wrote:

> In Russia, beneath this official layer, formed by the autocrat and his valets, a living image of all the calamities of Hell, we have found at least a nation, a People. The People, despite its brutalization and demoralization, yet possesses a vitality, a force, a future. Let us in fact suppose the overturn of the Emperor, his family, and his executors; Russia would not perish from that. Quite the contrary, then and only then would she begin to live, while giving back their liberty to the Peoples, which the ambition of the autocracy have forcibly linked to her.[94]

Upon Herzen's return to Paris at the end of the year, he involved himself in the paper's operation (his only workaday experience in journalism before *Poliarnaia zvezda*), established relatively friendly relations with both Proudhon and other staff members, and became close to Chojecki.[95] But despite his presence, there was no increase in the paper's coverage of foreign affairs. His influence is most clearly reflected in the appearance of a two-part article on German unification by his protégé Ludwig Bamberger. The author rejected mystical notions of nationhood, and even denied that there was a genuine

German nationalism. He called for German unification without mystification on the grounds of common sense, as a fundamental measure of political and administrative reform.⁹⁶ In April there was a series by Ernest Coeurderoy, who became a great admirer of Herzen, but there is no evidence that Herzen was aware of this or had helped place the articles.⁹⁷

Meanwhile, Herzen himself was represented by several pieces. His "Donoso Cortes, Marquis de Valdegamas, et Julien, empereur romain," which later became part of *S togo berega*, was the lead article on March 18. The April 1 supplement included his "Lettre d'un Russe à Mazzini," reprinted from *L'Italia del Popolo*. The editors of the Academy Edition of Herzen's works have also identified an unsigned review of a play, *Charlotte Corday*, as belonging to Herzen.⁹⁸

All in all, it was a small return on Herzen's investment. In a letter to Emma Herwegh in the first days of the paper he had complained, "Oh well, I was right, it was only a question of taking the bond. One lesson more."⁹⁹ There is, however, some evidence contradicting Herzen's cynicism.

In general, Proudhon did not share Herzen's concerns with international revolution and the international community of revolutionaries. Nonetheless, at least in the paper's planning stages, the alliance with Herzen was reflected in the paper's position. As he had indicated in his August 23 letter, at the time the negotiations were concluded, Proudhon saw one of the paper's three goals to "form a democratic league in Europe." In his own notes, he wrote, "We shall respond . . . to the fall of the Italian and Hungarian Republics and to the reaction of the northern monarchies by the formation of a democratic league in all of Europe." He planned at least brief mention (presumably in the first issue) of Hungary, Rome, Baden, and the expulsion of republicans from "everywhere."¹⁰⁰ It seems, then, that Proudhon intended to honor Herzen's concerns, and that he was not the one responsible for limiting the paper's involvement in this area.

Nonetheless, Proudhon's instructions to his staff are not concerned with international affairs, and Herzen himself does not appear to have made a very great impression on him. There is only one reference to "M. H***" in his correspondence regarding the paper, and this is in the context of the loss of his bond to fines.¹⁰¹ In Proudhon's *Carnets* Herzen's visits are not recorded, and his interests are not reflected. When the paper was finally going down, in April, Proudhon remarked, "Three horses have been killed under me in this war," and regretted the loss of the 24,000 francs.[102] The only personal reference to Herzen in the journals is an inaccurate account of the plans of some of the principals involved in the paper. On May 30, he wrote, "Charles Edmond is forced to leave, his letters of naturalization have been withdrawn from him; he is taking a passport for Egypt—M. Herzen is in the same situation;—he is withdrawing to England.—Mme. Herwegh rejoins her husband in Switzerland. We are annihilated."[103]

Despite disappointment, and ultimately failure, the period of collaboration with Proudhon was far from a futile episode in Herzen's life. He wrote and published actively during these months, not only in *La Voix du Peuple,* but also in other radical journals whose columns were now open to him. He had come far toward establishing himself as a representative of Russian revolutionary thought abroad and an interpreter of Russian conditions and potentialities. In a series of important works published by the end of 1850, he had expounded the fundamentals of his philosophical, theoretical, and political positions, and henceforward not just his personal friends but also the wider world of European radicalism could react to him on the basis of his views. Herzen's intellectual development at this period will be the subject of the following chapter.

6

THE UNCENSORED VOICE

HERZEN made one of his clearest political statements in the short farewell he addressed to his friends in 1849. His aim, he asserted with all the typographical emphasis he could manage, was "*Human Dignity and Free Speech,*" and to those goals he had decided to "sacrifice everything." And so, he told his friends, he had decided not to return to Russia, but to remain in the West, despite his disillusionment with European life.

> Life here is very hard, venomous malignity mingles with love, bile with tears, feverish anxiety infects the whole organism, the time of former illusions and hopes has passed. I believe in nothing here, except in a handful of people, a few ideas, and the fact that one cannot arrest movement; I see the inevitable doom of old Europe and feel no pity for anything that now exists, neither the peaks of its culture nor its institutions. . . . I love nothing in this world except that which it persecutes, I respect nothing except that which it kills—and I stay . . . stay to suffer doubly, to suffer my own personal anguish and that of this world, which will perish, perhaps to the sound of the thunder and destruction towards which it is racing at full steam. . . . Why then do I stay?[1]

In response to his own question, he went on:

> I stay because the struggle is *here,* because despite the blood and tears it is here that the social problems are being decided, because it is here that the suffering is painful, sharp, but *articulate.* The struggle is open, no one hides. Woe to the vanquished, but they are not vanquished without a struggle, nor deprived of speech before they can utter a word; the violence inflicted is great, but the protest is loud; the fighters often march to the galleys, chained hand and foot, but with heads uplifted, with free speech. Where the word has not perished, neither has the deed.

> For the sake of this open struggle, for this free speech, this right to be heard—I stay here; for its sake I give up everything; I give up you for it, a portion of my heritage and perhaps shall give my life in the ranks of an energetic minority of "the persecuted but undefeated."

Herzen went on to assure his friends that by emigrating he was also providing the greatest possible service to the cause of freedom in his homeland. From the West, he could be their "uncensored voice," and in so doing would be part of a revolutionary tradition: "In every country, at the beginning of an upheaval, while thought is still feeble and material power unbridled, men of energy and devotion withdraw, their free speech rings out from the distance and this very *distance* gives their words strength and authority because behind their words lie deeds and sacrifices. The mightiness of their words grows with the distance. . . . Emigration is the first symptom of approaching upheaval."

But the émigré had another role, which was to acquaint the West with Russia, and as he described this task, something very like nationalism sounded in Herzen's words:

> Let her learn to know better a people whose youthful force she has tried in battle, in battle from which it emerged victorious; let us tell her about this mighty and still unfathomed people which in its unobtrusive way has managed to create a state of sixty millions, which has grown in such a vigorous, marvelous fashion without losing the principle of community, and which was the first to maintain this principle through the initial upheavals of national development; about a people which has somehow miraculously contrived to preserve itself under the yoke of Mongol hordes and German bureaucrats, under the barrack-room discipline of the corporal's baton, and the degrading Tartar knout; which has retained the noble features, the lively mind and the generous sweep of a rich nature beneath the yoke of serfdom, and which in answer to the Tsar's order to educate itself, replied a hundred years later with the prodigious phenomenon of Pushkin. Let the Europeans get to know their neighbour: they only fear him, but they should know what it is that they fear.[2]

It was not, however, merely Russia's greatness and potential that Herzen would have Westerners know. He would have them understand that his country was not necessarily an enemy of the revolutionary ideals he still cherished; indeed, he argued, the best chance for revolution would come from Russia. In the process of making that claim, Herzen defined Russian intellectual history as the history of revolution, and made of himself not an isolated, lonely exception, but an heir to and a continuer of a substantial tradition. Through his interpretation of Russian history, Herzen attempted to rehabilitate his country's reputation and at the same time established himself as the representative abroad of its noblest tendencies.

The few pages written to his friends adumbrate a substantial portion of the themes that would continue to occupy Herzen; among them, his career as a theorist would owe most to his revulsion against the West and his emotional return to Russia. In their conciseness, however, these lines capture Herzen's mood, but omit the substantive content of his thought. This chapter will be devoted to an explication of that content.

Between the continuing violence and crisis in the West, to which Herzen had committed himseelf, and the pain of separation from a Russia he had decided to leave—probably forever—both sides of the Russia-West duality carried their load of conflict in Herzen's mind. At the time he decided to stay in France, Herzen for the first time expressed nostalgia not just for his friends, but also for "our poor nature, the village, our peasants." The nostalgia, fueled by distaste for so much in European experience, turned into an idealization of Russia. For the most part, Herzen the revolutionary idealized not the past or the present—Russia had never suffered greater repression than Nicholas imposed after the 1848 revolutions—but the future. Nonetheless, past and present were not entirely dismissed; Herzen increasingly was able to discern the seeds of future greatness in elements of Russia's tradition (as he interpreted it).

A few years after his emigration, Herzen himself described how faith in Russia compensated for his rage at the West:

> In [the *Pis'ma iz Frantsii i Italii*] is the first meeting with Europe, gay at first—and how not be gay, having burst out of Nicholaevan Russia.... The letters' gay tone soon darkens—ominous reflections and pathological analysis begin. The motley decorations of constitutional France could not long conceal the inner illness profoundly consuming it.... Suddenly, there was the thunder clap of February 24 [1848], and following it thrones scattered—tsars started to flee,... jostling each other on the highways. The ironic spirit of revolution again led European man to the summit, showed him a republic in France, barricades in Vienna, Italy and

> Lombardy—and again shoved him into prison.... My letters... again become gloomy, and this gloom grows and grows until December 2, 1851 wrings the cry from me, "Vive la mort!" When the last hope disappeared, when nothing remained but to bow the head meekly and accept silently the final blows as the consequences of terrible events,—then instead of despair, the youthful faith of the 1830s returned to my heart, and with hope and love I returned.... Beginning with a shout of joy at crossing the border, I finished [the *Letters*] with my spiritual return to my homeland.
>
> Faith in Russia saved me at the verge of moral ruin.[3]

This statement, although much disputed by authors attempting to chart Herzen's attitude to Russia and the West, appears to be a fairly accurate depiction of his changes in mood. As chapter 2 showed, he had arrived in the West skeptical of constitutional forms and ready for hostility to the dominant bourgeoisie. The hostility became much more acute, however, once he had actually experienced life in Paris, so much so that the journey to Italy in the autumn of 1847 was something of a flight from an oppressive milieu. He arrived back in Paris in 1848 after the first burst of revolutionary enthusiasm had passed and conflict between the conservative National Assembly and the radical crowds had replaced the union between people and politicians that had colored the first days after the abdication of Louis Philippe. The June Days left scars that would never heal, and Paris, for Herzen, would henceforth be the site where the bourgeoisie had first defended its prerogatives by butchering the working people.

By 1850, after Herzen had spent six months in simple, republican Switzerland, France seemed more alien than ever. He wrote to his friends from Geneva at the end of 1849: "Believe me, I find Paris so repugnant that I can't think about the possibility that in winter I will have to live there without horror."[4] He was indeed overwhelmed with disgust and despair upon his return to the French capital at the turn of the year. During his stay in France, both his private and his published writing is full of imagery of death and decomposition; the sense that the West was "rotten" and its culture moribund is almost palpable.

> I delude myself with no hope, yes, this is dissolution, the world is *decomposing*, but the principle of decomposition has changed character, and has developed from a slow fever to galloping consump-

tion. There is something sad and horrible in this spectacle of triumphant death. Everything remains upright and has a strong, solid appearance, but as soon as it is touched, it collapses, the muscles do not exist, there is only skin and bones.

There may be convulsive efforts, torrents of blood, shed through vengeance, spite, or despair—but triumph is as impossible for the old man as it is today for the child.[5]

The philosopher's pessimism was, however, often interrupted by the journalist's optimism, lending a certain inconsistency to Herzen's writing. As each election approached, all possibilities were thoroughly scouted, and often, like contemporary political analysts, he took a transitory episode for the portent of fundamental change. Thus, he could write early in April 1850, after the March elections, "The great question of the future is completely altered [since February]. France is democratizing herself before our eyes, and the elections of March 10 constitute a complete revolution."[6] Such momentary bursts of enthusiasm (in this case, probably also somewhat exaggerated for the benefit of his reader) do not reflect changes in his basic perceptions.

Herzen fashioned his ideology out of this combination of nostalgia and revulsion. In the work originally written for a Russian audience (*S togo berega*), the despair at the West is paramount; in the essays whose intended audience was Western radicals, the emphasis shifts to Russia's potential. While it is tempting to see Herzen adapting his position to his audience, there are other explanations for this apparent inconsistency. Most obvious, the works written with Westerners in mind from the start were also written with the purpose of informing a Western audience about Russia. It was only natural that his new theory of "Russian socialism" should find its place in them. The notion seems to have developed in the course of his writing, and after he finished the articles, he intended to translate them into Russian, to share his ideas with his countrymen. (See chapter 7.) Coincidentally, the works permeated with the sense that Western civilization was collapsing, designed for Russian readers, were written in times of political or personal stress, while the major works on Russia were written either in the quiet of Geneva, or in Nice, during periods of domestic harmony, when nostalgia could outweigh revulsion.

Herzen's work is not without inconsistencies, and attempts to analyze it with great precision are misplaced. Once past his youthful

Hegelianism, he made no attempt to produce a systematic and consistent theoretical structure, either in an individual work or through a large corpus. He was, rather, a journalist or essayist who wrote relatively popular, rather short pieces, usually with a specific audience in mind. His writing captures moods and impressions, develops large general propositions about Russian or European historical development, and comments on current political or intellectual concerns. There is a set of philosophical assumptions behind his work—the Feuerbachian left Hegelianism he had arrived at by the time he left Moscow—but most of the time this intellectual armature is invisible. Frequently he repeats himself; whole passages that originally appeared in a European article will turn up in their original Russian in a piece in *Poliarnaia zvezda* a few years later, although perhaps as part of a different argument. An explication of Herzen's theoretical views, consequently, must be derived from a number of works, with the connections between them often supplied by the interpreter. Other readers, of his time or our own, especially if they read a different selection of Herzen's works, could validly derive a picture similar in essentials, but with a somewhat different balance and nuance.

Belief that Western civilization had come to the end of its historical path, that its creativity was played out, was the primary assumption underlying the dichotomy between Russia and the West. This feeling gave rise to the view that any renewal would have to come from outside the civilization that had dominated European life since the time of the Romans, and this view in turn opened the possibility that Russia might be the source of renewal.

The experience of the 1848 revolutions convinced Herzen that Western Europe could not develop a free and just social order in which the individual would be able to develop all his capacities and would not serve as a means to other people's ends. The excesses of the privileged classes, for all their horror, did not shake Herzen's political faith; they merely proved he had been right all along in his denunciations.[7] More devastating was the realization that the democratic opposition had presented no viable alternative to the July Monarchy. Herzen was convinced that genuine freedom was possible only in conjunction with a social revolution that would overturn all existing property arrangements: "The more closely I looked, the more clearly I saw that France could rise again only through a radical economic revolution [*perevorot*], a '93 of socialism."[8] That 1848 had not produced this kind of radical transformation was the fault not of the old regime and the bourgeoisie, but of the so-called democrats who had led the opposition to Louis Philippe. They had shown themselves either more fearful of the people than they were of dictatorship, or else incapable, despite good intentions, of leading a revolutionary movement. It was the failure of the revolutionary alternative to the establishment that convinced Herzen that hope for political and social renewal in the West was groundless. "The democratic side, or the side of movement, was defeated BECAUSE IT WAS UNWORTHY OF VICTORY and it was unworthy of victory because it made mistakes everywhere, it feared everywhere to be revolutionary to the end, everywhere it furiously threw itself onto the empty throne and ruled in its own way. . . . With empty people like Ledru-Rollin, Louis Blanc the revolution could not succeed."[9]

The revolutionaries could not succeed because they were were part of the old regime and unable to separate themselves emotionally from its values. Dualism, the notion that Herzen had begun to develop in the immediate wake of the revolution, continued to provide an explanation for the value system which guided the opposition, just as it had the prerevolutionary establishment. All Western society was constructed around the ultimately Christian idea that the individual must be subordinate to abstract, higher ideals:

> The submission of the individual to society, to the people, to humanity, to the Idea, is merely a continuation of human sacrifice, of the immolation of the lamb to pacify God, of the crucifixion of the innocent for the sake of the guilty. . . . Christianity, the religion of contradictions, recognized on the one hand the infinite worth of the individual, as if only for the purpose of destroying him all the more solemnly before Redemption, the church, the Father in Heaven! These notions impregnated the whole of social life, were elaborated into a complete system of moral subjection, into a perverted but completely consistent dialectic. The world becoming more worldly . . . introduced its own elements into the Christian moral doctrine, but the foundation remained the same. The individual . . . has always been sacrificed to some social concept, some collective noun, some banner or other. . . . The general foundation of that attitude upon which the moral subjection of man and the "debasement" of his personality so firmly rest, is almost exclusively the dualism with which all our judgments are imbued. Dualism is Christianity raised to the power of logic, Christianity freed from tradition, from mysticism.

Imbued with dualistic notions, the revolutionaries of 1848 could not conceive of genuine freedom without submission to the state:

> The year which has passed, to end worthily, to fill the cup of moral degradation and torment, offered us a terrible spectacle: the fight of *a free man against the liberators of humanity*. The bold words, the mordant skepticism, the fierce denial, the merciless irony of Proudhon angered the official revolutionaries no less than the conservatives. They attacked him bitterly, they defended their traditions with the inflexibility of legitimists, they were terrified of his atheism and his anarchism, they could not understand how one could be free without a state, without a democratic government. In amazement they listened to the immoral statement that the republic is for man, not man for the republic. And when logic and eloquence failed them, they declared Proudhon a suspect, they placed him under a revolutionary anathema, expelling him from their communion of true believers.[10]

In Herzen's view, the dualistic civilization of the West, which included both the establishment and middle-class revolutionaries, did not and never had encompassed the entire population. The poor had been left outside and remained many centuries behind the culture of the rich and educated. Before he perceived Russia as a possible source of renewal, Herzen believed that it would be the disinherited of Western Europe itself who would serve as the new wave of barbarians that would overthrow and replace the European cultural tradition.[11]

Thus, the political opposition's inability to separate itself from the dying world did not mean that revolution would not come to the West—merely that when it came it would be a spontaneous movement of the ignorant masses, carried out without guidance by enlightened leaders. And that meant that revolution, when it came, would be indifferent to the ideals of individual freedom and autonomy that were part of the democratic opposition's creed:

> The masses want to stay the hand that impudently snatches from them the bread they have earned—that is their fundamental desire. They are indifferent to individual freedom, to freedom of speech; the masses love authority. They are still dazzled by the arrogant glitter of power, they are affronted by the sight of someone who stands apart. By equality, they understand equality of oppression; afraid of monopolies and privileges, they look askance at talent and allow no one not to do what they do. The masses want a social government that would govern *for* them,

and not like this existing one, *against* them. To govern themselves doesn't enter their minds.[12]

The result of 1848, he wrote in 1851, was the alienation of the people from the political opposition, which still stood on the old monarchist and Christian ground, and, like the Bourbons, had learned nothing from the revolution.

> The people are not with them; they have learned terribly much; the masses, like women, do not learn from school, but from misfortunes, and apprehend concrete truth at once through some instinct and observation.... In general, the people is overpraised; this revolutionary French people is in no way ready either for socialism or for freedom—but they are ready for revolution; their strengths are their awareness of social injustice, their anger, and a surprising unity. The French people is an army—an army not of democracy, as the Montagnards imagine, but an army of communism. But in a struggle, an army is necessary, and that is why the French now, as in the past, are in the avant garde.[13]

Communism, he went on to say, was inevitable and would constitute the true liquidation of the old society.[14]

This view of the people—alienated from both the establishment and the doctrines of the opposition, moved by a combination of rage and a primitive instinct for social justice, provides a link between Russia and the West in Herzen's thought. In his theory of "Russian socialism," as will be discussed below, he merely shifted the locus of revolutionary action from the alienated Western workers to the alienated Russian peasants.

But before Herzen arrived at this view, he had already linked the repressive Russia of the Empire to the Western civilization he saw in decline. He insisted in all his Western works that the difference between the Russian government and that of the European states was one of degree and not of kind, and that increasing repression in the West was daily reducing the difference:

> I am furious at the injustice of those narrow-hearted publicists who can only recognize tsarism at the 59th degree of northern latitude. Why these two standards? Insult Petersburg absolutism and our continued resignation as much as you like and crush them with reproaches; but insult everyone, and recognize despotism under whatever forms it presents itself, whether it's called a president of a Republic, a provisional government, or a National Assembly.

It is a shame, in the year 1849, after having lost all that was hoped for, all that was gained, alongside the corpses of those who fell and who were shot, alongside those who were chained and deported, at the sight of the unfortunate ones who are hounded from country to country; ... in 1849, I say, it is a shame to stop at the narrow point of view of liberal constitutionalism, of this platonic and sterile love for politics.

The optical illustion, which let us give slavery the aspect of liberty, has vanished; the masks have fallen; now we all know, *au juste*, what the republican liberty of France and the constitutional liberty of Germany are worth. We see now (or, if we do not, it is our own fault) that all existing governments, from the most modest canton in Switzerland to the autocrat of all the Russias, are only variations on one and the same theme.

"It is necessary to sacrifice liberty to order, the individual to society; therefore, the stronger the government, the more valuable it is."[15]

Russia was, indeed, marginally more repressive than the states of Western Europe; as Herzen had said in the "Addio," and as he repeated to Westerners in "La Russie," the fight could still be waged in the West, and that was the reason he had remained abroad. He had sacrificed everything to human dignity and freedom of speech, and should these disappear altogether in Europe Herzen would be forced to move on, to America.[16] But greater repression did not mean that Russia was a stable buttress of reaction. Quite the contratry; in the most controversial part of his propaganda, Herzen argued that only in Russia was real revolution possible, and only through Russia could revolution come to the West.

Russia

Herzen delivered the message of Russia's revolutionary potential in a series of works that were designed from the start for an audience of Western European radicals. (*S togo berega* and the "Pis'ma" were first published in German, but they had been planned for Russian readers.) "La Russie," written in the form of an open letter to Herwegh, and published in *La Voix du Peuple*, was the first; major works were the letter to Michelet (*Le Peuple russe et le socialisme*) and *Du Développement des idées révolutionnaires en Russie*. After he had settled in England, Herzen further developed his views in a series for William Linton, "La Russie et le vieux monde."[17]

A major aim of these works was to counteract the view of Russia dominant in the West, and particularly strong among the radicals and revolutionaries. Most Western Europeans could perceive only menace in the tsarist empire. They were influenced by travelers' tales of repression and the frozen terror of Siberia, they were moved by the plight and the propaganda of the Polish refugees, and most recently they were informed, or misinformed, by *La Russie en 1839,* the work of the French conservative Astolphe de Custine, who came to the autocratic empire to admire and left to denounce.[18] For the educated European, as for Michelet, "The sole stable impression is that Russia presents a monstrous visage: carnival mask or Medusa head? Should one laugh or be frightened?"[19] In the political context of 1848, Russia was seen as the potential savior of reactionary regimes, ready to intervene to crush revolutions and restore legitimate monarchs. Western rulers, particularly in Germany, were regularly accused by the left of becoming puppets of the Russian emperor.[20] The intervention in Hungary confirmed the prevailing view.[21]

Herzen countered this opinion with several arguments. He denied that the West was much freer than Russia; he argued that Russia had greater potential for revolution than had the tired and moribund West; and, finally, the fact of this revolutionary potential, he believed, greatly weakened the tsarist state—the Russian bear was, he thought, a paper tiger.

His views of Russia's potential role derived from his image of his native country. There were three essential elements in Herzen's comparison of Russia and the West: the state, the people, and the educated minority. The first of these, as discussed above, repressive and savage as it was, differed in degree, but not in kind, from the states of the West.

When responding to Westerners' negative views of Russia, Herzen had no wish to exculpate the Russian government; not only was he personally animated by hatred for it, but also his own international stature as a revolutionary hero was based on his victimization. If that government was not the threat to freedom and independence it was perceived to be, this was, he argued, simply a result of its incapacity, and not from any lack of ill will. Indeed, in his own negative depiction of the autocracy, Herzen was more than generous to the violently anti-Russian Custine, whom he called "a good and faithful observer." Custine's picture of Russia was not so much inaccurate, Herzen argued, as one-sided—it was the picture one received if, like the Frenchman, one limited one's experience to the court and official Russia. He was to be reproached for the narrow range of his observation, but not for his interpretation of what he did see.[22]

Herzen's strategy was to separate the Russian state from its citizens, whom he portrayed not as accomplices, but as victims of autocracy. "Surely we all love [Poland]," he said to Michelet, "but can we not do so without having to persecute some other country no less wretched in its fate—and persecute it merely because it was press-ganged into serving its tyrannical government in a career of crime.[23] Moreover, this oppressive Russian government, held in place only by coercion, was not the solid bulwark of reaction it seemed, but was itself threatened by volcanic revolutionary forces.

The Russian state had never become embedded in the consciousness of its subjects, and never could do so. The featureless plain of Russian life, temporal as well as spatial, gave it no organic link with the people over whom it ruled; the webs of tradition, of deference, of custom that made a complete break with existing institutions so difficult in the West, were lacking in Russia, where the state ruled by brute force alone. "The Europeans fail to understand that there is nothing solid, ultimately established, in the entire Imperial period in Russia; this is a revolutionary dictatorship in the name of autocracy: it is maintained by terror without any laws, without any rights. Perhaps this period was necessary for the merging of all Rus' into a single strong and concentrated state, but all the same this is not a normal situation, not a status quo, but a crisis, a revolution, a state of siege, a 1793 suspension of the rights of man!"[24] Repression and weakness were thus inseparable aspects of the autocratic state. It was isolated, and hence weak, because its repression made it hated by the people; and this lack of genuine support meant that it could not rule by consensus, and had no recourse but still greater repression.

The fragility of the autocracy was of major importance in Herzen's propaganda directed to the Western left. In effect, he denied that there was a Russian menace; fearful as the autocracy was of the spread of liberal revolution, it was almost equally afraid of intervening, for neither the army nor the social order itself were fully reliable. Major intervention, even if it came, would be liberating; the West would only temporarily lose pseudo-liberty, while the bulwark of reaction would itself collapse into revolution.[25]

The strategy of separating the Russian people from the state, in addition to freeing the people from the burden of guilt for the country's external and internal aggression, also gave Herzen a focus for his growing nostalgia. His home, the home he missed so acutely as Europe continued to slide into reaction, was not the barracks of Nicholas I, but the country where revolution just might happen. Nostalgia was first expressed at the same time he began to see his future in Western Europe. With each additional disappointment, his homesickness grew, and with it came his belief that Russia was the country of the future, however that might be defined. On his first arrival in Geneva, alone in a strange city, and halfway to being a refugee, he wrote his wife: "I often think that if it were only an iota better in Russia than it is now, then it would simply be logical to go to Moscow. There the future is painfully being born, in Europe, the past is painfully dying."[26]

And after his return to Paris, he told Herwegh:

> Sometimes I think that I will return to Russia; it is certain that we will not have a republic there in a year, but the emperor can die like any dog, and after a lapse of time, it will be possible to live there. Lermontov has said, "Russia is entirely in the future"; men who have the misfortune of being so well aware that the world that surrounds them is departing, must involuntarily turn their head toward the country which has no past—but which has an immense future. There one can at least do something, *one can be deceived*. Here one cannot.[27]

The repressive past and present had created a people with the potential for a revolutionary future. For the Russian people, the state was a source of suffering, both from government officials, and from the landowners, whose enserfment of the peasantry had been condoned by the state. Seeing only oppression from the world outside their villages, the peasants had retreated to their own inner world; they had retained the archaic peasant commune, and the commune had preserved them from the impact, for good or ill, of government policy.[28]

Thus, the commune, to which Herzen had turned his attention from time to time with differing evaluations, assumed far greater importance for him after 1848. The notion of "Russian socialism" that he now developed entailed the belief that the commune might serve as the basis for Russia's revolutionary transformation.[29] In deriving his theory, Herzen drew on a body of fact and speculation that had appeared only recently, but already was providing a rich harvest for speculative social thought. He produced a radical view of an institution that a few years earlier had been brought to the attention of

European readers by the conservative observer, August Haxthausen.[30] Haxthausen, and following him the Slavophiles, were the first important publicizers of the view that the commune offered an alternative, noncompetitive form of economic organization.[31]

Once the basic facts about the commune had been publicized by these conservatives, parallels with communist notions were bound to arise, particularly among socialists. Boris Nikolaevskii argued that Bakunin was the first to give the idea a revolutionary twist. He discussed the role of the commune and the potential for peasant revolution in Russia in *Russische Zustände*, a brochure published in 1849.[32] Bakunin asserted that the peasantry was a powerful revolutionary force, and he also insisted that the potential for revolution in Russia made the government fear overextending itself with foreign intervention. Both these points were used by Herzen, who drew on Bakunin's article and at times repeated his friend's ideas word for word. However, Bakunin's brochure is unlikely to have inspired Herzen's view of the commune, which it discusses only briefly.[33]

The attempt to develop a socialist theory that would fit Russian conditions was not confined to the emigration. Within Russia the task was taken up by the young people who formed a study circle and revolutionary group around Mikhail Butashevich-Petrashevskii. The ideas of the Petrashevtsy may have exerted some influence on Herzen's developing theory of Russian socialism. Vladimir Engel'son, who was Herzen's close companion in 1851 and 1852, had been associated with the Petrashevtsy and shared their ideas; he came to Western Europe too late to influence "La Russie," but was close to Herzen when he wrote his later, and fuller, expositions of the notion that socialism could come to Russia through a peasant uprising.[34]

Yet another radical who looked to the commune was Herzen's old, if somewhat problematic friend Sazonov, who as "Ivan Woinof" had written articles in *La Tribune des Peuples* that were close in spirit to Herzen. At the end of 1851, he proposed to write a series on the "revolutionary elements" in Russia. These included the communist element, "preserved in all its purity through the centuries in the Slavic *mir*." In articles projected, but never published, he intended to show "that Republican Europe had nothing to fear from Tsarist Russia, and that social Europe would find in communist Russia precious elements in view of the construction of a new world."[35]

Herzen was thus only one of a number of thinkers who perceived a relationship between the Russian peasant commune and the possibilities of a noncapitalist future for the country. He publicized the idea, and in so doing took it from its conservative origin and made it part of radical ideology. However, his use of the commune in his ideology was quite limited; "Russian socialism" never meant that the commune could provide the Russian people with a ready-made socialist society. Nor was Herzen's use of the idea nationalistic; he did not see the commune as a distinctively Russian or Slavic institution, but merely as an archaic form that chance had spared in Russia.

The possibility of revolution meant for Herzen that Russia was the land with a future; and he associated this hope with the belief, derived from Chaadaev, that Russia had no meaningful past.[36] In his published work, Herzen developed the idea more fully than he had in the February 14, 1850, letter to Herwegh quoted above. Harking back to his comparison of Pskov peasants and East Prussian burghers, made originally to the circle on the journey outward (see chapter 2), he once again portrayed the Russian peasants as living outside the historical process; generations followed one another, the men almost unchanged in an unchanging landscape:

> On the vast plains among the snow-dusted pine woods, little Russian villages appeared; they stood out sharply against a background of dazzling whiteness. I find something deeply moving in the appearance of these poor rural communes. The cottages huddle next to each other, preferring to burn together than to disperse. The fields, without hedges or fences, fade into an infinite distance behind the houses. The little hut belongs to the individual, the family; the land to everyone, to the commune.[37]

The notion of "Russian socialism" took this primitive, timeless peasant commune, and turned it into the potential for Russia's revolutionary development. The significance of the commune, however, lay not so much in the form of social and property organization that it represented, as in its defensive qualities. Immured in the little world of the commune, the Russian peasants were immunized against the ideology emanating from St. Petersburg. Knowing only oppression from the state and the landlords, they were untempted by the forms of civilization these groups represented. Herzen's analysis of the impact of the commune is thus fundamentally ideological and political. The Russian peasantry is potentially revolutionary because the commune gives it a solid position from which it can reject all that St. Petersburg demands of it: respect for law, Western civilization (as filtered through the despotic state), and so forth. Socialism may come more easily to Russia because the peasant in his commune has been attracted neither by feudalism nor by bourgeois private property—the Russians are still traveling very lightly, while the Western Europeans will have to divest themselves of a centuries-old cargo of values if they are ever to arrive at the other shore.

Thus national life remained intact in Russia, but so did economic backwardness. Herzen's economic analysis is cursory, but it is clear that he does not naively perceive the commune as a native phalanstery. He repeats Haxthausen's arguments that the guarantee of a livelihood in the countryside has resulted in elevated urban wages and has acted as a brake on urbanization. For Haxthausen this supposed influence was an argument against the commune, for it meant that Russia's economic development was thereby retarded. Herzen, however, was not concerned. He acknowledged that the commune was less productive than scientific private agriculture, but felt that, in the first place, increased agricultural productivity had only worsened the conditions of the laborers in the West, and, second, he did not see the need for efficient agriculture in Russia, given its vast spaces and sparse population. The Marxian dialectic, which associated the rise of the bourgeoisie with fundamental, and ultimately favorable, changes in productivity, as well as with economic oppression, is entirely lacking in Herzen; with a lordly look around his vast holdings, he simply doesn't care about the economic revolution and per capita production.

Moreover, the commune's way of life was not enlightened socialism, but communism, and, like all communism, it was itself repressive. It completely subordinated the individual to itself, absorbed the personality:

> The individual, used to relying on the commune for everything, is lost as soon as he is separated from it; he becomes feeble, he finds in himself neither strength nor resilience; at the least peril he runs quite quickly to take refuge under the protection of this mother, who thus holds her children in an eternal minority and exacts of them passive obedience. There is too little movement in the commune; it receives no impulsion from outside which would stimulate progress in it, no competition, no interior struggle, which would produce variety and movement; in giving a man his share of the earth, it dispenses him from all care.[38]

The "communism" of the peasantry, he felt, was important primarily for its impact on the educated class, which easily adopted a

The Uncensored Voice

socialist rather than a liberal creed because peasant customs had habituated it to land communes, periodic redistributions, and *arteli*.[39] But Herzen's primary interest in the commune concerned its role in maintaining the Russian national character and its potential for rebellion. He was, moreover, too much of an individualist to idealize the commune as a way of life for modern times; indeed, his clearest demands for individual freedom come in precisely those works in which he introduces Western readers to the revolutionary potential of the commune. (The contrast with Proudhon's acceptance of prevailing mores is instructive in this regard.) The Russian peasant, in Herzen's view, was no more a socialist individualist than the Paris worker; like him, however, he was a potent force against the status quo. Both were equally outcasts from the civilization of European gentlemen: "I have never said that I thought the sole possibility of renewal of the old world was by a new race; I always put to the side the other element, the volcanic element [of Western society]. But that too is a new race, which has received nothing from this civilization but misfortune."[40]

Indeed, Herzen's ultimate apocalyptic hope is for an alliance between Slavic and Western rebels against the old order.[41] In the West change would come not from the advanced strata of the population, but from the masses, who still lived in a medieval mental universe. The Russians were still more alienated from and less corrupted by the values of modern civilization than were Western proletarians, and so would find it easier to leap into the revolutionary future.

The Russian peasant commune, thus, was no model for future social organization in this early formulation of "Russian socialism." Indeed, given the obvious parallels between current descriptions of the commune and socialist ideas, and the degree of interest in it, it is perhaps less remarkable that Herzen perceived these similarities, than that he made such sparing use of them. Russian socialism demanded that the commune be thoroughly transformed in any future socialist society; however, this task, Herzen thought, was less difficult than transforming bourgeois society.

More original than Herzen's analysis of the commune was his view of the educated minority that would take on the role of revolutionary leadership. In the works designed for Western audiences of this immediate postrevolutionary period, Herzen introduced the notion of an intelligentsia (without using the word, which became current with its modern meaning only in the 1860s). He thereby created a role for men like himself in the task of revolutionizing Russian society.

Herzen, in common with later theorists, found the source of the revolutionary class in the nobility. He described a nobility of essentially two tiers; the great Petersburg courtiers, and the middle nobility, with its center in Moscow. Although this second group was generally corrupt, "the germ and the intellectual center of the coming Revolution" resided in it.

> The position of this educated minority (a rather considerable minority) is very tragic; it is separated from the people because its forefathers for several generations attached themselves to the civilizing government, and separated from the government because it has become civilized. The people see them as Germans, the government as French.
>
> In this order, so absurdly placed between civilization and the planter's right, between the yoke of an unlimited power and the seigniorial rights that it possesses over the peasants, in this order, where one finds the highest scientific culture of Europe, without freedom of speech, with no other activity than state service, a mass of passions and forces are in motion; precisely because these have no outlet, they ferment, increase, and often see the light of day in producing some striking individuality, full of eccentricity.[42]

Herzen presented Russia's intellectual history, from the Decembrists to the debates of the Moscow circles, as a series of various forms of rejection of the Petersburg despotism. Alienation from the government's position was universal among the educated minority, with disagreement arising only over alternatives.

Herzen's discussion of Russian intellectual history ends with the Slavophile-Westernizer controversy. The representative Westernizer to whom he introduced his Western readers was Belinskii—in this way, he avoided mentioning the names of people who were still alive and might be endangered. But he also gave an image of Westernism that coincided with his and Belinskii's radicalism, but differed considerably from the far more hesitant liberalism of his friends from the circle. He argued that the Westernizers differed from the Slavophiles because, while they rejected the Petersburg state, they accepted at least part of the civilization brought to Russia at the cost of "so much suffering, of torrents of blood." They were unwilling "to exchange a German yoke of slavery for an Orthodox-Slavic one; they wished to liberate themselves from all possible yokes." On the other hand, Herzen asserted that Westernism was not anti-Russian; it saw nothing hostile to the West in what was native to Russia, but foresaw the time when Russia, having transcended the Petersburg period, and Europe, having transcended constitutionalism, would meet.[43] In opposition to both the Russian present and the Russian past, as well as to their ideological opponents, the Westernizers demanded personal independence and respect for the individual.[44] Here, then, was the voice of authentic radicalism, driven by its alienation to reject its own heritage, but also capable of seeing the falsehood in the modest reform offered by Western liberalism.

> Do not accuse us of being immoral merely because we do not respect the things that you respect. Would you condemn a foundling for having no respect for his parents? We are free agents because we are self-made. . . . We are independent, because we possess nothing. There are literally no demands upon our affections. All our memories are tinged with bitterness and resentment. The fruits of civilization and learning were offered us at the end of the knout.
>
> What obligation, then, have we, the younger sons, the castaways of the family, to acknowledge any of your traditional duties? And how could we in all honesty accept this threadbare morality of yours, a morality which is neither humane nor Christian. . . .
>
> Russia will never be Protestant.
>
> Russia will never be *juste-milieu*.
>
> Russia will never stage a revolution with the sole aim of ridding herself of Tsar Nicholas only to replace him by a multitude of other Tsars—Tsar-deputies, Tsar-tribunals, Tsar-policemen, Tsar-laws.[45]

Herzen would never predict that these alienated, and hence liberated, Russians would achieve revolutionary victory; merely that here was the only group capable of making the attempt. Nor did he provide a mechanism whereby this doubly isolated and alienated group would be able to make contact with the Russian people, and so become an effective force. He did argue, however, that the alienation of the educated minority from the government signaled the end of any legitimation of the monarchy. At one time Peter's state had been an agent of civilization, however heavy-handed and repressive its methods had been. Now, however, civilized Russia had moved into opposition, and the government was forced into a wholly untenable position of attempting to maintain itself while fighting civilization, itself alienated both from the people and from the forces of enlightenment. Since the Decembrist uprising this was a government that had maintained itself solely by force, and hence it was fragile.

The theory of Russian socialism was thus complete and encompassed all three vital elements in contemporary Russia. The people were so oppressed and so alienated that they had vast revolutionary potential. The educated class, which lacked its Western counterpart's ties to the existing system, could lead the revolutionary forces without the hesitation and equivocation of Western radicals. And the despotic state, with no roots in Russian soil, would be unable to withstand a major assault. Herzen, who rejected all doctrines of historical progress and inevitability, would never predict that revolution must come to Russia. But if any country were to initiate the revolutionary process, Russia was the most likely candidate.

Herzen and His Audience

Herzen's message to the Western left received a wide hearing—by the time he settled in London in 1852, he had become well known within the radical community, and, in the absence of other spokesmen, he was the one primarily responsible for interpreting Russia to this audience. His work had appeared in French, German, and Italian publications (and would soon appear in English as well). His books and articles were also relatively widely reviewed in publications directed to the same audience; the *Deutsche Monatsschrift*, where parts of *S togo berega* first appeared, also published reviews and criticism by Reinhold Solger, Ludwig Bamberger, Karl Nauwerk, and Philipp Fallermayer.[46] In Cologne, Herzen's former secretary Friedrich Kapp publicized this work and the *Briefe aus Italien und Frankreich* (the first, German edition of the "Pis'ma"), and arranged to have excerpts printed in local newspapers.[47] The Belgian *La Réforme* (Verviers) printed excerpts from "La Russie," with a laudatory introduction, and *Du Développement* had a favorable review in Piedmont.[48] In addition to his new work, Herzen also brought out a German translation of his 1845 novella, "Who Is to Blame," which was well received.[49]

One of Herzen's most important conquests of this period was the democratic French historian, Jules Michelet. They met in 1851, while Herzen was staying in Paris. Herzen protested Michelet's depiction of Russia in his *Légendes démocratiques du nord*, a work that publicized the Polish cause and extolled Polish martyrs to Russian brutality. With exceptional graciousness, when Michelet brought out the *Légendes* in book form he not only revised the text, publicly apologized for some of his statements in the original edition, and gave an acknowledgement to Herzen, but also gave the Russian space in the book to reply. The result was *Le Peuple russe et le socialisme*, probably Herzen's single most accessible and influential work. For the rest of Herzen's life, he and Michelet were literary allies, praising and even puffing each other in the press, arranging favorable reviews of the other's works, and giving each other moral support.[50] Links between the men were a common interest in the "martyred" Bakunin and the assertion of the unity of aims of free Russia and free Poland. The contact with Michelet (arranged in the first instance by a Pole, A. Bernacki) thus reinforced Herzen's identification with the Polish independence movement.[51]

But for all Herzen's personal success, his message was received selectively and critically. His impact is most visible in attempts by Western writers not to merge the Russian people and the tsarist state into a single, monolithic barbaric and repressive force. In addition to Michelet, one might cite Hermann Ewerbeck, the veteran German communist, and one of Herzen's Paris contacts. In an 1851 work on Germany, published for a French audience, Ewerbeck divided Europe into three groups: the progressive countries, those East European peoples who were striving for freedom (Poles and Magyars), and reactionary Russia. However, condemnation of this last is phrased more delicately than normal antitsarist polemics: "The Russians are growing. Less by popular instinct than by the policy of their frightful government, they are hostile ... [to Western Europe], and at the present time are the mortal enemies of democratic development."[52]

It is also likely that Herzen's work, and most importantly *Du Développement*, henceforth provided most liberal and radical Western Europeans with their information on Russia's social institutions. The peasant commune would thus come to be seen not through the conservative eyes of Haxthausen and Custine, or the propaganda of the government's publicists, but from the point of view of a socialist looking for revolutionary possibilities.[53] And Westerners now had information about a new group in Russia—an alienated educated minority that had carried on a revolutionary tradition for half a century. Moreover, they learned from Herzen, a few of its representatives were right there among them in Western Europe.

Not surprisingly, Herzen met far more resistance to his notion that the Western left was futile, and that the West itself was a decaying corpse that could not bring about social regeneration. Even as he was planning to print the Italian translation of "La Russie," Mazzini told the author that he did not share his views, particularly on Europe's decline. Quite the contrary: "We are not in decrepitude; we are in the first age; we are being born today to national life properly understood as the organization of Humanity; and we have all the unreflection, all the methodological ignorance, in a word, all the faults of youth."[54]

Herzen's friend Ludwig Bamberger wrote a very favorable review of one of the *S togo berega* essays, "Omnia mea mecum porto," in the *Deutsche Monatsschrift*.[55] But most of the Germans associated with the journal, who by and large represented the left wing of the 1848 political assemblies, found *S togo berega* too extreme for their taste. Karl Solger, a personal friend, rejected Herzen's pessimism and argued that Herzen himself provided a living refutation to his own views by his personal activity in the revolutionary cause.[56] (For Herzen, the inability wholly to break with the cause was not a refutation of his views, but simply one more element in the "tragedy" of his position.)[57] Solger was particularly offended by Herzen's view of the European people as a spontaneous revolutionary force impelled by material injustice and desperation, but not moved by the noble ideologies of the socialist leaders.[58] Karl Nauwerk, in refuting Herzen's views in the same journal, gave an overly biological interpretation to the notion of "old" Europe and "young" Russia, and added an element of national hostility missing in the author he criticized. He asserted that "in the near future, the Western spear of freedom will penetrate deep into the heart of Eastern barbarism."[59] Nor was Nauwerk the only one to see in Herzen an apocalyptic vision of "race" war—Marx refused to have anything to do with the Russian, because, he claimed, "I do not have the view that old Europe will be renewed through Russian blood."[60]

The most substantial effort to criticize Herzen from the Marxist left came not from Marx himself, but from Moses Hess. He responded to *S togo berega* with a series of long letters, written in March and early April 1850; in November 1851, he wrote a much shorter, more private letter reacting to the *Briefen*.[61] In effect, Hess argued that Herzen's pessimism resulted from his inability to enter into the class struggle as a participant on the side of the proletariat; the time called for apostles, not alienated philosophers, pagan Romans redivivus, who could only bemoan the loss of a civilization that was irrelevant to the masses:

> Along with Proudhon and the German philosophers, you protest against "liberticide" communism. If you understood communism not as a utopia, but from its political side, as a historical movement, as a proletarian revolution, as the struggle of the proletariat for liberation from the domination of the bourgeoisie, as the striving of the workers to be rid of their guardians, from their present managers, and to manage their work themselves—in a word, if you understood communism as class struggle, then you would be able to judge appropriately the catch phrases about the destruction of "personal freedom" and all the other banal reproaches that are still being addressed to the proletariat from the real or ideological standpoint of the bourgeoisie.[62]

The criticism seems irrelevant; Herzen, after all, never denied that history might (or might not) march—but he was asserting in *S togo berega* the individual's right to perceive and judge the events and developments, even if he could not control them. Whatever the definition of proletarian communism, he was free to dislike it.

Hess also attacked Herzen's belief in the coming Slavic regeneration of Europe, although here he oversimplified Herzen's position. Hess, almost as far to the left as Herzen, agreed with him that the predominant culture of bourgeois Europe was doomed; however, he denied that the only possible source of renewal were new barbarians represented by the Slavic peoples: Hess hoped for a proletarian revolution instead. There was nothing here that Herzen would not have accepted. However, Hess went on to argue that the destruction of prevailing Western culture by "the Cossacks" would lead not to "progressive socialism," but to "reactionary socialism." The Slavic character, he felt, is stable, passive, and unhistoric: "I grant that the Slavs can shape a modern Byzantium, a Western China, but not a social democratic republic of our Europe, if Europe does not free itself. . . . I grant that there can be no free Europe without a free Russia, but I also believe that there can be no free Russia, no free Slavdom without a free Europe."[63] As his biographer noted, the argument was a strange one for a person who believed he was presenting a Marxist case against Herzen's idealism.[64]

Considerably more interesting was Hess's recommendation that Herzen should read Marx and his exposition of Marxian views on Western development. Herzen, the product of the circles, still saw

Great Britain with the eyes of 1840 Moscow, as the example of a rooted, traditional society in which alienation was at a minimum; Hess responded to this image as a historical materialist:

> You see the English situation as more consolidated than that of the Continent—probably because during the revolutionizing of the Continent from 1789 to 1830 England followed its "traditions" without a "break." As a political ideologist you have no sense for the *economic* revolution, the form under which England has participated in the movement of our time; . . . the *non-illusory*, practical part of the economic ideal for which Proudhon and his party . . . strive has already come about in England, and . . . therefore England is closer to a proletarian revolution than the Continent, than France itself.[65]

Hess posits the existence of two camps on the radical left, the historical materialists, led by Marx, and the Proudhonian idealists, of whom Herzen is one. His loyalty to the notion of a materialist camp is the more striking, since it is accompanied by an attack on the person of Marx himself. But despite adherence to the idea of Marx's ideology, Hess did not succeed in providing a lucid Marxist critique of Herzen's work.

As Michelet had been more than gracious in accepting Herzen's criticism of his work, so Herzen responded in the same manner to Hess, and suggested that he expand his first letter and print it. Indeed, he even suggested the title for the series of letters—"Briefen an Iscander."[66] Despite a number of efforts to publish the critique, both in Germany, by Herzen's publisher, and through Cabet's publications in France, for some reason it was never issued. Only in the twentieth century was the manuscript discovered and made public.[67]

Hess's failure is to be lamented, for a clear intellectual confrontation between Herzen and Marx would have been most interesting. For all their theoretical differences, the two men shared a number of traits. Intellectually, their common left-Hegelian heritage often led them to approach problems in similar fashion. Their judgment of events, too, was often similar; both were far too radical to see hope for peaceful transformations and social amelioration on the horizon; on the other hand, as strategists, both opposed revolutionary adventurism on each individual occasion when a choice had to be made. The more romantic Herzen, however, would continue to admire the adventurers, even as he rejected their actions, while Marx would dismiss the actors as well, charging them with petit-bourgeois radicalism and an inability to perceive that genuine revolution could come only from the revolutionary class.

However, the most important difference between the two men is the essentially political nature of Marx's activity; as we have seen in chapter 4, he was building a party of loyal followers capable of translating his will into political action. Ideology meant less than providing aid in building the working-class political instrument Marx knew he was seeking. Herzen, on the other hand, was far more a traditional man of the circles turned utopian socialist. For him, the exchange of views and knitting the bonds of friendship and loyalty among the international community of dedicated individuals was primary. Apart from the vague "public" that might be reached by his journalism (and which, at this stage, was confined almost wholly to the members of the community), he had no sense of political action and forging the tools for it. He could easily interact with men whose views were less or more radical than his own, so long as they were part of the community. The manipulative and domineering Marx put himself outside that fold and at the same time became a historical actor of far greater importance than Herzen or any of his friends.

While most of the opinions expressed on Herzen's early work were critical, Herzen did have keen admirers in Western Europe. There were those who shared his disillusionment and were enthusiastic at his interpretation of the meaning of the revolutionary experience. Malwida von Meysenbug, a participant in some phases of the German events and later the governess of Herzen's daughters, was moved by the moods and tone of *S togo berega* and found in it a welcome, unsparing criticism of the illusions of 1848.[68] Another admirer, the French physician Ernest Coeurderoy, shared the apocalyptic interpretation of Herzen's work, but where the Germans of the *Deutsche Monatsschrift* disapproved, he applauded. Coeurderoy expected the regeneration of old Europe to come through new "barbarian" invasions, with the Cossacks playing the role of the first-century Germans. "Let the barbarians descend, let them transfuse their young blood into the veins of our decrepit societies, which are constitutionally and organically bourgeois."[69] Herzen never took his own words so literally. The apocalyptic interpretation of his work by critics and admirers alike was no doubt encouraged by Herzen's references to himself as a "barbarian." This self-definition also spared his readers from pondering how sharply he had criticized their enterprise. Because it was easier for Western radicals to deal with, the apocalyptic interpretation of Herzen's thought was the one that prevailed in the early years of his journalism. The depth of Herzen's alienation was difficult for the radical community to grasp, especially in one who was so much a part of their world of polite behavior and comfortable living.

The Response in Russia

Whlie the West was willing to listen to Herzen, if critically, the response from Russia was harsher. In Herzen's justification of his emigration one could sense an apprehension that his friends in Moscow would feel he was deserting them. This apprehension was justified; apparently only Granovskii of the circle members defended his decision to remain in the West, arguing that he could not act effectively in Russia. The others, however, felt Herzen had abandoned them; and Ketcher, in particular, was driven in part by his angry sense of loss into repudiating Herzen's political views.[70] The circle was now irreparably destroyed, although it would be some time before the full scope of the breach became apparent. Herzen continued to contact his friends whenever possible and to try to convince them that his course was the right one. In 1851, he responded to their complaints by showing how successful he had been as a propagandist of their Russia:

> Leaving aside self-love and modesty—when did Russia have such an organ [as his own writing] in Europe? All my strength, all my thoughts are turned to you—and my voice has received weight. Only two days ago I spoke to Michelet for two hours about Russia, I have interested them in Russia. What would I have done in Russia, with its iron muzzle? A propos, see how in the local "Liberté de penser" everything I have said about Russia is expounded in detail—from this side, I cannot reproach myself that I have been inactive, and I cannot think that I would have done more there.[71]

His arguments were unavailing. Later the same year, even Granovskii bitterly attacked him for publishing *Du Développement*, although he could scarcely be a fair judge of a book he had been unable to read. Granovskii, viewing the subject from a purely Russian point of view (although the work was clearly designed primarily for a Western audience), argued that censorship rendered the book accessible only

The Uncensored Voice

to the authorities, and thus it could have no readers among those who might be convinced by it. The effect, he said, was merely to tighten censorship and intensify the government's attacks on Herzen. Moreover, by his discussion of the contributions of individual Russians, Herzen had put his friends in danger. "You took a heavy responsibility on your soul, Herzen, and you will hear no thanks from a single decent [*poriadochnyi*] Russian."[72]

Increasingly isolated from Russia and his friends by the tightened restrictions imposed by the government, Herzen continued his work in the West. Not until 1853, for the first time since his departure six years earlier, did he meet one of the members of the circle: the actor Mikhail Shchepkin traveled to London especially to see Herzen. Only after his friend's arrival did Herzen realize that he had come as a spokesman for the circle to implore him to give up his mission and emigrate to America. Shchepkin and all his friends starkly repudiated Herzen's work.[73] Formed as Herzen and his ideas had been by the ambience of the circle, the circle members nonetheless could not accept the conclusions he drew from premises they had worked out together; Herzen would ultimately have to find a different audience in Russia.

The Outcome

Herzen's bleak estimation of the prospects for political improvement, and his scorn for the democratic politicians who had failed so signally when they had the chance to change society, logically added up to a thorough pessimism and withdrawal from active politics. To some extent, his activity as a propagandist contradicted his assessment of the possibility of action, as was pointed out by Solger in his review of *S togo berega*. The final segments of that book did indeed counsel withdrawal; like the last Roman patricians, there was nothing for the politically sensitive elite to do but enjoy each other's civilized company and wait for the barbarians.[74]

There were, however, more positive forms of withdrawal from Europe. The obvious one that suggested itself to Herzen was transatlantic emigration; many of his friends, particularly among the German forty-eighters did indeed go to America—Carl Schurz, Friedrich Kapp, August Willich, Julius Fröbel among the most prominent. Before the catastrophes that overwhelmed him in 1851 and 1852, Herzen discussed the possibility with Herwegh and later with Vogt, Mazzini, and others.⁷⁵ America always remained the ultimate escape, if conditions in Europe became unbearable.⁷⁶

There was yet another possibility, one which in the end would have tragic consequences for Herzen. That was to create a microcosm of the good society for himself and his friends and withdraw to it from the corruption and injustice of the world around them. Herzen had two sources for this notion: on the level of practice, his own life had been enormously enriched by the circle—which was, in its way, just such a secular "city on the hill," living by its own values. As Malia has pointed out, "[The circle] was Herzen's introduction to society, and hence of crucial importance in the formation of his future social ideal, for the circle represented at the same time freedom for the flowering of the personality of each of its members, and full equality and fraternity among all of them. . . . Long before he heard of the word, the circle was his first taste of what he later called "socialism."⁷⁷

Utopian socialism confirmed Herzen's personal experience of the circle. Unlike later Marxian socialism, the early movement was focused on living in such a way that each individual's capacities could develop to their fullest potential. Although the utopians are best known for their attempts to establish socialist communities such as Brook Farm or New Harmony in the United States, such major and expensive undertakings were not necessary, especially for those whose means enabled them to be personally unconcerned with the problem of how to live a full life while still earning their livelihood. A recreation of the circle, a gathering together of like-minded friends who would live today with the freedom, honesty, and tolerance that they hoped would eventually be the lot of everyone, became an acceptable option, if the struggle in the broader world seemed futile.

Withdrawal to an isolated little world of kindred spirits led to personal crisis, because the spirits in question were Georg and Emma Herwegh, and the idea of withdrawal became part of the emotional and ideological ambience that Georg Herwegh and Natalie Herzen used to rationalize their love affair. It was also Herwegh and Natalie who supported the idea of withdrawal most clearly, so their testimony is of major importance in understanding this phase of Herzen's life and thought.

By the end of 1848, Natalie, probably under Herwegh's influence, was expressing a disillusionment and loss of interest in politics; nature became more enticing than the bustle of human activity:⁷⁸ "I have become . . . indifferent to everything going on outside my own inner world—to all uprisings and revolutions. . . . This indfference has become terrible even to me. . . . In the country, on a vibrant, warm day, when I see the trees and the high grass I would like to get lost in it, to forget everyone and be forgotten. I merge with the warm, perfumed breath of nature, disappear with it into the air, or like a playful, colorful butterfly flit from flower to flower (I don't want to be a bee—they are too industrious)."[79]

In Geneva, the ideology of withdrawal took form. One major ingredient was George Sand's novel, *La Petite Fadette*,[80] which Herwegh and Natalie misread and used as a model for their lives. The characters in the novel do in fact bear striking resemblance to the Herzen party. It tells of twin sons of a substantial peasant family. One, Landry, is strong, capable, and perfectly adapted to the world he inhabits; at the same time, he is devoted to his weaker, gentler brother Sylvinet. The more capable brother moves into mature life, taking a job away from home and planning his marriage. Landry's love, Fadette, bears some similarity to Natalie herself—a child of a somewhat dishonorable union, brought up by her cruel and outcast grandmother in isolation from the rest of society, she falls in love with Landry while still a child. Once Landry acknowledges and returns her feeling, he educates her to life in society, and she matures into a beautiful, wise, and wealthy woman. The two are forced to undergo a long separation before his family is reconciled to the match. Sylvinet, who is wholly consumed by love for his brother, cannot accept Landry's move to independent life. Pathologically jealous, he becomes ill and at the same time embitters the lives of everyone around him. As the marriage approaches, Sylvinet's illness becomes dangerous; Fadette cures him by pointing out his selfishness and ultimately inspiring him with love for her. In sharp contrast to the real life dénouement, Sylvinet, hopelessly in love with his brother's bride, leaves home forever.

Herwegh and Natalie enthusiastically applied the situation of the novel to their own lives. Herzen was the stronger twin, Landry, and Herwegh the weak Sylvinet, so consumed by love himself that he in turn consumed all about him. Natalie was Fadette. It is certainly not flattering to Herwegh to see him in the role of Sylvinet, but it does in fact seem quite a good likeness of his emotional constitution; in any case, for Herwegh and Natalie, Sylvinet he became. But whereas for Sand the "happy ending" involved the hero and heroine leaving home and becoming integated into their simple society, for Herwegh and Natalie the *bessonerie*, or nest of twins, became the goal, an idealized refuge from the world.

The Fourierist notion of "harmony" became the guiding ideal behind the lovers' notion of their *bessonerie*. They would leave the world and find harmony in a simple commune made up of the Herzen and Herwegh families. Somehow, the love of Herwegh and Natalie for each other would irradiate the whole group, all of whom would be ennobled and love each other in its warmth. Toward the end of the summer of 1849, the Herzens and Herwegh planned to leave the grand Hôtel de Bergues in Geneva, and move to a rustic retreat at Veytaux, a small village on the lake. Emma Herwegh, still in Paris and deeply suspicious of her husband's relationship with Natalie, was not eager to join the others. Natalie wrote to persuade her: "I will repeat what I already said long ago, that I feel that there will be no harmony and happiness for us until our families are reunited. I imagine such a beautiful life, I imagine a new life with you in a little corner of the world."[81]

The ultimate joy that Natalie could imagine would be for their little group to be expanded by the addition of Ogarev and Natalie Tuchkova, who were living together in Russia and hoping one day to rejoin their friends in the West.[82] The dream of their ultimate harmony kept her going through the months of separation, illness, and Emma's jealousy which she endured in Paris during the first half of 1850. "Yes, we must bear everything. In these few instants I believe in the future—we will have it, despite everything, it is as certain as death! As *inevitable*—without that, I do not understand the present.... I transport myself into the future—all, all are happy—harmony, serenity in our circle—the children's gaiety, even sympathy among them—what must be their development in such an atmosphere—perfect tranquillity, beautiful nature."[83]

Herwegh shared the dream. He wrote to Herzen after Natalie had rejoined her husband early in 1850, "This wrings my heart. Your wife was the last pledge of the realization of our sublime projects and of that formation of a world apart, which is now so cruelly aborted."[84]

Herzen shared the hope for a communal life; his recorded remarks, however, came after his return to Paris. By this time he was feeling his first serious doubts about Herwegh, stimulated by Emma's pain at her husband's treatment of her and his jealousy regarding Natalie. For weeks Herzen had sent his friend angry, reproachful letters, and Herwegh had returned defensive, petulant replies; this long altercation, Herzen explained, was an effort to clear the air before "definitively, irrevocably engaging [them]selves to a communal life."[85]

When, finally, the two families did settle in Nice at the end of the summer of 1850, Herzen wrote, "I peacefully enter this harbor, and on the gatepost of my house I inscribe the ancient pentagram to ward off every evil spirit of care and human madness."[86] But the harbor was mined, and no invocation of charms could salvage the enterprise. Alexander, Natalie, Georg, and Emma could not succeed in their attempt to build a new life behind an "ancient pentagram"; the dream of harmony they were trying to put into practice was already too tarnished by jealousy, adultery, and falsehood.

Alexander Herzen, 1847
From *Sobranie Sochinenii*, vol. 5 (Moscow, 1955).

Natalie Herzen
From Alexander Herzen, *Byloe i Dumy*, vol. 1 (Moscow, 1962).

Georg Herwegh, 1845
Dichtermuseum Liestal.

Alexander Herzen, early 1850s
From *Sobranie Sochinenii*, vol. 7 (Moscow, 1956).

"The Barricades," Edouard Detaille, 1848
Courtesy Bettmann Archive, Inc.

Revolutionaries on the Barricades, February 1848
Courtesy Bettmann Archive, Inc.

"The Uprising," Honoré Daumier, c. 1849
Courtesy Phillips Collection, Washington, D.C.

Invasion of the Paris Assembly, 15 May 1848
From T. J. Clark, *The Absolute Bourgeois: Artists and Politics in France, 1848–1851* (Greenwich, Conn.: New York Graphic Society, Ltd., 1973).

7
THE CRISIS

BETWEEN 1850 and 1852 acute and painful transitions confronted Herzen in many aspects of his life; the mature Herzen emerged from this series of trials. His relation to his family, his homeland, and Western revolution all arrived at a point of crisis and disillusionment. By the spring of 1852, all his hopes and expectations had foundered. Herzen recovered from the wreck of his dreams, but henceforth he would operate on new principles, and his old enthusiasm would be replaced by a cooler view of the rewards offered by both political and personal life. But despite the new irony that marked most of his public and private relations after 1852, Herzen also learned that friendship and cooperation were possible, even without the total commitment he had long demanded, and that he could make noticeable contributions to the cause to which he had dedicated himself, even though hopes for final victory remained remote. It is a thoroughly disenchanted, and yet still active, vital, and committed Herzen, who speaks to us from the pages of *Byloe i dumy*. Only the bond with Ogarev remained unaffected by the crisis, and even that link was greatly attenuated in this period because of the difficulties of communicating across the Russian frontier.

Herzen's disenchantment was progressive: his retreat from belief in the revolutions of 1848, to a search for a new world of action and sympathy among the revolutionaries, to a vision of an isolated "commune" consisting of his and the Herwegh families, has already been detailed. In 1851–1852, this last hope was shattered, first by the end of the friendship with Herwegh and then by the death of Natalie Herzen. Rather than succumb to isolation, Herzen worked his way back from it to a new relationship with the exile community, one based less on ideological agreement or political alliance than on the common problems they faced in accommodating to the rigors of exile life.

The Crisis

Exile status itself finally caught up with Herzen, and the legal break with Russia parallels his loss of contact with his primary Russian audience. Swiss citizenship eventually provided a solution to the legal problems created by the loss of his homeland. Politically, the decision to return to Russia through the press brought with it the creation of a new, remote, impersonal audience of young Russian strangers, as a replacement for his old, intimate circle of friends.

Overshadowing all of Herzen's other problems was his family crisis, which turned this period into one of genuine torment for him. The love affair between Natalie Herzen and Georg Herwegh shattered Herzen's romantic idealism. He claimed later, with considerable exaggeration, that his personal life ended with Natalie's death.[1] It is true, however, that the Herzen of the 1850s and 1860s is a person far less ready for close personal relations than the romantic youth of the circles, or even the man seeking an intimate extended family of the postrevolutionary days. An indication of the new reserve is that he appears not to have been on a second-person-singular basis with anyone whom he met after 1848.

His personality remained resilient, however, and this contributed greatly to his ability to pick up the pieces of his life after his move to London. Although he lost much of his capacity for intimate friendship, his sociability revived. It is the London Herzen whose portrait has come down to us in many memoir accounts, with his hospitality, his high spirits, the "fireworks" of his conversation, his booming laugh, and a boldness of thought that often dismayed men less resolute than himself. It is also this Herzen whose views and personality are reflected in *Byloe i dumy*, written in the 1850s and 1860s.

Paris 1850: The Crisis Begins

The relationship between Georg Herwegh and Natalie Herzen forms the backdrop to this period of Herzen's life. Fifty years ago, E. H. Carr first read Natalie's letters to Georg and other materials remaining in the possession of the Herwegh family (and now in the British Library), and described the affair in *The Romantic Exiles*. Carr did a masterful job of piecing together the documentation to create a sustained and convincing narrative; there is no need to repeat his work. Discussion here will, therefore, largely be limited to providing the framework necessary for understanding Herzen's situation.

Herzen, Natalie, Herwegh, and two of the Herzen children spent the summer of 1849 together in Geneva, leaving Emma and the Herwegh children in Paris. (Luisa Haag, Mariia Ern, and Kolia Herzen were in Zurich, where the child was enrolled in a school for the deaf.) Herwegh stayed at the Hôtel de Bergues, as did the Herzens; contact between Herwegh and the Herzens was thus almost continuous, and the sense of two separate ménages was broken down both by Herwegh's bachelor life and by the reduced domestic involvement that hotel living provided Natalie Herzen. It was at this time, during a brief absence of Herzen's, that the friendship between Natalie and Herwegh turned into a love affair. Herzen remained ignorant and unsuspecting; when she suffered a miscarriage in the autumn each man assumed that the lost child was his own. (Natalie believed Herwegh was the father.) Natalie was passionately attached to Herwegh, but at the same time never seems to have entertained the notion of separating herself from her family, to which she was also devoted, or from Herzen. Her dream instead, as we have seen, was of a communal life involving both families—and possibly Ogarev and Natalie Tuchkova as well—the life of the entire group irradiated by love for each other and by Natalie's and Herwegh's encompassing love.

The first plan for communal life, a shared house outside Geneva at Veytaux, failed; Emma was not willing to come to Switzerland to join the group, referring to the need to remain in Paris to try to salvage something of the family's finances. She argued that Herwegh should return to Paris, but he refused, pleading anxiety about his legal status. Instead, it was Herzen, impelled by pressure exerted by the Russian government, who at the very end of the year returned to France. The Herzen family went first to Zurich. Natalie with the two children remained there with Kolia, and Luisa Haag accompanied Herzen on the journey to Paris. On the way, they stopped in Bern, where Herzen had a joyful reunion with Herwegh, although they had been separated only a short time. It was, said Herzen, "almost the last moment that I still really loved that man."[2] From Bern Herzen went to Paris and Emma, while Herwegh traveled to Zurich and joined Natalie.

Herzen's return to France was spurred by the need to protect his property from the Russian government. As we have seen, he had concealed his intent to emigrate long enough to transfer most of his own assets to the West. His mother's fortune, however, was still tied up in Russia, and once the authorities became convinced that she planned to remain abroad, they proceeded to sequester it. Herzen went to Paris to enlist the aid of the Rothschild bank in releasing the funds; Luisa Haag transferred her property to Rothschild, and then the banker collected. The stratagem was successful only after six months of negotiation, a six months that Herzen spent in Paris consumed by inactivity and uncertainty.³

He stayed at first with Emma Herwegh, who immediately confronted him with her misery at her husband's neglect of her, her suspicions regarding Georg's relationship with Natalie, and her belief that he was exaggerating the danger of returning to France in order to stay away from her. Natalie's letters further disturbed Herzen; they were full of admiration for Herwegh, he said later; at the time, he described them as "having a mordant nature that made me tremble at first, and then to respond with the same mordancy." His suspicions now aroused, he summoned Natalie to come alone to Paris to resolve the situation, even if this ultimately should mean their separation. Faced with the implicit choice between her husband and Herwegh, Natalie took decisive action to preserve her marriage. Instead of coming by herself for a visit, she brought Sasha and Tata and settled in with Herzen for the duration of his stay. At least at the beginning of the Paris sojourn, she believed that this move had ended the affair with Herwegh.⁴

Herzen's letters to Herwegh, *Byloe i dumy*, and Natalie's letters to Herwegh are virtually the only sources for this period. The latter are almost entirely concentrated on personal relations within the two families. Herzen's are filled with the progress and setbacks of the financial project, with reproaches to Herwegh for his conduct (see chapter 8), and, on a general plane, with commentary on current politics and his dire view of the impending moral and political collapse of French civilization. They too provide little information about Herzen's life outside the family.

The general tone of Herzen's letters is depressed and fatigued. Natalie was ill almost the entire winter, and as soon as she recovered, other members of the family took to their beds, with an especially grave malady afflicting five-year-old Tata.⁵ Herwegh and Herzen wearied themselves and each other with mutual accusations and defenses. Herwegh objected to Herzen's obsession with his money and found him unsympathetic toward what had in fact become a separation from Emma. Herzen was indeed unsympathetic, and criticized what he considered the poet's infantile attitude, expressed both in his refusal to concern himself with economic reality and in his treatment of his wife.

The silence of this correspondence with regard to the radical community is an indication of Herzen's withdrawal from day-to-day political involvement. He did occasionally mention Proudhon and *La Voix du peuple*, but unfortunately gave no account of his participation in the editorial process. Apart from Proudhon and Turgenev, who was almost a part of the family circle at this time, Herzen scarcely mentioned his outside contacts.

The radical community in Paris had been decimated; the leaders, at least, had either been expelled from France or, fearing reprisals, had left voluntarily. The extent to which Herzen withdrew from the surviving remnant cannot be determined; the silence of his letters should not be interpreted to mean he had completely isolated himself. It is clear, however, that he was no longer interested in wooing the refugees, as he had done the previous winter. Even before his departure from Switzerland, he wrote to Emma:

> You can do me a great favor, and please do it, if, when you have nothing to say to our mutual friends, you warn them that I am poorer by a third [owing to the loss of his Kostroma estate] and seriously wish to change my way of life—that in addition to proofs of friendship, that I appreciate with all my heart, I wish a little free time; that I am in despair—but I will not be able to offer hospitality; that I am desolated, but I will be unable to provide a field hospital, a monastery, a meditation room . . . , an asylum for lovers—when the lady of their thoughts does not have time to receive them, a branch office for the men who, after having lost their country in space, wish to waste their time in Paris. . . . Do all this with the goodness that you have and I lack, do it in a way that everyone thinks that I love them still more, which is true, finally, repeat it often enough, strike the imagination, agitate the fantasy, don't spare allegories, rise to hyperbole.
> *Et libera nos*—from friends.[6]

Herzen's indifference to the refugees' political life can be gauged from two important pieces of negative evidence. First, there was no follow-up to *La Voix du Peuple;* although the paper itself was not a failure and Herzen maintained relatively cordial relations with his co-workers, the experience still seems to have disillusioned him. Nor did he associate himself with any political group, and there were no more attempts to involve himself with a publication speaking to a European audience. For the moment, he was content with the ability to place his own work in any of a number of publications, none of

The Crisis

which he was in essential ideological agreement with. When he did decide to become involved again in his own journal, he would write in Russian for an audience in his homeland.

His choice of residence was the second indication of Herzen's withdrawal. The success of political reaction steadily increased the pressure on the refugees. Threats from the great powers impelled Switzerland gradually to expel radical foreigners; by 1850, Swiss pressure had pushed the center of émigré life to London. Soon at least one—often several—rival organizations were established there by French, Polish, German, Italian, Hungarian, and other, smaller national groups. Conspiracy, organization, and publishing were all centered in the tolerant English capital. And London was the one accessible place where Herzen did not consider settling. In his letters to Herwegh, he often raised the question of where the families should live; the possibilities included the south of France, Switzerland, Nice (where they eventually did go), remote parts of Britain like Cornwall or the Channel Islands,[7] or possibly Spain. As a last resort, there was always America, with its mixed promise of freedom on the one hand, and on the other a complete break with Europe, its culture and its concerns. But, although he no longer wished to work with the other refugees, Herzen still hoped to stay in Europe and work for the cause. America, therefore, was not so much an option as a symbol of giving up the fight. Thus he searched for isolation within Europe, a remote commune away from day-to-day activity, but not too far from the theater of future drama. Sometimes he mentioned withdrawing for a year, as if to imply that at the end of that term he might rejoin the revolutionary camp; but if this was his intention, it was never clearly spelled out.[8]

Although Western Europe had lost much of its charm, the impossibility of turning back was underscored by the much more intense reaction in Russia.[9] Pressure on the Herzen family in exile was only one symptom of tsarist implacability. Simultaneously, the government at home struck at Herzen's closest friend and his most recent Russian contacts; Ogarev, Aleksei Tuchkov, Nikolai Satin, and Ivan Selivanov were arrested and brought from Penza to St. Petersburg. For months the Herzens were unable to decipher the cryptic message they received; they knew only that disaster had struck, but could not judge its extent.[10] In the case of Selivanov at least (the only one of the four to undergo a severe and prolonged punishment, with a term of administrative exile), his contact with Herzen was almost certainly the reason for his persecution. (See chapter 4.) Meanwhile, Herzen's old Moscow friends, fearful of the intensified repression, rejected his work, thus breaking almost the last ties holding the circle together.[11] Thus, by the spring of 1850, a weary Herzen was politically almost completely alone.

Nice, 1850–1852: Betrayal, Reconciliation, Death

In mid-March Herzen's "Donoso Cortes, Marquis de Valdegamas, et Julien, Empereur romain" appeared in *La Voix du Peuple*.[12] This was a slashing attack on the theory and practice of conservatism in which he argued that the hangman is the hero of the reactionary regime: "All the virtues, admired by Donoso-Cortes, are modestly united in the hangman, and moreover to the highest degree: obedience to authority, blind execution of orders, unlimited self-dedication. . . . Let us render the man of social vengeance his due and say, imitating our orator: 'The hangman is a great deal closer to the priest than is usually believed.' "[13]

The right-wing press attacked the work, and called for Herzen's prosecution.[14] Possibly as a result, in April Herzen suddenly received orders of expulsion from Paris.[15] The financial project was now complicated by the need to pursue a second line of negotiations, with the French police, in order to extend his already uncomfortable stay. By the end of April, he had settled on Nice as his next destination and wished nothing so much as simply to get out.[16] In May he began setting departure dates, always postponed either because of illness in the family or because there had been one more delay in the negotiations.[17]

Meanwhile, repression continued; the last issue of *La Voix du Peuple* appeared on May 14, and at about the same time Emma Herwegh was expelled from Paris[18] and Chojecki's French naturalization was revoked. On May 21, Emma left alone for Nice, with the Herzens planning to follow her as soon as possible.[19] It was still another three weeks before the Herzen family finally set out for the south. They were accompanied as far as Marseilles by Chojecki, who had decided to leave Europe altogether and go to Alexandria. "It is time," he wrote Emma, "to abandon poli-tics for poli-gamy."[20] Nice was much less remote than Egypt: nonetheless, the Herzens hoped the move would mark the beginning of a new life.[21]

It became apparent almost at once that the complicated relationships among the parties would make it extremely difficult to establish a life together. Herwegh had confessed his infidelity to Emma when she visited him in Zurich in March, and from then on she was very much involved in the lives of her husband and his mistress, discussing the affair with both of them, expressing her own jealousy and anger, and also facilitating their secret correspondence. Now, in Nice, despite her greatly reduced means, she hoped to settle her own family apart from the Herzens in their own house. She was, however, unable to find anything acceptable at a price she could afford, and Herzen, ignorant of the reason for her unwillingness to share a ménage, persuaded her to join his family in a large house outside town. Emma remained discontented; it must have seemed she was being treated like a poor relation—invited to share quarters, but in the cramped upstairs apartment and as part of a general scheme she must have dreaded. Her resentment, conveyed to Georg and thence back to Herzen, became one more element in the tangle of conflicting emotions.

Georg also had trouble dealing with Natalie's desires and emotions. She was the one most eager to restore their relationship, and to do it in the context of communal life. Her letters to him were full of passionate devotion. On the other hand, she had also made clear that she had no intention of leaving Alexander, and she insisted that her husband remain ignorant of the affair. As to the future of her relations with Georg himself, she sent mixed signals. When first contemplating their life together, she had believed it would not be possible to renew their physical relationship; however, once arrived in Nice, she was carried away by the fanatasy of going back to the delights of the time they had been together in Geneva. Moreover, she was pregnant once again, and Herwegh was both angry and jealous at the idea of her carrying Herzen's child.[22]

Herwegh responded to this complex situation by delaying his departure for Nice, sending a series of excuses and complaints to both Herzen and Natalie. Ironically, it took repeated urging from Herzen to convince him finally to come. He arrived in Nice only on August 22, accompanied by Luisa Haag, Kolia, and, probably, Mariia Ern.[23]

Once in Nice, Herzen burned his last Russian boats. In the autumn the government summoned him home; his refusal to return now officially put him outside Russian law.[24] The pressures exerted on the refugees by the European states meant that he could not now be certain of a safe place for himself and his family to live. London remained the only sure refuge, and in the fall of 1850 he was still unwilling to go there.[25] The expulsion from France, before his renunciation of Russian citizenship, had first demonstrated his vulnerability; in 1851 he was threatened with expulsion from Nice and was directly faced with the difficulties created by statelessness. Permission to remain in Piedmont was received only in July of that year, more than a month after his expulsion.[26] Moreover, he feared that if he were to die, his family would be forcibly returned to Russia.[27] Travel and residence throughout the European continent had become an uncertain proposition even for someone like Herzen, with the financial means to shield him from the worst kinds of arbitrary action.

From September 1850 until the summer of 1851 he sought to protect himself and his family by attaining new citizenship. Geneva was his first and obvious choice, but—a symptom of changing times—Fazy, who had welcomed him so warmly a year earlier, now was reluctant to commit himself to giving Herzen permission to remain in Geneva. Finally, through the good offices of Karl Vogt, Herzen was granted citizenship by the canton of Fribourg in June 1851. Cantonal citizenship carried with it citizenship in the confederation; henceforth, Herzen was a proud, if somewhat ironic, Swiss subject.[28]

Despite these difficulties, Herzen found life in Nice congenial, at first. The relative freedom of Piedmont, combined with French language and culture, made Nice a natural gathering place for radicals, so despite Herzen's expressed desire for isolation the little commune was not entirely alone. Although we have few details, we do know that there was an important group of Italian radicals spread between Nice and Genoa, among whom Herzen found his most congenial companions. Among them, Felice Orsini (who after a life of revolutionary adventure was guillotined in 1858 for an attempt to assassinate Napoleon III) seems to have been a regular contact. There were enough Poles in residence to hold a benefit ball that was attended by the Herzen family in February.[29] French refugees also found Nice a convenient haven; their colony expanded considerably after the coup d'état in France in December 1851. Karl Vogt, who came to Nice before the end of 1850 to undertake research in marine biology and also tutored Sasha Herzen, became a part of Herzen's immediate circle. In the summer of 1851, Chojecki returned to Europe from Egypt and joined the Herzen colony.[30] A few months earlier, a young couple from Russia, Vladimir and Aleksandra Engel'son, who had long been admirers of Herzen, had come to Nice. Venturi has described Herzen as at the center of a Russian colony; by the end of 1851, he writes, "Herzen and his little group of Russian emigrés had

The Crisis

achieved the position and significance of a political group, small in numbers but rich in debates and intuition, closely associated with the Italian and, especially after December 2, 1851, with the French groups."[31] This seems a considerable overstatement of Herzen's role and influence; nonetheless, it is clear that even in Nice he was to some degree functioning on a political level within an international framework.

The hiatus between the move to Nice and the discovery of Natalie's infidelity was a productive period for Herzen. He wrote *Du Développement des idées révolutionnaires en Russie* in this brief interval, and published it in Nice.[32] In October Herwegh made inquiries for him about the possibility of establishing a Russian press and finding typesetters for it in Stuttgart.[33] This seems to indicate that he was once again thinking about publishing Russian works in the safety of exile, picking up the idea where he had left it off in Paris in 1849.

This peaceful and productive period ended at the turn of 1851, when Natalie finally confessed to a now suspicious Herzen. Amid stormy scenes, he expelled the Herwegh family from the house. There were confrontations between Herzen and both Georg and Emma, as well as long letters combining recrimination, pleas not to terminate the foursome, and then efforts by Herwegh and Emma to persuade Natalie to leave Herzen. (This will be discussed later.) Aftershocks continued for months; there was an unpaid loan that Herzen now tried to collect and bills from servants and tradespeople that ended up with him. In a bizarre episode, the Herweghs sent their young son back to Nice from Menton to ask the Herzens to take him in; getting the child back to his parents was another time- and emotion-consuming complication.[34] The lovers' correspondence continued for some months after the rupture, but Herwegh's letters to Natalie became increasingly demanding and unreasonable; as far as he was concerned, her only options were to to join him or commit suicide. She recoiled from his selfish hysteria and by spring cut off the correspondence. Her disillusionment in her lover shattered the last fragments of her dreams of a year earlier.

Termination of the affair did not end the Herzen family crisis. From Natalie's letters to Herwegh, and Herzen's to Natalie, written in the summer of 1851, it appears that there were many hours of explanation and recrimination between husband and wife; reconciliation was by no means complete by the spring, and doubt remained about the future of their marriage.[35] Herzen thought about voluntarily moving from Nice, the scene of his disillusionment, made still more unat-

175

tractive by Emma Herwegh's return in the spring. Once again there were inquiries about possible places of residence, complicated by the naturalization issue. These personal cares appear to have fully absorbed Herzen for six months.

After weeks of abortive plans to leave Nice either for good or temporarily, at the end of May Herzen suddenly was expelled on twenty-four hours' notice (extended to a few days). He went at once to Paris, accompanied only by his young Russian friend Vladimir Engel'son, to await the documentation needed for his Swiss naturalization and to try to settle the problem of where to live. He remained there for close to a month, then went alone to Geneva and Fribourg, where he received his new citizenship. Shortly before his departure from France, he also learned that he would be able to return to Piedmont.[36]

At some point during this unhappy half year, Herzen conceived the idea of publishing his own collected works. While in Paris, he wrote the dedication to the proposed collection. The state of his emotions is indicated by the fact that the sole dedicatee was to be Ogarev—for now, Natalie was excluded. As for his mood, the text of the dedication is explicit:

> I have arrived . . . not at the end, but at the point where descent begins . . . for I expect nothing for myself, nothing will evoke either astonishment or profound rejoicing. Astonishment and happiness are restrained in me by memories of the past and by fears of the future. I have acquired such a force of indifference, of resignation, of skepticism, I wish to say of old age, that I will survive all the blows of fate, although I have neither the desire to live long nor that of dying tomorrow. . . .
>
> [I] find in myself neither the energy, nor the freshness necessary to undertake new work, and involuntarily the senile idea of gathering all that I have written into a single volume came to me.[37]

Herzen's depression followed him to Paris; he was bored, Paris amusements had palled, and he waited impatiently to leave. Mariia Ern and her new husband, Adolph Reichel, who were expecting their first child, were his closest Parisian contacts. But he also discovered that his publications had found an audience and he was in demand. Among his new acquaintances was the historian Jules Michelet; they met and exchanged books at this time, thus initiating their long, friendly relationship.

The Crisis

Natalie met Herzen in Turin on his homeward journey. The couple was finally fully reconciled, and their other problems seemed settled as well; they could count on staying in Nice as long as they wished and had Swiss citizenship to fall back on in case of an emergency. They headed back to Nice, for what would be the last happy period in their lives. As always when he was contented, Herzen was productive; in the autumn of 1851, he wrote *Le Peuple russe et le socialisme*, his response to Michelet's negative characterization of the Russians. This little work was probably Herzen's most successful statement of his views, and it remains his one political essay still in print and easily accessible in most languages. Also at Michelet's behest, he wrote an article memorializing Bakunin, whose fate at the hands of the Russian police was still unknown. Michelet intended to place the article over the name of an impoverished French radical who needed the honorarium. A brief notice appeared in *L'Événement*, but he seems to have failed to place a larger version, and the work was published only in 1908 by Herzen's son-in-law and Michelet's admirer, Gabriel Monod.[38]

In November the Herzens were struck and overwhelmed by tragedy. Luisa Haag and Kolia, who were returning to Nice from a visit to the Reichels in Paris, were killed in a shipwreck off Hyères. A stunned Natalie became ill shortly afterward; she never recovered and died of pneumonia in May. Herzen, half mad from grief and rage, blamed Herwegh for Natalie's death (see chapter 8). He placed his two young daughters into the care of Mariia Reichel and with thirteen-year old Sasha wandered about central Europe in the hopes of organizing revenge. He went to Turin, Genoa, Lausanne, and finally, in the autumn, to London. It took some time for him to realize it, but he had come home.

The Exiles in London: Mazzini and International Revolution

The move to London meant turning once again to the organized exile community, and this Herzen had resisted as long as possible. As late as the summer of 1851, when it seemed that Great Britain might be the only European option left for him, it was Edinburgh he considered. "I do not want to live in London," he wrote to the Moscow circle. "I have so many friends there that the city is antipathetic to me."[39]

Herzen was reluctant to rejoin the main exile community, for to do so meant becoming embroiled in a whole new set of conflicts. While he had been living in France and Piedmont, in London the exile world assumed new form. Before the revolutions that community had been made up of revolutionaries, that is, men who had actively resisted their governments and faced prosecution if they returned home. Italians, led by Mazzini, and Poles dominated the upper- and middle-class groups;[40] there was also the substantial group of German artisans of the Communist League. During their years in England, the émigrés had developed political and public relations networks that linked them to sources of influence in Britain (as discussed in chapter 3). With the outbreak of revolution, many had returned home to take part; now they were back, defeated again, more bitter than before and forced to resume the weary life of emigration.

The colony was now much augmented. Before 1848, London was only one of several centers of émigré life; Paris, Switzerland, and Belgium were each used as a base by groups of foreign political refugees. Now they came to London—the Germans Ruge and Marx, and left-wing Poles from the Polish Democratic Society. (The conservatives, led by Prince Adam Czartoryski, remained in France.) In addition, whole new groups now joined the emigration, people who previously had functioned in their own countries either as part of a tolerated opposition or outside of politics, but now had been drawn beyond the limits acceptable to the governments in office. The prerevolutionary French opposition, which had briefly come to power in 1848–Blanc, Caussidière, Ledru-Rollin, and many others who had participated in clubs and assemblies—were now consigned to exile. So too were middle-class German democrats and radicals—Baden rebels, members of the Frankfurt and other assemblies, and others who had participated actively in the political process in 1848–1849.

The new arrivals, who had to compete with the Italians and Poles for public sympathy,[41] differed considerably from the prerevolutionary group. They had participated actively in political life, at least for a short time, and they had lost. Now there were recriminations and bitterness regarding their compatriots who had taken different positions or followed different tactics. At the same time, these men were not wholly committed to the idea of revolution, as were the heroes of the earlier emigration. They had functioned before 1848 in an imperfect political system and were ready to do so again—indeed, most of them eventually did return home. They had also functioned professionally before the revolutions, instead of dedicating themselves wholeheartedly to politics; as a result, they were able to integrate themselves, at least to a limited extent, into English academic and professional life.

For the first few years after the 1848 revolutions, the character of émigré action was largely determined by Giuseppe Mazzini. In 1849, Herzen had attempted to define a revolutionary internationalist niche for himself. A year later Mazzini had taken control of this position and begun to give it organizational shape. He attempted to coordinate an international revolutionary movement that would achieve the nationalist goals he had defined almost two decades earlier. Herzen watched this process from a distance, and wished no part of it. Mazzini's efforts only exacerbated conflicts among the émigrés; nonetheless, they also provided grounds for the myth of international revolutionary conspiracy, and thereby intensified repression.

During the spring and summer of 1850, Mazzini had traveled secretly to Lausanne and Paris, as well as working in London, to lay the foundation for an organization that would coordinate and centralize the activities of émigré groups representing as many European nations as possible. He called it the European Central Democratic Committee. The first members were Mazzini himself, representing the Italians, Arnold Ruge representing the Germans, Albert Darasz for the Poles, and Ledru-Rollin for the French. In its first few months the committee expanded somewhat; by late November, it could claim adherence by national Italian, Polish, German, Austrian, and Dutch organizations (for some reason, no specifically French group is included in the committee's statements).[42] The Romanian national movement was also represented, and eventually there was a Romanian seat on the Central Committee.

In making his plans, Mazzini was by no means indifferent to Herzen; indeed, he actively courted the Russian. They met in Paris in the spring of 1850, and Mazzini invited Herzen to become the Russian representative on the committee. Herzen put Mazzini off. He was not impressed by the project, and after Mazzini's visit he wrote to Johann Jacoby, expressing his fears that the Italian leader was no longer ahead of his times, but in danger of falling behind them: "a noble individuality," he said, "but not progressive."[43] After the move to Nice, Orsini presented him with a formal offer from Mazzini to represent Russia on the committee, and this was met with an extremely cordial, but implacable, refusal.[44] For Mazzini himself Herzen had nothing but praise: "You are the only political actor of the recent period whose name is still surrounded with respect, glory, and sympathy. One can disagree with you, but it is impossible not to hold you in esteem." He had erred, however, in choosing his allies, "incapable men who have compromised an admirable position, who remind us only of the disasters they brought about. . . . Neither you nor history has any more need of them, all one can do for them is to amnesty them. You wish to cover them with your name, you wish to share your influence, your past, with them—they will share their unpopularity and their past with you."

According to Herzen, the committee's first public statements were retrograde because of the influence of his collaborators: "This is the continuation of the old liberalism, and not the beginning of the new liberty; these are epilogues, not prologues. These men cannot organize as you would like because one organizes oneself on the basis not of a vague sympathy, but of a profound, active thought—where is it? Where is the progress since the Mountain of '92? These men are the Bourbons of the revolution: they have learned nothing."

The only member of the committee whom Herzen singled out was Arnold Ruge, "whom I know well and whom I respect." However, Ruge, the well-known Hegelian atheist, had signed the committee's first document, a proclamation "that speaks in the name of God and Providence." Who could read this "without an ironical smile?" Herzen asked. "This concession is a matter of diplomacy, of politics—our enemies' methods," and useless to boot.

In attacking Ruge's adherence to the deism of the committee's statements, Herzen was indirectly criticizing Mazzini himself, for the fuzzy religiosity that permeated the committee's propaganda was the Italian's own, and Herzen almost certainly was aware of this.

Herzen confined his specific criticism to this issue of religion and hypocrisy, in an attack that dodged the main issue. He must have known that it was not Ruge, but Ledru-Rollin, whose presence on the committee both aroused the most serious controversy and also pushed revolutionary internationalism away from the socialism that Herzen espoused.

The enmity between Louis Blanc and Ledru-Rollin (which went back to the revolutionary period, when the then minister of the interior had sounded the tocsin against the April 16 workers' demonstration) divided the French exiles, even though most of the leaders agreed on the need to create a united front against Napoleon III. Blanc attempted to coordinate the socialists and spread out a network that reached as far as Nauvoo, Illinois, where the communist Étienne Cabet had retreated to a utopian colony. Cabet, however, while generally supporting Blanc, mourned the divisions within the French opposition (of which Blanc's effort was a symptom, though Cabet did not say so):

> it is not autocracy that kills democracy, but democracy that is committing suicide in continuing its divisions. What a depressing spectacle it has presented since the February Revolution, as before it! How many scandalous hostilities among its leaders recently! how our enemies must rub their hands.... Nonetheless, like you, I think that we must neither despair, nor cease to work for our deliverance.... I see only one means: that is to unite, to organize, to discipline ourselves, to march together.[45]

The high-minded Barbès was another who felt that the continuing conflict crippled the opposition to Napoleon; from his prison, he requested George Sand to act as mediator between Blanc and Ledru-Rollin.[46] She contemplated a trip to London to speak directly to the principals, but ultimately merely wrote to Blanc, urging him "to display a patience, a spirit of conciliation and fraternity superior to discussions of principles."[47] Blanc responded with a set of minimum demands for cooperation, but these did no more than crystallize the disagreement.[48]

Ledru-Rollin's presence on the Mazzini's European Central Democratic Committee, coming as it did in the middle of the former minister's ongoing conflict with Blanc, extended the conflict to the new international enterprise. Blanc himself made sure that Barbès, the would-be conciliator, knew how coldly the left had been excluded:

> You have learned, no doubt, that L[edru-Rollin], along with Mazzini, who is no more a socialist than he, has formed a so-called Central European Committee, on his own authority, and with no electoral mandate. Leaving aside the character of usurpation that sullies the formation of the committee, and the antisocialist color that it has given to its first publications, you should also know that all this was surrounded with the deepest mystery. Not only were ... all the socialists of the emigration not asked for our view, but they even kept it a calculated secret from us. This was accomplished so effectively that we learned of the matter only ... after it was done, although Landolphe and I see Mazzini almost every day and dine at the same table as M[artin] B[ernard], your friend and mine.[49]

Even the moderate Sand was shocked by Mazzini's alliance with Ledru-Rollin; like Herzen, she charged that Mazzini was mistakenly sacrificing principle to politics: "You believe that an entirely political association between several men who represent the republican situation, such as it may be for the moment, is a duty for you. You do it, you "overcome your repugnance" (you wrote me that . . .), you believe finally, that there is nothing else to be done. Perhaps there is nothing else to be done, but is that a reason to do this? That is the question?"[50]

Meanwhile, Blanc himself was also reaching beyond his compatriots, to the British radicals, looking for support and favorable publicity. Thus, he promised to inform George Holyoake of the radical *Leader* about the activities of his "Association," "not only to serve our cause but also for your sake."[51] Victor Hugo's correspondence provides a tantalizing hint that a year later Blanc was attempting to establish his own broad-based, but socialist-oriented, international organization. Hugo wrote to his wife: "They have brought me a *confidential* letter from Louis Blanc. They are going to establish in London a weekly, French-language journal. The committee will be composed of three French, three Germans, and three Italians. I would be one of the three French, along with Louis Blanc and Pierre Leroux."[52]

The European Central Democratic Committee exacerbated conflicts in the German colony, as well as among the French. The group affiliated with the committee, the German National Democratic Committee, was ideologically moderate; it included, in addition to Ruge, Gottfried Kinkel, the Bonn democrat and mentor of Carl Schurz; Gustav Struve, the Baden hero whom Herzen had found so ridiculous; Ernst Haug, the former Austrian officer; and Johannes Ronge, a leader of the German Catholic movement.[53] Farther to the left were the communists. These were split between those willing to form a common front with the moderates and Marx, who combined a rather moderate strategy with the intransigent refusal to cooperate with any but his own followers. The majority in the Communist League, led by August Willich and Karl Schapper, wished to work with Ruge and the committee; Marx and his followers were totally opposed. This was the issue that completed the rift between Marx and his Cologne opponents (and some of his Cologne allies) of 1848. In a maneuver that he would repeat against Bakunin years later, Marx moved the league's central authority out of the active colony in London to the weak underground in Cologne; there his wishes prevailed, but they

The Crisis

did so in a political vacuum.[54] The London majority and minority would not again attempt to work together.

The Hungarians and radical Poles were less obviously divided, for a single leader so overshadowed each of these colonies that disagreements remained muted. Lajos Kossuth and Stanislas Worcell each enjoyed enough authority not only to dominate his respective group, but also to speak for it in an international forum. For the moment, Kossuth held the Hungarians relatively aloof, while Worcell, despite quite significant ideological differences with Mazzini, brought the Poles into the organization for which the Italian provided the dominant public voice.[55]

The committee's activity was based on the premise that the revolutionary movement was still in progress, suffering only a momentary setback and not a long-term defeat. Its ultimate aim was to coordinate revolutionary activity by the national groups—a task at which it failed completely. More immediately, the committee or groups affiliated with it regularly dispatched propaganda and agents back to the home countries, in order to maintain contact between the exiles and their constituencies and to try to organize local committees.[56]

The European Committee's propaganda mission, in the end, was probably its most important. In addition to using agents to send printed materials back home, it also attempted to establish an exile voice abroad. Ledru-Rollin's biographer wrote that "it had its organ in each language."[57] This was an overstatement; the French paper turned into the committee's major outlet; in addition, Mazzini's own paper, the *Italia del Popolo,* provided an Italian voice. The attempt to reach an English-speaking audience was complex and not entirely successful.

The foundations for English support of the committee were established before 1848, with the formation of internationalist support groups for Mazzini and cooperation between the Italian and Polish exile organizations. Politically and socially, Mazzini's British followers ranged from the radical end of parliamentary liberalism to the moderate end of Chartism. The People's International League, discussed in chapter 3, which institutionalized this support, also extended it to the considerably more radical Polish Democratic Society, or Centralization, led by Worcell and Karl Stolzmann.

One of Mazzini's greatest British admirers and a leader of prerevolutionary organizational efforts was a moderate Chartist engraver and journalist, William Linton. When, in 1849, Linton was invited to participate in a new radical journal, *The Leader*, he eagerly agreed and proceeded to attempt to make of it an outlet for British Mazzinianism.[58] He traveled to Switzerland in the spring of 1850 to see Mazzini and get instructions for his activity on *The Leader*, stopping on the way home in Paris, where the Italian had provided an introduction to Herzen. Linton was to be disappointed, however. *The Leader*'s editorial group simply was not interested in serving as Mazzini's mouthpiece.[59] As early as July 2, 1850, Worcell had realized that Linton's hopes of turning the new magazine into the British arm of the committee were an illusion.[60] Linton soon left *The Leader*, and only a year later was he able to inaugurate a magazine that truly would be the British voice of Mazzinian theory and internationalism, *The English Republic*.[61]

It was the French, however, writing in the lingua franca of all the refugees, who provided the committee's voice—first in *Le Proscrit*, which appeared monthly in July and August 1850, and then in the weekly *La Voix du Proscrit*, which carried on for about one year. The editorial board reflected the journal's international mission. It included, in addition to French journalists, the Poles Darasz, Worcell, and Podolecki, the Viennese Ernst Haug, and Mazzini. According to Worcell, the Polish Democratic Committee was part of the planning and organizational group, and Arnold Ruge would also join.[62] Despite the internationalism of the board, however, this was essentially a French Jacobin paper controlled by Ledru-Rollin's follower Charles Delescluze; its internationalism primarily consisted of printing all the statements of the committee and providing a fairly extensive column covering international events and entitled "Chronique de l'étranger."

Like the French radical tradition from which Ledru-Rollin had emerged, *La Voix du Proscrit* was broad-based programatically; in addition to calling for Jacobin democracy, the paper also advocated nationalized credit and social reform measures. Indeed, one article went so far as to insist that "there is no democracy without socialism, no socialism without revolution."[63] Its most startling ideological innovation was its advocacy of direct democracy, an idea developed and supported by Ledru-Rollin himself.[64] But if its programmatic tolerance was broad, *La Voix du Proscrit*'s acceptance of other politicians was correspondingly narrow. It quarreled first with its confrères still at home, the Mountain, headed by Michel de Bourges.[65] Then it turned on the socialists, especially those in exile, and made public the conflict that had been seething quietly since the committee's foundation. It charged that the narrow-mindedness of the socialists had resulted in the vice of "doctrinairism," which was largely responsible for the fate of democracy in France.[66] Not surprisingly, the journal, far from serving as a unifying force, exacerbated the conflicts among the French left.[67]

Eventually Mazzini himself was involved in the conflict, which turned into an ugly repudiation of French socialism by the leader most identified with the policies of the European Committee. In February 1852, in a speech to his moderate English supporters, the Friends of Italy, Mazzini praised the Italian revolution of 1848, in which he had played so important a role, for its moderation: "They were not atheists, unbelievers or skeptics—they were not anarchists, the destroyers of authority, the followers of Proudhon, the Mephistopheles of democracy—nor were they terrorists. . . . Their object was not to suppress, but to improve—not to transplant the activity and comfort of one class to another, but to open wide the hand of activity and comfort to all—not to enthrone their own individual ideas, but to afford free scope to all ideas, and under the guidance of the best and the wisest to think, feel and legislate for themselves."[68]

In March 1852, *Le Nation* of Belgium printed an attack by Mazzini on French socialists,[69] and in English the leader who was at the time planning an armed insurrection against socialist resistance wrote bitterly:

> Mere talkers have destroyed France, and they will destroy Europe, if a holy reaction is not got up against them. . . . By dint of discussing on the future, we have abandoned the present to the first-comer. By dint of substituting each his little sect, his little system, his little organization of humanity, for the common faith, for the association of forces to make a conquest of the position, we have thrown disorganization into the ranks. The sacred phalanx which ought to press forward always as a single man, drawing closer together at each martyr's death, has become an assemblage of free corps, a veritable camp of Wallestein [sic], minus the genius of the master. . . . The enemy was one, discussing nothing but acting always, and it is not by arguing on the best means of cutting and clipping human kind to a fixed standard that the foe can be dislodged. The time has come to speak the truth plainly to our friends. They have done all the evil possible to the best of causes; they would have killed it by excess of love or by want of intelligence, if it was not immortal. I accuse the socialists . . . of having falsified, mutilated, diminished our grand idea, by impris-

oning our law, common for all, within absolute systems, which usurp at the same time power over the sovereignty of the country, and over the continuity of progress.[70]

Even those French socialists who were not wholly in disagreement with Mazzini were stunned by the attack: Thoré wrote privately:[71]

> I approve Mazzini's general sentiment on the unity of the European revolution, on the necessity for action, on the critique of the February Revolution, which accomplished nothing, on the initiative that belongs to all while the French sleep.... But I differ with Mazzini in his negation of socialism ... and also on his love for authority and his dictatorial instinct in the Napoleonic tradition. In my view, the revolution should not use the methods of Cavaignac and Bonaparte.

Thoré hoped that the entire French emigration could draw together to respond to Mazzini's charges, but in the end it was the socialists who answered the Italian. First they responded to the nature of his attack on them. "For a man who up to the very day of the battle was allied with the socialists," they wrote,

> violently to attack the socialists on the day after that battle had been lost; to waste on them, the oppressed, the hatred due to their oppressors; and in the very heart of the party, to fan the flames of discord which a common disaster might have extinguished; and all this by recriminations devoid of justice, and incapable of usefulness, without a pretext, without an excuse; thus to stir up a civil war among fellow-exiles in proscription, and to mingle a voice, which had hitherto given itself out as one of our own, with that odious concert of anathemas, in which the people's enemies vent all their fury; this is the office which M. Mazzini has undertaken to fulfill.

The socialists defended the moral purpose of their ideology against the charge that theirs was an appeal to purely material interests rather than to high-minded idealism. Finally, they publicly leveled charges against Mazzini that came from his own opponents within the Italian movement: that his conspiratorial methods endangered others while he remained safe in London; that experience had shown him to be a bungler when he did act; that he was an incompetent ideologist. Finally, the French socialists felt he should confine himself to the struggle for Italian unification, instead of attempting to assign roles to other nations in an international movement and behaving like a Caesar.[72]

British journals soon reflected the dispute. *The Reasoner* published pro-Mazzini statements by Linton, who also supported his friend in *The English Republic*. Meanwhile, Holyoake tried to find a middle ground in *The Reasoner* and gradually brought *The Leader* around to a prosocialist position. Even Ruge, the German representative on the European Committee, was pleased when *The Leader* finally came out against Mazzini, "Linton and other melodramatic democrats."[73] Personal as well as political relations were disrupted; although Blanc and Mazzini themselves were able eventually to patch up their quarrel, Mazzini's closest English supporters felt the need to choose sides. After the quarrel, wrote an English admirer of Mazzini, Louis Blanc "entered no house of ours or of our belongings since."[74]

This dispute did not directly concern the European Committee, which had been reduced to a very shadowy existence by the time it broke out. But during its heyday, in 1851, its own manifestos had combined ideological broadness with the preachiness that had irritated Herzen and with a revolutionary activism inspired by Mazzini's recklessness. They also contained the antisocialist code words that Mazzini would translate in 1852, although the potential dispute was still muted.

Throughout its statements, the committee insisted that the reactionary setback was both temporary and useful, for it had compelled the democratic forces to unite. "The task of the persecutors—which consisted of watering the idea with blood so that it would grow more quickly—is fulfilled; what will be their role in the world henceforth? Like all the scourges of God, they have only to disappear. What does their apparent triumph matter? Like the legendary knight of the Middle Ages, they walk, they still fight, and yet they are dead!"[75]

The committee's raison d'être was the assumption that a successful revolution must be international. The great task was to provide the revolutionary movement with an organization hitherto lacking, and this would be possible only when it had overcome its two great faults: exaggerating individual rights at the expense of duties, and "doctrinairism." The slogan of the committee was liberty, equality, fraternity and association; the details would come with experience.[76] Meanwhile, international solidarity was a duty imposed on all the liberation movements, and the various actors of 1848 were castigated for their failures of international mutual support.[77] This stress on the moral obligations and responsibilities of national groups, together with a refusal to acknowledge political reality, served to alienate almost every radical thinker who could not see a way to use the committee for the benefit of his own organization. Herzen, in his isolation, kept his distance, while the French socialists raged and Marx mocked the enterprise.

In its faith in the undifferentiated revolutionary "people," the committee was unable to devise much of a revolutionary strategy. The one positive recommendation—and it is one that Herzen would echo a few years later—was a call to the multinational armies of the despotic states, especially Austria and Russia, to mutiny; the soldiers should either rise in revolt, desert with arms, or, if all else failed, martyr themselves by refusing to fire on the opposing army.[78]

The other tactic, not specifically discussed on the pages of *La Voix du Proscrit* but publicly defended by Mazzini elsewhere,[79] was "action," that is, recourse to armed revolution, prepared by conspiracy. Mazzini's revolutionism was well known, and it was this that gave him and his committee notoriety among the police forces of the European states. The myth of international revolution, if not created by Mazzini, was certainly greatly furthered by him. An expression of the fears that the archconspirator aroused in the minds of government officials was made by the Lyons *procureur-général*, for example, who was frustrated by Swiss reluctance to allow the French to pursue "anarchists" across the borders:

> Mazzini's presence [in Geneva] is bearing fruit. The journal *L'Italia del Popolo* which had ceased to appear last summer, due to lack of funds, at the moment when Mazzini left for England, reappeared a few days ago. The first issue contains an article by Mazzini on democracy, its organizations, and its *official acts*. These official acts are the proclamations that emanate from the great machine of the central committee of European Democracy, composed of Mazzini Ledru-Rollin, Arnold Ruge and Darasz, and from the Italian National Committee. . . . A proclamation of the Italian National Committee. . . . speaks of the loan, the funds from which must serve for the *purchase of military supplies for the moment when the political circumstances of Europe, incalculable and unforeseen, will provide the occasion for insurrection.* . . . This is surely a new situation in history, . . . [when] a party gathered from revolutionaries of several nations is constituted thus in the middle of Europe, without being stopped by the powers, as a sort of government, with its official acts, making preparations for war, levying finances and an army, promising general insurrection.[80]

The authorities did not stop at an exaggerated view of the menace presented by the committee; they also consistently broadened its base, and moved it to the left. Thus, in February 1851, the Besançon *procureur-général*, describing the nest of French refugees in Switzerland, stated that they were in contact with "M. Arney, Secrétaire général de l'Association chartiste anglaise."[81] The reference is to George Harney, who was indeed deeply committed to revolutionary internationalism, but through the Fraternal Democrats, a group that cooperated with Marx and was far to the left of Linton and his pro-Mazzinian Friends of Italy.

If the French charged Switzerland with harboring dangerous refugees, both France and the German states made the same charges with regard to Great Britain. Again, the continental authorities expressed concern that London and/or Jersey had become the headquarters for international revolutionary conspiracy. Describing the "Central Committee of the European Republic," the police chief of Saxony, Eberhardt, wrote: "It appears in the most unequivocal manner from the contents of several correspondences, either intercepted or seized in the possession of different agents or emissaries, that from London itself they were increasingly working to bring about an overthrow of all existing government and the establishment of one common socialist republic, even England itself is included."

According to the Saxons, large numbers of radicalized German workers had been recruited to leave their homeland and come to Britain to proselytize the English workers. The Central Committee was described as being "in connection with the decided revolutionary party in England, France and Hungary," with contacts extending to the "properly proletarian [German] party" and the French Blanquistes. The German on the European Central Democratic Committee, Arnold Ruge, "along with Mazzini and Ledru-Rollin is one of the most exalted and persevering revolutionists, and therefore everything is to be feared from him." As well as generally pressuring the British goverment to act against the refugees, the German police chief asked that he be provided with the names of German refugees in England.[82] In one police report, originating in Paris, but finding its way into Moses Hess's German dossier, even Herzen—along with Hess, Herwegh, and Vogt, among others—were associated vaguely with what may have been a reference to a misunderstood European Central Democratic Committee.[83]

The British authorities, less inclined to political hysteria, did investigate the reports, but consistently dismissed the notion that bloody revolution was imminent.[84] As far as the committee itself was concerned, the most reliable British agent, Jonathan Sanders, reported:

> There is now only one democratic committee in existence, who [sic] has been established now nearly 3 years. The principle members are Ledru-Rollin, Caussidière, Louis Blanc, Ribeyrolle [sic], Landolfe [sic], Martin Bernard, Arago, Mazzini, Ronge, and others. That is the only committee capable of sending such [incendiary] proclamations to France. They have correspondents in every department of France and several of them are writers to the newspapers in France. Their private meetings are watched, as often as the circumstances will permit, but never was heard the [violent] cries alluded to . . . and their proclamations *known* are generally moderate, though certainly against the government.[85]

The list of men ascribed to the committee by Sanders shows that even a fluent French speaker who had apparently infiltrated some at least of the refugee organizations was unable to sort out French exile politics. On the positive side, Sanders certainly did help the British police establishment maintain a balanced, nonhysterical view of the revolutionary threat.

Although fears of an imminent universal socialist upheaval were the stuff of nightmare, this does not mean that Mazzini and others were not actively pursuing this dream of revolution, either by individual national groups or in cooperation with like-minded fellow refugees. Kossuth too hoped for an insurrection. In 1851 he made a triumphant fund-raising tour to the United States and returned to England with $96,000; three-quarters of that was spent on arms. At the end of October 1851, he and Mazzini did decide to attempt coordinated uprisings in Hungary, Lombardy, and Venetia.[86] In 1852, Sanders reported that the Jersey French exiles had also been brought in; a forthcoming exile invasion of France was to be aided with arms and ammunition provided by Mazzini and Kossuth. In the event the uprising succeeded, the revolutionary French government in its turn would aid the Italian and Hungarian democratic revolutions.[87]

Whatever the ultimate plans of the French, there appears to have been no attempt actually to put them into operation. Also, it seems likely that Sanders got some important facts wrong, for in his report he refers to cooperation between Mazzini and the French socialists—those same socialists who had been engaged in such bitter dispute

The Crisis

with him a few months earlier. It is more likely that the socialists refused to collaborate in the plan, thus evoking the Italian's anger, and that his Jersey supporters were from an ideologically more moderate and less clearly defined group. (Sanders mentioned no names except those of the Victor Hugo family, whom he described as opposed to the venture: "Victor Hugo and his sons cannot calm them, excited as they are with the hope of revenge.")

Indeed, even before this report was filed, Hugo, speaking on behalf of colleagues, had personally attempted to dissuade Mazzini from rash, revolutionary actions. And while the Italians in London continued loyally to support Mazzini in all his ventures, compatriots outside Britain had begun to question him; some of this doubt was reflected in the socialists' response to Mazzini's attacks on them, cited above. The Piedmont colony was opposed to this latest revolutionary attempt; when Alexander Herzen arrived in London in the late summer, he carried this message from Piedmont to Mazzini.[88] And Kossuth, while apparently not telling the Italian that the Hungarian revolution was off, did nothing to further it.

Despite the lack of enthusiasm around the rest of the European exile community, Mazzini went ahead with his plans. In February 1853, an uprising he had organized broke out at Milan. Mazzini addressed the rebels in the language of a blazing internationalism:

> The entire surface of Europe, from Spain to our own land, from Greece to holy Poland, is a volcanic crust, beneath which sleeps a lava which will burst forth in torrents at the upheaving of Italy. Four years ago the insurrection of Sicily was followed by ten European Revolutions; twenty European revolutions will follow yours.—All bound by one compact, all sworn to one fraternal aim. We have friends even in the ranks of the armies who rule us; there are entire peoples whose alarum-cry will answer yours. The national democracies of Europe form one organized camp. Vanguard of the great army of the people, Fear not isolation. The initiative of Italy is the initiative of Europe.[89]

The uprising was easily suppressed, there was no European echo, and even among his British supporters Mazzini lost credibility. It was the last, pitiful reflection of the 1848 revolution; and its failure was also the failure of nonsocialist revolutionary internationalism. Herzen, as we have seen, far from supporting the position, came as a herald of its demise.

Herzen and the London Exiles

The political turmoil in the émigré community canceled out any possibility of Herzen joining one of the mutually squabbling groups. What could he, a Russian socialist, gain from the insurrectionists of the European Central Democratic Committee with their dreams of conspiracies and successful democratic revolutions? The parochial quarrels of the French did not interest him; and he found the German moderates sentimental and foolish, while the autocratic Dr. Marx was already, sight unseen, on the other side of a barrier.

Only the Poles, who at least had a common enemy in the autocracy of Nicholas I and who had spent decades establishing networks for smuggling information out of and propaganda into the Empire, seemed possible allies. But the Poles could only be allies, not comrades in arms; Herzen, just because he sympathized with the cause of Polish independence, could not, as a Russian, be a part of their struggle any more than they could be part of his.

Herzen realized soon after his arrival in London that his mission was to Russia; the first indication is in a letter to Mariia Reichel: "An amazing project is turning around in my head—to undertake agitation for the liberation of the peasants."[90] By early February 1853, he was attempting to collect material from Russia on the peasant question for what would be the Free Russian Press, which he established with the cooperation of Worcell and the Polish Centralization.[91] In March, the press announced itself to the world; it is time, Herzen told his countrymen, for Russian works to be printed freely outside Russia and for Herzen himself to turn away from attempts to explain Russia to foreigners and to return to his native tongue. The Poles would provide transportation, and it was up to the Russians to provide material. "I am not as ardent and hopeful as I was when you liked my work," he told his friends, "but those convictions which remained have grown stronger. Meet me like a returned soldier, who has become older, been wounded, but who has honorably held to his banner, both in prison and in foreign lands, and with your former unlimited love give me your hand in our old union in the name of Russian and Polish freedom"[92]

But if his work henceforth would be Russian, his life would be European. Whatever their political differences, the émigrés rallied around Herzen in his bereavement, and, as will be discussed in the next chapter, some of the most prominent supported him in his struggle with Herwegh. In Turin and in Switzerland, friends were there to help him. When he arrived in London late in August 1852, in the company of Mazzini's friend Ernst Haug, Mazzini made him welcome, as did the Italian leader's English friends. Through Gottfried Kinkel he met Malwida von Meysenbug, who would be his daughters' governess for several years and would serve as a second mother to the younger one, Ol'ga. As long as Malwida was part of the ménage, contacts with the German colony were numerous.[93] Among the French, Louis Blanc became a good friend. Even at his most isolated, Herzen was surrounded by people to whom he was linked by the situation of exile; since he was not attempting to collaborate with them, differences in political ideologies rarely mattered.

Herzen brought to the refugees his personality, hospitality, and also his money. He contributed to all their subscription funds, he hired members of the exile community to work for him as teachers, physicians, and secretaries, and he helped find positions for others. And although he considered that his primary mission was to Russia, he continued to play an important role as interpreter of Russia to the West. Much was done by word of mouth; his contacts were numerous, and Herzen was voluble. He also continued to publish to a limited extent in Western languages, particularly French. The segments of *Byloe i dumy* that began to appear in the late 1850s were quickly translated, bringing Herzen to a fairly wide audience. Moreover, his stature was such that his Russian work was brought to the attention of the European public by specialist authors.[94]

Although Herzen turned back to Russia for his audience after 1851, he did so as not merely a Russian, but as a member of the international radical community. His program was uniquely Russian, and much of his ideology was unique as well; however, they evolved within the context of European radicalism. The international community provided him not only with material aid, but also with the authority to speak as part of a functioning political movement. Herzen's characteristic double focus on individual freedom and social justice made him an appropriate intermediary between the worlds of European radicalism and Russian revolution.

8

THE REVOLUTIONARY COMMUNITY

THROUGHOUT this work there have been frequent references to the "revolutionary" or "radical" community. This chapter will explore the meaning of this notion, and how its contents changed for Herzen in consequence of his own experiences.

The roots of Herzen's participation in the radical community go back to the Moscow circle. That closed little universe provided an environment in which values opposed to those reigning in the larger community could be fostered and nourished. The circle, and comfortable economic circumstances, enabled the members simply to opt out of some aspects of Russian life—they did not serve in the military and rarely in the civil service, thus avoiding both the service ethos and the bureaucratic mentality characteristic of most men of their class.

The circle also provided an alternative value system for those areas of adult life from which the members did not wish to isolate themselves, namely marriage and the family. It helped them replace the teachings of Christianity and the practice of the marriage market with a set of values that derived from utopian socialism, filtered, for the most part, through the works of George Sand.

The fundamental proposition regarding family life adopted by the circle members was the acceptance of women as truly human and equal to themselves. A number of corollaries flowed from this axiom. They supported education for women, so that their human qualities could become manifest. They sought companionate marriages, and believed women had the same right to friendship, companionship, and sexual gratification as did their husbands. They scorned marriages of convenience and the oppression of women, and tried, with only limited success, to do better.[1]

Once they were married and had become parents, circle members found it necessary to determine how to protect their own children

The Revolutionary Community

from the social values that they had already rejected in their own lives. Thus, the Herzens' concern for their children's education is an indicator of their alienation from prevailing social values. They could not be sent to schools, since the parents did not accept the schools' aims in socialization. Both Herzen and Natalie had themselves been educated at home, but in neither case had that experience represented a satisfactory alternative; Herzen had been subjected to a motley set of teachers with widely differing value systems, none of which were consonant with his father's ideals and actions—themselves not in harmony. Natalie had received a limited lady's education—French, needlework, and religion—which was not suited for the open, equal life demanded by the circle's ideology.[2] They would have to do a better job with their own children.

During her lifetime, Natalie was the parent predominantly concerned with the children's development and education. That this concern was not entirely maternal, but also had a prophylactic element, she made clear in describing her response to the revolution of 1848: "Looking at the children, I thought: Lucky ones! You will pass by all the contradictions through which life pushed us, as through a gauntlet, and from the wounds of which we would still not be healed, had it not been for this great transformation. . . . My mournful concern with education is ended—now schools will be founded on new bases; they will give you good nourishment, you will grow, develop freely, you will be good and your life will be good!"[3]

The need to provide the children with an ideologically consistent education explains Herzen's habit, already noted, of hiring tutors from within the radical camp—a practice that also helped provide jobs for the often needy radicals. After Herzen moved to London in 1852, when he had full responsibility for the now adolescent Sasha, he engaged a whole roster of tutors who were also a good sample of the radical émigré world: Hermann Müller-Strübing, Herzen's first German radical contact, for Latin and German; Ernst Haug for English: Louis Bulewsky, "escapee from . . . the prisons of Posnania," for drawing; Louis Vasbenter, an old colleague from *La Voix du peuple*, for French; Domagalsky, a military engineer active in the Polish Democratic Society, for mathematics; and Herzen himself took on the role of tutor for history.[4]

Herzen was also concerned that his daughters be properly educated, both academically and politically. After the girls joined him in 1853, he chose as Tata's governess Malwida von Meysenbug, a woman who was exceptional in seeking out and inhabiting the radical community on her own as a single woman. She had broken with her family, moved about Germany for personal and political reasons, and finally taken the hard road to exile. She was also a professional, progressive teacher, and had studied educational theory and taught in a progressive school in Germany. Herzen, more traditional than she, felt her training of the girls in deportment was lax, but he had nothing but admiration for her moral influence.[5] He later encouraged his older daughter to develop either her art or her music into a career, but in this he failed; as her father said, "She will not be a Rosa Bonheur, but she will have *'les bonheurs et les roses'* of a human development."[6] Not entirely consistent with his feminism, Herzen felt that this, while not ideal, was enough for a woman; on the other hand, he insisted that his son pursue a serious career.[7]

Herzen, Herwegh, and a Socialist Moral Code

When Herzen first arrived in the West, he had been a wealthy, sociable, sophisticated man of the world who mixed most easily with people of his own social background. His attempt to create a personal life on basis different from those prevailing in his class and country did not markedly set him apart. His cosmopolitanism and fluency in two European languages were useful preparation for exile life, but at the time they were simply part of the equipment a man of his background would be expected to carry. The experiences of the next five years would cause him to move from his old world into the new community of radicalism.

Between 1847 and 1850, his social life broadened, as he became acquainted—and in some cases made friends—with a segment of international radicalism; the number of his contacts increased even as repression limited their potential for effective action. At the same time, he was almost entirely cut off from contact with Russians after the autumn of 1848. (The last remaining nonémigré Russian was Turgenev, who returned home early in 1850.) In 1850, disillusioned by the radicals and largely by his own choice, he narrowed in again to the few people with whom he was intimate—his family and the Herweghs. He did not break with the other radicals; indeed, he continued to broaden his acquaintance, but he kept them at a considerable, formal distance.

Throughout these first years in the West, there was no need for any great change or development in the value system he had brought with him from Moscow. The test of his principles, and a turn to the radicals as a community in an effort to enforce them, would come in 1852, as a result of the tangled relationships between the Herzen and Herwegh families.

The principles of socialist morality were first strained by the crisis in the Herwegh marriage. This couple was bound together by strong, but conflicting, forms of dependency. Emma's devotion to her husband meant that for her maintaining the marriage took priority over almost everything else. She had learned to live with Georg's infidelity, and at least one of his early mistresses, Marie d'Agoult, had become Emma's friend and supporter.[8] Georg, on the other hand, was hopelessly impractical and relied completely on his wife to manage all aspects of their household. Throughout the marriage, they had also been financially dependent on Emma's family; Georg's readiness to separate in 1850 may have been due in part to the loss of Siegmund family funds.

Once embarked on his affair with Natalie Herzen, Herwegh found his marriage and the obligations it entailed burdensome. Physically separated from his family when the relationship began, he had no desire to return to Paris and Emma, and made excuses for remaining in Geneva with the Herzens instead. His letters to his wife became infrequent and casual. Gradually he came to the conclusion that he did not wish to return to Emma, but he never was able to make a definitive breach and ask to end the marriage.

When Herzen arrived in Paris in late December 1849, he found Emma distraught. He wrote to Georg charging him with irresponsibility toward her. "I found Emma very sad; she is deeply distressed—it is not purely and simply the separation which afflicts her; she (and many others) believe that the visa [for Georg's return to France, which could not be obtained] is not all that necessary—so you see that she has to explain everything by an absence of active love, etc. etc. This has led her to think and reflect, and . . . so she has come to rebel ever so slightly against Your Dominion."[9]

In the next few days, the situation got worse; Georg forgot his infant son's birthday, and he wrote to Herzen in care of Emma, without enclosing even a note to her. Herzen, forced into the role of consoling and reassuring his friend's wife (not entirely truthfully), angrily accused Herwegh of improper conduct: "Whether a man loves a woman or not is involuntary, and I would never dare touch these oceanic depths of the human soul. But it is another thing not to allow oneself, not even to desire, to be capriciously cruel. The man who thinks that it is enough to love him to bear oppression and lack of consideration, has a defect in his heart. . . . I give no one the right to torture, either by love or by hatred. . . . You have taken something which you ought to have rejected as an element unworthy of you, and elevated it to the height of a theory."[10]

Herwegh, not surprisingly, resented what he considered interference in his personal life; he insisted that despite his love for Emma, the bonds of family life had become entirely too burdensome, and he demanded another year's separation. "You are fortunate," he told Herzen, "that your head is always in the right place. . . . I lose mine sometimes, and then I don't understand anything. The anarchy of the external world reaches even inside me. I expect the same will happen to you one day. . . . I have shaken off the dust of the family for some time, not because I don't love, but because this infamous institution is the best means of not being able to love even the most noble, devoted, generous and loving thing in the world, a beautiful and great nature like Emma."[11]

Herzen reiterated his belief that a person had the right to free himself of a burdensome attachment, or even "to remain free for several months." But he still felt that Herwegh had failed to give his wife the explanation demanded by "simple humanity." "You think that you can tell a woman, 'Wait a year, and I will again permit you to love me,' but that is tyranny. Instead, tell her that you want to remain alone, to focus your thoughts; she will understand that."[12]

The issue of Herwegh's responsibility was never really resolved. He finally agreed to see Emma; she went to Zurich in March, when he confessed the affair with Natalie to her. Upon her return to Paris, she had become, however unwillingly, an accomplice and thus no longer could voice her resentment to Herzen.

Incomplete and inconclusive as was the exchange between the two men, it did clarify two fundamental propositions. First, there could be no coercion of the emotions, or the behavior, of a marriage partner. Herzen agreed that if his friend wished to terminate the relationship with Emma, it was legitimate for him to do so. It was also legitimate for him to withdraw from her for a time. She had no proprietary rights over him, not he over her. Second, there was the problem of the injured party. Herzen might assert that Emma would "understand" a temporary separation, and perhaps she would have done; but such understanding would not have eased her pain or healed her wounded pride.

In this period, before he realized why Herwegh was neglecting his wife, Herzen was the only one of the four to analyze the situation from what he thought was a disinterested standpoint. Nonetheless, the same propositions held when the affair betweeen Natalie and Georg was viewed from the inside by the lovers. Moreover, Herzen continued to defend them later, when it had become evident to him that he too was a deeply injured partner.

Only Natalie's side of the affair itself survives; she destroyed Georg's letters, while he, and later his family, carefully preserved hers, despite her regular pleas to "BURN THIS LETTER!" She felt that her love for Herwegh was justification enough for her conduct. She wrote defiantly about her "purity" shortly after initiating the affair, and it became a leitmotif in the letters she sent to her lover. And she wrote to her husband only a month before the couple's final reconciliation: "I feel myself to be completely pure. I could not be different, I always acted out of the complete fullness of my soul."[13]

On the other hand, she regretted the grief caused to Emma, and once the revelation had taken place she was profoundly saddened by her husband's pain. Compassion was involved in her return to Herzen in 1850, when she thought this would terminate the affair; it was one of the motives in her refusal to tell him of it, and in the first period after the break with Herwegh, it was also one of the ties that continued to bind her to him. Enlightened socialist mores might resolve some problems, but there was no way to avoid contradictory and conflicting emotional demands.

Thus despite Herzen's rage and grief, it was not he but the Herwegh couple who made the first accusations of a breach of revolutionary morality. Emma charged Natalie with hypocrisy for refusing to make a commitment to Georg. Once she had learned that Natalie had no intention of leaving Herzen, she told the other woman, "I no longer understood anything; I believed this was only an exaltation, and not a love. . . . My heart did not understand this dualism, did not understand how a woman whom Georg loved, for whom he could forget our love, could carry the child of one in her heart, and write love letters to the other."

After the break, Emma called on Natalie either to go with Georg, and make him happy, or else persuade him to take his wife back.[14] She justified her request that Natalie leave her own husband for

Emma's by portraying herself as a martyr to the new morality: "[I have] had to support a widowhood of three years, with all the sad and terrible occasions for humiliation and calumny. . . . [I have] allowed [my] heart to be torn out piece by piece without succumbing, with the *sole* aim of avoiding as much ill as possible, and of buying a solution in honor of the *truth*, of *complete liberty* [and *of true love—* added in the second draft] at the price of [my] own happiness, [my] own existence, and not of enforcing the conventions imposed by a false society."[15]

Georg, on the other hand, charged Herzen with violating the code by refusing to give his wife the freedom to choose her own life. In January 1852 (a year after the break), Herwegh challenged Herzen to a duel. In direct contradiction to the standards of the surrounding society, he asserted that it was the lover, not the husband, who was the injured party.

The charge, moreover, was a serious one. Herzen, who had no desire for a duel, as we shall see, asked their mutual friend Sazonov to mediate. Sazonov did attempt to dissuade Herwegh from pursuing his plans; he also told Herzen that on the whole he supported him in the conflict. Nonetheless, Sazonov also acknowledged the justice of Herwegh's primary argument; it was wrong, he said, for Herzen to force his wife to remain with him.[16]

Herzen did not respond to Sazonov by asserting his "right" to his wife; instead, he denied that there was any coercion. Moreover, the terminally ill Natalie herself wrote from her sickbed, "I have no need for my husband's magnanimity, in the sense you mean. . . . As a woman returning to her senses after a mad infatuation, and as the wife of your friend, I ask you to join with him and defend me from my enemy."[17]

Herzen began to attempt to apply sanctions against Herwegh only in response to his rival's challenge. In line with the code, he did not consider the affair itself grounds for taking any action, as he acknowledged to Proudhon: "If this had been purely and simply an individual affair, one of those fatal collisions when the passions, once unleashed, drag innocent and guilty to their destruction with the irresponsibility of a thunderbolt, then it would have been no one's business. Then, I would never have suffered any intervention in the case. There was a time when Herwegh's treason, his ignominious conduct, still bore this private character, and so during an entire year no one heard a word from me."[18]

It was only after the affair had ended that Herwegh behaved in a manner that violated the radical code. While on his travels in the summer of 1851, Herzen learned that Herwegh had spoken of the affair to outsiders and had said that Natalie was remaining with Herzen only "for a few months until he calmed down" and then would leave him for her lover.[19] Herzen felt that this intelligence fundamentally altered the situation; Herwegh had now committed at least one, perhaps two, major sins against Herzen's conception of morality. In the first place, he had publicized the scandal; Herzen found this airing of his family's private, and not entirely reputable, activities intolerable. The second issue was the statement imputed to Natalie—if she had been telling Herzen the truth for the past six months, then Herwegh was spreading lies and "calumny" about her.

Herwegh's treatment of her in letters written after the break constituted additional grievances. Herzen described the situation in a letter to Ernst Haug: "In the entire *first* letter he addressed to N., he implored her not to justify herself at his expense, to take all the responsibility; in the following ones threats of scandal, of murder, and astonishing proposals, such as rehabilitating herself in my eyes and then taking him on as tutor for my children, began again."[20]

Still Herzen, involved first in his reconciliation with Natalie, then shattered by his son's death and Natalie's terminal illness, did nothing. He reacted only when Herwegh issued his challenge and, at the same time, compounded the insult by making sure that all his and Herzen's acquaintances knew of it. He had Emma, who had returned to Nice almost a year earlier, spread a rumor of a "terrible letter"[21] he would send to Herzen; Vogt, Orsini, and Chojecki had all been informed of the challenge several days before it actually arrived, and they informed Engel' son. Moreover, Orsini sent a letter detailing the events to Mazzini in London. Thus, the entire affair had, in more or less distorted form, become the common property of the revolutionary community.[22]

Now that the affair had become public, Herzen prepared countermeasures. He rejected his rival's challenge; instead, he would bring him before the bar of the only public opinion that mattered to him—that of the revolutionaries. In doing so, he was taking a major step toward citizenship in the revolutionary community. He was also attempting to clarify and use the tenets of the heretofore largely implicit code of revolutionary morality.

Herzen decided that his enemy should be excommunicated from

the revolutionary congregation. To this end he wrote to Mazzini, in a letter that has been lost, and told the story from his point of view. The request for support by the victimized and bereaved Herzen was transmitted to Mazzini's supporters. It met a sympathetic response from the Italian radicals in Piedmont and from the Austrian rebel general Ernst Haug. The latter wrote Herzen a sympathetic letter expressing admiration for Natalie and her husband so exalted that it no doubt did much to assuage Herzen's injured feelings.[23] He sent Haug a long reply (quoted above) in which, for the first of many times, he gave his side of the story in great detail. This exchange marks the beginning of the friendship and alliance between Herzen and Haug that would last for several years.

Herzen now discovered the need to develop sanctions to enforce the radicals' code. With case and countercase established, he had to consider the appropriate punishment for his enemy. Civil or criminal legal action against a fellow outlaw was unthinkable. He asserted his own view at the same time he attacked Herwegh for threatening to have recourse to the police against Herzen's friends: "Herwegh has denounced us to the police; he has put himself under the protection of gendarmes, thus he understands the solidarity which links him to the police, to the society which owes him protection and assistance. And we others . . . do not accept police justice, . . . are put outside the law . . . and do not wish to re-enter it."[24]

Unable to have recourse to state justice, radicals attempted, without great success, to work out their own techniques. Herwegh had resorted to the most common, if least satisfactory—the duel. The frequency with which duels were threatened or actually fought among the radicals reflects the absence of other mechanisms for resolving disputes among them. Just before Herzen's arrival in London later the same year, the exile community was shocked by the fatal duel between two personal enemies who also represented rival French political factions, Frédéric Cournet and Emanuel Barthélemy. Herzen himself was later nearly challenged by Felice Orsini. Both Barthélemy and Orsini were men of violent temperament. Eventually one was hanged for murder in England, and the other guillotined for attempted regicide in France; they were the sort of men one might expect to find involved in duels.[25] But they were not the only ones to have recourse to this nonlegal manner of settling differences. Proudhon's rather absurd engagement in one has already been mentioned in chapter 5. Yet rational people who were also socialists and democrats could hardly find this remnant of feudalism acceptable. Not only was it a remnant of an obsolete social system, but also it was unable to settle differences of principle, its outcome was arbitrary, and, of course, only males could avail themselves of it.

Herzen had considered, and then decided against, challenging Herwegh in 1851; when challenged himself, he refused to fight. To justify his refusal he would have to redefine the honor supposedly defended by the duel; and to satisfy his own anger he would have to find another form of vengeance.

> The duel would repair nothing; it was stupid, it was a snare; the only person who could rehabilitate himself through a duel was he. As to my honor—I did not think much about it; I wished to punish the scoundrel, to avenge myself, but I was only moderately concerned to defend my honor against him. Frankly, my antecedents—to begin by prison and exile of five years at the frontiers of Siberia, and to end with my expulsion from Paris—have given me if not rights, at least some confidence in myself. If my honor could depend on a traitor, whose antecedents are not less well known then my own, I would wish to be dishonored.[26]

To the aristocrat, honor was defined by birth, and duels could be fought only with persons of equal status. Herzen, an aristocrat himself, here takes this notion and transforms it, while still asserting that his opponent was not worthy of fighting; "honorable antecedents" have become revolutionary exploits, dishonor derived from Herwegh's supposed cowardice in fleeing from the battlefield in Baden.

Herzen, however, went beyond rejecting Herwegh as an opponent; he rejected the duel itself, as an unworthy gauge of revolutionary honor and as a violation of the respect for women that was also part of the radical code: "I wished [by his refusal] . . . to recognize definitively, solemnly, and in reality the liberty of woman. I wished to give all the plenitude of independence to the woman for her to rehabilitate herself. Only imbeciles, minors, and the weak must be defended by others—but this woman is strong, and she is stronger alone."[27]

Thus it was Natalie who condemned her former lover. As soon as she was physically strong enough, she wrote a letter to Herwegh denouncing his conduct and expressing regret that she should have been so deluded about him in the past.[28] Herzen circulated this letter among his radical contacts, and thus it became a semipublic denunciation of the poet at the bar of radical public opinon. This was the first stage of Herzen's vengeance, his alternative to either a duel or legal redress.

Herwegh returned the letter, claiming he had never opened it; Herzen believed that in fact he had read it and replaced the seal. Somehow, this piece of deceit became the capstone of Herzen's case against the poet.[29] After Natalie's death in May, the story of the letter took yet another bizarre turn. Two of Herzen's supporters—acting, according to Herzen, to fulfill Natalie's wish—assaulted the poet in a hotel room in Zurich, insulted him, and forced him to listen to Natalie's letter. They then publicized the event, which probably did do a good deal to undermine Herwegh's reputation. It is unlikely it helped Herzen's much, however, especially since the poet took the opportunity to present his side just as publicly as possible, in long letters to the *Neue Zürcher Zeitung*, published July 18 and August 8, 1852.[30] Herzen replied publicly to the first of these letters on July 27.[31]

The inspiration for the public humiliation of Herwegh seems to have come less from Herzen himself than from Natalie and his friends. Herzen wanted something more formal, some sort of institutionalized condemnation. After Natalie's death, the campaign to activate radical opinion against Herwegh became his sole occupation—he was embarked on a crusade to prove that the radical community did exist, that it did indeed have a moral code, which Herwegh had violated, and that it was the obligation of the community to validate its existence by punishing the man whom Herzen considered his wife's murderer. He clearly justified the need for the radical community to impose sanctions in his letter to Proudhon:

> The democracy to which I belong understands perfectly the solidarity of all for each one and the moral duty to brand traitors. I belong to that new society to which you and your friends belong, I belong to the revolution to which Mazzini and his friends belong, and that is why I was in no way astonished that, regardless of the grave controversies that divide you from Mazzini, you and he have expressed the same opinion in this affair. . . . A new society must have all the ardor of youth, and if it does not feel itself either pure enough or moral enough or strong enough to desire and accomplish the defense of its own against the family scoundrels, it will be condemned to die as a foetus, to pass away without any real existence, as an abstract hope, as a utopian dream.[32]

Herzen traveled first to Genoa, then to Switzerland, and finally to London to canvass opinion and search for retribution. He collected letters that condemned Herwegh and supported his own decision not to fight the duel. In addition to his original supporters—the Italians, Haug, his Nice contacts Vogt and Engel'son, he wrote to outstanding French radicals—Proudhon, Michelet, and Sand. He contacted Richard Wagner, who wanted no part of the business, and the German community in London, which was divided on the question. Meanwhile, Marx and Engels mocked.[33]

English opinion was also solicited, although to what extent Herzen ventured onto this unfamiliar ground is uncertain. The one Englishman with whom Herzen had established contact prior to the crisis, William Linton, never mentioned anything about the scandal, and claimed in his memoirs not to know when Herzen lost his wife. This may, however, have been discretion on his part. Linton's collaborator on *The Leader*, Edward Piggott, received a letter from Haug that shows the campaign in action: "Mr. De Herzen will have the opportunity to explain his own affaire, which is also a general democratic and social one, and to ask your kind assistance for his proposed plan to let the representatives of modern ideas and principles judge how a traitor of human as well as social duties has to be treated."[34] One would like to know the British response to such an appeal.

The form of vindication Herzen sought was condemnation of Herwegh by a "court of honor," an idea which he stated originated with his Italian friends in Nice.[35] The court of honor, a solemn if unofficial tribunal made up of leading members of the radical community, was the one institutional device for resolving conflicts that had developed as an alternative to duels. Normally, a court of honor judged such matters as charges that a revolutionary was a police spy or a government agent or had in some other way acted against the interests of the revolutionary cause.[36] It did not have a tradition of judging personal conduct or enforcing the radical moral code. Therefore Herzen had to argue that Herwegh's conduct had gone beyond personal immorality and had undermined the norms of the community. His position was: "This is in no way an unfortunate tragedy, but a colossal question—a question of the whole revolutionary religion, of all the last hopes for me. Truly, I acknowledge myself as a *new* person. . . . And so I am attempting to punish a malefactor without the old court, without the old single combat—by the force of democratic opinion alone." Failure, he feared, would be "a microscopic proof, that not only on a large scale, but even on the pettiest, democracy is sterile and incompetent.[37]

Those radicals who shared the sense of community sympathized with Herzen, but they were also embarrassed by the airing of such private matters and were not willing to take the steps Herzen envisioned. Thus, Michelet was tactful and sympathetic. He accepted Herzen's basic premise, stating that the radicals constituted a "democratic church" with the right to excommunicate its erring members. He suggested, however, that it would be time for this church to weed out sinners after the revolution had triumphed.[38] By implication, nothing could be done in the here and now. Sand, with whom Herzen was not personally acquainted, appears not to have answered his letter at all.[39]

The attempt to have Herwegh formally condemned met with resistance even within his closest circle of friends. Karl Vogt eagerly, even maliciously, pursued the Herwegh couple on Herzen's behalf. His primary aim was to protect Natalie's reputation by gaining control of her letters. In the ultimately unsuccessful attempt to persuade the Herweghs to give up the letters, he did his best to blacken their reputation among their fellow radicals. He also attempted to use financial pressure, urging Emma's family to cut off all support unless the letters were turned over. He felt, however, that the public pursuit of vengeance merely added to everyone's embarrassment and hindered him in his task.[40]

Herzen did receive strong statements of sympathetic support from a cosmopolitan sprinkling of radicals: Mazzini, Kinkel, Willich, and Proudhon. Only Proudhon's response has survived, and it was all that Herzen could have hoped; it touched on so many of the themes Herzen was trying to develop that it deserves extensive citation. Beginning with outrage at Herwegh's conduct, Proudhon went on to a consideration of Herzen's response:

> I understand that in your first horror you did not crush the coward who so abused hospitality and friendship. That moment passed, I no longer assume that it is up to you to render justice. I approve, therefore, all that you and your friends have done; only I believe not enough has been done. Everyone in Europe who professes the ideas of social renovation has the right to consider himself henceforth a member of a superior society, whose first prerogative is the right of justice in regard to all the individuals who compose it. Therefore, why should we not . . . have our own holy *Wehm* for

the facts which concern us; it would be charged with vengeance for crimes which endanger our oath of progress and fraternity. A scoundrel abused the title of democrat, socialist, and revolutionary for ten years; he enjoyed the popularity attached to these titles; . . . this imposter will get off with only moral stigma that makes the old world laugh, leaves the culprit's skin untouched, and leaves him the entire enjoyment of his crime. . . . Against such outrages there is no recourse, neither justice, nor laws, nor vengeance among men.

Listen, Herzen, you may inform whomever you wish of what I have just said to you.

I inscribe my name the first on the list of true reformers who are resolved to resist tyranny by all useful means, and for that I do not hesitate before the formation of a tribunal of *franc juges*.

I consign Herwegh, cowardly suborner, faithless friend, traitor to honor and hospitality to shame and punishment. I pledge for my part that as soon as the *association wehmique* is constituted, to pursue the extermination of the said Herwegh by all the means in my power, and to strike him, without according him any reparation, and if I can, I will kill him.

It is time, my dear friend, for European democracy, reformist and revolutionary, to become something more than an empty word. We have the appearance of a coterie, of a coalition of coteries, cooperating to usurp, each in its own country, the bar of government, and to exploit in our turn the miserable humans. What then is our protestation, if finally it is not supported by acts? As long as the popular masses are not decidedly with us, perhaps we do not have the right to act harshly—by secret justice—against their tyrants; we must admit the sad necessities of humanitarian education. But the false brothers, the traitors, who sell us out, or, still worse, dishonor us, shall we leave them unpunished!. . . . No, no, it is impossible. For myself I accept neither this inconsequence nor this indignity.[41]

But for all its fervor, Proudhon's letter did not indicate how an "association wehmique" was to be constituted, and this, indeed, was an insuperable problem. Among Herzen's most devoted supporters were the Italians living in Piedmont, spread between Nice and Genoa. They wrote a joint letter that supported his refusal to fight Herwegh on the grounds that the poet was not worthy to fight a duel, but even they did not support any more formal condemnation.[42] They argued that they could not constitute themselves as a court, since only one party in the dispute acknowledged their jurisdiction.[43]

Unable to achieve the formal condemnation he was seeking, Herzen made do with the support he did have, interpreting it as tantamount to a court of honor. The letters he had collected amounted in themselves to a court, he claimed, and Herwegh had indeed been condemned; he also planned to publish a detailed "memoir" on the case, along with the letters, to complete the indictment and punishment of the renegade:

> The affair is not to be judged; the tribunal is not to be formed. The affair has been judged, a formal tribunal is impossible, a moral tribunal has pronounced its verdict. The general reprobation that has enveloped this man is proof of it. Do you think that men such as Mazzini, Willich, Proudhon, Kinkel, etc., would have expressed themselves with so much energy if the facts were not proven, if there were not documents and witnesses? To unmask this man before those whom I esteem and love is a need of my heart, an act of high morality. Socialist and revolutionary, I address myself only to our brothers. I am indifferent to the opinion of others.[44]

Shortly after his arrival in London, Herzen set about writing his memoir. Gradually he discovered that he could only explain recent events by going back to their antecedents. Almost without realizing it, the memoir turned into the "Memoirs"—*Byloe i dumy* was launched. His friends were relieved. Herzen, however, felt betrayed and self-betrayed. He wrote to Vogt,

> Et tu Brutus—you too pay me a compliment on the commencement of my memoirs, you and Engels[on], and Ed[mond Chojecki] and Tessié. But my friends, reflect that there is more friendship than reason in your contentment. I have no illusions. To write memoirs instead of a memoir is almost to abdicate, it is to be a perjurer, almost a traitor—and it covers moral downfall with literary success. I scorn myself for it. Then why do I do it? *Kastraten sind wir, impotente Wüstlinge,* instead of an erection we make to do with dirty words.[45]

He had felt that a moral condemnation of Herwegh by the revolutionary community would be a test of its vitality; his failure removed his last faith. Three years later he wrote, with regard to another dispute among the radicals: "The absence of a public opinion is one of the most terrible plagues of the revolutionary party. I think that it is legal and necessary not to tolerate scum in the party and to mount a collective defense of pure men. None of that exists, our party has no moral sense.... My old idea of a tribunal still haunts me. We do not have it because we do not form a party, we are not parts of a living organism, but bearers of a dead idea, of a cadaver."[46]

England: The Institutions of a New Society

Although Herzen did not achieve the new justice he had sought, the quest had important consequences for him. It forced him into contact with leading émigrés, even those with whom he disagreed. He could no longer withdraw from them in arrogant isolation; he needed their support in his struggle, and he no longer had his own satisfactory primary group within which to isolate himself. Although he consistently attempted to avoid immersion in exile affairs and would very soon turn most of his attention to what turned out to be his real vocation—Russian revolutionary journalism—he would henceforth be an active citizen of the exile community. The search for support also brought him to England, where he found the conditions he needed for his life's work. Six weeks after announcing the abandonment of the memoir, he told Mariia Reichel of his "amazing project ... to undertake an agitation for the liberation of the peasants."[47] Soon after, *Poliarnaia zvezda* was born.

In Britain, the exile community actively developed a network of institutions to give structure to their lives and protect their ideals. Ideology, practical needs, and the thirst for a ritual framework to express their beliefs combined to create a special set of customs. British popular radicalism, which had a long tradition of its own that drew on the customs of Dissenting Christianity and on a reworking of the norms of the dominant society to express socialist themes, was a major component of the new culture.[48] It combined with a more ideologically sophisticated continental radicalism to provide a matrix for the émigrés' lives. The revolutionary culture crossed both national and ideological lines; those who lived within it were comrades in arms, despite serious disagreements on programs and tactics. Those, like Marx, who scorned it remained outsiders to the larger radical community, regardless of their importance within their own faction. On the other hand, some individuals on the left wing of British parliamentary radicalism were able to participate in the culture, thus enlarging the reach of the community.

Radical culture helped create a new radical image. The personal rivalries and the ideological splits that characterized the real world of European exile politics were displaced by the portrayal of a universal struggle against "despotism" and "oppression" in favor of "freedom" and "republicanism." The struggle was international in scope, and Britons were invited to help in a movement that included Italians, Poles, Hungarians, French, Germans, and others. Building on the foundations laid by Mazzini and his supporters in the period before the revolution, the style of modern left-wing propaganda was taking form.

A symbolic structure soon emerged to provide the radical community with self-definition. Iconography and ritual were important elements in this process. Thus, in 1853, the London exiles provided a rich example of the former when they attempted to raise money by establishing a "Central European Fund." Subscribers to the fund received a card, suitable for framing, that included the following elements: "The flag bears an emblematical engraving of a battle, . . . the flags of Hungary and Italia, with figures weeping for the fallen; a tomb inscribed with the names of Bandiera, Bakounin, Batthany, Blum, Konarski: a war horse without a rider: at the foot of a field piece lie crown and mitre: the flag of Italy, on which you read *Dio e Popolo*, floats near St. Peter's: and the signatures of G. Mazzini and Louis Kossuth (from autographs) complete the circle of emblems."[49]

In the refugees' public life, the most important needs were to keep alive the tradition for which they had given up their homeland and to aid those of their fellows who were in need. Many of the exiles were poor footsoldiers of the revolution who were unable to find work in a country whose language and customs remained hopelessly alien to them. Benefit and commemoration often coincided; a meeting would bring together the leaders, possibly of several different revolutionary movements; a great moment of the radical past would be celebrated; and the proceeds would benefit the destitute refugees.[50] The anniversaries of the February Revolution in Paris and the Polish uprising of 1831 were major commemorative occasions, but others could easily be found: the events of the French Revolution of 1789 were celebrated and the deaths of revolutionary martyrs were memorialized. At the commemorative meeting, there would be a series of speeches in which the ideals of the movement and the solidarity of the peoples were reaffirmed to loud applause and revolutionary songs were sung. Full reports of the proceedings in the radical press *(Reynolds' Newspa-*

per, *The People's Paper, l'Homme,* etc.) further sanctified and legitimized the tradition.[51]

A special form of ritual, which affirmed more clearly perhaps than any other that revolution went beyond politics to citizenship in a new community, was the funeral. The final service the good radical gave to his cause was to be the centerpiece in a symbolic manifestation of international solidarity and rejection of the Christianity of the surrounding society. For example, in 1853, the Jersey colony paid its last respects to Louis-Halin Dutailis: "The column set out. The four proscribed nations, the Polish, Hungarian, Italian, French, served as pallbearers. An enormous red flag followed. Afterward came the entire proscription, where could be seen Pierre Leroux, Félix Mathé, Victor Hugo; for the rest, no priest, no mass; a crowd of English and Jerseyites profoundly astonished at this singular cortege."[52]

There was also a special rhetoric for these occasions, exemplified in Charles Bradlaugh's account of the funeral of Herzen's friend Simon Bernard.

> The proscribed of all the nationalities of Europe mustered round his coffin to do him honor. Italy, Germany, Russia, Poland, Hungary, and France were numerously represented: and long ranks of the best and bravest of banished men trod in sadness in the rear of the funeral hearse.... Among the hundreds of intellectual looking men [at the graveside] might be seen most noticeably the bearded figure of that most omniscient of political writers Alexander Herzen; here the stalwart frame of the escaped Bakunin; here the saddened features of an old Englishman who had borne part with him in his political struggles and who had loved the dead man with the fullest friendliness of his most honest nature.[53]

Herzen and the Mores of a New Social Order

Upon his arrival in England, Herzen became a participant in the institutions of the exile community. He contributed to the philanthropies, attended occasional political rallies, and on a few occasions spoke himself in commemoration of the Polish uprising.[54] He even headed one fund drive that was organized to provide a defense for his friend Simon Bernard, accused of collaboration in the Orsini assassination plot.[55]

He and his family made their own contributions to the evolution of revolutionary ritual. At the turn of the new year of 1855, he presented fifteen-year-old Sasha with the dedication of the new edition of *S togo berega*, and in it stated: "The religion of the coming revolution is the only one that I bequeath to you. It has no paradise to offer, no rewards except your own awareness, except conscience."[56] The presentation took place in a special rite of passage, during a small party to celebrate the new year. Malwida von Meysenbug described and memorialized the scene:

> The youth fell into his father's arms, tears in his eyes. We were all deeply moved. Each of us thought about our far away homes, melancholy with the thought of how far, how far the time might be, if it ever came, when we could return and freely profess that religion. But at the same time, each of us also felt that in this small, interesting circle we could sense a breath of that spirit, a consequence of our hope that all mankind would one day be joined in a beautiful union. It was with a heartfelt feeling that we shook hands for the New Year—a small congregation of free people in exile that knew full well that even should their greeting be repeated year after year in banishment, they still already belonged to the true church of the future, that of a nobler, . . . freer mankind.[57]

Herzen the publisher also did his part to establish Russian radical tradition and the iconography to support it. His historical publications gave the Russian left the "usable past" that continues to form the armature of the modern vision of Russian history.[58] The symbolism he employed was part of the same task. Thus, *Poliarnais zvezda* was named in memory of a Decembrist paper, and the magazine's logo was an engraving of the profiles of the five Decembrists who were hanged. The engraving was made by Herzen's Chartist friend William Linton. Both journalist and artist, Linton's combination of talents gave him considerable importance in defining radical symbolism. He was keenly aware of the revolutionary community, for its presence legitimated his own efforts to link moderate Chartists, parliamentary radicals, Polish democrats, and Italian nationalists in a single cause. The engraving itself served as part of Sasha's initiation into revolutionary adulthood. For his name day, just a few weeks before the New Year's present of the dedication, Sasha received from his father "a gift already that of a youth, and not of a child, and full of honor for me—the portrait of the five sacrifices of December 14."[59]

Herzen attempted to make his family life a microcosm of life within the radical community. His practice of surrounding himself with fellow exiles as tutors, secretaries, and physicians has already been noted. All of those associated with Herzen's publications as printers, typesetters, and distributors, were also in the radical camp. Some issues seem trivial—for example, Herzen wrote a long letter to the wife of a member of Parliament who was giving a ball for the children of émigrés explaining that eight-year-old Tata could not attend, because balls were not appropriate entertainment for revolutionaries.[60] Others, however, raised serious issues of defining the good life for self-conscious rebels agaist prevailing mores.

Within the family, Herzen and, after 1855, Ogarev as well, were concerned to inculcate the children with the political ideals and the accompanying moral principles that to them defined the radical creed. As the children grew older, Herzen worried that they might instead absorb the values of the society around them. Privacy and domesticity were threats, for they would divert the young people from the life of political commitment to which their elders were dedicated. Marriage to a person outside the community was the greatest danger. Thus, Herzen advised Tata's new governess, Emily Reeve: "She is fifteen. What I would like is to remove from her, as far as possible, the banal idea of marriage, the bourgeois preoccupation with her position, and with that all the little vices of those who aspire to marriage—coquetry, and the rage for adornment (a young girl must dress up; I am concerned about clothes-mania)."[61]

On an occasion when Sasha wished to marry, Ogarev wrote to him in defense of the special values of the world of revolution, and showed how they were threatened by domesticity:

> It is impossible to make it your goal to be the father of a family. If there is no other human goal alongside this anthropological necessity, then the goal is bourgeois. . . . The more I think about it, the more I come to the conclusion that you are attracted to this goal by self love and by criticism of our home, a criticism, however, which is quite narrow. . . . Reflect a bit, that it is much purer, broader, and more intelligent to pose serious intellectual labor for oneself, where you would be able to perfect yourself and be useful for others and for science, i.e., for the development of human understanding, than to inscribe yourself as a paterfamilias.[62]

Even more serious than Sasha's early desires to get married, was his possible influence on Tata, for whom, in Herzen's view, early marriage would be a disaster. In refusing to allow her to spend a winter with her brother, he wrote, "here she will become an autonomous and thinking individual, and then she will want to get married; if she finds a truly worthy man she will marry—if not, not. With you, moved by what you consider the normal happiness of [Sasha's newly married friend] Schiff, she would marry . . . I don't know whom, and would destroy her development. . . . Throwing an eighteen- or nineteen-year old girl into marriage is a crime."[63]

As Herzen's children grew up, there were, as Ogarev's and Herzen's letters both implied, painful conflicts between Sasha and his elders. Running through them was the tension between individual, domestic virtues on the one hand and social obligation on the other—a private morality valuable in itself against a way of life concerned more with enabling people to act effectively in the larger world. The tenets of the revolutionary code were questioned and clarified in these discussions; and enough documentation survives to throw an unusually clear light on the issues of socialist personal morality.

A series of questions were illuminated by the relationship between Herzen and Ogarev's wife, Natalie Tuchkova-Ogareva. Shortly after the Ogarevs joined Herzen in London in 1855, Herzen and Natalie Tuchkova became lovers. Unlike Herwegh and Natalie Herzen a few years earlier, this couple conducted their affair in accord with the tenets of the code—they informed Ogarev of their intentions before initiating the affair, and he acquiesced.[64] Natalie eventually bore three children by Herzen, a daughter, Liza, and a younger set of twins.[65]

Perhaps more than any of the family, Ogarev was the spokesman for the new morality. The fact that his marriage to Natalie was already strained when they arrived in London no doubt simplified matters for him; nonetheless, his response to her was a model of revolutionary morality:

> You fell in love with my brother [Herzen]. Without dwelling on my relationship to you, I will say only that instead of the influence I had dreamed of exerting on you, I felt that I was subordinate, and instead of elevating, I was lowering you. I was certain that [my] brother's love would elevate you—and life would be placed on such an exalted footing as rarely happens. You could love my brother and be the mother of my sister's children. . . . Indeed, what a great relation would be established between all of us.[66]

And when the time came to inform Herzen's daughter Ol'ga that Liza Ogareva was her half-sister, it was Ogarev who wrote to her: "I love, and always have loved, your father, as my only brother in the world. Also, I considered his children as my own. I loved your mother as a true sister, and I have always loved all of you as my own children. I love Lisa as my own child, since she too is the daughter of your father and Natalie, whom I consider as a sister."[67]

The relationship between Herzen and Natalie Tuchkova turned out to be unhappy for everyone. Natalie, once the young girl who had inspired Natalie Herzen's devotion, her "Conseulo," had developed into a difficult, neurotic person. Her relationship with Herzen's older children was so bad that eventually Herzen had to move his daughters out of the house.[68] The twins died in 1864, while alone with Natalie in Paris, and this blow severely undermined her mental stability. Herzen could no longer live easily with her, nor could he break with her altogether, for fear of the consequences to their surviving child.

Herzen expressed his concern for Natalie in a letter to Tata, the content of which she passed on to her brother. Misinterpreting his solicitude to mean that Natalie was pregnant again, Sasha attacked his father in a furious letter to Ogarev. In it, the definition of "marriage" in the radical community is made clear; in the absence of civil or religious solemnization of unions, the essential element in defining a marriage was the creation of a family. Sasha specifically condemned his father for renewing his commitment to Natalie, in effect re-solemnizing a very bad "marriage" by producing another child. He also charged his father with sacrificing the interests of his children to his feelings for Natalie. On the other hand, he condoned, though with bad grace, Herzen's initial action in bringing Natalie into their family as his mistress/wife. His father, in Sasha's view, had the right to emotional and sexual fulfillment and to a second marriage (and this is the way he refers to the union throughout); but once the relationship had turned sour, by Herzen's own admission, and in view of the distress it brought everyone else, he did not have the right to renew it by fathering yet another child.[69]

Ogarev showed Sasha's letter to Herzen (as Sasha had suggested). Herzen reacted in a letter to Malwida; though saddened and angered, he acknowledged that his own commitment to a larger world had had a part in bringing misfortune to him. "It was Alex[ander]'s *tone* [that deeply offended and upset me]; it is the facility with which he undertakes the role of censor, judge, and even executioner toward me which has angered me. As to the substance . . . I am guilty of much and horribly punished and censured. The family, family life, was always secondary for me—twice it has taken vengeance on me."[70]

Herzen left it to Ogarev to respond directly to Sasha. His friend's letter, he said, was a "masterpiece," and its author was "a man of the new morality—in all its poetry."[71] Unfortunately, this explication of the "new morality" appears not to have survived. It is, however, a measure of the distance separating the Herzens' socialist morality from that of surrounding Victorian society, that this correspondence took place at all, and was discussed among at least five people, two of them unmarried women: Sasha, Ogarev, Herzen, Tata, and Malwida.

In 1863, twenty-four-year-old Sasha fathered an illegitimate son. Before the baby's birth he had left England to study in Switzerland. Herzen treated this situation with the same openness that would later prevail in the discussions of his own relationship with Natalie Tuchkova. Letters from Herzen and Ogarev regularly sent news of the boy, and all the members of Herzen's family knew and visited mother and child.[72] There was apparently some discussion of Herzen's taking the child from his mother, a working-class woman named Charlotte Hutson, and bringing him into his own household,[73] but instead mother and son were lodged with Ludwik Czerniecki, manager of the Free Russian Press.

After the Herzens left England for Switzerland in 1865, Charlotte and the baby moved in with Ogarev's mistress Mary Sutherland and her son. In May 1867, they came to stay with Ogarev in Geneva. Shortly thereafter, Charlotte Hutson disappeared, and it was suspected, correctly, that she had committed suicide.[74] This tragedy provoked an exchange of letters between Ogarev and Sasha that once again dealt with the questions of family responsibility and individual morality for people who had to develop their own code, since they did not subscribe to the one that prevailed in the society about them.

Ogarev charged that Sasha was evading taking responsibility for Charlotte's fate.[75] To this Sasha replied that the fact of fathering an illegitimate child had forced him to rethink the whole problem of sexual morality. He had come to the conclusion that the danger of pregnancy was such that "noncriminal" sexual relations were impossible outside of marriage. He had, therefore, taken a vow of chastity, to which he intended to adhere until his marriage. With this decision, plus financial support he had provided for his former mistress and their child, he seemed to feel that he had met his obligations; he also felt himself to be morally superior to Ogarev and his father, with their much looser standards of sexual conduct.[76]

Ogarev was not impressed. His disapproval of Sasha's self-righteousness, expressed in a July 1867 letter, counterposed the essentially social nature of the older generation's commitment to the younger man's individualism:

> First of all, [your letter] consists entirely of self-justification—to such an extent, that you even forgot to mention the poor woman with a word of regret—and you write entirely of yourself, of your self-purification, after which you have the right to forgive yourself and to look upon yourself as a pure person. I have indeed little faith in these moral purges. Physiologically they can lead to impotence, and nothing else. For me the eternity of marriage has not existed since the Reformation. And asceticism itself, so highly valued in Christianity's monastic life, seems to me not a virtue, but masturbation with self-love and self-justification. I demand from a person simply the humanity of a humane mercy—and should repentance be necessary, then not in order to forgive oneself the past (forgive or not—you cannot wipe it out), but so that you become aware of what was evil in the unconscious act, answer for its consequences, and summon one's strength for a more common cause than your own marriage.[77]

These exchanges show how intertwined were the issues of political commitment and moral-cultural values. Just as Sasha was torn between his father's political dedication and his own inclination toward the quiet life of a Swiss professor of physiology, so his code of sexual conduct approached Victorian standards in practice without, however, any acknowledgement of the religious bases for those standards. Unlike Sasha, caught between the worlds of revolution and Victorianism, Ogarev identified solidly with the morality of the revolutionary code. This by no means resolved or even simplified moral issues, as he well knew, but it did mean that questions of appropriate conduct would be approached with a different set of values and priorities.

The conflicts within the Herzen family display the working out of a revolutionary code with unusual clarity. To what extent was their behavior characteristic of the subculture which they inhabited? This question cannot be answered with any great precision, but on the whole, their conduct appears to be not inconsistent with the mores of their society. The one major exception to this was Herzen's airing of the

Herwegh affair, in the attempt to achieve public condemnation of his rival; for the most part, this merely embarrassed his fellow radicals.

The revolutionary was a person dedicated to the cause; a few among them were so dedicated that they gave up personal gratification and comfort. Mazzini, Worcell, and Bakunin[78] were admired for their selflessness; and here the later, Nechaevan, demand for revolutionary asceticism is foreshadowed. However, most members of the radical community lived in more or less stable families. Companionate marriages and shared commitment to the revolutionary cause were qualities that aroused admiration; exploitative unions were condemned.

In their disregard of marriage laws, the socialists were, of course, regularly charged with undermining the family and morality. Occasionally, the socialists would respond. Marx's answer is the most familiar: "But you Communists would introduce community of women, screams the whole bourgeoisie in chorus. The bourgeois sees in his wife a mere instrument of production. He hears that the instruments of production are to be exploited in common, and, naturally, can come to no other conclusion than that the lot of being common to all will likewise fall to the women. He has not even a suspicion that the real point aimed at is to do away with the status of women as mere instruments of production."[79]

The strategy of turning criticism into an attack on the mores of the bourgeoisie seems to have been a radical commonplace. Proudhon resorted to it, and so, in his early writings, did Herzen. Proudhon even asserted that he had acquaintances for whom it was a point of honor not to have their marriage legally solemnized, "to such an extent the matrimonial contract, dishonored by interest, seems to them to be contrary to the dignity of love and inspires them with horror." If such people were in error, he went on, it was merely from "excessive delicacy."[80]

Occasionally, the radicals would attempt to expound their moral code, and on two occasions, Herzen had a part in it. Arnold Ruge wrote a play, *Die Neue Welt*, in which the plot, if not the characters, were largely based on the Herzen-Herwegh-Natalie triangle. He sent it to Herzen for comment, and an angry Herzen responded, "It is the apotheosis of a criminal, the canonization of a coward, a traitor."[81] Ruge was hurt by this reaction; he denied first that his character was based on that of the "Zurich criminal"; Herwegh, he said, could not serve him as a poetic inspiration. All he had done was take some of the facts from Herzen's experience, in order to illustrate the problems with which his play was concerned, but he had changed the characters. Moreover, Ruge denied that he sided with his "crazy subject." The point was that the play was of general interest, he said, because it posed "the major problems of the freest people."[82]

The Herwegh episode was far too painful for Herzen ever to contemplate with equanimity, and the "moral" of the story, as Herzen perceived it, could be grasped only with the aid of substantial commentary; not unnaturally he resented Ruge's use of it to illustrate the new code. But Herzen himself was eager to illustrate the code in the proper circumstances. A year earlier, in April 1853, Vogt had written to him of the hasty marriage of his sister to an Austrian émigré Hans Kudlich. Faced with the fianceś's expulsion from Bern and unable to arrange a religious wedding before his departure, Vogt's father "assumed the role of patriarch; he gathered the friends of the family, and he gave the nuptial benediction."[83] Herzen was delighted: "I esteemed [your father before] with all my heart, but now I esteem him with all my heart and a half. Sacristi! This marriage is a historical event, a revolutionary antecedent. Tell me, as soon as possible, if you will allow me to make of it a little article for *The Leader*, which will pass into the *Nation*, etc.—But he has rewarmed, moralized, the stupid institution of marriage."[84]

The story duly appeared at the end of August, under Linton's initials, in *The English Republic*. The action of the elder Vogt was praised, and its political meaning stressed: "For it is not only in political affairs but in every department of life that the same spirit of self-dependence should actuate us, as actuated those of whom I . . . speak."[85]

Herzen became a citizen of the radical community at the same time he became a professional Russian revolutionary journalist, shortly after he moved to London in 1852. The community may have helped inspire the venture, since journalism was the most important political activity the Western European émigrés could still perform. The community thus provided Herzen with the self-definition he needed to legitimate his new activity. Such legitimation did not come from his primary audience; his friends at home rejected his new life, and it would be several years before he found a new Russian readership.

He lacked a Russian personal support network, as well as distant followers. Of the adult members of his Russian extended family, Mariia Reichel alone remained; she unfailingly supported him, but she was far off in Paris and primarily involved with her own family. Ogarev was able to join him only in 1855. In the intervening period, Herzen could find support for his enterprise only among the other émigrés—most practically, from the Polish Democratic Society, which outfitted him with type, typesetters, and channels to send his materials back to Russia, in exchange for his political and financial support for the cause of Polish independence. Moral support came from the larger community, and this allowed him to speak not simply as a Russian who supported Polish aspirations, but also as a Russian who was part of the great cause of European liberation.

Life among the émigrés was punctuated by quarrels and feuds from which Herzen always attempted to insulate himself. The existence of a sense of communal mores and values that overrode ideology and nationality provided a centripetal force that helped keep the persistent quarrels from destroying all sense of solidarity. It kept the sense of mission alive, and enabled the émigrés to avoid assimilation by English society. (Those English people with whom Herzen and his European friends had regular contacts were themselves at least peripheral members of the international community.) The community developed a rhetoric and iconography that is still drawn upon by some elements on the left.

The integrity of the community was most threatened by international conflict and, ironically, by revolutionary success. The Crimean War, which pitted almost all the radical émigrés against Russia, was a difficult time for Herzen; he succeeded in defining himself as that Russian who opposed the villainy of his government, but at some cost. The unification of Italy and Germany and the establishment of the Third Republic in France made it possible for many of the exiles to find accomodation with their governments and to return home. Conflict now arose between national and international loyalties. But there had already been time to establish the myth of international revolution, and in *Byloe i dumy* Herzen had had time to write its chronicle.

CONCLUSION

HISTORIANS have perceived the revolutions of 1848 as paradoxical defeats for the revolutionary ideal. The dreams of political romanticism died on the barricades in Paris in June, or in Vienna in October; the makers of the revolution went to prison, or to exile, or to their deaths. The age of generous ideals and of simple, clear visions of political morality came to an end, to be succeeded by a new "toughness" and "realism." Yet within a quarter century, the victors had put into place many of the reforms the vanquished had fought for; the radical and democratic exiles were amnestied and could come home to a world of civil liberties, parliamentary government, and national unification. But if the victory of the government forces was paradoxical, so too was the ultimate vindication of the revolutionaries. The worlds to which they could return at the end of their lives were arenas of business as usual. Constitutions and broad suffrage did not translate into the virtuous republicanism that had been their sustaining vision, and the new national, constitutional states had as little use for their exalted political dreams as had the reactionary regimes of 1847.

The fate of the revolutionaries' political vision reflects their own strengths and failings. For years before the revolution, they had worked to develop and propagandize their programs. Occasionally, they fought and died for their views, and if each individual revolutionary effort failed, the series of noble failures created a mythology and martyrology for radicalism. The heroic legends and the noble ideals were made known to the public at large through journalism, art, public demonstrations, and manipulation of the establishment media. The methods of political propaganda developed by this generation of radicals would last for well over a century and are not yet completely out of date.

Through their efforts the revolutionaries had put the program of democratic and socialist reform on the agenda. Their success as propagandists meant that in most of Europe their ideals had become so entrenched in the awareness of politically active sectors of the population that it had become almost impossible to repudiate them. Thus, their programs were enacted by the governments that defeated them.

But although they succeeded in setting the political agenda, the radicals had no mechanism for translating their ideas into political reality. Revolutionary processes brought many of them close to governmental power in 1848, but they proved to be incapable of holding on to it and using it creatively. Once the revolution was over, they were reduced to squabbling over the mistakes of 1848 and plotting futile armed insurgencies. In the decades to come it would be men who could command the political power of the state and who were not afraid to use this power for change rather than cautious retrenchment—men like Cavour, Bismarck, and even Alexander II—who were able to set their imprint on political events, not small bands of dedicated souls acting out of love for ideals and the people.

Alexander Herzen's mature life was shaped by his response to the European radicals, just as his youthful social vision had owed much to their propaganda. His expectations of the West had been formed by reading radical critics—Blanc, Proudhon, and George Sand being the most important—and linking their denunciations of European conditions to his left-Hegelian radicalism. He had therefore been expecting to find an imperfect and unjust social order, with a dominant bourgeoisie unworthy of its power and influence, when he came to Western Europe in 1847. But reality exceeded all his expectations; he was shocked and appalled by what he perceived as the corruption, vulgarity, and hypocrisy in the Bourgeois Monarchy of Louis Philippe. New acquaintances among the French and émigré radicals, whom he met after his arrival in Paris, helped him sharpen his analysis of the failings of European society.

The outbreak of revolution found Herzen in Italy. He was entranced by the revolutionary process in its operatic Italian form, and his respect for the Italian heroes of the *Risorgimento* would last the rest of his life. But revolution in Italy was not powerful enough to break the strength of the Hapsburg monarchy. The movement was doomed without outside help, and Herzen appears to have been aware of this by the time he left the peninsula to follow events farther north.

Conclusion

The Paris uprising and the establishment of the republic drew Herzen back to France. He arrived too late for the ebullience of February and found, instead, the first stages of reaction; even the moderate policies of the Provisional Government were repudiated by the conservative National Assembly. Herzen's response was critical and his view of the revolutionary movement complex. He now differentiated between the crowds who had made the revolution and the opposition politicians who has emerged with governmental power. It was the inadequacy, the timidity, and the fundamental conservatism of the politicians that had held them back from joining with the Paris populace to make a clean sweep of the old order. Forced into confrontation with revolutionary forces, they had lost their democratic veneer altogether. The French revolutionary government had been unable to take the measures necessary for victory, and Herzen had arrived in Paris just in time to see its defeat. This was registered by the election of the conservative National Assembly, followed soon after by the bloody defeat of the revolutionary Paris crowd.

The more radical leaders, who had never held power, might be admirable and heroic, and Herzen often could admire them as human beings; however, their theories and programs could no longer attract him. His political disillusionment was complete. Herzen perceived the exploited and oppressed Paris workers, and eventually the Russian peasants, as truly revolutionary forces and thought they might well ultimately win; but he also felt that these forces were themselves indifferent to the values of individual freedom that he cherished. There seemed no way of linking the call for freedom and individual autonomy of the middle-class radicals with the urgent demand for social justice that animated the Paris workers.

Despite his disenchantment with the revolution, Herzen renewed and extended his acquaintance with French and exiled radicals in Paris, as well as socialist politicians and journalists. If he could no longer admire them as leaders, he could still appreciate them as potential colleagues and friends. He entered into the world of political action with his move to Geneva in the summer of 1849. Soon, he was involved in the collaboration with Proudhon on *La Voix du Peuple* and in addition was developing networks of contacts among the Italian and German exile colonies. He began to write extensively for French and German audiences, thus discovering his dual Western journalist's role as gadfly of the radical movement on the one hand, and as the interpreter of Russia to the Western left on the other.

Throughout his first years in the West, Herzen appears to have been seeking a community in which he could find both liberty and fraternity—the individualism lacking in Russia combined with the harmonious friendship of his old Moscow circle. Constitutionalism, revolution, and the Geneva exiles all failed to satisfy his political demands, and by 1852 the circle itself was irrevocably lost, not only by his emigration, but also by his friends' repudiation of his work. Finally, he attempted to create his own little high-minded commune on the narrowest conceivable scale—his family and the Herweghs, living in relative isolation from the mainstream of exile life. The family crisis shattered this dream forever, and his faith that private life offered a sanctuary for his values was destroyed once and for all.

Nor was there any hope of going back, retreating to a pre-European innocence. From the latter part of 1848 onward, nostalgia for friends and youthful memories in Russia became a major motif; it inspired many of the best pages of *Byloe i dumy*. But Herzen never entertained the slightest illusion that he could return in fact to his homeland.[1] (In the memoirs of Herzen's Russian acquaintances, he is frequently portrayed as expressing a painful homesickness and fantasizing about going back, but it is unlikely that he ever believed this was a possible option. More often than not, the fantasy revolved around his children returning to Russia after his own death.) Russia was more repressive, politically more hopeless than the West. Emigration offered the only practical way to work for radical change in Russia.

Herzen retained his illusions about the circle for a longer time; the reality of his isolation from the friends he had loved so much and trusted so long was unbearable. His emotional disengagement from the circle, to the extent it ever took place, came only in 1855–1856. First Granovskii died, leaving the circle without its most important member, and then Ogarev joined him in London, and the two men were able to recreate in part the world of friendship.

Yet, even as Herzen lost his youthful idealism, he became a tougher, more realistic, and more effective political figure. He rejected grand theoretical schemes and dismissed socialist panaceas, but he established the press and edited his journals, and thereby did provide a vehicle for uncensored Russian thought. In the short run he had some influence on the reform effort of Alexander II, and in the long run he helped shape Russian revolutionary thought. During his career as a journalist, he kept his sights fixed on his goals; and like

Conclusion

Proudhon in 1849, he was willing to find short-term alliances wherever possible, from the provincial estate to the Winter Palace, and was also willing to give up his stake in revolution for the sake of meaningful reform in the present.

He also found a community in which he could function—the world of exile as it crystallized in London during the 1850s. He often found the émigrés naive or foolish. The controversies that periodically tore the community apart seemed futile and pointless to him, and the tactics even of the men he most admired he found unacceptable. Nonetheless, he joined them, and found in their midst sociability, if not the profound affection he had earlier sought from his friends. The exiles also provided a set of moral and cultural standards that helped give shape to a life that was otherwise threatened by a loss of all values. On a more practical level, the revolutionary community provided Herzen with legitimation of his own activity and with practical experience in publishing and disseminating émigré literature.

Always, however, he remained something of an outsider, the stranger, the Russian "barbarian," observing even the most sympathetic men with the unsentimental gaze of one who was not himself involved. Since he had not been a participant himself, he did not need to rationalize or defend the measures taken during the revolutionary struggle. The very absence of a Russian émigré community helped him in this; there was no "party" to establish a "party line" in interpreting events; there was no revolutionary strategy that could be harmed by a misplaced word or a too harsh and too public assessment of an ally. This disengagement from the revolutionary milieu enabled Herzen to write one of the best analyses of the French revolution of 1848, that contained in the *Pis'ma* series, as well as the frequently mordant portraits of the members of the international revolutionary community found in *Byloe i dumy*.

One Western 1848 revolutionary politician stood at least as far from his fellow exiles as did Herzen—Karl Marx. Even before revolution broke out in 1848, Marx had separated himself from the community of middle-class intellectual radicals and journalists in order to build a modern political movement. He sought primarily working-class groups,[2] which he then attempted to forge into obedient executors of his commands. He was uninterested in working with other middle-class theorists; they were potential rivals, and at best they confused the drive for action by offering alternative strategies and visions. We have seen that even before 1848 Marx was more likely to drive such intellectuals out of his organization than deal with them.

In Cologne during the revolutionary period, Marx's special style had matured. He had attempted, ultimately successfully, to seize control of the workers' movement from the more popular and more responsive Andreas Gottschalk, at considerable cost in bitterness. He had also insisted on complete tactical flexibility, attempting to forge an alliance with non–working class radicals and rejecting the demands from his own constituency for revolutionary purity. Ultimately he alienated not only the Cologne organization and his would-be liberal-democratic allies, but also even his own lieutenants who had come from London to work with him. The cost, by 1851, was the dissolution of the Communist League, the arrest of the Cologne leadership, and the splitting of the London communist organization. The same pattern would be repeated later on, most spectacularly in the case of the First International.

Marx thus failed as dismally in 1848 as all the other revolutionaries. However, he had begun the process of creating a modern, working-class party. Social Democracy, once Marx had forged it, would understand power and would be able to utilize the new political structures to organize a strong constituency and wield very considerable influence. By the time Marx died, such a party would have been created in Germany, and by the end of the nineteenth century parties heavily influenced by the Marxist and German Social Democratic example would have been established throughout Western Europe. To be sure, the socialist parties did not develop as Marx had predicted, and their very success in organizing and representing the workers may well have been a factor in the exhaustion of the revolutionary impulse in Europe. Nonetheless, it is Marx's imprint that the modern socialist movement bears.

Herzen and Marx—this unbalanced pair continues to force comparisons. Both lived for over a decade in London, at times not more than a mile or two apart. Both stood apart from the enthusiasms and the squabbles of the main émigré groups. Both also stood apart from Mazzini's attempts to establish émigré organizations, and they both rejected the Italian's old-fashioned liberal nationalism. Both saw the motive force of revolutionary change coming from the exploited depths of society. And they refused to have anything to do with each other. Marx charged that Herzen was a Russian nationalist who called for European revitalization through a barbarian Russian invasion. On at least one occasion, he refused to share a speaker's podium with the Russian, and he was not at all pleased that his English ally Ernest Jones was also an ally of Herzen.[3] Herzen charged that Marx purposely fomented the rumors that Bakunin was a Russian agent[4] and undermined his socialist credibility by allying himself with the conservative Russophobe David Urquhart. Herzen's portrait of Marx's followers is the most biting in *Byloe i dumy*. One has the sense that the mutual antipathy between these two men was fueled by the fact that each felt that the other presented an alternative vision of socialist organization.

What was Herzen's alternative? Like Marx, he turned away from the maneuvering within the radical exile community; however, instead of seeking a different constituency and a more modern type of organization, as had Marx, he turned back to Russia. His mission became the one that the first wave of exiles had carried out well in the period preceding the outbreak of revolution. Fröbel had established a press to smuggle forbidden work into Germany; the poetry of Herwegh had had pride of place in this activity. Herzen's press made available to Russian readers the poetry of Pushkin and other classic writers which for political or moral reasons could not pass the censors, as well as that of his friend Ogarev. Herwegh and Ruge had attempted to create written symposia to expose the viewpoints of a variety of political thinkers who could not publish in their homeland; Herzen would accomplish this goal for Russia with *Poliarnaia zvezda*. The Poles and Germans in Paris had popularized their respective causes among the French politicians and journalists; Herzen did the same in London. In general, the pre-1848 emigrations had established the legitimacy of demands for democratic and socialist change in their homelands; Herzen did the same for his. In so doing, he implicitly asserted the validity of the program of middle-class, intellectual revolutionaries, while Marx's entire career repudiated that program.

The Russian dimension to his work made it unnecessary for Herzen to involve himself too deeply in émigré life. But, unlike Marx, his avoidance of the squabbles did not constitute a condemnation of the men and women who made up the exile community. On the contrary, he continued in his personal life to be a traditional middle-class intellectual radical who operated through the written word and social interaction, not political organization. He shunned hierarchical organizations, seeking instead egalitarian communities. He acknowledged the norms of the radical subculture and contributed to elaborating the sense that this culture possessed its own mores and values that were more rational and humane than those of surrounding Victorianism. Russian backwardness meant that there was a fruitful field of work for a tough-minded survivor who retained the ideals of a gentler, more romantic age.

NOTES
BIBLIOGRAPHY
INDEX

NOTES

Preface

All translations, unless published sources are indicated, are my own. French words in quoted passages indicate French in the original.

1. From Herzen's "Addio" to his Moscow friends, March 1849. Printed in Alexander Herzen, *From the Other Shore* and *The Russian People and Socialism*, intro. Isaiah Berlin (Cleveland and New York, 1963), p. 15. These two works were each originally published in a Western language. The first, written in Russian, appeared as *Vom anderen Ufer* (Zurich, Hoffman und Campe, 1850); the second appeared in its original French as *Le Peuple russe et le socialisme*. The definitive versions, along with publishing histories and variations, are in Herzen's collected works: Aleksandr Gertsen [Alexander Herzen], *Sobranie sochinenii v tridtsati tomakh* [Collected Works in Thirty Volumes] (Moscow, 1954–55), 6:7–133, 436–76, 495–513; and 7:271–340, 407–08, 435–42. Unless otherwise stated, all subsequent references to Herzen's collected works will be to this edition.

2. For discussion of other early, oppositional radicals see Martin A. Miller, *The Russian Revolutionary Emigres, 1825–1870* (Baltimore, 1986), pp. 16–111, *passim;* O. V. Orlik, *Peredovaia Rossiia i revoliutsionnaia Frantsiia (I polovina XIX v.)* (Moscow, 1973), esp. pp. 212–27. For more discussion of Herzen and emigration, see chapter 6.

3. Paul Miliukov's liberal propaganda, with its image of two Russias, strongly recalls Herzen's dichotomy. See his 1904 work, *Russia and its Crisis*, foreword by Donald W. Treadgold (New York, 1962).

4. Gertsen, *Sobranie sochinenii* 25:251–291, *passim.*

5. "K Nashim," ibid. 25:297 (first published in *Poliarnaia zvezda*, no. 1). He further elaborated on the importance of these greetings in response to objections from a reader: "Otvet," ibid., p. 317 (first published in *Poliarnaia zvezda*, no. 2).

6. Utopian socialism has not received a great deal of scholarly attention,

and the efforts of its adherents to make their lives a microcosm of rational society remains to be fully analyzed. Feminist scholarship, stressing the crucial link between feminism and early socialism, has made a good start. See, for example, Barbara Taylor, *Eve and the New Jerusalem: Socialism and Feminism in the Nineteenth Century* (London, 1983), pp. 19–24, *et passim.*

7. For an analysis of the composition of *Byloe i dumy,* see Lidiia Chukovskaia, *"Byloe i Dumy" Gertsena* (Moscow, 1966).

8. Ia. El'sberg, *Gertsen: Zhizn' i tvorchestvo,* 3d ed. (Moscow, 1955).

9. Martin Malia, *Alexander Herzen and the Birth of Russian Socialism: 1812–1855* (Cambridge, Mass., 1961).

10. E. H. Carr, *The Romantic Exiles* (1933; rpt. New York, 1975).

11. See, for example, Edward Acton, *Alexander Herzen and the Role of the Intellectual Revolutionary* (Cambridge, 1979); Z. V. Smirnova, *Sotsial'naia filosofiia A. I. Gertsena* (Moscow, 1973).

12. N. Ia. Eidel'man, *Gertsen protiv samoderzhaviia. Sekretnaia politicheskaia istoriia Rossii xviii–xix vv. i Vol'naia pechat'* (Moscow, 1973); and esp. *Tainye korrespondenty 'Poliarnoi zvezdy'* (Moscow, 1966).

Chapter 1. The Background

1. Ivan Turgenev, *Rudin,* trans Richard Freeborn (New York, 1975), pp. 97–99.

2. I have limited the background material to the matters that I feel are most relevant for understanding Herzen's journey to Western Europe and his activities there. For a fuller account of Herzen's background and early life, see *Byloe i dumy,* available in English as *My Past and Thoughts: The Memoirs of Alexander Herzen,* 4 vols., intro. Isaiah Berlin, trans. Constance Garnett, rev. Humphrey Higgins (New York, 1968); or Malia, *Herzen.*

3. On the importance of the circle for Herzen's development, see Malia, *Herzen,* p. 68; and Judith Zimmerman, "Friends and Lovers: The Sources of Alexander Herzen's Feminism," Dept. of History, University of Pittsburgh at Greensburg, Greensburg, Pa., 15601.

4. The wives were Natalie Herzen and Elizaveta Granovskaia; widows were Tatiana Astrakova, and, much more peripherally, Mariia Ivanovna Poludenskaia, widow of a Moscow University professor and sister of Nikolai Sazonov; Mariia Korsh, sister of Evgenyi Korsh, was an active circle member.

5. "Friends and Lovers" deals with this subject in more detail. Herzen responded to Granovskii's criticism of Ogarev in a letter of September 21, 1849 (Gertsen, *Sobranie sochinenii* 23:182).

6. Ibid. 9:21–24.

7. For a modern discussion of the Hegel phenomenon, see Andrzej Walicki, *The Slavophile Controversy: History of a Conservative Utopia in Nineteenth-*

Century Russian Thought, trans. Hilda Andrews-Rusiecka (Oxford, 1975), pp. 287–393.

8. Gertsen, *Sobranie sochinenii* 3:5–88. For details, see Malia, *Herzen*, pp. 236–44.

9. Diary entries for January 7 and 28, 1843, in Gertsen, *Sobranie sochinenii* 2:256–57, 265.

10. The views of the professor who most influenced the Russians, Karl Werder, are summarized in Arthur P. Mendel, *Michael Bakunin: Roots of Apocalypse* (New York, 1981), pp. 154–56.

11. Granovskii to Elizaveta Granovskaia, June 29, 1844, in A. Stankevich, *T. N. Granovskii i ego perepiska* (Moscow, 1897), 2:261.

12. Gertsen, *Sobranie sochinenii* 2:111–15, 121–37.

13. By the time Herzen left Russia, the Westernizers, led by Belinskii, had abandoned Kraevskii's *Otechestvennyie zapiski* for *Sovremennik* [The Contemporary], which had just been taken over by the poet Nikolai Nekrasov and Ivan Panaev.

14. On this, see Herzen's correspondence, Gertsen, *Sobranie sochinenii* 22:212, and his diary, 2:386, 397 (entries for October 21 and December 27, 1844).

15. Ibid. 3:89–316. For commentary, see Malia, *Herzen*, pp. 313–18.

16. See Gertsen, *Sobranie sochinenii* 9:92–133, for descriptions of the circles.

17. Ibid. 9:207–08; P. V. Annenkov, *The Extraordinary Decade: Literary Memoirs*, trans. Irwin R. Titunik, ed. Arthur P. Mendel (Ann Arbor, Mich., 1968), pp. 129–38; Isaiah Berlin, *Russian Thinkers* (New York, 1979), pp. 131–35, *et passim*.

18. On this point, see the remarks of Tatiana Astrakova in T. P. Passek, *Iz dal'nykh let: Vospominaniia* (Moscow, 1963), 2:327–28.

19. On Ketcher, see Gertsen, *Sobranie sochinenii* 9:223–55, *et passim*; see also Natalie Herzen to Elizaveta Granovskaia, March 3 (February 19), 1847, and Natalie Herzen to Tatiana Astrakova, September 1 (August 20), 1847, in ibid. 23:11, 39.

20. The need to find something new to talk about was expressed humorously in his open letters home; see the beginning of the "Pis'ma iz Avenue Marigny" (ibid. 5:15). [Throughout I shall refer to the first version of the 'Pis'ma," the published and unpublished series "Pis'ma iz Avenue Marigny," "Pis'ma s via del Corso," and "Opiat' v Parizhe" (ibid. 5:229–44, 245–302, 303–82). Only the first few letters appeared in Russian at the time; others came out later in German translation. The citations, however, may come from the later, published version of the complete set, "Pis'ma iz Frantsii i Italii," when the latter reprinted the original version unchanged.] Orlik cites a number of other Russian travelers whose published Letters from France informed readers at home about advanced doctrines (*Peredovaia Rossiia*, pp.

195–96). Annenkov, who was far less radical than Herzen, and whose 1842 "Pis'ma iz-za granitsy" Orlik cites in this context, maintained his interest in the European left. He met and described Marx and Weitling, among others, and in 1847 accompanied Herzen and Bakunin in their Paris activities.

21. Gertsen, *Sobranie sochinenii* 5:7–385; vol. 23, *passim* (Letters to "Moskovskim druz'iam").

22. Mariia Korsh's contribution is discussed in K. I. Butina, ed., "Materialy A. I. Gertsen iz Arkhiva Korshei," *Zapiski Otdela rukopisei, Gosudarstvennaia Biblioteka SSSR imeni V.I. Lenina* 32 (1971), 182–200.

23. On Blanc, see Leo Loubere, *Louis Blanc: His Life and His Contribution to the Rise of French Jacobin Socialism* (Evanston, Ill., 1961), esp. pp. 22–48; on Proudhon, see Robert L. Hoffman, *Revolutionary Justice: The Social and Political Theory of P.-J. Proudhon* (Urbana, Ill., 1972); George Woodcock, *Pierre-Joseph Proudhon: A Biography* (London, 1955), pp. 44–65, 76–80, 87–103; see also Pierre Haubtmann, *Proudhon, Marx et la pensée allemande* (Grenoble, 1981). For the sense of a new crystallization of social thought in the 1840s, see William H. Sewell, *Work and Revolution in France: The Language of Labor from the Old Regime to 1848* (Cambridge, Mass., 1980), esp. pp. 219–20, 232–36.

24. David Owen Evans, *Le Socialisme romantique: Pierre Leroux et ses contemporains* (Paris, 1948), pp. 39–40; for a far more detailed discussion of the relationship between Leroux and Sand, see Jean-Pierre Lacassagne, *Pierre Leroux et George Sand: Histoire d'une amitié (D'après une correspondance inédite 1836–1866)* (Paris, 1973); see also Alexandre Zévaès, "Félix Pyat: Homme de lettres et homme politique," *La Nouvelle revue*, 4th series, October 1930, p. 265.

25. On Poncy and Perdiguer, see Sewell, *Work and Revolution*, pp. 220–22, 236–42, *et passim*; for Sand's relations with them, see George Sand, *Correspondance*, ed. Georges Lubin (Paris, 1964–   ), vol. 5ff., *passim*.

26. See, for example, Sand's negotiations to review Blanc's *History of the French Revolution* in the manner he would find satisfactory and to place the reviews (ibid. 8:107–08, 122–24).

27. As an example, one young journalist from the provinces who had long struggled to make his career finally felt he had arrived. After years of begging every available sou from his mother, he invited her to visit him in Paris, where, he boasted, he could introduce her to the leading lights of French socialism, "Père Leroux," "Père Buchez," and George Sand, and where she would "see" the press magnate Emile Girardin and the conservative politician Guizot (Théophile Thoré to his mother, April 3, 1839, Papiers de Thoré-Bürger, Bibliothèque de l'Arsenal, Paris, 7909, f. 51).

28. For overviews, see Claude Bellanger, Jacques Godechot, Pierre Guiral, and Fernand Terrou, eds. *Histoire générale de la presse française* (Paris, 1969), 2:91–114: John Plamenatz, *The Revolutionary Movement in France, 1815–71* (London, 1958), pp. 35–62; see also works cited dealing with individual political figures.

29. Evans, *Le Socialisme romantique*, p. 39 and n.
30. Bellanger et al., *Histoire générale de la presse française* 2:129.
31. As did the ex-Saint-Simonian socialist with secret society contacts, Théophile Thoré (Thoré to Félix Delhasse, August, 1843, Papiers de Thoré-Bürger, 7911, f. 113).
32. Zévaès, "Pyat," pp. 264–65.
33. Plamenatz, *The Revolutionary Movement*, pp. 58–62.
34. Bernard H. Moss, *The Origins of the French Labor Movement, 1830–1914: The Socialism of Skilled Workers* (Berkeley, Calif., 1976), pp. 38–39.
35. On the working-class movement, see Sewell, *Work and Revolution*.
36. On the attraction Paris offered foreign exiles, particularly intellectuals, see Lloyd S. Kramer, "Exile and European Thought: Heine, Marx, and Mickiewicz in July Monarchy Paris," *Historical Reflections/Réflexions Historiques* 11, no. 1 (1984), 50–53.
37. E. Kandel' and S. Levtsova, "Marks i Engel's—vospitateli pervykh proletarskikh revoliutsionerov," in *Mark i Engel's i pervye proletarskie revoliutsionery*, ed. E. Kandel' (Moscow, 1961), p. 10.
38. Edmund Silberner, *Moses Hess: Geschichte seines Lebens* (Leiden, 1966), pp. 149–50; Hermann Ewerbeck, *L'Allemagne et les Allemands* (Paris, 1851), pp. 589–93.
39. Ibid.; Arthur Mueller Lehning, "The International Association (1855–1859)," *International Review for Social History* 3 (1938), 192–99.
40. Sidney Hook, *From Hegel to Marx: Studies in the Intellectual Development of Karl Marx* (Ann Arbor, 1962), pp. 126–28.
41. Since the two men lived in a relatively small community of exile, the categorical statement that they never met is perhaps too strong—they may have accidentally encountered each other; but they did attempt to avoid each other, and left no record of any personal contact.
42. Victor Fleury, *Le Poète Georges Herwegh (1817–1875)*, Bibliothèque de la "Révolution de 1848," no. 6 (Paris, 1911), p. 69.
43. Julius Fröbel, *Ein Lebenslauf. Aufzeichnungen, Erinnerungen und Bekentnisse* (Stuttgart, 1890–91), 1:95–97.
44. Fleury *Le Poète Georges Herwegh*, pp. 85–95.
45. Herwegh's testimony in the trial of the League of the Just is revealing: "I have always found it an honor to frequent from time to time the inferior classes, who are rude, clumsy, but healthy and robust, and to search in the dreams and castles in Spain of popular poetry for the fundamental plan of the future society. I entered into relations with the Geneva group in this spirit; I have had discussions with its members; I have even dined with them, without belonging to their group, nor without ever having been invited to join, for I hate leagues and conspiracies, not from cowardice or loyalism, but from a profound moral sentiment: the cause of the people seems to me to be too great to be resolved in coteries which vainly

compromise it vis-à-vis the power which disposes of force" (in ibid., pp. 115–16).

46. Ruge to Fröbel, August 18, 1843, in Arnold Ruge, *Briefwechsel und Tagebuchblätter aus den Jahren 1825–1880,* ed. Paul Herrlich (Berlin, 1886), 1:327; Fröbel, *Ein Lebenslauf* 1:134.

47. Marie d'Agoult to Herwegh, 1844, "Lettres de Marie d'Agoult," Bibliothèque Nationale, Nouvelles Acquisitions Françaises, 25,183, f. 370.

48. Hook *From Hegel to Marx,* pp. 153–64, analyzes the theoretical disagreements; see also David McLellan, *Karl Marx: His Life and Thought* (New York, 1973), p. 78; Ruge to Fröbel, June 4 and December 6, 1844, in *Briefwechsel* 1:357–58, 380–81.

49. For bibliography on *Vorwärts,* see Wolfgang Büttner, "Das Feuilleton des Pariser 'Vorwärts!' " *Jahrbuch für Geschichte* 32 (1985), 172.

50. McLellan, *Marx,* pp. 100–03, 135–36.

51. For a strong statement of Marx's indebtedness to French social thought, see David Gregory, "The Influence of French Socialism on the Thought of Karl Marx, 1843–45," *Proceedings of the Sixth Annual Meeting of the Western Society of French Historians* (Santa Barbara, Calif., 1979), pp. 242–51.

52. The most substantial biography of d'Agoult is Jacques Vier, *La Comtesse d'Agoult et son temps* (Paris, 1955–63), although Vier is somewhat too partial to and protective of his subject and denies that there was an affair. However, the letters published by Marcel Herwegh in *Au Printemps des dieux: Correspondance inédite de la Comtesse Marie d'Agoult et du poète Georges Herwegh,* 5th ed. (Paris, 1929) suggest that the two were on intimate terms until late 1844. Among d'Agoult's unpublished letters is one complaining that Marx and his friends were spreading rumors abut Emma's jealousy, and another, attributed to the end of 1844, in which the countess was looking for an excuse to write Herwegh, and included a misquotation (in English) from Robert Burns: "Have you never loved so kindly, / Have you never loved so blindly, / Never meet and never parted / You have never been broken hearted." (Lettres de Marie d'Agoult, ff. 427, 450).

53. Michel Cadot, *La Russie dans la vie intellectuelle française (1829–1856)* (Paris, 1967), pp. 36–37; E. H. Carr, *Michael Bakunin* (1937; rpt. New York, n.d.), pp. 135–37.

54. Oscar J. Hammen, *The Red '48ers: Karl Marx and Friedrich Engels* (New York, 1969), pp. 40, 119–20.

55. This process is discussed in considerable detail in David Felix, *Marx as Politician* (Carbondale, Ill., 1983), pp. 60–78. I agree with Felix's thesis, but find his argumentation unconvincing. Much of the later discussion of relations between Marx and the other radicals will be based on the assumption that "Marx was primarily a politician and not a thinker. . . . As great as Marx was as thinker, I shall argue that he was a greater politician" (p. ix).

56. Herwegh to d'Agoult, September 23, 1844, in *Au Printemps des dieux,* ed. Herwegh, pp. 107–08.

57. Ludwig Bernays to Moses Hess and friends, January 21, 1846, in Moses Hess, *Briefwechsel,* ed. Edmund Silberner (The Hague, 1959), pp. 146–48. Bernays thought Bakunin, whom he hated, was a bad influence on Herwegh. Fröbel in his memoirs *(Ein Lebenslauf* 1:140–41) charged that in 1843 Bakunin, by his political tactlessness, had undermined Fröbel's position as editor of the liberal *Schweizerisch Republikaner.* Fleury, however, attributed Fröbel's loss of his position to Herwegh's involvement in the trial of the League of the Just *(Le Poète Georges Herwegh,* p. 115).

58. Joan S. Skurnowicz, *Romantic Nationalism and Liberalism: Joachim Lelewel and the Polish National Idea,* East European Monographs, no. 83 (Boulder, Colo., 1981), pp. 73–83.

59. R. F. Leslie, *Reform and Insurrection in Russian Poland, 1856–65* (London, 1963), p. 5; B. Nikolaevskii, "Za vashu i nashu vol'nost'! (Stranitsy iz istorii russko-polskikh otnoshenii)," *Novyi Zhurnal* 7 (1944), 266; Skurnowicz, *Romantic Nationalism,* p. 88.

60. Skurnowicz, *Romantic Nationalism,* p. 87.

61. E.E.Y. Hales, *Mazzini and the Secret Societies: The Making of a Myth* (New York, n.d.), pp. 111–35.

62. Leslie, *Reform and Revolution,* pp. 7–8; Peter Brock, *Polish Revolutionary Populism: A Study in Agrarian Socialist Thought from the 1830's to the 1850's* (Toronto, 1977), *passim.*

63. Peter Brock, "Polish Democrats and English Radicals, 1832–1862: A Chapter in the History of Anglo-Polish Relations," *Journal of Modern History* 25, no. 2 (June 1953), 147–48; Henry Weisser, "Chartist Internationalism, 1845–1848," *Historical Journal* 14 (1971), 58–62.

64. Cadot, *La Russie dans la vie intellectuelle française,* p. 446; for details of the articles' coverage of Herzen, see B. F. Egorov, K. N. Lomanov, I. G. Prushkina, and Ia. E. El'sberg, eds., *Letopis' zhizni i tvorchestva A. I. Gertsen: 1812–1870* (Moscow, 1974), 1:396, 397, 398.

65. Carr, *Bakunin,* pp. 137–47.

66. Iu. Kamenev, "Samyi ostroumnyi protivnik Gertsena," *Vestnik Evropy* 49, no. 4 (April 1914), 124–25.

67. In March 1846, Marie d'Agoult turned to Herwegh for news of Poland (d'Agoult to Herwegh, March 6, 1846, in Lettres de Marie d'Agoult, f. 494).

68. Marcel Herwegh, ed., *1848: Briefe von und an Georg Herwegh,* 2d ed. (Munich, 1899), pp. 42–43, 49–50, 52–62, 64–78, 80–81.

69. Letter to his Moscow friends, February 8 (February 20), 1847, in Gertsen, *Sobranie sochinenii* 23:9.

70. Letter to his Moscow friends, March 12 (February 28), 1847, in ibid. 23:13.

71. On Jacoby, see Edmund Silberner, *Johann Jacoby: Politiker und*

Mensch, Veröffentlichungen des Instituts für Sozialgeschichte (Braunschweig-Bonn; Bonn–Bad Godesberg, 1976); Silberner, ed., *Johann Jacoby Briefwechsel: 1816–1849*, Veröffentlichungen des Instituts für Sozialgeschichte (Braunschweig; Hanover, 1979). See also Jacques Droz, *Les Révolutions allemandes de 1848* (Paris, 1957), pp. 30–69, *passim;* Theodore Hamerow, *Restoration, Revolution, Reaction: Economics and Politics in Germany, 1815–1871* (Princeton, N.J., 1958), esp. p. 65; Peter Wende, *Radikalismus in Vormärz: Untersuchungen zur politischen Theorie der fruhen deutschen Demokratie*, Frankfurter Historischer Abhandlungen, vol. 11 (Wiesbaden, 1975), p. 32.

72. Dietmar U. Wagner, "The German Students and the Failure of the 'Progressive Movement,' 1840–46," Consortium on Revolutionary Europe, 1750–1850, *Proceedings* (1977), p. 53.

73. Ibid., pp. 58–60.

74. Ibid., pp. 54, 62.

75. Bernays to Hess, letter cited in n. 57 (above), p. 147.

76. On the relations between Mazzini and Sand, see Sand, *Correspondance* 6:603–04; 7:717; 8:125–27, 234–36, 281. The "Letter to the Pope" and Sand's article appeared in *Le Constitutionnel*, February 7, 1848.

Chapter 2. The Traveler

1. For her memoirs, and a glimpse of the domestic side of Herzen's life generally, see M. K. Reikhel, *Otryvki iz vospominanii*, Materialy dlia biografii Gertsena, vyp. 1 (Moscow, 1909).

2. Livonia was one of the three Baltic provinces of the Russian Empire. Its territory is divided between present-day Latvia and Estonia. The native rural population was Latvian and Estonian, while the cities were dominated by Germans. The territory had originally been colonized by German crusader knights, then annexed by Sweden, and won by Russia early in the eighteenth century. This history is reflected in Herzen's impressions.

3. Luisa Haag, Mariia Ern, and Kolia Herzen went to Württemburg, to see Haag's relatives, and later joined the rest of the family in Paris, taking an apartment near theirs. The separate accommodations suggest some domestic problems, but their nature is unknown. To understand the separate apartment, Natalie wrote her friend Tatiana Astrakova, one would have to understand all the backstairs details, and these she did not provide (Natalie Herzen to Tatiana Astrakova, October 13 and 15, 1847, in A. I. Gertsen [Herzen], *Neizdannye pis'ma A. I. Gertsena k N. I. i T. A. Astrakovym*, ed. L. L. Domger [New York, 1957], p. 116). Haag and Ern also visited England during this summer, leaving Kolia with his parents. Avenue Marigny is in one of the most exclusive sections of Paris, extending between the Champs-Elysées and the Rue St. Honoré, in a section dominated by government administration

and couturiers. Today, almost all the private buildings are gone, replaced by parks or offices. The street ends at, of all things, the Ministry of the Interior, and it also includes the back of the Elysée Palace, home for twenty years to Louis Napoleon Bonaparte, as well as subsequent presidents of the republic.

4. Gertsen, *Sobranie sochinenii* 5:17–18, 19.
5. Ibid. 5:22, 23.
6. Ibid. 5:20.
7. Ibid. 5:21.
8. Ibid. 7:9–10; for more detailed discussion, see chapter 6.
9. Herzen to Moscow friends, February 20, 21, 1847, in ibid. 23:8. On Turgenev's peregrinations in the wake of Pauline Viardot, see Leonard Schapiro, *Turgenev: His Life and Times* (New York, 1978), pp. 55–60; Turgenev to Mariia Korsh, around September 1, 1847, I. S. Turgenev, *Pis'ma v trinadtsati tomakh* I, *1831–1850* (Moscow-Leningrad, 1961), p. 259.
10. Herzen sent greetings to them from Müller in his first letter from Berlin, Herzen to Moscow friends, February 20, 1847, *Sobranie sochinenii* 23:8.
11. Ibid. 11:168–71; M. A. Bakunin, *Pis'ma M. A. Bakunina k A. I. Gertsenu i N. P. Ogarevu*, ed. M. P. Dragomanov (St. Petersburg, 1906), p. 29n.
12. In *Byloe i dumy* Herzen reported that he ran into Bakunin in the street immediately upon his arrival in Paris: Bakunin was busily arguing with several companions, just as he had been accustomed to do in the old days in Moscow. The story may be true, but it is surely misleading, for it implies a closer relationship between Herzen and Bakunin than ever existed in Russia, and it ignores the prosaic problem of how Herzen knew where to look for him (Gertsen, *Sobranie sochinenii* 11:16–17).
13. Herzen to Moscow friends, March 12–19, 1847, in ibid. 23:12–16. The recommendation to see the hospital came from a respectable Russian source, a diplomat named Titov whom Herzen ran into at a customs station.
14. Ibid. 5:16.
15. Natalie Herzen to Tatiana Astrakova, July 3, 1847, in ibid. 23:32.
16. Ibid. 6:498.
17. After returning to St. Petersburg, Belinskii vigorously defended Herzen's "Pis'ma iz Avenue Marigny" against criticism from the Moscow friends (Belinskii to Botkin, December 2–6, 1847, in V. G. Belinskii, *Polnoe sobranie sochinenii*, vol. 12: *Pis'ma, 1841–1848* [Moscow, 1956], pp. 446–52). However, just before his death, he defended the historical role of the bourgeoisie (see Walicki, *The Slavophile Controversy*, pp. 443–44).
18. Natalie Herzen to Tatiana Astrakova, May 3, 1847, in Gertsen, *Sobranie sochinenii* 23:25; Herzen to Astrakova, July 4, 1847, in ibid. 23:33; Natalie to Astrakova, June 29, 1849, and undated (Autumn 1849), in Herzen Family Papers, Bakhmetev Archive, Columbia University.
19. On Sazonov, see N. Riazanov, "Karl Marks i russkie liudi sorokovykh godov," *Sovremennyi mir*, no. 9 (1912), 146–68.

20. Natalie Herzen to Tatiana Astrakova, September 1, 1848, in Gertsen, *Sobranie sochinenii* 23:39.

21. Thus, a note from Natalie Herzen to Astrakova from the mid-1840s arranged to transmit a letter from Mariia Ivanovna to her brother through Annenkov, who was going abroad (undated note, Herzen Family Papers).

22. Katkov later became editor of the arch-conservative *Moskovskie vedomosti*.

23. Ogarev to Herzen, in a letter cited by Dragomanov in his introduction to Bakunin, *Pis'ma*, pp. 12–13.

24. On the subsidy, see ibid.; on Herzen's friendliness, see Bakunin to his relatives, July 13–15, 1840, in M. A. Bakunin, *Sobranie sochinenii i pisem, 1826–1876*, ed. Iu. M. Steklov (Moscow, 1935), 3:13–15.

25. Cadot, *La Russie dans la vie intellectuelle française*, p. 42.

26. Malia, *Herzen*, pp. 345–49.

27. Gertsen, "Pis'ma iz Frantsii i Italii," in *Sobranie sochinenii* 5:141.

28. Herzen to P. B. Annenkov, in ibid. 23:68. The friendship lasted throughout Herzen's life. See Bocquet's condolence letter to Sasha Herzen, in L. P. Lanskii, "Otkliki na smert' Gertsena: Po materialam inostrannoi pechati i 'Prazhskoi Kollektsii,' " *Literaturnoe nasledstvo* 63 (1956), 533–34.

29. Herzen to Moscow friends, June 21, 1847, in *Sobranie sochinenii* 23:31.

30. Ibid. 10:190.

31. Herzen got into the habit of writing to Mariia Reichel on a regular basis in 1852–1853, when, after Natalie's death, she cared for his daughters for a year in Paris until he got settled in London.

32. Kamenev, "Samyi ostroumnyi protivnik," pp. 124–25.

33. Gertsen, *Sobranie sochinenii* 11:128. Orlik suggests, without evidence, that Herzen was a visitor at the Decembrist Nikolai Turgenev's salon, where Poles also gathered (*Peredovaia Rossiia*, p. 224). This seems quite likely.

34. Neither in the published Herwegh, *Au Printemps des dieux*, ed. Marcel Herwegh, nor in the unpublished Lettres de Marie d'Agoult, have I found reference to Herzen, aside from one oblique mention in a letter to Emma Herwegh written after the crisis in 1851, in which the countess merely asks, "Où est votre mari? Où sont les Herzens?" (N.A. Fr., 25, 183, f. 313). Other Russians—Sazonov, Bakunin, and Ivan Golovin, are occasionally mentioned by d'Agoult, leading to the suspicion that the Herwegh family destroyed letters referring to Herzen before returning the correspondence to d'Agoult's family. One not very reliable witness, Ivan Golovin, places Herzen at d'Agoult's salon in 1848 (Iwan Golownin [Ivan Golovin], *Der Russische Nihilismus. Meine Beziehungen zu Herzen und zu Bakunin* [Leipzig, n.d.], p. 61).

35. Malia, *Herzen*, p. 337. For a more traditional view of Herzen's reaction to the West, see El'sberg, *Gertsen*, pp. 212–310. Z. V. Smirnova, while agreeing with Malia that Herzen's disillusionment began early and was the

inevitable result of his illusions, nonetheless feels that the effect of living through a revolution cannot be ignored: "And if it is indubitable that the germ of a series of ideas, developed by Herzen in the future, were already present before his departure abroad . . . it is equally indubitable . . . that the revolution of 1848 placed a series of new problems before Herzen's thought and brought him into contact with new situations" (*Sotsial'naia filosofiia*, p. 85).

36. Herzen to Shchepkin, April 23, 1847, in *Sobranie sochinenii* 23:19–23; see also Natalie to Astrakova, May 3, 1847, in ibid. 23:24, which confirms Herzen's impressions. The real thrust of the letter was understood in Moscow, where Botkin disapproved of it (Botkin to Annenkov, July 19, 1847, in P. V. Annenkov, *P. V. Annenkov i ego druz'ia. Literaturnyia vospominaniia i perepiska 1835–1885 godov* [St. Petersburg, 1892], pp. 541–42).

37. Gertsen, *Sobranie sochinenii* 5:42–55.

38. Natalie mentioned seeing it in a letter to Astrakova written toward the end of May (in ibid. 23:26).

39. Ibid. 5:42–55.

40. Zévaès, "Félix Pyat," p. 267. See also James H. Billington, *Fire in the Minds of Men: Origins of the Revolutionary Faith* (New York, 1980), p. 237.

41. Diary entry, October 29, 1842, in *Sobranie sochinenii* 2:313; Billington, *Fire in the Minds of Men*, p. 156. Herzen intended to translate, abridge and improve Pyat's play as a vehicle for Shchepkin (Herzen to Sergei and Tatiana Astrakov, end of May, 1847, in *Sobranie sochinenii* 23:25).

42. Thoré to his mother, late 1847 (Thoré-Bürger Papers, 7909, f. 116); d'Agoult to Herwegh, September 1847 (Lettres de Marie d'Agoult, ff. 524, 525). D'Agoult invited Thoré to attend her salon in 1847; if he did so, there might be a common source for these two similar, dire predictions (Thoré-Bürger Papers, 7913, ff. 42–46). See also d'Agoult's view of these events as part of the prologue to revolution in Daniel Stern [Marie d'Agoult], *Histoire de la Révolution de 1848* (Paris, 1850), 1:10–13.

43. Gertsen, *Sobranie sochinenii* 5:245.

44. See, for example, Herzen to Natalie, June 7, 1837, in ibid. 21:173–74.

45. Ibid. 23:246.

46. A. J. Whyte, *The Evolution of Modern Italy* (New York, 1965), pp. 51–53.

47. Gertsen, *Sobranie sochinenii* 5:252.

48. See ibid. 5:255–56, for Herzen's account of going to hear a concert that advertised a new hymn to Pius IX, but learning that under pressure the piece had been replaced by a selection from "The Thieving Magpie" ("Pie neuf" replaced by "Pie voleuse").

49. Terminology is confusing here. "Savoy," "Piedmont," and "the Kingdom of Sardinia" all refer to the same political entity.

50. Herzen to Granovskii, August 4, 1849, *Sobranie sochinenii* 23:171.

51. Ibid. 23:245–66.
52. Ibid. 23:252.
53. For this discussion I have used the early, manuscript form of this article, in ibid. 6:324–40, and commentary, p. 497.
54. Ibid. 5:247. Clôtre St.-Merry, in Paris, was the scene of heavy street fighting in an insurrection in June 1832. The "September Days" refer to the September massacres of 1792, which inaugurated the radical Jacobin period of the French Revolution.
55. Ibid.
56. Ibid. 5:267–70, and Herzen to Moscow friends, January 30, 1848, in ibid. 23:56–57. See also Smirnova, *Sotsial'naia filosofiia*, pp. 99–100, and Malia, *Herzen*, pp. 362–64.
57. For a discussion of the extent to which Herzen can be called an existentialist, which largely centers on *S togo berega*, see William Cannon Weidemaier, "Herzen and the Existential World View: A New Approach to an Old Debate," *Slavic Review* 40 (Winter 1981), 557–69. Weidemaier surveys the literature on this subject and strongly asserts the validity of the label. Without going into details of philosophic arguments, this author agrees with the other historians cited by Weidemaier, Raeff, Berlin, and Malia, that it seems reasonable to use the term *existentialist* to describe Herzen's demand that individuals maintain their freedom, humanity, and sense of humor, while suspended over a moral and metaphysical void. The persuasiveness of Herzen's thought in his own household is reflected in a letter that Natalie Herzen wrote to the Tuchkov sisters at this time: "Don't scorn the present, there is no future; none at all. Think well—there is only what *is*. You think that I wish to preach morality to you—not at all, I am only showing you how shameless it is to take the present from others. It is possible that we will see each other at Akshino [Ogarev's Penza estate], it is possible. But, what may be also may not be, while it is true that you are here in Rome" (in Natalie Herzen, "Dnevnik i pis'ma N. A. Gertsena," ed. M. Gershenzon, *Russkie Propylei: Materialy po istorii russkoi mysli i literatury* 1 [1915], p. 292).
58. On the background of the Tuchkov family, see Nataliia Ogareva-Tuchkova, *Vospominaniia, 1848–1870* (Moscow, 1903).
59. On the intensely emotional quality of this relationship, see Carr, *Romantic Exiles*, pp. 37–52, and Natalie Herzen's letters to Tuchkova in "Dnevnik i pis'ma." See also Lillian Faderman, *Surpassing the Love of Men: Romantic Friendship and Love Between Women from the Sixteenth Century to the Present* (New York, 1981), pp. 145–231, for a general discussion of relationships between women in the nineteenth century. Faderman argues that such intense friendships, while not overtly sexual, were a manifestation of a basically homosexual orientation; Carr suggests that in Natalie Herzen's case her "unrestrained yet innocent passion" for Natalie Tuchkova helped prepare her emotionally for the affair with Georg Herwegh. The whole question of the

nature of emotional bonding between friends and lovers in the nineteenth century still needs a great deal of exploration; in the case of the Herzens the manifest heterosexual orientation of both spouses in no way precluded strong emotional attachment to friends of the same sex.

The impact of the friendship between the two Natalies on the family's future life was very great; because of it, the Herzens encouraged the relationship between Ogarev and Natalie Tuchkova as the completion of their circle of friendship; and it was as a person loved by both Natalie Herzen and Ogarev that Natalie Tuchkova later appealed to Herzen.

60. Gertsen, *Sobranie sochinenii* 23:48. Galakhov's letter is quoted in *Letopis' Gertsena* 1:421.

61. Herzen found the book a "crime," while Ivanov "passionately loved" its author ("A. Ivanov," Gertsen, *Sobranie sochinenii* 13:326). Gogol's book stimulated Belinskii's "Open Letter to Gogol'," his strongest and clearest statement of liberal Westernism, and one of the classic Westernist statements. The "Letter" was written in July 1847, in Salzbrünn, and Herzen learned of it when Belinskii came to Paris (see Ralph E. Matlaw, ed., *Belinsky, Chernyshevsky and Dobrolyubov: Selected Criticism* [New York, 1962], pp. 83–92).

62. Herzen to Annenkov, March 5, 1848, in *Sobranie sochinenii* 23:66; Herzen to Moscow friends, August 2–8, 1848, in ibid. 23:90; Z. M. Tsypkina, "Gertsen i deiateli ital'ianskogo natsional'no-osvoboditel'nogo dvizheniia (1848–1852 gg.)," in *Ob'edinenie Italii: 100 let bor'by za nezavisimost' i demokratiiu. Sbornik statei* (Moscow, 1962), p. 32.

63. Gertsen, *Sobranie sochinenii* 5:275–81.

64. Ibid. 5:281. Natalie Herzen to Tatiana Astrakova, March 16, 1848, in "N. A. Gertsen (Otryvki iz neizdannykh pisem)," *Russkiia zapiski* 14 (February 1939), 104. Mariia Korsh was severely crippled, which meant that she was often the one left behind.

65. Herzen to Annenkov, March 5, 1848, in *Sobranie sochinenii* 23:66.

66. Ibid. 23:65; Natalie Herzen to Tatiana Astrakova, March 16, 1848, in "N. A. Gertsen . . . pisem," p. 105.

67. Gertsen, *Sobranie sochinenii* 5:292.

68. Herzen's delay in returning to Paris is discussed by Allen McConnell, "Against All Idols: Alexander Herzen and the Revolutions of 1848. A Chapter in the History of Tragic Liberalism," Ph.D. diss., Columbia University, 1954, pp. 114–16.

69. Herzen to Annenkov, March 5, 1848, in *Sobranie sochinenii* 23:66–68.

70. Natalie Herzen to Tatiana Astrakova, March 16, 1848, Herzen Family Papers. At this time the Herzens were still intending to return to Russia, and were thus very careful about what they put down on paper in letters destined for home.

71. "A. Ivanov," Gertsen, *Sobranie sochinenii* 13:326.

72. Ibid. 10:27–28.

73. Natalie Tuchkova to Tatiana Passek, late 1880s, in N. P. and N. A. Ogarev, *Arkhiv N. A. in N. P. Ogarevykh*, ed. M. Gershenzon (Moscow, 1930), p. 267. Tuchkova said only three Russian women were involved because Natalie Herzen was physically too weak to participate.

74. Gertsen, *Sobranie sochinenii* 5:298–301.

Chapter 3. Paris: The First Months

1. For this section, I have relied primarily on Stern [Marie d'Agoult], *Histoire de la Révolution de 1848;* Maurice Agulhon, *The Republican Experiment: 1848–1852* (New York, 1983), pp. 22–49; Marc Caussidière, *Mémoires* (Paris, 1849); Louis Blanc, *1848: Historical Revelations* (rpt. New York, 1971); and Georges Duveau, *1848: The Making of a Revolution,* trans. Ann Carter, intro. George Rude (New York, 1968). In this summary I have attempted to explain briefly the dynamics of the political situation in France as they appear to me, and to provide an explanation of those aspects of the revolutionary experience that Herzen dealt with in his "Opiat' v Parizhe." The general perspective is that of the revolution as seen from the club left; for a very different modern view, see William Fortescue, *Alphonse de Lamartine: A Political Biography* (New York, 1983). The first section of this chapter will explain the revolution as Herzen saw it, and introduce Herzen's 1848 *Pis'ma iz Frantsii i Italii,* in *Sobranie sochinenii,* vol. 5.

2. This was on the Left Bank and included the working-class Faubourg St. Marcel, the proposed site for the banquet (Duveau, *1848,* p. 9).

3. Lead article, *La Vraie République,* August 17, 1848, p. 1; Stern, *Histoire* 1:100–01; Caussidière, *Mémoires* 1:36–37.

4. Similarly, in 1830, economic crisis lay behind popular restiveness, but does not appear to have played a part in the demands of the crowd that brought down Charles X. See David Pinkney, *The French Revolution of 1830* (Princeton, N.J., 1973), pp. 60–61, 63–67, *et passim.*

5. Duveau, *1848,* pp. 54–55. His real name was Alexandre Martin.

6. On Lamartine, see Stern, *Histoire* 1:19–23; and Fortescue, *Lamartine.*

7. Fortescue, *Lamartine,* pp. 140–43, 152.

8. Ibid., p. 187.

9. Gertsen, *Sobranie sochinenii* 5:340.

10. See below. George Sand worked in the ministry for a short time, and prepared some of the propaganda.

11. For Blanc's account of the positive contributions of the commission, see his *1848,* pp. 122–87.

12. On the clubs, see Peter H. Amann, *Revolution and Mass Democracy: The Paris Club Movement in 1848* (Princeton, N.J., 1975).

13. For examples of admiration of Barbès, see Stern, *Histoire* 2:160–61;

and Sand, letter to Maurice Dudevant, April 16–17, 1848, in *Correspondance* 8:418–19.

14. On Blanqui and the so-called Taschereau document, see Maurice Dommanget, *Un Drame politique de 1848: Blanqui et le Document Taschereau* (Paris, 1948). Herzen himself was not unaffected by the hostility generated against Blanqui; he wrote to his friends in August that Blanqui was very influential and the most intelligent of the socialists, but dishonorable. "Barbès, before whose charm and nobility even his enemies kneel, is a man of character and astonishing courage; his talent to attract people to him is great, but he cannot lead, manage, organize" (Herzen to Moscow friends, August 5, 1848, in *Sobranie sochinenii* 23:88). A year later, he saw Blanqui and Proudhon as the only significant leaders of the French left (Herzen to Moscow friends, September 27, 1849, in ibid. 23:189).

15. Lead article, *La Vraie République*, no. 102, August 19, 1848, p. 1.

16. Louis Blanc had made his reputation as a socialist theoretician by arguing in favor of "social workshops," which were to be set up with government aid, but would be essentially self-governing producers' cooperatives. The "national workshops," which were established by the government of which he was a part, were frequently taken to be the realization of his theories. After the failure of the revolution, Blanc bitterly denied this, and he never took credit for them (Blanc, *1848*, pp. 193–208). Although there remains some disagreement on this point (for instance, Fortescue, in his recent biography of Lamartine, implies Blanc's support for the workshops, but does not directly assert it; p. 154), most contemporary scholars accept Blanc's view (see Agulhon, *The Republican Experiment*, pp. 36–37).

17. See, on this point, Stern, *Histoire* 2:209–15.

18. On this point, see Sand to Henri Martin, March 9, 1848, and to Louis Viardot, March 17, 1848, in *Correspondance* 8:333, 349; Blanc, *1848*, pp. 296–99; Loubere, *Louis Blanc*, pp. 96–97. The Jacobin left was less certain that the elections should be delayed; see Caussidière, *Mémoires* 2:9–11; and Marcel Dessal, *Un Révolutionnaire jacobin: Charles Delescluze 1809–1871* (Paris, 1952), p. 62.

19. *Sobranie sochinenii* 5:352.

20. Caussidière, *Mémoires* 2:11–12.

21. *Sobranie sochinenii* 5:355.

22. Ibid.

23. On this point, Marx's criticism was trenchant, though similar in content to that of others. See "The Class Struggles in France: 1848–1850," in Karl Marx and Friedrich Engels, *Selected Works in Two Volumes* (Moscow, 1958), 1:150–54.

24. John M. Merriman, *The Agony of the Republic: The Repression of the Left in Revolutionary France, 1848–1851* (New Haven, Conn.: 1978), pp. 2–21; see also Agulhon, *The Republican Experiment*, pp. 46–47.

25. "L'Ordre en Pologne," *La Vraie République*, May 15, 1848, p. 1.
26. Cited in Louis Gottschalk, *The Era of the French Revolution (1715–1815)* (Boston, 1929), p. 223.
27. Edward Royle, *Victorian Infidels: The Origins of the British Secularist Movement, 1791–1866* (Manchester, 1974), p. 252.
28. Lehning, "The International Association," pp. 189–90.
29. Ibid., pp. 191–93.
30. W. J. Linton, *Memories* (London, 1895), pp. 98–102.
31. Ibid., pp. 103–04.
32. A. R. Schoyen, *The Chartist Challenge: A Portrait of George Julian Harney* (London, 1958), pp. 158–59. Jones and Harney were closely associated with the militant leader Feargus O'Conner, editor of the Leeds *Northern Star*. O'Connor himself, however, was opposed to the Chartists involving themselves in foreign movements.
33. McLellan, *Marx*, pp. 155–59; Silberner, *Hess*, pp. 257–58.
34. Felix, *Marx as Politician*, pp. 64–67.
35. Quoted in McLellan, *Marx*, p. 154. For discussion of the attempt to recruit Proudhon, and the Frenchman's response, see Haubtmann, *Proudhon*, pp. 103–04, 110–11.
36. Ibid., pp. 69–72, 78.
37. McLellan, *Marx*, pp. 175–76; Hammen, *The Red '48ers*, pp. 154–56; Engels to Marx, January 14, 1848, in Karl Marx and Friedrich Engels, *Werke* (Berlin, 1945–67), 17:111; Felix, *Marx as Politician*, p. 68.
38. Stern, *Histoire* 1:33–36.
39. Sand interceded to get Mazzini's proscription removed and obtain a passport for him. Sand to Bastide, March 5, 1848, in *Correspondance* 8:320–21; McLellan, *Marx*, pp. 189–92; Carr, *Bakunin*, p. 155. Bakunin's expulsion will be discussed below.
40. *La Voix des Clubs*, no. 15, March 26, 1848; Alphonse Lucas, *Les Clubs et les Clubistes: Histoire complète* (Paris, 1851), pp. 131–32; *Le Représentant du Peuple*, no. 2, March 13, 1848; J. Tchernoff, *Associations et sociétés secrètes sous la deuxième république, 1848–1851, d'après des documents inédits* (rpt. New York, 1973), p. 207.
41. *La Voix des Clubs*, no. 2, March 14, 1848; *Le Représentant du Peuple*, no. 2, March 13, 1848; Tchernoff, *Associations et sociétés secrètes*, p. 206.
42. *La Voix des Clubs*, March 13, 1848, p. 2.
43. Golovin, a former civil servant, appeared in Paris in 1842, where he made contact with radical circles. Herzen met him in June 1848, after doing his utmost, he later claimed, to avoid him. Herzen's remarks about Golovin in *Byloe i dumy* are unrelievedly and bitterly hostile, and none of his contemporary correspondence suggests anything but scorn for his compatriot. See, for example, Herzen to Herwegh, April 21, 1850, *Sobranie sochinenii* 24:28–29, and, for the way his friends spoke of Golovin to Herzen, Moritz

Hartmann to Herzen, April 24, 1850, in I. A. Zhelvakova, *et al.*, eds., "Perepiska s nemetskimi demokratami," *Literaturnoe nasledstvo* 96 (1985), 176. On the other hand, for some years Golovin participated in the same causes as Herzen, and their names were frequently bracketed. Moreover, his involvement with the international émigré publication, *l'Almanach de l'exil*, brought him to the unfavorable notice of the French police. See J. Tchernoff, *Le Parti républicain au coup d'état et sous le Second Empire* (Paris, 1906), p. 112. See, on Golovin, in addition to Gertsen, *Sobranie sochinenii* 11:404–27; Miller, *Russian Revolutionary Emigrés*, pp. 50–64; Cadot, *La Russie dans la vie intellectuelle française*, pp. 28–29; Marc Vuilleumier, Michel Aucouturier, Sven Stelling-Michaud, and Michel Cadot, eds., *Autour d'Alexandre Herzen: Révolutionnaires et exilés du xixe siècle: Documents inédits* (Geneva, 1973), pp. 18–27.

44. *Sobranie sochinenii* 7:403; Golownin, *Der Russische Nihilismus*, p. 62.
45. *La Souveraineté du Peuple*, no. 3, April 8, 1848, p. 2.
46. *Sobranie sochinenii* 10:329; Riazanov, "Kark Marks," *Sovremennyi mir*, no. 8 (1912), 168.
47. *La Voix des Clubs*, March 13, 1848, p. 2.
48. Ibid., March 14, 1848, p. 2.
49. Both statements are printed in Herwegh, *1848*, pp. 121–25.
50. [Otto von] Corvin[-Wiersbitzki], *Aus der Leben eines Volkskampfers. Errinerungen* (Amsterdam, 1861) 3:29.
51. Amann, *Revolution and Mass Democracy*, p. 172.
52. Stern, *Histoire* 2:306–10; Caussidière, *Mémoires* 1:199–208.
53. Sources for this section include Fleury, Corvin, McLellan and Hammen, plus other works as specifically cited. The Russian authorities Lemke and Riazanov are inaccurate on this episode; Lemke notes in A. I. Gertsen [Alexander Herzen], *Polnoe sobranie sochinenii i pisem*, ed. M. K. Lemke (22 vols.; St. Petersburg, 1915–1925) [hereafter cited as Lemke], 14:29, 32, *et passim*, and Riazanov, "Marks," *Sovremennyi mir*, no. 12.
54. Lucas, *Les Clubs*, pp. 10–13, describes the regular functioning of the Association; Bruno Kaiser, *Der Freiheit eine Gasse: Aus den Leben und Werk Georg Herwegh* (Berlin, 1948), pp. 39–43, describes its most impressive public performance, its greeting to the Provisional Government.
55. Hammen, *The Red '48ers*, p. 201; Marx to Engels, March 16, 1848, *Werke* 28:119.
56. Herwig Förder, Martin Handt, Jefim Kandel, Sofia Lewiowa, eds., *Der Bund der Kommunisten: Dokumente und Materialen*, vol. 1, *1836–1849* (Berlin, 1970), pp. 715–48, *passim*.
57. "Zur Geschichte der deutschen Legion aus Paris," in Herwegh, *1848*, p. 134.
58. See Gottschalk to Herwegh, March 22, 1849, in ibid., p. 265; see chapter 4 for a fuller discussion of Gottschalk.

59. Gottschalk to Hess, March 26, 1848, in Hess, *Briefwechsel,* p. 175.
60. The "Appeal" was printed in *La Voix des Clubs,* no. 14, March 25, 1848, p. 3.
61. Corvin, *Aus der Leben eines Volkskampfers* 3:34–36.
62. D'Agoult to Emma Herwegh, Lettres de Marie d'Agoult, N.A. Fr. 25,183, f. 291; Stern, *Histoire* 2:311.
63. "Appeal."
64. Communiqué of the Societé Allemande, *La Voix des Clubs,* no. 14, March 25, 1848, p. 3.
65. Corvin, *Aus der Leben eines Volkskampfers* 3:62–63. On Willich, see Loyd D. Easton, "August Willich, Marx and Left-Hegelian Socialism," *Cahiers de l'ISEA,* August 1965, pp. 101–37.
66. Corvin, *Aus der Leben eines Volkskampfers* 3:62–63.
67. Ibid., *passim;* Carr, *Romantic Exiles,* pp. 50–51.
68. For an example of Herwegh giving this impression, see Gustav Rasch, *Aus meiner Festungszeit. Ein Beitrag zur Geschichte der preussischen Reaction* (Pest, Vienna, Leipzig, 1868), pp. 23–24.
69. Bakunin to Emma Herwegh, October 18–19, 1847, in Bakunin, *Sobranie sochinenii* 3:268.
70. Bakunin to Sand, December 14, 1847; Sand to Bakunin, January 1, 1848, in Sand, *Correspondance* 7:232–33 and nn.; Bakunin's speech is in Bakunin, *Sobranie sochinenii* 3:270–79.
71. Entry for December 22, 1847, in [K.] A. Varnhagen von Ense, *Tagebücher* (Bern, 1972), 4:170.
72. Bakunin to Annenkov, December 28, 1847, in Bakunin, *Sobranie sochinenii* 3:284.
73. Carr, *Bakunin,* pp. 157–60; Corvin, *Aus der Leben eines Volkskampfers* 3:43.
74. Bakunin to Annenkov, April 17, 1848, in Bakunin, *Sobranie sochinenii* 3:297–98.
75. Carr, *Bakunin,* pp. 161–70; Fröbel, *Ein Lebenslauf* 1:181, 190–91; Varnhagen von Ense, *Tagebücher* 5:120, 130, 133, 174, 203, 224.
76. Carr, *Bakunin,* pp. 170–71; Sand, *Correspondance* 7:547n.
77. Marx to Engels, September 8, 1853, in *Werke* 28:281; Edmund Silberner, ed., "La Correspondance Moses Hess–Louis Krolikowski, 1850–53," *Annali Istituto Giangiacomo Feltrinelli* 3 (1960), 608n.
78. Establishing the revolutionary bona fides of the émigrés was a serious problem. Herzen's daughter, Tata (Natalie) believed that one of her father's major activities had been to defend Russian revolutionaries from charges of working for the government, and she criticized Carr's *Romantic Exiles* for failing sufficiently to stress this. Natalie (Tata) Herzen to Boris Nikolaevskii, February 6, 1936, copy in Rodicheva Collection, Bakhmetev Archive, Columbia University.

79. Carr, *Bakunin*, pp. 204–18; "Novye materialy o Bakunin i Gertsene," *Golos minuvshago*, January 1913, p. 185.
80. *The English Republic* (Chronicle from October 22 to November 22, 1851), 1:369.
81. *Sobranie sochinenii* 25:126–27.
82. For Michelet's concern, see letters to Herzen from October and November 1851, in Gabriel Monod, ed., "Jules Michelet et Alexandre Herzen d'après leurs correspondance intime (1851–1869)," *La Revue* 68 (1907), 150–52, 156.

Chapter 4. Herzen and the Paris Revolution

1. Schapiro, *Turgenev*, pp. 55, 60, 61.
2. I. V. Selivanov, "Zapiski dvorianina-pomeshchika," *Russkaia starina* 28 (June 1880) 289–316.
3. Levitskii to his brother-in-law, A. V. Polenov, June 2, 1848, in Lemke, ed., *Polnoe sobranie sochinenii* 5:260–61. This letter was intercepted by the Russian police and led to the initiation of Russian government interest in Herzen's activities. See below for a discussion of the results of this interest.
4. Gertsen, *Sobranie sochinenii* 23:81, 89, 97, 101–02.
5. See, for example, ibid. 5:357, 360, 368.
6. Thoré editorial, *La Vraie République*, no. 34, April 29, 1848, p. 1.
7. Herzen to Moscow friends, August 2–8, 1848, in *Sobranie sochinenii* 23:86. (This was, of course, written after the June Days, and may be influenced by them.)
8. The members of the Directory were Arago, Garnier-Pages, Marie, Lamartine, and Ledru-Rollin.
9. *La Vraie République*, no. 50, May 15, 1848, p. 3.
10. "L'Ordre en Pologne," ibid., p. 1.
11. Editorial, ibid., no. 54, May 19, 1848, p. 1.
12. Amann, *Revolution and Mass Democracy*, pp. 240–47.
13. Blanc, *1848*, p. 391.
14. Sand to Thoré, May 28, 1848, in *Correspondance* 8:477–82.
15. Herzen to Moscow friends, August 2–8, 1848, in *Sobranie sochinenii* 23:86–87.
16. Natalie Herzen to Tatiana Astrakova, June 8, 1848, in ibid., pp. 75–76.
17. Natalie Herzen to Tatiana Astrakova, June 23–30, 1848, in ibid., pp. 78–79. For other reactions to the June Days in the Herzen party, see Herzen to his Moscow friends, August 2–8, in ibid., pp. 79–92; an unidentified writer (Mariia Ern or Mariia Korsh?) to unidentified recipient, in Herzen Family Papers. See also Herzen, *From the Other Shore*, pp. 43–49; Gertsen, *Sobranie sochinenii* 11:28–35, for his later descriptions.

18. Golownin, *Der russische Nihilismus*, p. 60; Gertsen, *Sobranie sochinenii* 10:29–35.

19. Herzen to Astrakova, June 30, 1848, in *Sobranie sochinenii* 23:81, 87.

20. See, for example, Fortescue, *Lamartine*, pp. 183–86; Stern, *Histoire*, 3:155, 264–69, *et passim*.

21. Herzen to Moscow friends, August 2–8, in *Sobranie sochinenii* 23:81, 87.

22. See, for example, "Le Dualisme, c'est la monarchie," in ibid. 12:217–25; "La Russie et le vieux monde" (1854), in ibid. 12:135. A future friend of Herzen's, the German communist August Willich, derived a very similar position from the same Feuerbachian premises (Easton, "August Willich," p. 124).

23. Gertsen, *Sobranie sochinenii* 5:363–64. See also Herzen to Moscow friends, September 6, 1848, in ibid. 23:95; on Herzen's anarchism, see Smirnova, *Sotsial'naia filosofiia*.

24. Fleury, *Le Poète Georges Herwegh*, p. 147; Kaiser, *Der Freiheit*, pp. 44–45.

25. For a detailed discussion of Proudhon's position and role in 1848, see chapter 5.

26. Natalie Herzen to Tatiana Astrakova, June 18, 1848, in Gertsen, *Sobranie sochinenii* 23:78. The health problems of Natalie and Sasha, which had been the official reason for the journey, and the need to provide special education for Kolia, may also have played a role in their decision.

27. Herzen to Kliucharev, March 25, 1848, in ibid., p. 71. The sale was completed in July. This move was later interpreted as the beginning of a series of actions designed to transfer his wealth abroad, to be discussed later. See Lemke, ed., *Polnoe sobranie sochinenii* 5:266.

28. Herzen to Moscow friends, August 2–8, 1848, in *Sobranie sochinenii* 23:79–80.

29. Natalie Herzen to Granovskii, in N. P. Antsiferov, ed., "N. A. Gertsen (Zakharina): Materialy dlia biografii," *Literaturnoe nasledstvo* 63 (1956), 382. (This exceptionally frank letter was carried back with Mariia Korsh and the Tuchkovs, as was Herzen's of August 2–8.)

30. *Sobranie sochinenii* 5:303–85.

31. After the publication of the first, German edition, Herzen added three more letters in 1850 and 1851 (ibid., pp. 190–217).

32. Herzen, *From the Other Shore*, p. 50.

33. On this continuing image in Herzen's thought, see Malia, *Herzen*, pp. 194–95; Smirnova, *Sotsial'naia filosofiia*, pp. 17, 63–65, 134–35.

34. Herzen, *From the Other Shore*, p. 92.

35. Ibid., p. 108.

36. Smirnova, *Sotsial'naia filosofiia*, p. 120; L. Ia. Ginzburg, " 'S togo berega' Gertsena (Problematika i postroenie)," *Izvestiia Akademii Nauk SSSR.*

Otdelenie literatury i iazyka 21, no. 2 (March–April 1962), 116, 117. Ginzburg feels the physician of "Consolatio" represents Herzen's position (p. 119).

37. On Jacoby, see Silberner, *Johann Jacoby*, and Silberner, ed., *Johann Jacoby Briefwechsel*.

38. Carl Schurz, *The Reminiscences of Carl Schurz* (New York, 1907–1908), 1:98–110, 139; Eberhard Kessel, introduction to *Die Briefe Carl Schurz an Gottfried Kinkel* (Heidelberg, 1965), pp. 30–31.

39. Droz, *Les Révolutions allemandes*, pp. 549, 576–79.

40. Hans-Ulrich Wehler, ed., *Friedrich Kapp: Vom radikalen Frühsozialisten des Vormärz zum liberalen Parteipolitiker des Bismarckreiches. Briefe 1843–1884* (Frankfurt a.M., 1969), pp. 9–10; Friedrich to Johanna Kapp, January 17, 1848, in ibid., p. 52.

41. The Cologne events are summarized in Felix, *Marx as Politician*, pp. 79–93, in an interpretation that sees Marx as more successful, and his rivals as more insignificant, than I do.

42. McLellan, *Marx*, p. 196.

43. Silberner, *Hess*, pp. 283–85; Felix, *Marx as Politician*, pp. 83–84.

44. [Ewerbeck], "Germany (Extract from a Letter from Berlin)," *The Spirit of the Age*, no. 12, October 14, 1848, p. 182.

45. Hammen, *The Red '48ers*, p. 371; Felix, *Marx as Politician*, pp. 86–89.

46. Easton, "August Willich," pp. 104, 109.

47. Schurz, *Reminiscences*, pp. 139–40.

48. Kapp to Ida Kapp, June 12, 1848, in Wehler, ed., *Friedrich Kapp . . . Briefe*, p. 57.

49. Hammen, *The Red '48ers*, p. 242; Droz, *Les Révolutions allemandes*, pp. 273–74.

50. Droz, *Les Révolutions allemandes*, pp. 548–49; Kamenev, "Samyi ostroumnyi protivnik," p. 128; Wehler, ed., *Friedrich Kapp . . . Briefe*, pp. 14–15, 57.

51. "Manifesto of the German Democracy," *The Spirit of the Age*, no. 17, November 18, 1848, p. 263.

52. Droz, *Les Révolutions allemandes*, pp. 385, 549.

53. Ibid., p. 385; Wehler, ed., *Friedrich Kapp . . . Briefe*, p. 16; Kamenev, "Samyi ostroumnyi protivnik," p. 130; Rasch, *Aus meiner Festungszeit*, pp. 18–20.

54. On Herwegh's despair, see Silberner, *Johann Jacoby*, p. 209, drawing on letters from the summer of 1848; Rasch, *Aus meiner Festungszeit*, pp. 23–24; on Herzen's rather despairing vivacity—"there is a revolution now, and soon it will be over, we do not wish to go home," he would say when staying out till five and six in the morning—see Lemke, ed., *Polnoe sobranie sochinenii* 5:260, citing Ruge correspondence for June 1849. Herzen already had some reputation in Germany as a writer of fiction (see *Letopis'* 1:473).

55. Natalie Herzen to Tatiana Astrakova, August 6, 1848, in Gertsen, *Sobranie sochinenii* 23:92.

56. Gustav Rasch commemorative article on Herzen, *Neue Freie Presse,* trans. and quoted in Lemke, ed., *Polnoe sobranie sochinenii* 5:269–70. The account in Rasch's memoirs, *Aus meiner Festungszeit,* p. 20, is similar, but not quite so expansive.

57. Natalie Herzen to M. F. Korsh, May 12, 1849, in Butina, ed., "Materialy A. I. Gertsen," p. 194. Sokolovo was the estate rented by the Herzens in the summers of 1845 and 1846.

58. Kamenev, "Samyi ostroumnyi protivnik," p. 128; Kapp to Hess, October 8, 1849, in Hess, *Briefwechsel,* pp. 228–29. Kapp went to the United States in 1850, where he had a successful legal and political career, and where he remained until the unification of Germany, when he returned, to become a member of the Reichstag. Although he had become significantly more conservative, he remained part of the liberal opposition to Bismarck. His son, however, was the Wolfgang Kapp who led the protofascist Kapp Putsch against the Weimar government in 1920.

59. While I feel that Herzen's hostility to Marx is directly related to the fact that most of Herzen's friends and allies resented Marx's treatment of them, Z. V. Smirnova sees the same phenomenon in Marx's hostility to Herzen. Along with ideological differences, she credits the "hostile relationship of Marx to people with whom Herzen maintained friendly relations," and gives as examples Vogt and Bakunin (Z. V. Smirnova, "Gertsen i Germaniia," *Literaturnoe nasledstvo,* no. 96 [1985], p. 84).

60. Ewerbeck to Hess, November 14, 1848, in Hess, *Briefwechsel,* p. 209.

61. Lucas, *Les Clubs,* pp. 15–16.

62. "Erklärung des deutschen Vereins in Paris" (September 12, 1848), in Hess, *Briefwechsel,* pp. 200–01.

63. Hess, *Briefwechsel,* pp. 202–03.

64. Friedrich Althaus, "Alexander Herzen," *Unsere Zeit: Deutsche Revue der Gegenwart,* n.s. 8 (1872), 44.

65. *Sobranie sochinenii* 10:153.

66. De Shpies note, appended to Kiselev report on Herzen, June 26, 1849, in Lemke, ed., *Polnoe sobranie sochinenii* 5:260.

67. Kiselev to Nesselrode, in ibid.

68. Ibid.

69. De Shpies note, in ibid. By the end of the year, Herzen heard through Golovin that Tausenau had been questioned about him (Herzen to Herwegh, December 21, 1849, in *Sobranie sochinenii* 23:218).

70. Siberner, *Hess,* pp. 294–99.

71. Ruge, June 6, 1849, in *Briefwechsel,* 2: 99.

72. Solger to Herwegh, November 24, 1848, cited Kamenev, "Samyi ostroumnyi protivnik," pp. 129–30n.

73. Mazzini to Herzen, November, 1849, in Vuilleumier et al., eds., *Autour de Herzen*, p. 77.
74. *Letopis'* 1:513, drawing on TsGAOR, d. 237, ll. 106–08.
75. Ibid. 1:520.
76. Ibid. 1:521. The archives of the Paris police were almost entirely destroyed in 1870 (legend has it that only the contents of two cartons used to wrap the Venus de Milo survived), and a search through existing materials in the Ministry of Foreign Affairs and the Ministry of the Interior has failed to turn up any confirmation of this material, which was drawn from the Russian Ministry of Foreign Affairs. Existing records show the French authorities very concerned about the activities of French exiles and Mazzini, but little interested in Germans, Russians, and Poles. Golovin is the only Russian exile whom I found mentioned in the French records (see Howard C. Payne and Henry Grosshans, "The Exiled Revolutionaries and the French Political Police in the 1850's," *American Historical Review* 68 [July 1963], 954–73; Tchernoff, *Associations et sociétés secrètes, passim*).
77. Kiselev report, in Lemke, ed., *Polnoe sobranie sochinenii* 5:266–67.
78. Levitskii to his sister, S. L. Polenova, June 24, 1849 (intercepted), quoted in ibid. 5:261–62.
79. Herzen to Kliucharev, November 24, 1848, in *Sobranie sochinenii* 23:115.
80. Ibid. 23:124.
81. These negotiations are described in *Byloe i dumy*, in ibid. 10:132–50.
82. See Herzen to Chumikov, August 9, 1851, where he advises another potential émigré to be sure to get his property out with him (ibid. 24:200).
83. N. A. Belogolovyi, *Vospominaniia i drugiia stat'i* (St. Petersburg, 1901), pp. 540–41.
84. Ladislas Mickiewicz, preface to Adam Mickiewicz, *La Tribune des Peuples* (Paris, 1907), p. 7.
85. Gertsen, *Sobranie sochinenii*, 10:38–41.
86. Stefan Kieniewicz, "Histoire de la 'Tribune des Peuples,'" in *L'Indépendance et la question agraire: Esquisses polonaises du xixe siècle. Opera Minora* (Warsaw, 1982), pp. 136–37.
87. On Chojecki, see Zygmunt Markiewicz, "Charles Edmond, Voyageur et comparatiste oublié," in *Connaissance de l'étranger: Mélanges offerts à la mémoire de Jean-Marie Carré* (Paris, 1964), pp. 292–301; and Z. L. Zaleski, *Attitudes et destinées: Faces et profiles d'écrivains polonais* (Paris, 1932), pp. 150ff.
88. Mickiewicz, preface, p. 9; Kieniewicz, "Histoire," p. 136.
89. Leader, *La Tribune des Peuples*, no. 1, March 15, 1849. Mickiewicz identification from L. Mickiewicz, *La Tribune des Peuples*, pp. 54–58.
90. Mickiewicz, preface, p. 11.
91. Franco Venturi, *Studies in Free Russia*, trans. Fausta Segre Walsby and Margaret O'Dell (Chicago, 1982), p. 190.

92. Iwan Woinof, "De la Russie," *La Tribune des Peuples*, no. 1, March 15, 1849.

93. Mickiewicz, preface, p. 7.

94. He sent in a report of public opposition to Russian intervention in Hungary that appeared on April 9.

95. Mickiewicz, preface, p. 7; Kieniewicz ("Histoire," p. 136) associates de la Sagra with the central, policy defining group on the paper, which would imply that he was Mickiewicz's appointee, rather than Chojecki's. However, this does not square with Herzen's account of de la Sagra's open opposition to Mickiewicz's views at the paper's founding banquet (*Sobranie sochinenii* 10:40–41).

96. "Réponse à M. Pulszky," *La Tribune des Peuples*, no. 3, March 17, 1849. The author was identified in the next issue.

97. Gottschalk to Herwegh, May 1, 1849, in Herwegh, ed., *1848*, p. 267.

98. Herzen, *From the Other Shore*, pp. 15–16.

99. "Vmesto predisloviia ili ob'iasneniia k sborniku," *Sobranie sochinenii* 6:145–49.

100. Herzen risked becoming the victim of violence by some of Bonaparte's street toughs in December, when he scornfully refused to shout "Vive l'Empereur" (*Letopis'* 1:475). The story was told by Turgenev, who was with Herzen, to P. A. Vasilchikov.

101. William L. Langer, *The Revolutions of 1848: Chapters from "Political and Social Upheaval"* (New York, 1969), pp. 152–53.

102. Natalie Herzen to Mariia Korsh, May 12, 1849, in Butina, ed., "Materialy A. I. Gertsen," pp. 193–94.

103. Sand to Mazzini, June 23, 1849, in *Correspondance* 9:199.

104. Rasch, *Aus meiner Festungszeit*, p. 25; Ruge diary, June 12, 1849, in *Briefwechsel* 2:100–01.

105. Herzen to Moscow friends, September 27, 1849, in *Sobranie sochinenii* 23:186; *Byloe i dumy*, in ibid. 10:44–54.

Chapter 5. Geneva and Proudhon

1. *Sobranie sochinenii* 10:116.
2. Herzen to Natalie, July 1, 1849, in ibid. 23:154.
3. Herzen to Emma Herwegh, July 11, 1849, in ibid. 23:163.
4. Natalie Herzen to the Granovskiis, September 8, 1849, in ibid. 23:182.
5. For Swiss background, see E. Bonjour, H. S. Offler, and G. R. Potter, *A Short History of Modern Switzerland* (Oxford, 1952); and Ann G. Imlah, *Britain and Switzerland, 1845–1860: A Study of Anglo-Swiss Relations during Some Critical Years for Swiss Neutrality* (Hamden, Conn., 1966).

6. James Fazy, *Les Mémoires de James Fazy, Homme d'état Genèvois (1794–1878)*, intro. François Ruchon (Geneva, 1947), p. 45.
7. Ibid., p. 32.
8. Imlah, *Britain and Switzerland*, pp. 45–47.
9. Loiseau (Besançon) to Minister of Justice, Archives Nationales, BB18 1480A, 8003A, f. 174.
10. De Lamoricière to Toqueville, Direction Politique, #66, Ministère des Affaires Étrangères, Correspondance Politique, La Russie, vol. 203, 226–28.
11. Imlah, *Britain and Switzerland*, pp. 46–47.
12. Fazy, *Mémoires*, pp. 153–54.
13. Vuilleumier dates Fazy's presence in Paris in mid-January, on the basis of Genevan records (intro. to "Révolutionnaires de 1848 et exilés," in Vuilleumier et al., eds., *Autour de Herzen*, p. 17 and n). A letter from Herzen to Ogarev, with an approximate date of December 1848 (or later), refers to a meeting with "your Genevan friend," identified by the editors of the *Sochineniia* as Fazy (*Sobranie sochinenii* 23:122, 380).
14. Cited in Vuilleumier, intro. to "Révolutionnaires de 1848 et exilés," in Vuilleumier et al., eds., *Autour de Herzen*, p. 22.
15. *Sobranie sochinenii* 10:102–03.
16. Herzen to Moscow friends, September 27, 1849, in ibid. 23:188.
17. Vuilleumier, intro. to "Révolutionnaires de 1848 et exilés," in Vuilleumier et al., eds., *Autour de Herzen*, pp. 17–18.
18. Herzen to Natalie, June 29, 1849, in *Sobranie sochinenii* 23:150. See also his response to the ceremony honoring the children, and his praise of Geneva to his friends (ibid. 23:158, *et passim*).
19. Herwegh to Emma, August 15, 1849, in Herwegh, ed., *1848*, p. 293.
20. Herzen to Moscow friends, September 27, 1849, in *Sobranie sochinenii* 23:187–88; see also his reminiscences in *Byloe i dumy*, in ibid. 10:59–64.
21. Herwegh to Emma, August 14, 1849, in Herwegh, ed., *1848*, p. 291.
22. Friedrich Kapp and August Willich were among those who emigrated; Ludwig Bamberger intended to do so, but stayed in England instead. Carl Schurz was another America-bound forty-eighter whom Herzen met and admired.
23. Friedrich Kapp to Joanna Kapp and to his father, August 1 and 13, 1849, in Wehler, ed., *Friedrich Kapp . . . Briefe*, pp. 62–63.
24. Stanley Zucker, *Ludwig Bamberger: German Liberal Politician and Social Critic, 1823–1899* (Pittsburgh, Pa., 1975), p. 31.
25. Among the members of the Frankfurt Parliament, he knew the Austrian poet Moritz Hartmann and the former vice-president of the assembly, Wilhelm Löwe-Kalbe, with both of whom he had at least limited later contact (Gertsen, *Sobranie sochinenii* 23:207).
26. Fröbel, *Ein Lebenslauf* 1:272–73; Jacoby to Herwegh, August 14, 1856, in Silberner, ed., *Johann Jacoby: Briefwechsel*, pp. 46–47.

27. Gertsen, *Sobranie sochinenii* 10:69–70; Herwegh to Emma, in Herwegh, ed., *1848*, p. 292.
28. Gertsen, *Sobranie sochinenii* 10:65–66.
29. Herzen to Moscow friends, September 27, 1849, in ibid. 23:188.
30. Ibid. 23:147, 149–52, *et passim*.
31. Herzen to Natalie and the Herweghs, July 4, 1848, in ibid. 23:159.
32. Galeer to Delargeaz, in Vuilleumier, intro. to "Révolutionnaires de 1848 et exilés," in Vuilleumier et al., eds., *Autour de Herzen*, pp. 38–39; for commentary, see ibid., pp. 37–39. Picking up the *Revue de Genève*'s description of him cited above, Galeer wrote, " 'A person of very independent fortune,' according to the *Revue de Genève*; according to us, a man of heart and intelligence, a citizen of the new world, a comrade of war."
33. *Sobranie sochinenii* 10:63–64.
34. Ibid. 23:64–65.
35. Vuilleumier, intro. to "Révolutionnaires de 1848 et exilés," in Vuilleumier et al., eds., *Autour de Herzen*, p. 38; Herzen to Herwegh, March 5, 1850, in *Sobranie sochinenii* 23:293, 437; however, despite his anger, Herzen was still concerned that a subscription to the paper he did support, *La Voix du Peuple*, be sent to the Genevans (Herzen to Chojecki, October 8, 1849, in ibid. 23:199).
36. Sazonov to Herzen, July 4, 1849, in N. E. Zastenker, ed. "N. I. Sazonov-Gertsenu," *Literaturnoe Nasledstvo* 62 (1955), 536–37.
37. Gertsen, *Sobranie sochinenii* 10:190.
38. On this point, see especially Daniel Halévy, *Le Mariage de Proudhon* (Paris, 1955), and Haubtmann, *Proudhon*.
39. Yet another Russian, Herzen's friend Ivan Galakhov, was described in January 1849 by the German author Fanny Lewald as a great admirer of Proudhon (Fanny Lewald to Johann Jacoby, January 20, 1849, in Silberner, ed., *Johann Jacoby: Briefwechsel*, p. 551). Chojecki also brought a Hegelian background to his appreciation of Proudhon's intellectual approach. Proudhon said to him, "Philosophy and the dialectic have not all deformed and depraved your understanding, as has happened with their glorious adepts" (Proudhon to Chojecki, June 12, 1850, in P.-J. Proudhon, *Correspondance* [Paris, 1875], 3:254).
40. The most useful works on the relationship, intellectual as well as personal, between Herzen and Proudhon are Raoul Labry, *Herzen et Proudhon* (Paris, 1928); and Michel Mervaud, "Herzen et Proudhon," *Cahiers du monde russe et soviètique* 12: nos. 1–2 (January–June, 1971), 110–89; in addition to Smirnova, *Sotsial'naia filosofiia*, pp. 83–143.
41. Halévy, *Le Mariage de Proudhon*, pp. 180–89.
42. Before the assembly met, he had argued that in the absence of a just social order that would create something like a Rousseauesque general will, mutually contradictory private interests would be reflected by universal suffrage. "The more one uses this system, before the economic revolution has

been accomplished, the more one will retrogress toward royalty, despotism, and barbarism" (P.-J. Proudhon, *Mélanges: Articles de Journaux, 1848–1852* [Paris, 1868], 1:15–16).

43. Hostility to the Jacobin left is pervasive in Proudhon. See his *Les Carnets de P.-J. Proudhon*, ed. Pierre Haubtmann, vol. 3, *1848–50* (Paris, 1968). For perceptions from the other side, see Zévaès, "Pyat," pp. 272; and Dessal, *Delescluze*, pp. 77–91. Delescluze, editor of *La Révolution Démocratique et Sociale*, almost had a duel with Proudhon himself. In late 1848, when Proudhon's conflicts with the left were at their height, George Sand wrote to Mazzini, comparing Proudhon to Pierre Leroux: "Proudhon is much stronger than he in absolute and personal theories. But this is the spirit of Satan, and woe to us if we thus disregard the ideal! Leroux has too much of it, but in having none at all, Proudhon is no more practical" (Sand to Mazzini, November 22, 1848, in *Correspondance* 8:716). But the following May, when Proudhon had received a shockingly harsh three-year sentence for press offenses, Sand chided the leftist democratic socialist journalist Théophile Thoré, editor of *La Vraie République*, for taking him on. "I am well aware of the aspects that wound us, . . . but what a useful and vigorous champion of democracy! What immense service he has rendered for the past year! It pains those who see things naively and from a somewhat distant perspective to find you at war . . . when it is necessary that all the living forces of the future march together" (ibid. 9:176). On the duel, see Halévy, *Le Mariage de Proudhon*, pp. 205–12.

44. Proudhon, *Mélanges*, esp. December 4, 1848, pp. 211–17.

45. P.-J. Proudhon, *Les Confessions d'un Révolutionnaire pour servir à l'histoire de la Révolution de Fevrier*, intro. Daniel Halévy (Paris, 1929), p. 114.

46. Stern, *Histoire* 2:172.

47. For Proudhon's biography and views, I am relying primarily on Hoffman, Halévy, and Edward Hyams, *Pierre-Joseph Proudhon: His Revolutionary Life, Mind and Works* (New York, 1979). All except Hoffman are partial to their subject; the collaboration with Herzen is either mentioned only in passing, or else follows the inaccurate account in Alfred Darimon, *À Travers une Révolution (1847–1855)* (Paris, 1884).

48. Sazonov to Herzen, June 27–29, 1849, in Zastenker, ed., "N. I. Sazonov," p. 532.

49. Herzen to Moscow friends, August 2–8, 1848, in *Sobranie sochinenii* 23:88.

50. Herzen to Moscow friends, November 5–8, 1848, in ibid. 23:189.

51. Herzen to Moscow friends, September 27–28, 1849, in ibid.

52. See Smirnova, *Sotsial'naia filosofiia*, pp. 115–17.

53. Proudhon, *Mélanges*, p. 15.

54. Gertsen, *Sobranie sochinenii* 5:354–56.

55. Compare Proudhon, *Mélanges*, p. 14 (April 29, 1849), rejecting club

activity as pointless parliamentarianism, to the view taken in his *Confessions* (which was exactly contemporaneous with the negotiations with Herzen) that one of the Provisional Government's sins of omission was not "organizing the clubs around the representatives of the people and causing them to enter into parliamentary life" (Proudhon, *Confessions*, p. 114).

56. Proudhon, *Carnets* 3:21 (March 1, 1848).

57. Ibid. 3:190–92 (June 6 and 13, 1849). In his influential *Le Mariage de Proudhon*, Halévy stated that Proudhon was unconcerned about the attack on Rome because he so disliked Mazzini and the actions of the Roman republic (pp. 88, 247–49). The *Carnets* contradict this view. See also the manifesto of *Le Peuple*, in *Mélanges*, p. 141.

58. Both men objected to the immoral lifestyle of the haute bourgeoisie, a condemnation that appears to have been a radical commonplace (cp. Herzen's second "Letter from the Avenue Marigny," in *Sobranie sochinenii* 5:37–38, and Proudhon, *Mélanges*, pp. 43–45, 137—from his campaign statement, and from the manifesto of *Le Peuple*).

59. Mervaud, "Herzen et Proudhon," pp. 120–28; Georges Gurvitch, "Proudhon et Marx," in *L'Actualité de Proudhon: Colloque des 24 et 25 novembre 1965* (Brussels, 1967), p. 93. Proudhon made many statements indicating his moderate tactics for *La Voix du Peuple*: see, for example, Proudhon to Maurice, October 29, 1849, in *Correspondance* 3:38–39; Proudhon, *Carnets* 3:219–247, 252–323. The strongest conservative statement was made at the end of *La Voix du Peuple*'s life: "What a pity that the government, aiming indiscriminately at everything which bears the name socialist, stops us in our career. Before six months we would have pacified, cleared up, smoothed everything. 'Utopia' vanquished by us, all that would be needed would be negotiations in regard to transitions: in concert with the disinterested intelligences of all the parties we would have founded the great party of the conservative, democratic and progressive republic. We could have become the pioneers not only of the revolution and the proletariat, but of the bourgeoisie and of the government itself" (Proudhon to Chojecki, in *Correspondance* 3:255).

60. On Girardin, see Bellanger et al., *Histoire générale de la presse française* 2:114–24; for the request for the bond, see Proudhon to Girardin, June 22, 1849, in *Correspondance* 3:5–7. On relations between Proudhon and Girardin, see Halévy, *Le Mariage de Proudhon*, pp. 254–57.

61. Ch. Ed., "Politique industrielle," *La Tribune des Peuples*, no. 24, April 7, 1849, pp. 1–2.

62. Sazonov to Herzen, July 4, 1849, in Zastenker, ed., "N. I. Sazonov," p. 537.

63. Sazonov to Herzen, June 17–19, 1849, in ibid., pp. 524, 532.

64. Gertsen, *Sobranie sochinenii* 10:190; Zastenker, ed., "N. I. Sazonov," p. 526. Zastenker, in discussing this deception, does not consider the possibility that Sazonov was responsible for it.

65. Zastenker, ed., "N. I. Sazonov," p. 524.
66. Natalie Herzen to Tatiana Astrakova, Autumn 1849, Herzen Family Papers.
67. Sazonov to Herzen, July 4, 1849, in Zastenker, ed., "N. I. Sazonov," pp. 537–38.
68. Herzen-Herwegh Papers, British Library, Add. Mss. 46,667, ff. 140–41, 142–45.
69. This analysis was first made by Labry, *Herzen et Proudhon*, pp. 88–89, and is based on Herzen's account in *Byloe i dumy*, *Sobranie sochinenii* 10:190.
70. Herzen expressed disagreement with Proudhon in an undated letter to Herwegh, written before his departure from Paris (ibid. 23:145).
71. This postscript, addressed to Herzen, and thus his first correspondence from Proudhon, was saved by him and put into an album that is now in the Herzen Archives, at the Internationaal Instituut voor Sociale Geschiedenis, Amsterdam. Lemke published a translation into Russian (the album was lent to him by Herzen's son at the beginning of this century), and Labry retranslated that into French. Michel Mervaud transcribed the French original in "Herzen et Proudhon," p. 146. The context would indicate that the postscript was originally appended to the letter under discussion.
72. Since Proudhon read and approved this letter, it seems reasonable to assume that this "indirect quote" does indeed represent what he wished to say to Herwegh and Herzen, and therefore it has considerable historical interest as a documentation of Proudhon's position.
73. Sazonov to Herzen July 22, 1849, in Zastenker, ed., "N. I. Sazonov," p. 539.
74. Emma Herwegh to Georg Herwegh, July 26, 1849, BRH 1836, Herwegh Archive, Dichtermuseum, Liestal, Switzerland.
75. Labry, *Herzen et Proudhon*, pp. 90–91; Proudhon to Charles Proudhon, August 12, 1849, in *Correspondance* 3:29; Emma Herwegh to Georg Herwegh, August 11, 1849, BRH 1837, Herwegh Archive.
76. Michel Mervaud, "Six Lettres de Herzen à Proudhon," *Cahiers du monde russe et soviètique* 12, no. 3 (July–September, 1971), 309.
77. Proudhon to Herzen, August 27, 1849, in Mervaud, "Herzen et Proudhon," p. 149.
78. Herzen to Proudhon, August 27, 1849, in *Sobranie sochinenii* 23:175–76.
79. Herzen to Emma Herwegh, early September, 1849, in ibid, 23:180.
80. Proudhon to Herzen, September 15, 1849, in Mervaud, "Herzen et Proudhon," pp. 152–53.
81. See Mervaud, "Herzen et Proudhon." Proudhon did not share Herzen's low opinion of *La Voix du Peuple:* it accomplished the ends he set for it (see his *Carnets*, vol. 3).
82. Herzen to Emma Herwegh, October 24, 1849, in *Sobranie sochinenii*

23:200; in a letter to Ogarev, Sazonov stated that he had only joined the paper at Herzen's request, but this is contradicted by his own eagerness to involve Herzen (Lemke, ed., *Polnoe sobranie sochinenii* 14:134).

83. The contents of the paper and Chojecki's own reaction suggest that he did this to the best of his ability, despite the fact that personally he knew Proudhon and his French collaborators far better than he did Herzen. One can infer from this that the young Pole, who had first written about Herzen's Hegelian works in 1847, really was an admirer who had recruited him for ideological as well as financial reasons.

84. *La Voix du Peuple*, September 25, 1849, p. 1.

85. Many of the accused were journalists, including some of Proudhon's former collaborators, and he and his staff were personally as well as journalistically involved. See Proudhon, *Correspondance*, vol. 3, and *Carnets*, vol. 3; Chojecki to Emma Herwegh, undated, in Herzen-Herwegh Papers, Add. Mss. 47,667, f. 157; Emma Herwegh to Herzen, November 11, 1849, BRH 1848, Herwegh Archive. Because this note was written on the back of a letter to her husband, it survived among the Herwegh papers. Herzen's frequent letters to her about *La Voix du peuple* suggest that they maintained a substantial correspondence that he must have subsequently destroyed.

86. "Revue de l'étranger," supplement to *La Voix du Peuple*, October 15, 1849, p. 1.

87. Herzen to Chojecki, October 20, 1849, in *Sobranie sochinenii* 23:199.

88. Chojecki to Emma Herwegh, undated letter, Herzen-Herwegh Papers, Add. Mss. 47,667, f.154. Chojecki may have been referring to Herzen's financial affairs, which he was attempting to help unravel, and which did indeed draw Herzen back to Paris at the end of the year. See chapter 7.

89. Ibid., ff. 150, 152.

90. Emma Herwegh to Herzen, November 11, 1849, BRH 1848, Herwegh Archive. The large number of letters from Herzen to Emma (*Sobranie sochinenii* vol. 23, summarized by Mervaud, "Herzen et Proudhon") show him regularly transmitting instructions through her.

91. *La Voix du Peuple*, November 5, 1849, p. 1. A few months later, Proudhon himself suggested that the paper play that card in attacking the reaction: "Recall the outrages of reaction, the confession made by one of its organs, 'rather the cossacks than the republicans' " (Proudhon to Darimon and Ch. Edmond [Chojecki], February 29 [?], 1850, in *Correspondance* 3:149–50). The presence of Russian troops suppressing the revolution in Hungary lent credence to the radicals' anti-Russianism.

92. C. H. Edmond [Chojecki], "Lettre première. Politique universelle. Solidarité des Peuples," supplement to *La Voix du Peuple*, November 12, 1849, pp. 1–2.

93. Un Russe, "Lettre deuxième," supplement to *La Voix du Peuple*, November 19, 1849, p. 2.

94. Ch. Edmond [Chojecki], "Politique universelle . . . L'Autriche," supplement to *La Voix du Peuple*, December 17, 1849, p. 1.

95. Natalie Herzen, on the other hand, found Chojecki courteous, but Darimon "beneath all criticism" (Natalie Herzen to Georg Herwegh, February 1850, in L. R. Lanskii, ed., "Pis'ma Natalii Aleksandrovny Gertsen k Gervegam," *Literaturnoe nasledstvo* 64 [1958], 272).

96. Un Allemand, "Lettre sur l'unité allemande et le Parlement d'Erfurth," supplement to *La Voix du Peuple*, March 4 and 11, 1850; Bamberger identification, in Mervaud, "Herzen et Proudhon," p. 151n; and Stanley Zucker, "Ludwig Bamberger and the Politics of the Cold Shoulder: German Liberalism's Response to Working Class Legislation in the 1870s," *European Studies Review* 2, no. 3 (July 1972), 203n. Herzen asked Herwegh's opinion of the article, and commented on its importance in a letter to the English journalist William Linton (Herzen to Herwegh, March 17, 1850, in *Sobranie sochinenii* 23:305; Herzen to Linton, in ibid. 24:7.

97. Ernest Coeurderoy, "Etudes sociales sur le canton du Vaud," supplement to *La Voix du Peuple*, April 29, May 6, May 13, 1850.

98. The Donoso Cortes article was signed "Is_____r, docteur en théologie, Cologne," and the letter to Mazzini by "Un Russe." The review was printed in the March 25 issue (Gertsen, *Sobranie sochinenii* 6:133–42, 224–31, 239–43).

99. Herzen to Emma Herwegh, October 10, 1849, in ibid. 23:197. At least one foreign reaader did notice and appreciate the foreign supplement and Proudhon's polemics as well. Herzen's friend and former employee Friedrich Kapp wrote from Cologne in January 1850, requesting copies of the Monday issue with the "Revue," as well as those numbers in which "Proudhon struggles against [Félix] Pyat and L[ouis] Blanc" (Kapp to Herzen, January 1, 1850, in Herzen-Herwegh Papers, Add. Mss. 47,664, f. 68).

100. Proudhon, August 26, 27, and September 12, 1849, in *Carnets* 3:228, 231, 245.

101. Proudhon to Darimon and "Edmond," February 29, 1850, in *Correspondance* 3:150.

102. Proudhon, *Carnets* 3:295–96.

103. Ibid. 3:375.

Chapter 6. The Uncensored Voice

1. Herzen, *The Russian People and Socialism*, pp. 11, 10.
2. Ibid., pp. 15, 16.
3. *Sobranie sochinenii* 5:9–10.
4. Ibid. 23:190.
5. Herzen to Herwegh, April 5, 1850, in ibid. 23:10–11. See also 24:34–

35, 44–46, 216–17, for similar statements. The one time he used vivid language to describe Europe's approaching "death" in his published work was in "Omnia mia mecum porto," which was dated April 1850 and was thus exactly contemporaneous with his private statements expressing the extreme of disgust and despair (Herzen, *From the Other Shore*, pp. 123–26).

6. Herzen to William Linton, April 1, 1850, in *Sobranie sochinenii* 24:7. Acton, *Alexander Herzen*, pp. 70–71, tends to overestimate the importance of these political discussions. They are, in fact, close in tone to the types of analysis that Proudhon sent his friends and collaborators in very long letters from his prison cell, and very possibly reflect the style of Proudhon and his friends.

7. Thus, part of his response to the June Days was the challenge to Botkin to cease quarreling about the bourgeoisie. See chapter 4.

8. Author's introduction, "Pis'ma iz Frantsii i Italii," *Sobrani sochinenii* 6:9. See also Ginzburg, " 'S togo berega' Gertsema," p. 113.

9. Herzen to Moscow friends, September 27, 1849, in *Sobranie sochinenii* 23:187.

10. Herzen, *From the Other Shore* ("Omnia mia mecum porto," 1850), pp. 134–36, 132–33; see also pp. 56–62 (from "Year LVII of the Republic," October 1848).

11. Since comparisons with Marx are inevitable, it is important to note here that Herzen differed profoundly from Marx in not perceiving that the industrialization process had a major impact on the mentality of the workers; he did indeed see the petite bourgeoisie as nonrevolutionary, even counter-revolutionary (see chapter 4), while the workers were revolutionary fighters; the difference he attributed to the corrupting influence of bourgeois civilization, to which the poorer workers were immune. Herzen also believed, in 1851, that the peasants had been radicalized by the events of 1848 (see Herzen to A. A. Chumikov, August 9, 1851, in *Sobranie sochinenii* 24:198–99). Herzen showed a much less sophisticated understanding of the impact of industrialism, which he had had little opportunity to observe first-hand; however, like Bakunin, he may have been closer to seeing where revolutionary action could come from than was the theoretically more acute Marx.

12. Herzen, *From the Other Shore*, pp. 133–34.

13. Herzen to Chumikov, in *Sobranie sochinenii* 24:198–99.

14. Herzen meant by "communism" a system of total collectivism such as that envisioned by Etienne Cabet.

15. "La Russie," *Sobranie sochinenii* 6:185.

16. Ibid. 6:186.

17. "La Russie et le vieux monde (Lettres à W. Linton, esq.)," in ibid. 12:134–67; first published in *The English Republic* in 1854 in English translation. The French original was published in *L'Homme* the same year, as was a separate French publication.

18. See George Kennan, *The Marquis de Custine and His "Russia in 1839"* (Princeton, N.J., 1971) for Custine and his book.

19. Michel Cadot, introduction to Jules Michelet, *Légendes démocratiques du nord* (Paris, 1968), p. xiv; see also Cadot, *La Russie dans la vie intellectuelle française.*

20. See, for example, "Le Comité Central Démocratique Européen, aux Allemands," *La Voix du Proscrit,* no. 4 (November 17, 1850), pp. 49–50. The choice, according to this statement, signed by the leaders of the European Central Democratic Committee, Ledru-Rollin, Mazzini, Albert Darasz, and Arnold Ruge, was between "absolutism and liberty, tyranny and democracy. . . . To be Russian or to be democratic, that is the alternative."

21. The unpublicized threat to intervene in Switzerland if the refugee situation were not regulated shows that European apprehension about Russia's intentions was not baseless. See chapter 5.

22. "La Russie," *Sobranie sochinenii* 6:158–60.

23. Herzen, *The Russian People and Socialism,* p. 171.

24. Gertsen, "Vmesto predisloviia," in *Sobranie sochinenii* 6:146.

25. See especially "Lettre d'un Russe à Mazzini," in ibid. 6:224–30.

26. Herzen to Natalie Herzen, June 29, 1849, in ibid. 24:151. There is something a bit pathetic in Herzen's statement to his friends, in which he tells them of his flight from France, and the plight of the refugees in Switzerland, but assures them that he is not one of that mistreated group (Herzen to Moscow friends, September 29, 1849, in ibid. 23:186).

27. Herzen to Herwegh, February 14, 1850, in ibid. 23:266.

28. Ibid. 7:44. See Smirnova, *Sotsial'naia filosofiia,* pp. 150–55, for an analysis in terms of Russian socialism.

29. On the changing role of the peasant commune in Herzen's thought, see ibid., pp. 78, 144–47; Malia, *Herzen,* pp. 396–415; and Acton, *Herzen,* pp. 65–69.

30. For Haxthausen's role in developing later views of the commune, see S. Frederick Starr, introduction to August von Haxthausen, *Studies on the Interior of Russia,* trans. by Eleanore L. M. Schmidt, ed. S. Frederick Starr (Chicago, 1972), pp. xxiv–xxv, xxx–xxxiv. Herzen had met Haxthausen during his stay in Russia in 1843.

31. On this point, see Malia, *Herzen,* pp. 310–12, 401–406.

32. Bakunin, *Sobranie sochinenii* 3:399–426 (in Russian translation).

33. Nikolaevskii, "Za vashu i nashu vol'nost'!" p. 261. For the discussion of the commune, see Bakunin, *Sobranie sochinenii* 3:408.

34. J. H. Seddon, "The Petrashevtsy: A Reappraisal," *Slavic Review* 43, no. 3 (Fall 1984), 451; see also El'sberg, *Gertsen,* p. 348. Seddon's argument is weak chronologically as presented; it is further weakened by an error in placing Engel'son at Herzen's side in 1850—he and his wife arrived in Nice and became acquainted with the Herzens only in 1851 (see Luisa Haag to

263

Mariia Reichel, February 23, 1851, in N. D. Efros, ed., "Iz pisem L. I. Gaag," *Literaturnoe nasledstvo* 63 [1956], 401–02).

35. Silberner, ed., "La Correspondance Hess-Krolikowski," p. 589.

36. Herzen informed his European readers about Chaadaev in *Du Développement des idées révolutionnaires en Russie*, written 1850, and originally published in 1851 (*Sobranie sochinenii* 7:91). See also *Byloe i dumy*, in ibid. 9:138–48 for Herzen's evaluation of Chaadaev, and his characterization of the first "Philosophical Letter" (published in 1836) as "a shot in the dark night." For Chaadaev, see Peter Ia. Chaadaev, *Philosophical Letters, and Apology of a Madman*, trans. and intro. Mary-Barbara Zeldin (Knoxville, Tenn., 1969).

37. Herzen described the commune in language so evocative that it should be quoted in the original: "Entre les bois de sapin saupoudrés de neige, dans de grandes plaines, apparaissaient les petits villages russes; ils se détachaient brusquement sur un fond d'une blancheur éblouissante. L'aspect de ces pauvres communes rurales a quelque chose de profondément touchant pour moi. Les maisonnettes se pressent l'une l'autre, aimant mieux brûler ensemble que de s'éparpiller. Les champs sans haies ni clôtures, se perdent dans un lointain infini derrière les maisons. La petite cabane pour l'individu, pour la famille; la terre à tout le monde, à la commune" (*Du Développement, Sobranie sochinenii* 7:9).

38. "La Russie," originally printed in *La Voix du peuple*, nos. 50, 57, 71, November 19, 26, and December 10, 1849; *Sobranie sochinenii* 6:167. The section on the commune, ibid. 7:163–72, was repeated, in condensed form, in *Du Développement*, as "Annexe sur la commune rurale en Russie," in ibid. 7:128–32. For "La Russie" as a stage in the development of the theory of Russian socialism, see Smirnova, *Sotsial'naia filosofiia*, pp. 148–49.

39. *Du Développement, Sobranie sochinenii* 7:121–23.

40. Herzen to Herwegh, August 2, 1850, in ibid. 24:131. In pointing to the parallels between the Western workers and the Russian people, it is perhaps worth remembering that Herzen characterized the French masses as "like women" in their apprehension of reality. In *Du Développement*, we learn that "the Slavic character presents something feminine; this intelligent, strong race, filled with varied dispositions, lacks initiative and energy. We could say that the Slavic nature, not sufficient in itself, awaits a shock that will awaken it" (ibid. 7:25). And in the letter to Michelet, he wrote, "The Slav world is like a woman who has never loved and so seems indifferent to all that goes on around her: listless, detached, remote. But we cannot tell what will happen in the future: the woman is young, and even now something seems to be stirring within her, making her heart beat faster" (Herzen, *The Russian People and Socialism*, pp. 175–76).

41. *Du Développement, Sobranie sochinenii* 7:17–18.

42. "La Russie," ibid. 6:178–79.

43. Ibid. 6:181.

44. *Du Développement*, ibid. 7:104–10.
45. Herzen, *The Russian People and Socialism*, pp. 199–200.
46. Kamenev, "Samyi ostroumnyi protivnik," pp. 145–60; Eberhard Wolfgramm, "Alexander Herzen und die 'Deutsche Monatsschrift,' " *Beiträge zur Geschichte der Beziehungen zwischen dem deutschen Volk und den Völkern der Sowjetunion* (Berlin, 1954), pp. 99–101.
47. G. Ziegengeist, "Über die Bedeutung von A. I. Herzens Schaffen für das progressive deutsche Geistesleben in der fünfziger Jahren des 19 Jahrhunderts. Zum 150. Geburtstag Alexander Herzens," *Zeitschrift für Slawistik* 7, no. 5 (1962), 515–16.
48. Venturi, *Studies*, pp. 144–94.
49. The work was originally serialized in 1845–1846, and the Russian edition of the book came out in 1847 (see Smirnova, "Gertsen i Germaniia," pp. 78–79). This work, with its depiction of the near seduction of a gentle wife, modeled in fact on Natalie, seems strangely to anticipate the Herzen-Herwegh triangle. More strangely still, the Herweghs kept their autographed copy of the book, and it remains today with their other belongings in the Herwegh Archive in Liestal.
50. Venturi, *Studies*, pp. 146–47, describes Michelet's own favorable published commentary on *Du Développement* and the reaction to it of *L'Avenir de Nice*.
51. Cadot, introduction to Michelet, *Légendes démocratiques*, provides the fullest discussion of the relationship between Herzen and Michelet. Michelet's letters to Herzen are in the Herzen Archive, Internationaal Instituut voor Sociale Geschiedenis, Amsterdam; Gabriel Monod edited and published a large selection of the correspondence in "Jules Michelet et Alexandre Herzen." Herzen's letters to Michelet are scattered through Gertsen, *Sobranie sochinenii* 24, *et. seq.*
52. Ewerbeck, *L'Allemagne et les Allemands*, p. 2.
53. See, for example, Venturi, *Studies*, pp. 144, 147–52, *et passim*.
54. Mazzini to Herzen, early November, 1849, in Vuilleumier et al., eds., *Autour de Herzen*, pp. 76–77.
55. Herzen to Bamberger, October 10, 1850, in Zhelvakova et al., eds., "Perepiska s nemetskimi demokratami," p. 180.
56. Wolfgramm, "Herzen," p. 99. Kamenev saw a similarity in the journal's criticism of Marx and Herzen, both of whom unmasked the "fetishism" of such democratic slogans as "liberty," "equality," and "justice." "For both Herzen and Marx, the most important result of 1848 was the complete revelation of those contradictions of contemporary society which could not be covered either by the republic, or by the slogans of "equality" and "brotherhood" (Kamenev, "Samyi ostroumnyi protivnik," pp. 141–42).
57. Herzen to Bamberger, October 10, 1850, in Zhelvakova et al., eds., "Perepiska s nemetskimi demokratami," p. 180.

58. Smirnova, "Gertsen i Germaniia," p. 78.
58. Wolfgramm, "Herzen," p. 101.
60. Marx to Engels, February 13, 1855, in *Werke* 18:434.
61. The draft of Hess's "Briefen an Iscander" are printed in Hess, *Briefwechsel*, pp. 239–67; a partial Russian translation of one was printed in A. I. Gertsen [Alexander Herzen], "Novonaidennyie stat'i i pis'ma," *Literaturnoe nasledstvo* 7–8 (1933), 84–85. The letter of November 18, 1851, is available in a number of places; I have used the version Herzen received, rather than one of Hess's drafts; this is printed in Vuilleumier et al., eds., *Autour de Herzen*, pp. 81–84.
62. From the third letter, in Hess, *Briefwechsel*, pp. 256–57.
63. From the first letter, in ibid., p. 245.
64. Silberner, *Hess*, p. 308.
65. Herzen to Hess, March 3, 1850, in Gertsen, *Sobranie sochinenii* 23:287; Hess, alternate third *Briefe an Iscander*, *Briefwechsel*, p. 258.
66. Herzen to Hess, in *Sobranie sochinenii*, 23:288.
67. Silberner, *Hess*, pp. 308–09.
68. Malwida von Meysenbug, *Memoiren einer Idealistin*, 9th ed. (Berlin and Leipzig, 1905), 2:89.
69. Coeurderoy quoting his own 1852 statement in 1854, *L'Homme*, April 26, 1854, p. 11, rebutting an assertion by the editor, Charles Ribeyrolles, that it was reaction, not the revolutionaries, that had welcomed Russia's intervention in 1849; it was the reactionaries, not the revolutionaries, who had destroyed "the civilization which we cherish" (ibid., April 12, 1854). The fullest account of Coeurderoy is Max Nettlau, "Notice bibliographique sur Ernest Coeurderoy (1826–62)," in Ernest Coeurderoy, *Oeuvres*, vols. 1–3, *Jours d'Exil* (Paris, 1910). See also Herzen on Coeurderoy, in *Sobranie sochinenii* 11:59–65; and Herzen to Coeurderoy, June 7, 1854, in ibid., 25:182–84.
70. Lemke, ed., *Polnoe sobranie sochinenii* 5:298, citing the reminiscences of the wife of N. M. Shchepkin.
71. Herzen to Moscow friends, June 19, 1851, in *Sobranie sochinenii* 24:184.
72. Cited in S. A. Perselenkov and Ia. Z. Cherniak, eds., "Gertsen i Ogarev: Novye materialy," *Zven'ia* 6 (1936), 356–58.
73. E. S. Nekrasova, "Akter M. S. Shchepkin i. A. I. Gertsen," *Russkaia mysl'* 25, no. 1 (1904), 2d pagination, 73–85, gives Shchepkin's letters to Herzen. Herzen's response to the Shchepkin visit can be traced in his correspondence with Mariia Reichel and the Moscow friends, in *Sobranie sochinenii*, vol. 25. The discussion of this episode in Laurence Senelick, *Serf Actor: The Life and Art of Mikhail Shchepkin* (Westport, Conn., 1984), pp. 197–201, is not well enough informed on the political background to be helpful.
74. For somewhat embarrassed Soviet responses to Herzen's counsels of

passive withdrawal, see Smirnova, *Sotsial'naia filosofiia,* pp. 134–35, and Ginzburg, " 'S togo berega' Gertsena," pp. 121–23. Herzen's interest in the period of transition to Christian Europe was rekindled by his reading Mommsen's *Primitives de l'eglise chrétienne* at the end of 1848 (Natalie Herzen to the Tuchkov sisters, December 8, 1848, in "Dnevnik i pis'ma," p. 252). Natalie compared the persecuted Christians of the early Church with the persecuted socialists of her own day; "the only difference is that now it is not enthusiasm for another extremity, not exaltation, but a simple, natural human demand, and for this people are persecuted as severely in the nineteenth century as they were for fanaticism in the first!"

75. Herzen to Herwegh, May 30, 1850, in *Sobranie sochinenii* 24:68; Herzen to Mariia Reichel, August 26–September 7, 1853, in ibid. 25:113. A number of Herzen's friends felt the need to dissuade him from emigrating to America, especially right after Natalie's death in 1852. See Mazzini to Herzen, May 27, 1852, in J. M., ed. "Lettres de Mazzini à Herzen," *Bulletin of the International Institute of Social History* 8 (1953), 19; Medici to Herzen, November 6, 1852, Herzen Album, Herzen Archive, Internationaal Instituut voor Sociale Geschiedenis, Russian translation in Lemke, ed., *Polnoe sobranie sochinenii* 7:60; Vogt to Herzen, October 14, 1853, in Marc Vuilleumier, ed., "Une lettre inédite de Carl Vogt à Herzen," *Musées de Genève* 147 (July–August, 1974), 19–20. Once he got to work on the press, America began to look less enticing. In 1854 he responded to a friend's suggestion that he emigrate with the following: "But we shall still wait a while. Affairs become ever more interesting, and to leave would be like a flight" (Herzen to Mariia Reichel, February 5, 1854, in *Sobranie sochinenii* 25:150).

76. This point was also made in his published work (ibid. 6:186 ["La Russie"], 7:19 [*Du Développement,* quoting *S togo berega*]). The problem was, "What shall we do in virgin forests, we who cannot spend a morning without reading five newspapers, we whose whole poetry is in the struggle with the old world.... No, let us be frank, and admit that we would make poor Robinson Crusoes. And those who went to America, did they not take old England with them there?" (*From the Other Shore,* p. 151).

77. Malia, *Herzen,* p. 68.

78. Natalie Herzen to the Tuchkov sisters, December 1848–January, 1849, in "Dnevnik i pis'ma," pp. 255, 258.

79. Natalie Herzen, "Zapiski 1848 goda," in Antsiferov, ed., "N. A. Gertsen," p. 374. Antsiferov tentatively dates these "Zapiski" to June 1848, but that seems too early. In a letter to Tatiana Astrakova, on November 4, 1848, Natalie said she was enclosing some pages from her journal; since the letter and the original of the "Zapiski" both were in the possession of Astrakova, and now are together at Columbia University, it is possible that the "Zapiski" are those pages (Domger, ed., *Neizdannye pis'ma,* p. 143). On the other hand, in a letter from Geneva, Herwegh mentioned to his wife that Natalie had

written an autobiographical fragment, and if this reference is to the "Zapiski" then they were composed in mid-1849 (Herwegh to Emma Herwegh [1849], Herwegh Archive, no. 1817).

80. The novel was first published in 1848. A recent English edition of the 1871 translation is *Fanchon the Cricket* (Chicago, 1977).

81. Natalie Herzen to Emma Herwegh, October 10, 1849, in Gertsen, *Sobranie sochinenii* 23:196.

82. Natalie Herzen to Herwegh, February 17, 1850, in ibid. 23:269; Natalie to Herwegh, February 23, 1850, in Lanskii, ed., "Pis'ma Natalii Aleksandrovny Gertsen k Gervegam," p. 276.

83. Natalie to Herwegh, April 12, 1850, in Herzen-Herwegh Papers, Add. Mss. 47,665, f. 112. There are far too many examples of Natalie's belief in or longing for "harmony" to cite.

84. Herwegh to Herzen, January 1850, in Lemke, ed., *Polnoe sobranie sochinenii* 14:43–44. See also Herwegh to Herzen, March 1850, ibid. 14:60.

85. Herzen to Herwegh, February 14, 1850, in *Sobranie sochinenii* 23:265. For the substance of their arguments, see chapter 8.

86. Ibid. 5:200. See Acton, *Herzen*, pp. 59–61, for a discussion of the communal notions lying behind the move to Nice.

Chapter 7. The Crisis

1. See, for example, Herzen to Malwida von Meysenbug, August 13, 1853, in *Sobranie sochinenii* 25:88; and Herzen to Moscow friends, September 2, 1853, in ibid. 25:109.

2. *Byloe i dumy*, ibid. 10:254.

3. The account in *Byloe i dumy* leaves out the uncertainty, and the agony, of waiting. See the series of letters to Herwegh, in ibid. 23:221–326, *passim*; 14:9–88, *passim*.

4. *Byloe i dumy*, in ibid. 10:254–55; Herzen to Herwegh, January 22, 1850, in ibid. 23:239–40; Natalie Herzen to Herwegh, February 8, 1850, in Herzen-Herwegh Papers, Add. Mss. 47,665, ff. 34–35.

5. Herzen to Herwegh, May 7, May 17, May 18, and May 19, 1850, in *Sobranie sochinenii* 24:43, 49, 51, 53, on Tata. Comments on Natalie's health, and the drain on Herzen, are scattered through these letters. See also Natalie's miserable letter to Tatiana Astrakova, June 7, 1850, in Domger, ed., *Neizdannye pis'ma*, pp. 162–63.

6. Herzen to Emma Herwegh, November 29, 1849, in *Sobranie sochinenii* 23:211.

7. The warm climate and French speech of Jersey made it a major exile colony for some years. See Frances Guille, ed., *Le Journal d'Adèle Hugo* (Paris, 1968, 1971) for a general description of émigré life there.

8. See, for example, Herzen to Herwegh, February 14, 1850, in *Sobranie sochinenii* 23:266.

9. "Granovskii writes me that things are terrible in Russia, that despotism, drunk with success, has even lost shame" (Herzen to Herwegh, March 17, 1850, in ibid. 23:304).

10. See Herzen to Herwegh, March 23, 24 and 26, in ibid. 23:301–17, 322.

11. For Herzen's anger at this rejection by his friends, see ibid. 24:159–61, 183–84.

12. Herzen to Herwegh, March 16 and 19, 1850; Herzen to Friedrich Kapp, March 28, 1850, in ibid. 23:303, 307, 320.

13. *From the Other Shore*, pp. 159–60. Donoso-Cortes had spoken of the soldier in these terms.

14. Ibid., p. 162n.

15. *Byloe i dumy, Sobranie sochinenii* 10:141.

16. Herzen to Herwegh, April 23, 1850, in ibid. 24:30.

17. Ibid. 24:43–90, *passim*.

18. Herzen to Herwegh, May 17, 1850, in ibid. 24:49–50.

19. Herzen to Herwegh, May 21, 1850, in ibid. 24:54.

20. Chojecki to Emma Herwegh, in Herzen-Herwegh Papers, Add. Mss. 47,667, f. 163.

21. Herzen to Herwegh, June 17, 1850, in *Sobranie sochinenii* 24:92.

22. In May, as the move to Nice became imminent, Natalie insisted that their relationship would have to be resumed on a new basis (Natalie Herzen to Herwegh, Herzen-Herwegh Papers, Add. Mss. 47,665, ff. 150, 153–54, letters reprinted in part in Lanskii, ed., "Pis'ma Natalii Aleksandrovny Gertsen," p. 287). In June and July, she justified her pregnancy against Herwegh's jealous attacks (Herzen-Herwegh Papers, Add. Mss., 47,665, ff. 217–19, 228; part of the latter is reprinted in Lanskii, ed., "Pis'ma Natalii Aleksandrovny Gertsen," pp. 228–29).

23. Gertsen, *Sobranie sochinenii* 24:486. Mariia Ern married Adolph Reichel in Paris in November, and settled there. Her itinerary between August and November is not clear.

24. Ibid. 10:156–60; Herzen to Orlov, September 23, 1850, in ibid. 24:143–44.

25. Herzen to Bamberger, in Zhelvakova et al., eds., "Perepiska," p. 180. At this time, Herzen realized he might be expelled from Piedmont, but thought it unlikely. He looked forward to two to three years in Nice's resort climate.

26. The letter from the Piedmont minister of the interior, dated July 12, 1851, and allowing Herzen to return to Nice and remain there as long as convenient, is in the Herzen Archive, Internationaal Instituut voor Sociale Geschiedenis.

27. See Luisa Haag to Mariia Reichel, February 1, 1851, in "Iz pisem L. I.

Gaag," p. 400, *et passim*, for continuing concern. See Venturi, *Studies*, p. 160, for the Piedmontese side of Herzen's defense.

28. Herzen to Fazy, January 22, 1851, in *Sobranie sochinenii* 24:155, raises the naturalization issue; most of the rest of this correspondence has been lost. The citizenship problem is one of the leitmotifs running through Luisa Haag's letters to Mariia Reichel. See "Iz pisem L. I. Gaag." On Vogt's role, see Vuilleumier, intro. to "Révolutionnaires de 1848 et exilés," in Vuilleumier et al., eds., *Autour de Herzen*, pp. 27–28. For the ceremonies in Chatel, see *Byloe i dumy, Sobranie sochinenii* 10:178–81. On his references to himself as Swiss, see, for example, Herzen to Mariia Reichel, March 18, 1853, in ibid. 25:30.

29. It was, wrote Luisa Haag, "one of the biggest soirées to take place in Nice" (Luisa Haag to Mariia Reichel, February 22, 1851, in "Iz pisem L. I. Gaag," p. 402).

30. Luisa Haag to Mariia Reichel, June 30, 1851, in ibid., p. 408. Chojecki's illegitimate child had previously been brought from Paris to Nice.

31. Venturi, *Studies*, p. 148.

32. Ibid., p. 143.

33. G. Ziegengeist, "Herzens Plan zur Gründung einer freien russischen Druckerei in Stuttgart im October 1850 (Aus dem ungedruckten Briefwechsel zwischen G. Herwegh und A. Kolatschek)," *Zeitschrift für Slawistik* 8, no. 5 (1963), 703.

34. These episodes are well documented in *Byloe i dumy, Sobranie sochinenii*, vol. 10, and in Carr, *The Romantic Exiles*. Luisa Haag's letters in "Iz pisem L. I. Gaag" provide a different perspective. For the moral issues involved, see below, chapter 8.

35. See Gertsen, *Sobranie sochinenii* 24:170–91, *passim*.

36. Herzen to Natalie, June 20, 1851, in ibid. 24:185.

37. "Dedicace (A Nicolas Ogareff)," ibid. 7:267.

38. "Michel Bakounine," ibid. 7:340–51, 442. Michelet discussed his plans in letters to Herzen of November 7, 11, and 24, 1851, now in the Herzen Archive, Internationaal Instituut voor Sociale Geschiedenis, 2.d.VI., and in letters of November 17 and 20, 1851, in Monod, ed., "Jules Michelet et Alexandre Herzen," pp. 156–57.

39. Herzen to Moscow friends, June 19, 1851, in *Sobranie sochinenii* 24:183. See also Herzen to Natalie, June 24, 1851, in ibid. 24:189.

40. The Polish refugees from the 1831 uprising were from all social groups; however, the leadership was dominated, even monopolized, by men from the gentry and aristocracy.

41. The sympathy they sought was not always forthcoming. As an example, the American ambassador in London (soon to be president) James Buchanan wrote, "I confess that my sympathies have been strongly enlisted in favor of the Poles, Hungarians & Italians. These people, almost to a man,

detest the foreign despotism which [has] blotted their nationalities from the map of Europe, & every lover of freedom must ardently desire that they should succeed in recovering their independence.... In regard to France, similar reasons do not exist. It has not been subject to a foreign power; and whatever may be thought of the usurpation of Louis Napoleon, this has been sanctioned by a vast majority of the French people. Should they become tired of his dominion, they are abundantly able to relieve themselves of it" (Buchanan to Marcy, December 27, 1854, in *The Works of James Buchanan*, ed. John Basset Moore [Philadelphia and London, 1909], 9:291–92).

42. Ch. Delescluze, "Archive et correspondance du Comité central démocratique européenne," *La Voix du Proscrit*, no. 7, November 21, 1850, pp. 93–95.

43. Herzen to Jacoby, April 24, 1850, in *Sobranie sochinenii* 24:35.

44. Herzen to Mazzini, September 13, 1850, in ibid. 24:139–41; Venturi, *Studies*, pp. 141–42.

45. Etienne Cabet to Louis Blanc, October 30, 1850 (responding to a letter of July 20), from Nauvoo, Ill. (Correspondance du Louis Blanc, Bibliothèque Nationale, N.A. Fr. 11,398, f. 33).

46. Alvin R. Calman, *Ledru-Rollin après 1848 et les proscrits français en Angleterre* (Paris, 1921), p. 33.

47. Sand to Barbès, August 27, 1850, in Sand, *Correspondance* 9:669–70.

48. Loubere, *Louis Blanc*, p. 147.

49. Blanc to Barbès, September 3, 1850, in J. F. Jeanjean, "Louis Blanc et Ledru-Rollin: Lettres inédites," *La Révolution de 1848* 7 (1910–1911), 107–14.

50. Sand to Mazzini, October 5, 1850, in Sand, *Correspondance* 9:731–32. As the biographers of both Blanc and Ledru-Rollin have pointed out, the appeal by Sand and Herzen to Mazzini's revolutionary idealism was misplaced; in fact, politically, his religious democratic nationalism was considerably closer to Ledru-Rollin than to the "materialism" of any consistent socialism (Loubere, *Louis Blanc*, p. 147; Calman, *Ledru-Rollin*, pp. 93–94).

51. Blanc to Holyoake, August 21, 1850, Library of the Cooperative Union, Ltd., Manchester, Holyoake Collection, f. 382.

52. Victor Hugo to his wife, December 31, 1851, in Victor Hugo, *Correspondance* (Paris, 1950), 2:39.

53. Kessel, introduction to *Briefe von Schurz an Kinkel*, p. 29.

54. Hammen, *The Red '48ers*, pp. 408–09. The crucial meeting of the Communist League was held on September 15, 1850.

55. Calman, *Ledru-Rollin*, p. 96. Albert Darasz was the Polish representative on the European Committee until his death in 1852, but the dominant figure in the Centralization always appears to have been Worcell.

56. Ibid., pp. 95–99.

57. Ibid., p. 100.

58. On Linton and *The Leader*, see F. B. Smith, *Radical Artisan: William*

James Linton, 1812–97 (Manchester, 1973), pp. 93–96; and Linton, *Memories*, pp. 119–23.

59. The editorial board was headed by Thornton Hunt, son of the radical poet Leigh Hunt, and included the journalist George Henry Lewes, common-law husband of George Eliot.

60. Worcell to Linton, July 2, 1850, in Stefan Kieniewicz, ed., "From the Polish Correspondence of William J. Linton, 1844–1854," *Annali Istituto Giangiacomo Feltrinelli* 3 (1960), 189, 190.

61. For a general description, see Smith, *Radical Artisan*, pp. 102–09.

62. Worcell to Linton, in Kieniewicz, ed., "From the Polish Correspondence," p. 190; Dessal, *Delescluze*, p. 145.

63. Théodore Karcher, "Point de Démocratie sans Socialisme! Point de socialisme sans révolution," *La Voix du Proscrit* 2, no. 2 (1851), 22–26; see also Gustave Naquet, "La Liberté sociale," ibid., no. 28 (1851), 367.

64. See Calman, *Ledru-Rollin, passim*, for Ledru-Rollin's postrevolutionary program of direct democracy.

65. Ibid., p. 78; Dessal, *Delescluze*, p. 152.

66. Karcher, "Point de Démocratie": "In a word, socialism is nothing more than the scientific development of the revolutionary program, with only this difference: the revolution, unlike certain sectarian leaders [*chefs d'école*] does not believe it possesses an arcane wisdom all ready to turn humanity into El Dorado instantaneously, and it does not demand a dictatorship to apply a metaphysical system." Ch. Delescluze, "Plus de doctrinaires! Plus de dictateurs!" *La Voix du Proscrit* 2, no. 5 (May 24, 1851) and supplement, pp. 57–74, was a direct and harsh attack on Louis Blanc.

67. Blanc was publishing his own *Le Nouveau monde* at this period, and in negotiations with Leroux and Cabet about the possibility (never realized) of a joint socialist paper (Cabet to Blanc, January 25, 1851, in Correspondance de Louis Blanc, f. 34). This may be the joint enterprise to which Hugo referred.

68. "Lecture by Joseph Mazzini," *Reynolds' Newspaper*, no. 79, February 15, 1852, p. 3.

69. Described by Linton in a letter to the editor of *The Leader*, defending Mazzini, March 31, 1852 (Holyoake Collection, f. 481).

70. "Mazzini on Democracy," *Reynolds' Newspaper*, no. 85, March 29, 1852, p. 7.

71. Théophile Thoré (in London) to Félix Delhasse, March 20, 1852, in Papiers de Thoré-Bürger, no. 7911/29.

72. "M. Mazzini and the French Democrats," *Reynolds' Newspaper*, no. 86, April 14, 1852, p. 13. The statement was signed by Louis Blanc, Cabet, Pierre and Jules Leroux, and others. Cabet also wrote an individual defense of the French and of socialism that appeared in *Reynolds' Newspaper*, no. 89, April 25, 1852, p. 7.

73. Ruge's comment is in a letter of October 6, 1852, to Holyoake, in

Holyoake Collection, f. 527. The dispute in *The Reasoner* is in vol. 12 (1852), 337–39, 353–56, 381, 395, 414. *The English Republic* 2 (1852), 121–24 expressed Linton's complete support for Mazzini. Blanc wrote to Holyoake, in a private letter, to persuade him (ultimately successfully) to support his side (Blanc to Holyoake, April 28, 1852, Holyoake Collection, f. 486).

74. James Stansfeld to Holyoake, January 30, 1860, in ibid., f. 1181.

75. "Le 24 Fevrier. La Comité central démocratique européen," *La Voix du Proscrit* 2, no. 18 (1851), 248.

76. "Aux peuples! Organisation de la démocratie," *Le Proscrit*, no. 2, August 1850, pp. 47–51.

77. "Le Comité central démocratique européen," *La Voix du Proscrit* 2, no. 7 (June 1, 1851), 101–07, summarized the criticism; individual charges can be found in manifestoes directed to the various nationalities and scattered through *La Voix du Proscrit*. The Germans had failed to understand that their nation could not be constituted at the expense of others; the Italians allowed their national thought to be effaced in the interest of the dynasty, and denied international solidarity; Hungary did not acknowledge the equal rights of the Slavs and Romanians; Poland did not respond to the international rising this time around; and France in its arrogance thought it could resolve the social question on its own, and ignored its international responsibilities.

78. *La Voix du Proscrit* 1, no. 6 (1850), 79–81.

79. For example, in a London speech in June 1852, reported in *Reynolds' Newspaper*, no. 95, June 6, 1852, p. 3.

80. The *Procureur Général* of the Lyons parquet of the court of appeal to M. le Garde des Sceaux, December 23, 1850, Archives Nationales, BB18, 1480A, 8003A. f. 8.

81. Note of *Procureur Général* of Besançon, February 13, 1851, that was transmitted to the Ministry of Justice, to the Ministry of the Interior, and back to Justice again (Archives nationales, BB18, 1480A, 8003A, f. 72). See also Tchernoff, *Parti républicaine*, p. 112.

82. Translation of statement by Eberhardt, forwarded to Palmerston, April 23, 1851 (Public Record Office, Kew, H.O. 45/O.S. 3518, f. 12). At about the same time, the Paris prefect of police was also interested in German refugees in London; he was able to distinguish between the working-class orientation of the followers of "Dr. Marx, who lives in Cologne," and the followers of the European Committee. But he stressed that both factions were laboring for a common goal, "the uprising of the German states" (Report of Paris Prefect of Police, June 21, 1851, transmitted from the French minister of the interior to Britain, in ibid., f. 7).

83. Silberner, *Hess*, p. 315.

84. For a discussion of the British response to the refugee situation, including the use of hired informers, never officially acknowledged, see Bernard Porter, *The Refugee Question in Mid-Victorian Politics* (Cambridge, 1979).

85. Sanders Report, November 1, 1850, PRO, H.O. 45/O.S. 3518, f. 11.
86. Thomas Kabdebo, *Diplomat in Exile: Francis Pulszky's Political Activities in England, 1849–1860* (Boulder, Colo., 1979), pp. 72, 79.
87. Sanders report, August 14, 1852, PRO, H.O. 45/O.S 4547A.
88. Victor Hugo to Madier de Montjou, August 8, 1852, in *Correspondance* 2:123–24; Adèle Hugo, *Journal* 1:240 (entry for August 5, 1852). For Herzen's opposition to an Italian uprising, see *Byloe i dumy*, in *Sobranie sochinenii* 10:67; for commentary, see Tsypkina, "Gertsen i deiateli," p. 59.
89. *The People's Paper*, February 12, 1853, p. 5.
90. Herzen to Mariia Reichel, December 23, 1852, in *Sobranie sochinenii* 24:375.
91. Herzen to Mariia Reichel, February 5, 1853, in ibid. 25:16.
92. "Vol'noe Russkoe Knigopechatanie v Londone. Brat'iam na Rusi," in ibid. 12:62–63. The document is dated February 21, 1853, but apparently only appeared in March; see Herzen to Mariia Reichel, March 18, 1853, in ibid. 25:30, promising a copy of the announcement in his next letter.
93. See the reminiscence of Herzen by Carl Schurz, who met him at the Kinkels soon after his arrival in England (Schurz, *Reminiscences* 2:53–54).
94. See, for example, H. Delaveau, "Le Roman contemporain en Russie: M. Alexandre Hertzen," *Revue des deux mondes*, July 1854, pp. 316–42; and the discussion in Monica Partridge, "Alexander Herzen and the English Press," *Slavonic and East European Review*, June 1958, pp. 453–70.

Chapter 8. The Revolutionary Community

1. Judith Zimmerman, "Alexander Herzen and George Sand: Influence and Empathy," Dept. of History, University of Pittsburgh at Greensburg, Greensburg, Pa., 15601, covers this subject in more detail.
2. For Herzen on his own education, see *Byloe i dumy*, *Sobranie sochinenii* 8:49–55. For Natalie's youth, see Judith Zimmerman, "Natalie Herzen and the Early Intelligentsia," *Russian Review* 41, no. 3 (July 1982), 249–72.
3. Antsiferov, "N. A. Gertsen," p. 372.
4. For the roster of teachers, see Herzen to Vogt, November 21, 1852, in *Sobranie sochinenii* 24:362; see also Herzen to Mariia Reichel, November 21, 1852, in ibid. 24:365.
5. Herzen to Malwida Meysenbug, October 1854, in ibid. 25:198; Herzen to Mariia Reichel, November 21, 1854, in ibid. 25:212.
6. Herzen to Malwida Meysenbug, February 28, 1866, in ibid. 28:159.
7. See, for example, Herzen to A. A. Herzen, February 7, 1864, in ibid. 28:426.
8. The countess's letters to Emma, testifying to this friendship, are in the Lettres de Marie d'Agoult at the Bibliothèque Nationale. Emma asked

d'Agoult to come to Nice that summer of 1850, to provide moral support; the countess, probably wisely, refused (Agoult to Emma Herwegh, in ibid., f. 308).

9. Herzen to Herwegh, December 28, 1849, in *Sobranie sochinenii* 23:222.

10. Herzen to Herwegh, December 31, 1849, in ibid. 23:226–27.

11. Herwegh to Herzen, January 4, 1850, in Lemke, ed., *Polnoe sobranie sochinenii* 14:38; for more of Herwegh's exculpation, see ibid. 14:44–57, *passim*.

12. Herzen to Herwegh, January 17, 1850, in *Sobranie sochinenii* 23:234.

13. Natalie to Herzen, June 9, 1851, in Lemke, ed., *Polnoe sobranie sochinenii* 6:188.

14. Emma Herwegh to Natalie Herzen, draft letter, undated (early 1852?), in Herzen-Herwegh Papers, Add. Mss. 47,664, ff. 290–304.

15. Drafts of letter, Emma Herwegh to Natalie Herzen, February 5 and 6, 1852, in ibid., ff. 306, 307.

16. Sazonov to Herzen, February 3, 1852, in Lemke, ed., *Polnoe sobranie sochinenii* 7:14.

17. Natalie Herzen to Sazonóv, February 15, 1852, in Gertsen, *Sobranie sochinenii* 24:231. Sazonov was caught in the middle. He sympathized with Herwegh for having the affair (he was himself partial to married women), and admired Natalie for flouting convention, under the impression, at this time, that she had chosen Herwegh (Sazonov to Herwegh, June 3, 1851, in Herzen-Herwegh Papers, 47,667, ff. 170–71). Later, after receiving Herzen's and Natalie's rebuttals, he declared his neutrality, and transmitted Herzen's response to Herwegh's charge: "He answers that his wife loves him more than ever, and has no love at all for you" (Sazonov to Herwegh, May 13, 1852, in ibid., f. 174). By November, he told Herwegh that he had absolutely no grievance against Herzen: "If he finally repossessed his goods you can be afflicted by it," but that was not grounds for a challenge. Sazonov found the provocation "mad" (Sazonov to Herwegh, November 3, 1852, in ibid., f. 172).

18. Herzen to Proudhon, September 8, 1852, in *Sobranie sochinenii* 24:326.

19. Herzen to Natalie, June 28, 1851, in ibid. 24:192–99; her responses to his renewed anguish were published by Lemke (*Polnoe sobranie sochinenii* 6:421–23). Natalie had promised to "see" Herwegh again in a year—it is not impossible that he honestly misinterpreted her promise to mean that she would come to live with him. Herwegh told Chojecki, as well as Sazonov, that his separation from her was temporary (Chojecki to Herwegh, February 15 [1851], in Herzen-Herwegh Papers, Add. Mss. 47,667, f. 164).

20. Herzen to Haug, approx. March 16, 1852, in *Sobranie sochinenii* 24:326.

21. The letter is recalled by Herzen in *Byloe i dumy*, and a draft is quoted at length by Carr in *The Romantic Exiles*. "He said that with my *slanders* against him I had *confused* Natalie, that I exploited her weakness and my influence over her, that she *betrayed* him. In conclusion, he *denounced her* and said that *fate* has decided between me and him, that 'it drowns your offspring and your family in the sea' " (*Sobranie sochinenii* 10:284). Other points in the letter included insistence that the miscarriage in Geneva was Herwegh's child. The challenge was based on Herzen's continuing to live with (and once again impregnate) his wife: "You will not continue this prostitution of a being whom I did not steal from you, but whom I took because she told me that you had never possessed her; at any rate, I shall not survive it if you do. To your gratuitous insults to Emma you have added the infamy of pretending that I seduced your wife" (Carr, *Romantic Exiles*, p. 109). Carr, in discussing the motive for Herwegh's belated challenge, suggests, among other possibilities, that news of Natalie's pregnancy "stung him to a new paroxysm of rage and hatred." The content of the draft letter, and the rage he had manifested in 1850, when she was carrying Ol'ga, suggest that this was indeed the motivating impulse.

22. Gertsen, *Sobranie sochinenii* 10:284–85.

23. A Russian translation of Haug's letter is quoted in Lemke, ed., *Polnoe sobranie sochinenii* 7:42–44. A French version is in the Rodicheva Papers, Columbia University.

24. Herzen to Proudhon, September 6, 1852, in Gertsen, *Sobranie sochinenii* 24:326.

25. On the Barthélemy-Cournet conflict, see Herzen's account in *Byloe i dumy*, ibid. 11:78–95; Alexandre Zévaès, "Les Proscrits français en 1848 et 1851 à Londres," *La Révolution de 1848* 21, no. 104 (May–June 1924), 95–96, both of which are sympathetic to the more radical Barthélemy; Calman, *Ledru-Rollin après 1848*, pp. 138–39, and Adèle Hugo, *Le Journal*, vol. 2, *passim*. The latter two take the side of the more moderate, Rolliniste, Cournet. On the Orsini affair, see Orsini to Herzen, undated, in Herzen Archive, Internationaal Instituut voor Sociale Geschiedenis, 2.d.ix; Herzen to Orsini, September 9, 1856, in *Sobranie sochinenii* 26:25–26; Herzen's account of the affair is in *Byloe i dumy*, ibid. 10:366–69; see also Ogareva-Tuchkova, *Vospominaniia*, pp. 102–04.

26. Herzen to Haug, approx. March 16, 1852, in *Sobranie sochinenii* 24:249.

27. Ibid.

28. The letter, dated February 18, is quoted in *Byloe i dumy*, ibid. 10:290–91; Carr discusses it in *The Romantic Exiles*, pp. 111–12.

29. Gertsen, *Sobranie sochinenii* 10:291–92. The envelope, with the dubious seal, was carefully saved by Herzen, and is now in the Collections Slaves of the Bibliothèque Nationale.

30. *Sobranie sochinenii* 10:305–12; for Herwegh's responses, see Lemke, ed., *Polnoe sobranie sochinenii* 7:112–19.

31. *Sobranie sochinenii* 7:390–91.

32. Herzen to Proudhon, September 9, 1852, in ibid. 24:36. The same argument was made in the letters to other prominent radicals.

33. Herzen's letters to Vogt, in particular, detail the campaign in London. The letters to the major radical figures are in the *Sochineniia*, and most have been quoted here. Marx wrote to Engels: "I already wrote you that Herzen is here and is circulating memoirs against Herwegh, that he not only put horns on him, but also squeezed 80,000 francs out of him" (Marx to Engels, September 29, 1852, in Marx and Engels, *Werke* 28:148.

34. Haug to Piggott, August 31, 1852, in Holyoake Collection, f. 1162. Spelling Haug's.

35. Gertsen, *Sobranie sochinenii* 10:288.

36. There is little literature on the court of honor, and what there is refers to specific cases. Blanqui refused to appear before one when charged, in 1848, with having been a police informer. A court of honor attempted unsuccessfully to resolve the Barthèlemy-Cournet conflict. At about the same time, the French community in London did manage to use a court to settle an issue involving the charge of misuse of funds collected by an exile charitable organization (Calman, *Ledru-Rollin,* pp. 139–40). As Vuilleumier states, "Doubtless there was a certain naiveté in this wish to have Herwegh judged by the tribunal of revolutionary democracy" (Vuilleumier, intro. to "Révolutionnaires de 1848 et exilés," in Vuilleumier et al., eds., *Autour de Herzen,* p. 43).

37. Herzen to Mariia Reichel, July 23, 1852, in *Sobranie sochinenii* 24:306.

38. Michelet to Herzen, July 29, 1852; in Monod, ed., "Jules Michelet et Alexandre Herzen," pp. 161–62.

39. Herzen to Müller-Strübing, October 18, 1852, in *Sobranie sochinenii* 24:350–51; for Müller's transmittal of the letter to Sand, see Sand, *Correspondance* 11:418–19 and n.

40. See Vogt to Herzen, June 4, July 2, and November 11, 1852, in Vuilleumier et al., eds., *Autour de Herzen,* pp. 91–98, *passim,* and a letter from early September, 1852, in N. Iu. Kolpinskii et al., "Perepiska s K. Fogtom," *Literaturnoe nasledstvo* 96 (1985), 96–97.

41. Proudhon to Herzen, August 7, 1852, in Michel Mervaud, ed., "A propos du conflit Herzen-Herwegh. Un inédit de Proudhon," *Cahiers du monde russe et soviètique* 14, no. 3 (1973), 346–47. Mervaud's article provides an analysis of the origin and content of the letter, and prints the entire document. Herzen, like Proudhon, in his search for a legitimation of some sort of tribunal, turned back from the medieval duel to the *Wehm* of the ancient Germans.

42. Lemke, ed., *Polnoe sobranie sochinenii* 7:80–81.
43. Engel'son to Herzen, July 30, 1852, in ibid. 7:78.
44. Herzen to Müller-Strübing, October 18, 1852, in *Sobranie sochinenii* 24:350.
45. Herzen to Vogt, November 21, 1852, in ibid. 24:361.
46. Herzen to Saffi, December 17, 1855, in ibid. 25:320.
47. Herzen to Mariia Reichel, December 23, 1852, in ibid. 24:375.
48. See especially E. P. Thompson, *The Making of the English Working Class* (New York, 1963). It is also likely that French working-class radical traditions influenced the form of radical culture. On this point, see Sewell, *Work and Revolution in France*.
49. *The Reasoner* 13, no. 7 (1852), 110.
50. For example, a tea party and meeting "in commemoration of the illustrious Robespierre" was held on April 13, 1853. According to the invitation, Blanc, Nadaud, and the English radical publisher Reynolds had promised to attend, and Kossuth, Ledru-Rollin, Saffi, Schoelcher, Holyoake, and others had been invited. The moderate Irish radical, Bronterre O'Brien, presided. The invitation was pasted into Holyoake's diary, and an entry confirms his attendance (Holyoake Collection).
51. Victor Hugo's son, Charles, praised the Jersey exile colony for its faithful accomplishment of the task of memorial and propaganda: "It multiplied as much as possible collective and individual protests. It celebrated, in unanimous meetings, the great republican anniversaries and gave speeches, in these solemn circumstances, which the free papers of England, Belgium, Spain, Italy and America reproduced in their columns and leaflets of which circulated from hand to hand in Paris from the workshops to the salons" (Charles Hugo, *Les Hommes de l'exil* [Paris, 1875], p. 178).
52. Adèle Hugo, *Journal* 2:55.
53. Hypatia Bradlaugh Bonner, *Charles Bradlaugh: A Record of His Life and Work* (London, 1908), 1:204 and n. Charles Bradlaugh (1833–1891) was a prominent British radical, atheist journalist. His greatest fame came in later years, with his and Annie Besant's indictment for publishing an "indecent pamphlet" that disseminated birth control information.
54. Herzen's position as a Russian was complex, at this period when Russia, along with Austria, symbolized to most radicals despotism incarnate, and when the tensions that would soon bring on the Crimean War were already very much in evidence. These circumstances limited his public participation, and defined the role he could play.
55. Victor Schoelcher to Herzen, July 26, 1858, in Herzen Album, 17, Herzen Archive, Internationaal Instituut voor Sociale Geschiedenis.
56. *From the Other Shore*, p. 4; Sasha said of the dedication that it was a gift "higher than all my hopes." A. A. Herzen to Mariia Reichel, January 4, 1855, in Gertsen, *Sobranie sochinenii* 25:223.

57. Meysenbug, *Memoiren* 2:255.

58. On Herzen's historical contribution, see esp. Eidel'man, *Gertsen protiv samoderzhaviia*.

59. A. A. Herzen to Mariia Reichel, December 15, 1854, in Gertsen, *Sobranie sochinenii* 25:220. The entire family was involved in consolidating revolutionary tradition and mythology that year. For Herzen, on the same occasion, the children and Sasha's tutor presented a series of *tableaux vivants* representing major episodes in Herzen's life and his involvement in radical activity (ibid. 25:219–20).

60. Herzen to Mariia Reichel, June 20, 1853, in ibid. 25:67.

61. Herzen to Emily Reeve, September 20, 1860, in ibid. 25:96. A few months earlier, he had written to Mariia Reichel: "If she sees a great deal of German *Liebelei*, and at sixteen years also gets married, that would truly destroy half of my life" (Herzen to Mariia Reichel, June 23, 1860, in ibid. 25:71).

62. Ogarev to A. A. Herzen, October, 1863, in Michel Mervaud, ed., *Nicolas Ogarev. Lettres inédites à Alexandre Herzen, Fils* (Rouen and Paris, 1978), pp. 70–71.

63. Herzen to A. A. Herzen, January 12, 1866, in *Sobranie sochinenii* 28:140.

64. On the Herzen-Tuchkova relationship, see Ogareva, "Moia Ispoved'," *Arkhiv Ogarevykh*, p. 264; Herzen to Ogarev, late 1856, in *Sobranie sochinenii* 26:62–63; Natalie Tuchkova to Ogarev, undated, in N. A. Roskina, "Iz perepiski N. A. Tuchkovoi-Ogarevoi," *Literaturnoe nasledstvo* 63 (1956), 506–07, *et passim*; Carr, *Romantic Exiles*, pp. 248–58.

65. The Herzens' independence of conventional morality did not extend to acknowledgment of this situation; the children were officially Ogarev's.

66. Ogarev to Natalie Tuchkova-Ogareva, November 6, [1865], in "Iz perepiska . . . Tuchkovoi," pp. 507–08.

67. Ogarev to Ol'ga Herzen, June 13, 1869, Michel Mervaud, ed. *Lettres inédites: Herzen, Ogarev, Bakounine* (Paris, 1975), p. 129.

68. On the separation, see Gertsen, *Sobranie sochinenii* 28:96; Ol'ga Herzen Monod later told of verbal abuse by Natalie, upon occasion so great that she ran and hid in the doghouse, where Malwida once found her asleep, hugging the dog (Notes of A. F. Rodicheva, Rodicheva Papers, Columbia University, Box 15.7.3.1). As for Natalie, she found it "a true misfortune" to live with the Herzen children: "Tata is the best, and yet her egoism is such that it repulses you despite yourself; as for Alex., he is the most disobliging and disagreeable man alive—the very services he renders his father, he does with the most terrible bad grace, and as to Ol'ga, in everything she is the worst example one could find for other children; lying, arrogant, impertinent, lazy, idle . . . , etc. etc." (Tuchkova to Mlle. Michel, Herzen Archive 3b[4], Internationaal Instituut voor Sociale Geschiedenis). Ogarev severely

condemned Natalie for her treatment of the Herzen children (see "Iz Perepiska . . . Tuchkovoi," *passim*).

69. A. A. Herzen to Ogarev, copy in Rodicheva papers, misdated 1863, probably 1866.

70. Herzen to Malwida Meysenbug, August 7, 1866, in *Sobranie sochinenii* 28:212–13.

71. Herzen to Malwida Meysenbug, July 25, 1866, in ibid. 28:208.

72. See, especially, Ogarev's letters to Sasha in Mervaud, *Nicolas Ogarev*, pp. 60–92.

73. Herzen to A. A. Herzen, February 7, 1864, in *Sobranie sochinenii* 27:426.

74. There appears to have been a sexual encounter between Charlotte Hutson and Henry Sutherland, Mary's young son, followed by an argument with Mary Sutherland (Ogarev to A. A. Herzen, June 21, 1867, in Mervaud, *Nicolas Ogarev*, p. 120).

75. Ibid.

76. A. A. Herzen to Ogarev, June 26, 1867, in Rodicheva Papers.

77. Ogarev to A. A. Herzen, July 13, 1867, in Mervaud, *Nicolas Ogarev*, p. 123.

78. See, for example, Herzen's "memorial" article on Bakunin and his praise of Worcell for giving up his family to dedicate himself to the cause (*Sobranie sochinenii* 7:343, on Bakunin; and ibid. 11:132, on Worcell).

79. "The Manifesto of the Communist Party," in Marx and Engels, *Selected Works* 1:50–51.

80. Proudhon, response to Cardinal Mathié, 1854, cited in Halévy, *Le Mariage de Proudhon*, p. 35.

81. Herzen to Ruge, February 15, 1854, in *Sobranie sochinenii* 25:154.

82. Ruge to Herzen, trans. by Lemke, ed., *Polnoe sobranie sochinenii* 8:21–22.

83. Vogt to Herzen, April 1, 1853, in Vuilleumier et al., eds., *Autour de Herzen*, p. 113.

84. Herzen to Vogt, April 5, 1853, in *Sobranie sochinenii* 25:40.

85. W.J.L., "The Marriage of Dr. Kudlich," *The English Republic* 2, no. 86 (August 30, 1853), 344. Herzen identified Linton as the author and promised to send it to Vogt, on August 15 (*Sobranie sochinenii* 25:90).

Conclusion

1. In 1861, Tolstoi told Proudhon of Herzen's desire to return; Herzen responded, "I do not think at all about going into the bear's mouth. Probably Count Tolstoy has taken my castles in Spain for castles on the banks of the Volga" (Herzen to Proudhon, in Mervaud, "Six Lettres," p. 314).

2. I am deliberately avoiding the term *proletariat*. Marx, of course, believed that revolution would come from the organized industrial workers, whom he called the proletariat. There are two problems with this usage. First, it appears to be a rather idiosyncratic definition used by some Saint-Simonians and by Marx, but not generally accepted. For other socialist thinkers of the time, the word meant the poorest and most oppressed of the poor, without regard to the source of their income; in actual fact, these would more likely be artisans, especially in decaying crafts, than industrial workers. Marx's *Lumpenproletariat* seems rather closer to the contemporary meaning of *proletariat*. (On the Saint-Simonian use of *proletariat* to mean industrial workers, see James Briscoe, "The Unfinished Revolution: The Saint-Simonians and the Social Question—Origins of Socialist Debate in the July Monarchy," The Consortium on Revolutionary Europe, *Proceedings* [1984], pp. 235–37. Second, Marx's own groups were more often made up of artisans than of industrial workers.

3. It is a measure of the hostility of Marx and Engels toward Herzen that Engels felt one of their friends had failed in his responsibility by allowing an article of Herzen's to be published in an English newspaper. Marx did not argue with Engels's desire for censorship, but pointed out that the friend in question worked for a different newspaper, and thus was not to blame for the article appearing (Engels to Marx, April 21, 1854; Marx to Engels, April 22, 1854, in Marx and Engels, *Werke* 28:344–46).

4. *Sobranie sochinenii* 11:158–60, recalls an episode in 1853; see also Marx to Engels, September 3 and 28, 1853, in Marx and Engels, *Werke* 28:280–84, 295. There was another episode in 1862.

BIBLIOGRAPHY

Archival Sources

Archives Nationales, BB18 (Ministry of Justice, political series), 1480A, 8003A. Paris.
Blanc, Louis. Correspondance de Louis Blanc. Bibliothèque Nationale, Nouvelles Acquisitions Françaises, 11,398. Paris.
D'Agoult, Marie. Lettres de Marie d'Agoult. Bibliothèque Nationale, Nouvelles Acquisitions Francaises, 25,183. Paris.
France. Ministère des Affaires Étrangères. Correspondance Politique, La Russie, vol. 203. Paris.
Herwegh Archiv. Dichtermuseum. Liestal, Switzerland.
Herzen Archives. Internationaal Instituut voor Sociale Geschiedenis. Amsterdam.
Herzen Family Papers. Bakhmetev Archive, Columbia University. New York.
Herzen-Herwegh Papers. British Library, Add. Mss. 47,664–47,668. London.
Holyoake Collection. Library of the Cooperative Union, Ltd., Manchester.
Proudhon, Pierre-Joseph. Correspondance (Lettres à Charles Edmond, 1850–1861). Bibliothèque Nationale, Nouvelles Acquisitions Françaises, 11,389. Paris.
Public Record Office. H.O. 45/O.S. 3518, 4547A. Kew.
Rodicheva Papers. Columbia University. New York.
Papiers de Thoré-Bürger. Bibliothèque de l'Arsenal, 7909-7922. Paris.

Works by Alexander Herzen

The standard edition of Herzen's works is the thirty-volume version produced by the Soviet Academy of Sciences, which is annotated in this work as Gertsen, *Sobranie sochinenii*. With the exception of *S togo berega*, for which I used the English version cited as *From the Other Shore*, and *Le Peuple russe et le socialisme*, translated in the same volume, all references to Herzen's works are from this edition. The most important of these are for this period of Herzen's life are: *Pis'ma iz Frantsii i Italii* [Letters from France and Italy] (vol. 5); *S togo berega* [From the Other Shore] (vol. 6); *La Russie* (vol. 6); *Du Développement des idées révolutionnaires en Russie* (vol. 7); *Le Peuple russe et le socialisme* (vol. 7). The correspondence for these years is in vols. 23 and 24.

Since the appearance of the Academy edition, some new Herzen documentation has been discovered and published; additional, recent Herzen citations reflect this.

Although the Academy edition made all others obsolete from the point of view of works actually written by Herzen, older editions have some special qualities which makes them retain their value. The first major collection of Herzen's works, that edited by Lemke (*Polnoe sobranie sochinenii i pisem*), contains invaluable notes, which include letters to Herzen, archival materials discovered by Lemke, and all manner of information. No serious student of Herzen can do without this treasury. The collection of private letters published by Domger in 1957 is based on the Herzen Family Papers at Columbia; Domger included all letters from Natalie Herzen to which Alexander appended a note, however insignificant, while the Academy edition is more sparing of Natalie's letters. I have cited these letters from the Academy edition, when possible, otherwise from Domger, or else, if they contain no material by Herzen himself, from the archival source.

Gertsen, Aleksandr. *Sobranie sochinenii v tridtsati tomakh.* Moscow, 1954–1965.

From the Other Shore [S togo berega] and *The Russian People and Socialism* [Le Peuple russe et le socialisme]. Intro. Isaiah Berlin. Cleveland, 1963.

My Past and Thoughts: The Memoirs of Alexander Herzen. Trans. Constance Garnett; rev. Humphrey Higgins; intro. Isaiah Berlin. 4 vols. New York, 1968.

Neizdannye pis'ma A. I. Gertsena k N. I. i T. A. Astrakovym, ed. L. L. Domger. New York, 1957.

"Novonaidennyie stat'i i pis'ma." *Literaturnoe nasledstvo* 7–8 (1933), 56–95.

Polnoe sobranie sochinenii i pisem. Ed. M. K. Lemke. 22 vols. Petrograd, 1914–1925.

"Six Lettres de Herzen à Proudhon." Ed. Michel Mervaud. *Cahiers du monde russe et soviétique* 12, no.3 (July–September 1971), 307–16.

Other Published Primary Sources and Memoirs

Althaus, Friedrich. "Alexander Herzen." *Unsere Zeit: Deutsche Revue der Gegenwart*, n.s. 8 (1872), 21–56.

BIBLIOGRAPHY

Annenkov, P. V. *The Extraordinary Decade; Literary Memoirs.* Trans. Irwin R. Titunik; ed. Arthur P. Mendel. Ann Arbor, Mich., 1968.
Annenkov, P. V. *P. V. Annenkov i ego druz'ia. Literaturnyia vospominaniia i perepiska 1835–1885 godov.* St. Petersburg, 1892.
Antsiferov, N. P., ed. "N. A. Gertsen (Zakharina): Materialy dlia biografii." *Literaturnoe nasledstvo* 63 (1956), 355–93.
[Bakunin, M. A.] "Novye materialy o Bakunine i Gertsene." *Golos minuvshago*, January, 1913, pp. 182–90.
[Bakunin, M. A.] *Pisma M. A. Bakunina k A. I. Gertsenu i N. P. Ogarevu.* Ed. M. P. Dragomanov. St. Petersburg, 1906.
Bakunin, M. A. *Sobranie sochinenii i pisem, 1826–1876.* Ed. Iu. M. Steklov. Vol. 3, *Period pervogo prebyvaniia za granitsei, 1840–49.* Moscow, 1935.
Belinskii, V. G. *Polnoe sobranie sochinenii.* Vol. 12, *Pis'ma, 1841–1848.* Moscow, 1956.
Belogolovyi, N. A. *Vospominaniia i drugiia stat'i.* 4th ed. St. Petersburg, 1901.
Blanc, Louis. *1848: Historical Revelations.* 1858. Reprint. New York, 1971.
[Buchanan, James.] *The Works of James Buchanan.* Ed. John Basset Moore. Vol. 9, *1853–55.* Philadelphia and London, 1909.
Butina, K. I., ed. "Materialy A. I. Gertsen iz Arkhiva Korshei." *Zapiski Otdela rukopisei, Gosudarstvennaia Biblioteka SSSR imeni V. I. Lenina* 32 (1971), 182–200.
Caussidière, Marc. *Mémoires.* 2 vols. Paris, 1849.
Chaadaev, Peter Ia. *Philosophial Letters, and Apology of a Madman.* Trans. and intro. Mary-Barbara Zeldin. Knoxville, Tenn., 1969.
[Chojecki,] C. H. Edmond. "Lettre première. Politique universelle. Solidarité des peuples." Supplement to *La Voix du Peuple*, no. 43, November 12, 1849, pp. 1–2.
[Chojecki,] C. H. Edmond. "Politique universelle. Solidarité des Peuples. Lettre troisième. L'Autriche." Supplement to *La Voix du Peuple*, no. 78, December 17, 1849, pp. 1–2; no. 85, December 24, 1849, pp. 1–2; no. 91, December 31, 1849, pp. 1–2.
Corvin [-Wiersbitzkii, Otto von]. *Aus der Leben eines Volkskämpfers. Erinnerungen.* 4 vols. Amsterdam, 1861.
Darimon, Alfred. *À Travers une Révolution (1847–1855).* Paris, 1884.
Delaveau, H. "Le Roman contemporain en Russie: M. Alexandre Hertzen." *Revue des deux mondes*, July 1854, pp. 316–42.
Efros, N. D., ed. "Iz pisem L. I. Gaag." *Literaturnoe nasledstvo* 63 (1956), 393–415.
Ewerbeck, Hermann. *L'Allemagne et les Allemands.* Paris, 1851.
Fazy, James. *Les Mémoires de James Fazy, Homme d'état Genèvois (1794–1878).* Intro. François Ruchon. Geneva, 1947.
Forder, Herwig, Martin Handt, Jefim Kandel, and Sofia Lewiowa, eds. *Der*

BIBLIOGRAPHY

Bund der Kommunisten: Dokumente und Materialen. Vol. 1, *1836–1849.* Berlin, 1970.

Fröbel, Julius. *Ein Lebenslauf. Aufzeichnungen, Erinnerungen und Bekentnisse.* 2 vols. Stuttgart, 1890–1891.

[Golovin, Ivan.] Golownin, Iwan. *Der Russische Nihilismus. Meine Beziehungen zu Herzen und zu Bakunin.* Leipzig, n.d.

Haxthausen, August von. *Studies on the Interior of Russia.* Trans. Eleanore L. M. Schmidt; ed. and intro. S. Frederick Starr. Chicago, 1972.

Herwegh, Marcel, ed. *Au Printemps des dieux: Correspondance inédite de la Comtesse Marie d'Agoult et du poète Georges Herwegh.* 5th ed. Paris, 1929.

Herwegh, Marcel, ed. *1848: Briefe von und an Georg Herwegh.* 2d ed. Munich, 1898.

[Herzen, Natalie.] "Pis'ma Natalii Aleksandrovny Gertsen k Gervegam." Ed. L. R. Lanskii. *Literaturnoe nasledstvo* 64 (1958), 259–319.

[Herzen, Natalie.] "Dnevnik i pis'ma N. A. Gertsena." Ed. M. Gershenzon. *Russkie Propylei: Materialy po istorii russkoi mysli i literatury* 1 (1915), 232–76.

[Herzen, Natalie.] "N. A. Gertsen (Otryvki iz neizdannykh pisem)." *Russkiia zapiski* 14 (February 1939), 99–119.

Hess, Moses. *Briefwechsel.* Ed. Edmund Silberner. Quellen und Untersuchungen zur Geschichte der deutschen und osterreichischen Arbeiterbewegung, herausgegeben vom Internationaal Instituut voor Sociale Geschiedenis, Amsterdam. The Hague, 1959.

Hugo, Adèle. *Le Journal d'Adèle Hugo.* Ed. Frances Guille. 2 vols. Paris, 1968, 1971.

Hugo, Victor. *Correspondance*, vol. 2. In *Oeuvres completes de Victor Hugo.* Paris, 1950.

J. M., ed. "Lettres de Mazzini à Herzen." *Bulletin of the International Institute of Social History* 8 (1953), 16–34.

[Jacoby, Johann.] *Johann Jacoby Briefwechsel: 1816–1849.* Ed. Edmund Silberner. Veröffentlichungen des Instituts für Sozialgeschichte. Braunschweig, Hanover, 1979.

Jeanjean, J. F. "Louis Blanc et Ledru-Rollin: Lettres inédites." *La Révolution de 1848* 7 (1910–1911), 107–14.

[Kapp, Friedrich.] *Friedrich Kapp: Vom radikalen Frühsozialisten des Vormärz zum liberalen Parteipolitiker des Bismarckreiches. Briefe 1843–1884.* Ed. Hans-Ulrich Wehler. Frankfurt a.M., 1969.

Kieniewicz, Stefan, ed. "From the Polish Correspondence of William J. Linton, 1844–1854." *Annali Istituto Giangiacomo Feltrinelli* 3 (1960).

Kolpinskii, N. Iu., et al. "Perepiska s K. Fogtom." *Literaturnoe Nasledstvo* 96 (1985), 85–175.

Lanskii, L. P. "Otkliki na smert' Gertsena: Po materialam inostrannoi pechati i 'Prazhskoi Kollektsii.' " *Literaturnoe nasledstvo* 63 (1956), 523–40.

BIBLIOGRAPHY

Linton, W. J. *Memories*. London, 1895.
Marx, Karl, and Friedrich Engels. "The Class Struggles in France, 1848–1850." In *Selected Works in Two Volumes*, 1:118–243. Moscow, 1958.
Marx, Karl, and Friedrich Engels. *Werke*. 42 vols. Berlin, 1956–1967.
Matlaw, Ralph E., ed. *Belinsky, Chernyshevsky and Dobrolyubov: Selected Criticism*. New York, 1962.
Mervaud, Michel. "À propos du conflit Herzen-Herwegh. Un inédit de Proudhon." *Cahiers du monde russe et soviétique* 14, no. 3 (1973), 333–48.
Mervaud, Michel, ed. *Lettres inédites: Herzen, Ogarev, Bakounine*. Vol. 7 of *Les inédits russes*. Paris, 1975.
Mervaud, Michel, ed. *Nicolas Ogarev. Lettres inédites à Alexandre Herzen, Fils*. Rouen and Paris, 1978.
Meysenbug, Malwida von. *Memoiren einer Idealistin*. 3 vols. 9th ed. Berlin and Leipzig, 1905.
Mickiewicz, Adam. *La Tribune des Peuples*. Pref. Ladislas Mickiewicz. Paris, 1907.
Monod, Gabriel, ed. "Jules Michelet et Alexandre Herzen d'après leurs correspondance intime (1851–1869)." *La Revue* 68 (1907), 145–64, 307–21.
Nekrasova, E. S. "Akter M. S. Shchepkin i A. I. Gertsen." *Russkaia mysl'* 25, no. 1 (1904), 2d pagination, 73–85.
Ogarev, N. P., and N. A. Ogareva. *Arkhiv N. A. i N. P. Ogarevykh*. Ed. M. Gershenzon. Moscow, 1930.
Ogareva-Tuchkova, Nataliia. *Vospominaniia, 1848–1879*. Moscow, 1903.
Passek, T. P. *Iz dal'nykh let: Vospominaniia*. 2 vols. Moscow, 1963.
Perselenkov, S. A., and Ia. Z. Cherniak, eds. "Gertsen i Ogarev: Novye materialy." *Zven'ia* 6 (1936), 338–413.
Proudhon, P.-J. *Correspondance*. 17 vols. Paris, 1875.
Proudhon, P.-J. *Mélanges: Articles de Journaux, 1848–1852*. Vol. 17 of *Oeuvres Complètes de P.-J. Proudhon*. Paris, 1868.
Proudhon, P.-J. *Les Carnets de P.-J. Proudhon*. Ed. Pierre Haubtmann. Vol. 3, *1848–50*. Paris, 1968.
Proudhon, P.-J. *Les Confessions d'un Révolutionnaire pour servir à l'Histoire de la Révolution de Fevrier*. Intro. Daniel Halévy. Vol. 7 of *Oeuvres Complètes de P.-J. Proudhon*, Nouvelle Edition. Paris, 1929.
Rasch, Gustav. *Aus meiner Festungszeit. Ein Beitrag zur Geschichte der preussischen Reaction*. Pest, Vienna, Leipzig, 1868.
Reikhel, M. K. *Otryvki iz vospominanii*. Vol. 1 of *Materialy dlia biografii Gertsena*. Moscow, 1909.
Roskina, N. A. "Iz perepiski N. A. Tuchkovoi-Ogarevoi." *Literaturnoe nasledstvo* 63 (1956), 505–22.

Ruge, Arnold. *Briefwechsel und Tagebuchblätter aus den Jahren 1825–1880.* Ed. Paul Herrlich. 2 vols. Berlin, 1886.
Sand, George. *Correspondance.* Ed. Georges Lubin. Vol. 7, *Juillet 1845–Juin 1847;* vol. 8, *Juillet 1847–Décembre 1848;* vol. 9, *Janvier 1849–Décembre 1850.* Paris, 1954– .
Sand, George. *Fanchon the Cricket.* Chicago, 1977. [Translation of *La Petite Fadette.*]
Schurz, Carl. *Die Briefe von Carl Schurz an Gottfried Kinkel.* Ed. and intro. Eberhard Kessel. Beihefte zum Jahrbuch fur Amerikstudien, 12. Heidelberg, 1965.
Schurz, Carl. *The Reminiscences of Carl Schurz.* 2 vols. New York, 1907–1908.
Selivanov, I. V. "Zapiski dvorianina-pomeshchika." *Russkaia starina* 28 (June 1880), 289–316.
Stankevich, A. *T. N. Granovskii i ego perepiska.* 2 vols. Moscow, 1897.
Stern, Daniel [Marie d'Agoult]. *Histoire de la Révolution de 1848.* Paris, 1850.
Tchernoff, J. *Associations et sociétés secrètes sous la deuxième république, 1848–1851, d'après des documents inédits.* Reprint. New York, 1973.
Tchernoff, J. *Le Parti républicain au coup d'état et sous le Second Empire.* Paris, 1906.
Turgenev, Ivan. *Rudin.* Trans. Richard Freeborn. New York, 1975.
Turgenev, Ivan. *Pis'ma v trinadtsati tomakh.* Vol. 1, *1831–1850.* Moscow-Leningrad, 1961.
Varnhagen von Ense, [K.] A. *Tagebucher. Aus dem Nachlass Varnhagen's von Ense.* 15 vols. Bern, 1972.
Vuilleumier, Marc, ed. "Une Lettre inédite de Carl Vogt à Herzen," *Musées de Genève* 147 (July–August 1974), 18–21.
Vuilleumier, Marc, Michel Aucouturier, Sven Stelling-Michaud, and Michel Cadot, eds. *Autour d'Alexandre Herzen: Révolutionnaires et exilés du XIXe siècle: Documents inédits.* Geneva, 1973.
Zastenker, N. E., ed. "N. I. Sazonov-Gertsenu." *Literaturnoe Nasledstvo* 62 (1955), 522–45.
Zhelvakova, I. A. et al., eds. "Perepiska s nemetskimi demokratami." *Literaturnoe Nasledstvo* 96 (1985), 175–99.
Ziegengeist, G. "Herzens Plan zur Gründung einer freien russischen Druckerei in Stuttgart im October 1850 (Aus dem ungedruckten Briefwechsel zwischen G. Herwegh und A. Kolatschek)." *Zeitschrift für Slawistik* 8, no. 5 (1953), 696–709.

Contemporary Periodicals

The English Republic. London, 1851–1855.
L'Homme. Jersey and London, 1853–1856.

The People's Paper. London, 1852–1858.
The Reasoner. London, 1852–1855.
Le Représentant du Peuple. Paris, 1848.
Reynolds' Newspaper. London, 1850–1869.
La Souveraineté du Peuple. Paris, 1848.
The Spirit of the Age. London, 1848–1849.
La Tribune des Peuples. Paris, 1849. (March 15–June 12; Sept. 12–Nov. 9).
La Voix des Clubs. Paris, 1848.
La Voix du Peuple. Paris, 1849.
La Voix du Proscrit. Weekly, London, 1850–1851. (First two issues, *Le Proscrit.*)
La Vraie République. Paris, 1848–1849.

Secondary Sources

Acton, Edward. *Alexander Herzen and the Role of the Intellectual Revolutionary.* Cambridge, 1979.
Agulhon, Maurice. *The Republican Experiment: 1848–1852.* The Cambridge History of Modern France, no. 2. New York, 1983.
Amann, Peter H. *Revolution and Mass Democracy: The Paris Club Movement in 1848.* Princeton, N.J., 1975.
Bellanger, Claude, Jacques Godechot, Pierre Guiral, and Fernand Terrou, eds. *Histoire général de la presse française.* 4 vols. Paris, 1969.
Berlin, Isaiah. *Russian Thinkers.* New York, 1979.
Billington, James H. *Fire in the Minds of Men: Origins of the Revolutionary Faith.* New York, 1980.
Bonjour, E., H. S. Offler, and G. R. Potter. *A Short History of Modern Switzerland.* Oxford, 1952.
Bonner, Hypatia Bradlaugh. *Charles Bradlaugh: A Record of his Life and Work.* 7th ed. London, 1908.
Briscoe, James. "The Unfinished Revolution: The Saint-Simonians and the Social Question—Origins of Socialist Debate in the July Monarchy." Consortium on Revolutionary Europe, *Proceedings* (1984), 231–42.
Brock, Peter. *Polish Revolutionary Populism: A Study in Agrarian Socialist Thought from the 1830's to the 1850's.* Toronto, 1977.
Brock, Peter. "Polish Democrats and English Radicals, 1832–1862: A Chapter in the History of Anglo-Polish Relations." *Journal of Modern History* 25, no. 2 (June 1953), 139–57.
Büttner, Wolfgang. "Das Feuilleton des Pariser 'Vorwärts!' " *Jahrbuch für Geschichte* 32 (1985), 171–202.
Cadot, Michel. *La Russie dans la vie intellectuelle française (1829–1856).* Paris, 1967.

Cadot, Michael. Introduction to Jules Michelet, *Légendes démocratiques du nord*. Nouvelle édition, avec introduction, notes, et index par Michel Cadot. Paris, 1968.
Calman, Alvin R. *Ledru-Rollin après 1848 et les proscrits français en Angleterre*. Paris, 1921.
Carr, E. H. *Michael Bakunin*. 1937. Reprint. New York, n.d.
Carr, E. H. *The Romantic Exiles*. 1933. Reprint. New York, 1975.
Chukovskaia, Lidiia. *"Byloe i Dumy" Gertsena*. Moscow, 1966.
Dessal, Marcel. *Un Révolutionnaire jacobin: Charles Delescluze 1809–1871*. Paris, 1952.
Dommanget, Maurice. *Un Drame politique de 1848: Blanqui et le Document Taschereau*. Paris, 1948.
Droz, Jacques. *Les Révolutions allemandes de 1848*. Paris, 1957.
Duveau, Georges. *1848: The Making of a Revolution*. Trans. Ann Carter. Intro. George Rude. New York, 1968.
Easton, Loyd D. "August Willich, Marx and Left-Hegelian Socialism." *Cahiers de l'ISEA*, August 1965, pp. 101–37.
Egorov, B. F., K. N. Lomanov, I. G. Prushkina, Ia. E. El'sberg, eds. *Letopis' zhizni i tvorchestva A. I. Gertsen: 1812–1870*. 2 vols. Moscow, 1974.
Eidel'man, N. Ia. *Gertsen protiv samoderzhaviia. Sekretnaia politicheskaia istoriia Rossii xviii–xix vv. i Vol'naia pechat'*. Moscow, 1973.
Eidel'man, N. Ia. *Tainye korrespondenty 'Poliarnoi zvezdy'*. Moscow, 1966.
El'sberg, Ia. *Gertsen: Zhizn' i tvorchestvo*. 3d and 4th eds. Moscow, 1955, 1963.
Evans, David Owen. *Le Socialisme romantique: Pierre Leroux et ses contemporains*. Paris, 1948.
Faderman, Lillian. *Surpassing the Love of Men: Romantic Friendship and Love Between Women from the Sixteenth Century to the Present*. New York, 1981.
Felix, David. *Marx as Politician*. Carbondale, Ill., 1983.
Fleury, Victor. *Le Poète Georges Herwegh (1817–1875)*. Bibliothèque de la "Révolution de 1848," no. 6. Paris, 1911.
Fortescue, William. *Alphonse de Lamartine: A Political Biography*. New York, 1983.
Ginzburg, L. Ia. " 'S togo berega' Gertsena (Problematika i postroenie)." *Izvestiia Akademii Nauk SSSR. Otdelenie literatury i iazyka* 21, no. 2 (March–April 1962), 112–25.
Gottschalk, Louis. *The Era of the French Revolution (1715–1815)*. Boston, 1929.
Gregory, David. "The Influence of French Socialism on the Thought of Karl Marx, 1843–45." *Proceedings of the Sixth Annual Meeting of the Western Society of French Historians*, Santa Barbara, 1979, pp. 242–51.
Gurvitch, Georges. "Proudhon et Marx." *L'Actualité de Proudhon: Colloque des 24 et 25 novembre 1965*. Brussels, 1967.
Hales, E.E.Y. *Mazzini and the Secret Societies: The Making of a Myth*. New York: n.d.

BIBLIOGRAPHY

Halévy, Daniel. *Le Mariage de Proudhon.* Paris, 1955.
Hamerow, Theodore. *Restoration, Revolution, Reaction: Economics and Politics in Germany, 1815–1871.* Princeton, N.J.: 1958.
Hammen, Oscar J. *The Red '48ers: Karl Marx and Friedrich Engels.* New York, 1969.
Haubtmann, Pierre. *Proudhon, Marx et la pensée allemande.* Grenoble, 1981.
Hoffman, Robert L. *Revolutionary Justice: The Social and Political Theory of P.-J. Proudhon.* Urbana, Ill., 1972.
Hook, Sidney. *From Hegel to Marx: Studies in the Intellectual Development of Karl Marx.* Ann Arbor, Mich., 1962.
Hugo, Charles. *Les Hommes de l'exil.* Paris, 1875.
Hyams, Edward. *Pierre-Joseph Proudhon: His Revolutionary Life, Mind and Works.* New York, 1979.
Imlah, Ann G. *Britain and Switzerland, 1845–1860: A Study of Anglo-Swiss Relations during some Critical Years for Swiss Neutrality.* Hamden, Conn., 1966.
Kabdebo, Thomas. *Diplomat in Exile: Francis Pulszky's Political Activities in England, 1849–1860.* Boulder, Colo., 1979.
Kaiser, Bruno. *Der Freiheit eine Gasse: Aus den Leben und Werk Georg Herwegh.* Berlin, 1948.
Kamenev, Iu. "Samyi ostroumnyi protivnik Gertsena." *Vestnik Evropy* 49, no. 4 (April 1914), 118–60.
Kandel', E., and S. Levtsova. "Marks i Engel's—vospitateli pervykh proletarskikh revoliutsionerov." In *Marks i Engel's i pervye proletarskie revoliutsionery,* ed. E. Kandel'. Moscow, 1961.
Kennan, George. *The Marquis de Custine and His "Russia in 1839."* Princeton, N.J., 1971.
Kieniewicz, Stefan. "Histoire de la 'Tribune des Peuples.' " In *L'Independence et la question agraire: Esquisses polonaises du xixe siècle. Opera Minora.* Polish Historical Library, no. 3, pp. 117–82. Warsaw, 1982.
Kramer, Lloyd S. "Exile and European Thought: Heine, Marx, and Mickiewicz in July Monarchy Paris." *Historical Reflections/Réflexions Historiques* 11, no. 1 (1984), 45–70.
Labry, Raoul. *Herzen et Proudhon.* Collection historique de l'Institut d'études slaves, no. 4. Paris, 1928.
Lacassagne, Jean-Pierre. *Pierre Leroux et George Sand: Histoire d'une amitié (D'après une correspondance inédite 1836–1866).* Paris, 1973.
Langer, William L. *The Revolutions of 1848: Chapters from "Political and Social Upheaval."* New York, 1969.
Lehning, Arthur Mueller. "The International Association (1855–1859)." *International Review for Social History* 3 (1938).
Leslie, R. F. *Reform and Insurrection in Russian Poland, 1856–65.* London, 1963.

Loubere, Leo. *Louis Blanc: His Life and His Contribution to the Rise of French Jacobin-Socialism.* Evanston, Ill., 1961.
Lucas, Alphonse. *Les Clubs et les Clubistes: Histoire complète.* Paris, 1851.
Malia, Martin. *Alexander Herzen and the Birth of Russian Socialism: 1812–1855.* Cambridge, Mass., 1961.
Markiewicz, Zygmunt. "Charles Edmond, Voyageur et comparatiste oublié." In *Connaissance de l'étranger: Mélanges offerts à la mémoire de Jean-Marie Carré.* Etudes de Littérature étrangère et comparée. Paris, 1964.
McConnell, Allen. "Against All Idols: Alexander Herzen and the Revolutions of 1848. A Chapter in the History of Tragic Liberalism." Ph.D. diss. Columbia University, 1954.
McLellan, David. *Karl Marx: His Life and Thought.* New York, 1973.
Mendel, Arthur. *Michael Bakunin: Roots of Apocalypse.* New York, 1981.
Merriman, John M. *The Agony of the Republic: The Repression of the Left in Revolutionary France, 1848–1851.* New Haven, Conn., 1978.
Mervaud, Michel. "Herzen et Proudhon," *Cahiers du monde russe et soviètique* 12, nos. 1–2 (January–June 1971), 110–89.
Miliukov, P. N. *Russia and its Crisis.* Foreword by Donald W. Treadgold. New York, 1962.
Miller, Martin A. *The Russian Revolutionary Emigres, 1825–1870.* Baltimore, 1986.
Moss, Bernard N. *The Origins of the French Labor Movement, 1830–1914: The Socialism of Skilled Workers.* Berkeley, Calif., 1976.
Nettlau, Max. "Notice biographique sur Ernest Coeurderoy (1826–62)." In Ernest Coeurderoy, *Oeuvres.* Vols. 1–3, *Jours d'Exil.* Bibliothèque sociologique, no. 44. Paris, 1910.
Nikolaevskii, B. "Za vashu i nashu vol'nost'! (Stranitsy iz istorii russko-polskikh otnoshenii)." *Novyi Zhurnal* 7 (1944), 252–76.
Orlik, O. V. *Peredovaia Rossiia i revoliutsionnaia Frantsiia (I polovina XIX v.).* Moscow, 1973.
Partridge, Monica. "Alexander Herzen and the English Press." *Slavonic and East European Review,* June 1958, pp. 453–70.
Payne, Howard C., and Henry Grosshans. "The Exiled Revolutionaries and the French Political Police in the 1850's." *American Historical Review* 68 (July 1963), 954–73.
Pinkney, David. *The French Revolution of 1830.* Princeton, N.J., 1973.
Plamenatz, John. *The Revolutionary Movement in France, 1815–71.* London, 1958.
Porter, Bernard. *The Refugee Question in Mid-Victorian Politics.* Cambridge, 1979.
Riazanov, N. "Karl Marks i russkie liudi sorokovykh godov." *Sovremennyi mir,* no. 8 (1912), pp. 154–74; no. 9, pp. 146–68; no. 11, pp. 192–209; no. 12, pp. 195–213.

Royle, Edward. *Victorian Infidels; The Origins of the British Secularist Movement, 1791–1866.* Manchester, 1974.
Schapiro, Leonard. *Turgenev: His Life and Times.* New York, 1978.
Schoyen, A. R. *The Chartist Challenge: A Portrait of George Julian Harney.* London, 1958.
Seddon, J. H. "The Petrashevtsy: A Reappraisal." *Slavic Review* 43, no. 3 (Fall 1984), 434–53.
Senelick, Laurence. *Serf Actor: The Life and Art of Mikhail Shchepkin.* Westport, Conn., 1984.
Sewell, William H. *Work and Revolution in France: The Language of Labor from the Old Regime to 1848.* Cambridge, Mass., 1980.
Silberner, Edmund. *Johann Jacoby: Politiker und Mensch.* Veröffentlichungen des Instituts für Sozialgeschichte. Braunschweig-Bonn; Bonn-Bad Godesberg, 1976.
Silberner, Edmund. *Moses Hess: Geschichte seines Lebens.* Leiden, 1966.
Silberner, Edmund, ed. "La Correspondance Moses Hess–Louis Krolikowski, 1850–53." *Annali Istituto Giangiacomo Feltrinelli* 3 (1960), 582–620.
Skurnowicz, Joan S. *Romantic Nationalism and Liberalism: Joachim Lelewel and the Polish National Idea.* East European Monographs, no. 83. Boulder, Colo., 1981.
Smirnova, Z. V. "Gertsen i Germaniia." *Literaturnoe nasledstvo* 96 (1985), 64–87.
Smirnova, Z. V. *Sotsial'naia filosofiia A. I. Gertsena.* Moscow, 1973.
Smith, F. B. *Radical Artisan: William James Linton, 1812–97.* Manchester, 1973.
Taylor, Barbara. *Eve and the New Jerusalem: Socialism and Feminism in the Nineteenth Century.* London, 1983.
Thompson, E. P. *The Making of the English Working Class.* New York, 1963.
Tsypkina, Z. M. "Gertsen i deiateli ital'ianskogo natsional'no-osvoboditel'nogo dvizheniia (1848–1852 gg.)." In *Ob'edinenii Italii: 100 let bor'by za nezavisimost' i demokratiiu. Sbornik statei.* Moscow, 1962.
Venturi, Franco. *Studies in Free Russia.* Trans. Fausta Segre Walsby and Margaret O'Dell. Chicago, 1982.
Vier, Jacques. *La Comtesse d'Agoult et son temps.* 6 vols. Paris, 1955–63.
Wagner, Dietmar U. "The German Students and the Failure of the 'Progressive Movement,' 1840–46." *Consortium on Revolutionary Europe, 1750–1850. Proceedings* (1977), pp. 50–68.
Walicki, Andrzej. *The Slavophile Controversy: History of a Conservative Utopia in Nineteenth-Century Russian Thought.* Trans. Hilda Andrews-Rusiecka. Oxford, 1975.
Weidemaier, William Cannon. "Herzen and the Existential World View: A New Approach to an Old Debate." *Slavic Review* 40, no. 4 (Winter 1981), 557–69.

BIBLIOGRAPHY

Weisser, Henry. "Chartist Internationalism, 1845–1848." *Historical Journal* 14 (1971), 49–67.
Wende, Peter. *Radikalismus in Vormärz: Untersuchungen zur politischen Theorie der fruhen deutschen Demokratie*. Frankfurter Historischer Abhandlungen, vol. 11. Wiesbaden, 1975.
Whyte, A. J. *The Evolution of Modern Italy*. New York, 1965.
Wolfgramm, Eberhard. "Alexander Herzen und die 'Deutsche Monatsschrift.' " *Beiträge zur Geschichte der Beziehungen zwischen dem deutschen Volk und den Völkern der Sowjetunion*. Zeitschrift für Geschichtswissenschaft, supplement 1. Berlin, 1954.
Woodcock, George. *Pierre-Joseph Proudhon: A Biography*. London, 1956.
Zaleski, Z. L. *Attitudes et destinées: Faces et profiles d'écrivains polonais*. Paris, 1932.
Zévaès, Alexandre. "Félix Pyat: Homme de lettres et homme politique." *La Nouvelle revue*, 4th series. October 1930, 60–69, 95–109, 161–74, 257–86.
Zévaès, Alexandre. "Les Proscrits français en 1848 et 1851 à Londres." *La Révolution de 1848* 20, no. 102 (January–February 1924), 345–76; 21, no. 104 (May–June 1924), 94–115.
Ziegengeist, G. "Über die Bedeutung von A.I. Herzens Schaffen für das progressive deutsche Geistesleben in der fünfziger Jahren des 19 Jahrhunderts. Zum 150. Geburtstag Alexander Herzens." *Zeitschrift für Slawistik* 7, no. 5 (1962), 515–29.
Zimmerman, Judith. "Alexander Herzen and George Sand: Influence and Empathy." Dept. of History, University of Pittsburgh at Greensburg, 1984.
Zimmerman, Judith. "Friends and Lovers."
Zimmerman, Judith. "Natalie Herzen and the Early Intelligentsia," *Russian Review* 41, no. 3 (July 1982), 249–72.
Zucker, Stanley. *Ludwig Bamberger: German Liberal Politician and Social Critic, 1823–1899*. Pittsburgh, Pa., 1975.
Zucker, Stanley. "Ludwig Bamberger and the Politics of the Cold Shoulder: German Liberalism's Response to Working Class Legislation in the 1870s." *European Studies Review* 2, no. 3 (July 1972), 201–27.

INDEX

Agoult, Comtesse Marie d': and *Deutsch-Französische Jahrbücher*, 20–21; salon of, 39, 41; *Histoire de la Révolution de 1848*, 71; and Proudhon, 118; and Emma Herwegh, 197; and Herweghs, 237n67
Agrarian socialism, Polish, 24
Albert. *See* Martin, Henri
Alexander II, emperor of Russia, 222, 224
Anneke, Friedrich, 91–92
Annenkov, Pavel, 35, 73, 77, 95, 233n17
Arago, Etienne, 20, 73, 190, 249n8
Arnim, Bettina von, 73
Astrakova, Tatiana, 82, 232n4
Austria: and the Italian revolution, 48–49, 222; as common enemy of liberal and nationalist movements, 61, 65; Bakunin in, 74; repression in, 94; Chojecki on, 132

Babeuf, Gracchus, 16
Baden: radicalism in, 27; German Legion in, 71–73; 1848 uprisings in, 71–73, 94; and Switzerland, 109–11; and Struve, 112; and Proudhon, 133; exiled veterans from, 178
Bakunin, Mikhail: Hegelian conservatism of, 6; "The Reaction in Germany" and left Hegelianism of, 7, 18; and Sand, 15, 21; and *Deutsche Jahrbücher*, 18; and Ruge, 19–20; and Adolph Reichel, 19; and Herwegh, 19–20; and Vogt family, 20; and *Deutsch-Französische Jahrbücher*, 20; Paris contacts of, 21, 25, 33; and *La Réforme*, 21; and Viardot, 21; and German radicals, 22; and Lelewel, 24; and Polish émigrés, 24–25; and Berlin University, 25; and Moscow circles, 36–37; and Herzen, 37–38, 98–99, 114, 155, 177, 234n20; activities of in 1848, 65, 69, 72–75; charged as Russian agent, 74, 227; and Proudhon, 114; views on peasantry and *Russische Zustände*, 148; and Michelet, 155, 177; and Marx, 182, 252n59; as exile, 211; celibacy of, 218; and d'Agoult, 240n34
Bamberger, Ludwig, 91, 129, 132, 255n22
Barbès, Armand: as imprisoned revolutionary, 13; and club movement, 56–57, 59; and May 15 demonstration, 79–80, 115; mentioned by Herzen, 81; and Herzen, 120; and unity of French émigrés, 181
Barrot, Odilon, 51
Barthélemy, Emanuel, 202
Bauer, Heinrich, 63, 70
Bauer, Otto, 27
Belgium, 16, 178
Belinskii, Vissarion, 6, 9, 24, 35–36, 104, 152, 243n61
Béranger, Pierre-Jean, 15
Berlin: Bakunin in, 19, 73; Herwegh in, 20; Herwegh on revolutionary prospects in, 25; Emma Herwegh in (1847), 25; Herzen response to, 25–

295

26; Herzen in, 32–33; in 1848 revolution, 90, 94, 97
Berlin University, 25, 26, 33
Bernacki, A., 155
Bernard, Simon, 211
Bismarck, Otto von, 222
Blanc, Louis: as influence on Herzen, 8, 11, 39; works of, 13; and *La Revue indépendante*, 14; and *La Réforme*, 15; and Sand, 20; role in French Provisional Government, 1848, 52–60; and Luxembourg Commission, 54; on 1848 elections, 59; in May 15 demonstration, 79–81; and Herzen, 81, 88, 141, 192, 222; emigration of, 84, 115, 178; and Proudhon, 114; and Ledru-Rollin, 180, 181, 272n66; émigré organizational attempts of, 180–82; and Mazzini attack on socialists, 187; as member of French émigré democratic committee (London), 188, 190
Blanqui, Auguste: as imprisoned revolutionary, 13; and Society of the Seasons, 17, 52; and club movement, 56–57, 59; refusal to appear before court of honor of, 56, 277n36; accused of planning coup d'état, 60; and May 15 demonstration, 79–80, 115
Blind, Carl, 96, 106
Blum, Robert, 93, 210
Bocquet, Camille, 78
Bocquet, Jean-Baptiste, 37, 78, 96
Bonaparte, Louis Napoleon: election of, 61, 76; as president, 105; and Proudhon, 115, 118, 121; and Herzen, 121; assassination attempt against, 174, 202, 211; coup d'état of, 174; émigrés' resistance to, 180–81; and Thoré, 186
Bonheur, Rosa, 197
Bonn, 90, 92
Bornstedt, Adalbert von, 69
Botkin, Nikolai Petrovich, 35
Botkin, Vasilii Petrovich, 12, 35, 36, 84, 241n36
Botkina, Ekaterina Nikolaevna, 35
Bradlaugh, Charles, 211

Branicki, Xavier, 102–03
Brentano, Lorenz, 112
Brunetti, Angelo (pseud. Cicerouacchio), 46, 48
Brussels, 21–22, 63–65, 73, 91
Bulewsky, Louis, 195
Buonarotti, Filippo, 28
Burschenschaften, 27

Cabet, Etienne, 17, 20, 158, 181, 272n67
Carbonari, 23, 28, 61
Carr, E. H., 74, 167, 248n78
Caussidière, Marc: and the Paris police, 1848, 55; on 1848, 59; and foreign radicals, 68–69; on Bakunin, 73; and Herzen, 81; emigration of, 84, 178; as member of émigré democratic committee (London), 188, 190
Cavaignac, Eugène, 83, 84, 87, 116, 121, 186
Cavour, Camille, 222
Central Committee of the German Democrats, 97, 112
Central European Fund, 210
Channel Islands, 23, 189–91, 211
Charles Albert, king of Savoy, 47, 48
Chartism, 24, 62–63, 183–84, 212
Chiffonier de Paris, Le, 40. *See also* Pyat, Félix
Chojecki, Charles Edmond: and *La Revue Indépendante*, 24; and internationalism, 67; and *La Tribune des Peuples*, 102–04; and Herzen, 118, 131, 132; and Girardin, 122; and *La Voix du Peuple*, 118, 123–29, 131; expulsion from France of, 134, 172; in Nice, 174; and Herzen-Herwegh conflict, 201, 275n19; on *Byloe i dumy*, 208; Hegelianism of, 256n39
Cicerouacchio. *See* Brunetti, Angelo
Circolo Popolare, 46
Clubs: in revolutionary France, 56–59, 65–68, 70; Club de la Révolution, 56, 79–80; Societé Centrale Repúblicaine, 56; Assemblée Nationale Italienne, 66; Club de l'Emigration Polonaise [Club des Polonais], 66; Club des Emigrés

INDEX

Italiens, 66–67; Club des Ouvriers Allemands, 66, 70; Emancipation des Peuples, 66; Fraternité des Peuples, 66; Club de la Naturalisation Française, 67; visited by Herzen, 78; and May 15 demonstration, 79–80; Club of the Rights of Man, 80; after the June Days, 84; as influence on Herzen, 88; Proudhon's criticism of, 120; exile of members of, 178
Coeurderoy, Ernest, 133, 159
Collett, J. D., 63
Cologne: Marx in, 18–19, 91–93, 182, 226; Hess in, 19, 92; Herwegh in, 20; Herzen on, 30–32, 34; and Gottschalk, 70; revolution of 1848 in, 91–93; Herzen's work publicized in, 154
Cologne Democratic Society, 92
Communist Correspondence Committee, 63–64
Communist League: formation and character of, 17, 64; response to February 1848 Revolution of, 63; and Marx, 64, 69–70; in Paris, 66, 69–70; Ewerbeck a member of, 74; in Cologne, 91–92, 226; in England, 178; split of English branch of, 182
Congress of Democratic Associations (Germany), 93
Congress of Vienna, 61, 65
Considerant, Victor, 20, 114
Constitutionnel, Le, 25, 238*n*76
Cournet, Frédéric, 202
Courtais, Vicomte de, 81
Corvin-Wiersbitzki, Otto von, 70–71
Cremieux, Adolphe, 53
Crimean War, 220
Custine, Astolphe de, 145, 155
Czartoryski, Prince Adam, 23, 178
Czerniecki, Ludwik, 216

Darasz, Albert, 68, 179, 184, 188, 271*n*55
Darimon, Alfred, 129, 131
Decembrists, 75, 104, 152, 154, 212
De la Sagra, Ramon, 104
Delescluze, Charles, 184

De Shpies, V. I., 98, 100
Deutsch-Franzöische Jahrbücher, 18–20
Deutsche Jahrbücher, 7, 18, 33
Deutsche Monatsschrift, 154
Deutsche Verein, 96–97, 99
Deutsche Volkszeitung, 112
Domagalsky (tutor to Sasha Herzen), 195
Dresden, 18, 19, 20, 74
Dupont de l'Eure, Jacques Charles, 52
Dutailis, Louis-Halin, 211

Emigrés:
—in England: international colony of, 16–17, 65, 171, 177–94, 210–11; and League of the Just, 22; Polish, 23, 24, 25, 68, 97, 178, 183, 192; and Marx, 28, 64, 69–70, 91–92, 226; and internationalism, 62, 67, 210; and French February Revolution, 67; and *Deutsche Monatsschrift*, 154; Italian, 178–79, 183, 191; German, 67, 178, 182, 205; Hungarian, 183; and Herzen, 192, 205, 220, 225, 226–27; French, 202, 211; and British politics, 209; impact of war and unification on, 220; and Marx, 226–27
—in France: German, 16–17, 20–22, 61–62, 64–65, 68–72; Polish, 22–26, 67–68, 156; and revolutionary government, 68–69, 71; and Herzen, 77, 95–98, 100–01; and 13 June 1849 demonstration, 106
—in Piedmont, 174
—in Switzerland: German, 16–17, 20, 107, 109–13, 223, 227; French, 113
Engels, Friedrich, 21, 22, 63–64, 69–70, 74, 91, 205
Engel'son, Vladimir, 148, 174, 176, 201, 205, 208
England: and Struve, 111; and Kapp and Bamberger, 112; Herzen in, 144, 211; Herzen's view of, 158; Shchepkin visit to, 161. *See also* Emigrés, in England
English Republic, The, 184, 187, 219
Ern, Mariia Kasparovna. *See* Reichel, Mariia

INDEX

European Central Democratic Committee, 100, 179–90
Ewerbeck, Hermann: as leader of League of the Just, 17; and *Vorwärts*, 21; and Bakunin, 74; and Herzen, 96, 98–99; political activity of, 96; and *La Tribune des Peuples*, 104; Herzen's possible influence on, 155
Exiles. *See* Emigrés

Fallermayer, Philipp, 154
Fazy, James, 109–11, 113–14, 174
Ferdinand II, king of the Two Sicilies, 47
Feuerbach, Ludwig, 27, 85, 94, 140
Fichte, Johann, 26
Fleury, Victor, 237n57
Flocon, Ferdinand, 15, 20, 55, 70
Fourier, Charles, 7, 13, 15, 163
France: 1840s radicalism in, 13–16; the press in, 14–16, 130; Herzen in (1847), 34–41; Herzen stay in, (1848–49), 76–90, 95–106, 222; Herzen in (1850), 168–71; Herzen expulsion from, 172; fears of international revolution in, 188–89. *See also* Emigrés, in France
—history of: 1789 Revolution and First Republic of, 61, 210, 242n54; Restoration, 14; 1839 uprising in, 56, 72; 13 June 1849 demonstration in, 98, 99, 106, 107, 110, 118, 120, 124, 130; the "Mountain" in, 105–06, 115–16, 119, 184; democrats of, 140, 143; Third Republic of, 220
—in 1848: 50–60, 130, 210, 223; and the banquet campaign, 50; Provisional Government of, 51, 52–59, 63, 65, 68, 70; and the National Guard, 51, 55, 58, 60, 80–81, 84, 121; and workers' associations, 54, 58; and the Garde Mobile, 55, 60, 71, 83; and the People's Guard, 55; March 16 and 17 demonstrations, 58, 78; elections in, 58–60; national workshops in, 58, 82–83; April 16 demonstration, 59; June Days, 59, 82–83, 99, 106, 115, 119, 138; Constitution of, 60, 115; May 15 demonstration, 67, 78–80, 83, 115, 120; and the forty-five centime surcharge, 59; and the National Assembly, the Directory, and Cavaignac, 60, 78–79, 81, 83–84, 88, 115, 223; Ministry of Labor of, 79
Frankfurt, 73, 178
Fraternal Democrats, 63, 67, 189
Frederick William, king of Prussia, 20
Free Russian Press, 101, 105, 167, 192
Freiligrath, Ferdinand, 94
Fribourg, 174, 176
Friends of Italy (England), 185, 189
Fröbel, Julius: and pre-1848 emigration, 19–20; and Bakunin, 73, 237n57; in Frankfurt Parliament and German Democratic Congress, 93–94; and Herzen, 105, 112, 227; and *La Voix du Peuple*, 129; emigration of, 161

Galakhov, Ivan, 35, 43, 46, 256n39
Galeer, Albert, 113
Garibaldi, Giuseppe, 106, 130
Garnier-Pages, Louis Antoine, 53, 249n8
Geneva: Herwegh in, 20, 99–100, 106–32, 168, 174, 176, 197, 223; Natalie's memories of, 173
Genoa, 177, 205
German committee. *See* Deutsche Verein
German Democratic Association, 68–70
German Legion, 68–73, 86, 92
German National Democratic Committee (London), 182
Germany: radicalism in, 18–20, 25–27; Landtags of, 26; and the 1848 Pre-Parliament, 26, 72–73, 90, 112; Frankfurt Parliament of, 26, 72, 90, 93–94, 111; Herzen in, 30–34; 1848 Revolution in, 61–72; Democratic Congresses of, 91, 94; and Prussia, 90, 94, 99; and Cologne Workers' Association, 92–93; and émigrés in Saxony, 189; unification of, 220
Girardin, Emile de, 122–24, 234n27
Gogol', Nikolai, 46
Golovin, Ivan, 66–67, 98–99, 104, 114, 240n34

298

INDEX

Goncharov, Ivan, 24
Gottschalk, Andreas, 70, 91–92, 96, 104, 129, 226
Goudchaux, Michel, 53
Granovskaia, Elizaveta, 8, 232$n4$
Granovskii, Timofei, 7–10, 24, 87, 105, 160
Gregory XVI, 28
Griboedov, Aleksandr, 104
Grün, Karl, 17, 21, 64
Guizot, François, 42, 50–51, 53, 55, 73, 234$n27$

Haag, Luisa (Herzen's mother): in Germany, 26; departure from Russia of, 30, 77, 238$n3$; and Bakunin, 75; property of, 100–01, 168–69; in Zurich, 109, 168; in Paris, 168; in Nice, 173; death of, 177
Hallische Jahrbücher für Wissenschaft und Kunst, 18
Harney, Julian, 63, 189
Haug, Ernst: and *La Tribune des peuples*, 104; in London, 182, 184, 193; as tutor for Sasha Herzen, 195; and Herzen-Herwegh conflict, 201, 202, 205
Haxthausen, August von, 150, 155
Hecker, Friedrich, 71–72
Hegel, G.F.W.: interpretation of in Russia, 5–7; Herzen's interpretation of, 6–9, 38, 114, 140, 222; and artisan communism, 17; and left Hegelians, 18–19, 21, 26–27, 33, 91, 158; and Chojecki, 103
Heidelberg meeting (1848), 71
Heine, Heinrich, 19, 21
Herweg, Emma: background of, 20, 38; and Polish revolutionaries, 25; in Paris (1849), 108, 168; correspondence of, 123; and *La Voix du Peuple*, 127–28; and Chojecki, 131, 172; and Herzen, 95, 133, 170; and private commune, 162–65; jealousy and family crisis of, 164, 168–69, 172–73, 175–76, 197–98, 199, 201; and revolutionary moral code, 199–200; family of, 205

Herwegh, Georg: early career of, 19–22; and Marie d'Agoult, 21, 41; and Polish radicalism, 24; and German Catholicism, 27; and Herzen, 38, 46, 72, 77, 86, 105, 138–39, 147, 149, 161, 169, 171, 227, 261$n96$; political activity of (1848), 66–69; and German Legion, 68–73, 91; as political contact for Herzen, 77, 95–96, 99, 102; and Gottschalk, 92; in Geneva (1849), 108, 110; on Geneva refugees, 111–12; and German refugees, 112–13; accused of contributing to socialist paper, 114; and *La Voix du Peuple*, 123–29; and "La Russie," 144; and Natalie Herzen, 162–69, 172–73, 175–76, 177, 193, 196, 203–08, 217–19; and private commune, 162–64, 166, 196, 224, and *La Petite Fadette* (Sand), 163–64; and proposed Russian press, 175; police report on, 189; and revolutionary moral code, 197–203, 205, 206–07, 214, 218
Herzen, Aleksandr Aleksandrovich (Sasha): and Karl Vogt, 20, 174; departure from Russia of, 30, 42, 77, 250$n26$; and Bocquet, 37, 78, 96, 240$n28$; and Natalie Herzen, 82, 87, 177; and Kapp, 96; in Geneva, 108; in Paris (1850), 169; education of, 195; and dedication of *S togo berega*, 211–12; and revolutionary moral code, 213–17
Herzen, Alexander
—life of: intellectual background of, 4–13, 139, 194; illegitimate birth of, 5; emigration of, 29–34, 86, 135–36, 144, 160, 171–72, 173; in Paris (1847), 34–40; and Bakunin, 38–39, 72–75, 177; and Herwegh, 38, 69, 72, 166–69, 175–76, 197–99; in Italy, 42–49; in Paris (1848–49), 60, 66–67, 76–78, 81–89, 91, 95–106; and Willich, 72; and Michelet, 75, 154–55, 160, 176–77; radical contacts of, 77–78, 95–97; journalism of, 86, 87, 105, 139; and Proudhon, 86, 112,

299

INDEX

114, 119–21, 142; property of, 86–87, 100–02, 168–70, 172, 197–98; and Bamberger, 91, 112; investigation of, 97–101, 189; and Ruge, 99, 180, 218–19; and Mazzini, 100, 179–82, 184, 187, 188, 191; and *La Tribune des Peuples*, 102–04; and the 13 June 1849 demonstration, 106; and *La Voix du Peuple*, 122–34; citizenship of, 111, 167, 174, 176–77; and Linton, 144, 184, 212, 219; Western audience of, 154–60, 176; and Hess, 156–58; Russian response to, 160–61, 172; possible U.S. emigration of, 161–62; in Nice, 162–65, 172–73, 174–75; in France (1850), 168–72; withdrawal from émigré activity of, 156, 161, 169–70, 191; expulsion from France and Piedmont of, 172, 173, 176; publication plans of, 176, 192, 208; and deaths of Kolia, Natalie, and Luisa Haag, 177; in London, 177, 192–93; and revolutionary community, 208, 211–13, 219–20; and Natalie Tuchkova, 214–15; summary, 221–30
—views of: and Marx, 18, 69, 74, 158–59; on 1848 revolutions, 45, 54, 59, 140–41, 143, 227; and revolutionary internationalism, 61, 149; on National Assembly, 78; on May 15 demonstration, 81–82; on the June Days, 82–84; on political democracy, 84–85; on dualism, 85–86, 88, 141–42; on Russia and the West, 87, 135–40, 156; on the masses, 89, 142–43, 151; on Russian socialism, 108, 139, 144–51, 154, 155, 224; on social revolution, 140; on "barbarians" and "cossacks," 142, 157, 159; on communism, 143, 148, 150, 157; on the educated minority, 145, 151–53, 155; on Custine, 145–46; on economic development, 150, 158; on peasant emancipation, 192, 212; value system of, 194–99; on education, 195–96; feminism of, 195–97, 204; and revolutionary moral code, 200–08, 213–16, 218–19

—works of:
Byloe i dumy, 5, 10, 13, 33, 38, 48, 66, 77, 97, 102, 166–67, 169, 209, 221, 225–57
Du Développement des idées révolutionnaires en Russie, 32, 66, 144, 149, 150, 154–55, 160, 174
Kolokol, 38
Kto vinovat', 154
Le Peuple Russe et le Socialisme, 143–44, 153, 155, 177
Pis'ma iz Frantsii i Italii (including "Pis'ma iz Avenue Marigny," "Pis'ma s Via del Corso," "Opiat' v Parizhe"), 12, 30–31, 34, 39–41, 43–44, 49, 87–88, 137–38, 144, 154, 156, 226
Poliarnaia zvezda, 38, 132, 140, 210, 213, 228
S togo berega, 35, 44–45, 88–89, 133, 139, 144, 154, 156–57, 159, 161, 172, 213
"Charlotte Corday," 133
"Dedication," 176
"Diletantizm v nauke," 6
"La Russie," 108, 131, 144, 148, 152, 154, 156
"Lettre d'un Russe à Mazzini," 133
"Pis'ma ob izuchenii prirody," 9
Herzen, Egor Ivanovich (half brother), 86, 100
Herzen, Nikolai Alexsandrovich (Kolia): departure from Russia of, 12, 30, 77, 238*n*4; in Zurich, 109, 168; in Nice, 173; death of, 177, 201
Herzen, Natalie: illegitimate birth of, 5; departure from Russia of, 11, 30, 77, 238*n*3; in Paris, 35–37, 40, 82, 87, 95, 106; in Italy, 42–43; and Natalie Tuchkova, 45, 215, 242*n*59; on emigration, 86; in Geneva, 108, 113; and Mariia Poludenskaia, 123; and Herwegh, 162–67, 172–73, 175, 197, 198, 199–201, 203–04, 206, 214, 218; reconciliation with Herzen of, 177, 201; death of, 177, 201, 204; on education, 195; and Emma Herwegh,

300

198–200; and Haug, 202; Herzen's influence over, 242n57; on Chojecki and Darimon, 261n95

Herzen, Natalie Aleksandrovna (Tata): departure from Russia of, 12, 30, 77, 108; in Paris, 169; illness of, 169; and Mariia Reichel, 177; and Meysenbug, 195–96; and Emily Reeve, 213; and Herzen, 213–14; and Natalia Tuchkova, 214–15; and revolutionary tradition, 248n78

Herzen, Ol'ga, 177, 193, 214–15

Hess, Moses: in Cologne, 18; in Paris, 20; and Marx, 64, 91–92; warned against German Legion, 70; and Democratic Congress, 94; and Herzen, 96, 156–58; "Briefen an Iscander," 156–58; police report on, 190

Holy Alliance, 61

Holyoake, George, 182, 187

Hugo, Victor, 182, 190, 211

Huber, Aloysius, 81

Hungarian Republic, 133, 145, 191

Hutson, Charlotte, 216, 217

Iakovlev, Ivan (Herzen's father), 10, 12, 195

International Democratic Association, 64

International Workingmen's Association, First, 91, 226

L'Italia del Popolo, 113, 133, 183

Italy: radicalism in, 28; revolution in, 42–49, 138, 222; Roman Republic of (1848–49), 106, 111, 113, 120, 133; unification of, 220

Ivanov, A. A., 46

Jacoby, Johann, 27, 73, 90, 112, 179

Jersey, 23, 189–91, 211

Jones, Ernest, 63, 227

Journal de Genève, 110

Kapp, Friedrich: in Cologne, 91; on the Frankfurt Parliament, 93; and the Democratic Congress, 94; emigration of, 95, 161; as tutor to Sasha Herzen, 96; as contact for Herzen, 112; and publication of Herzen's work, 154; on Proudhon, 261n99

Karamzin, Mikhail, 12

Katkov, Mikhail, 36

Kavelin, Konstantin, 24

Ketcher, Nikolai, 11, 160

Ketcher, Serafima, 11

Kinkel, Gottfried, 90, 94–95, 182, 193, 206, 208

Kiselev, Nikolai, 98

Klapka, George, 130

Kliucharev, Grigorii, 100–01

Kol'tsov, Viktor, 24

Königsburg, 27, 90, 112

Korsh, Evgenyi, 12

Korsh, Mariia, 12, 30, 38, 47, 77, 95, 232n4, 250n29

Kossuth, Lajos, 132, 183, 190–91, 210

Kudlich, Hans, 219

Lamartine, Alphonse de, contact with Ruge of, 20; as foreign minister of the Provisional Government, 53, 65, 68, 79; and Blanqui, 80; and Herzen, 81, 85; on Directory, 249n8

Lammenais, Félicité, 20

Landolphe, 190

Lausanne, 177, 179

Leader, The, 182, 184, 187, 205, 219

League of Proscripts, 16

League of the Just: formation and ideology of, 16–20; and Herwegh, 20, 235n45, 237n57; and the Chartists, 62; and Communist League, 63–64; and Marx, 63, 70; and Ewerbeck, 74

Lechevalier, Jules, 104

Ledru-Rollin, Alexandre: and *La Réforme*, 15; in the French opposition, 50; as minister of the interior in the Provisional Government, 54–55, 58–59, 78, 80; and foreign radicals, 68, 70; and Herzen, 81, 141; and the "Mountain," 105; and the 13 June 1849 demonstration, 105–06; and Proudhon, 116; emigration of, 178; and European Central Democratic Committee, 179, 180, 181; and Blanc,

180–82; and *La Voix du Proscrit*, 184; police reports on, 188–90
Left Hegelianism. *See* Hegel
Lelewel, Joachim, 23–24, 34, 73
Lemaître, Frédéric, 40
Lermontov, Mikhail, 104, 147
Leroux, Pierre, 7, 14–15, 88, 114, 182, 212, 234n27, 257n43, 272n67
Levitskii, Sergei, 77, 97, 101
Limoges, 60
Linton, William J.: and February 1848 Revolution, 63; and Herzen, 144, 261n96; and Mazzini, 184–85, 187; and Herzen-Herwegh conflict,.205; and *Poliarnaia zvezda*, 212; and "The Marriage of Doctor Kudlich," 219
London Workingmen's Association, 62–63
Louis Philippe, king of France, 8, 13–14, 51, 138, 140, 222
Luxembourg Commission, 54–55

McGrath, Philip, 63
Mainz, 90
Malia, Martin, 39, 162
Marrast, Armand, 53
Martin, Henri [Albert], 52, 55
Marx, Karl: *The Reaction in Germany*, 7, 18, 37; *Communist Manifesto*, 17, 22, 63; and the Communist League, 17, 182; and Ruge, 18; and Herzen, 18, 34, 150, 156, 157–59, 226–27; in Cologne, 18–19, 91–92, 226; in Paris, 20–22, 65–66, 69–70; *Holy Family*, 21, 91; in Brussels, 25, 27, 65; and Sazonov, 36; *Economic and Philosophical Manuscripts*, 63; organizational activity of, 63–64, 225; and Weitling, 64; and Hess, 64; and Proudhon, 64, 114; and the German Legion, 69–70; and Bakunin, 73–74; in 1848 German politics, 92–94; Herzen's friends' opposition to, 96, 102, 104, 192; *Poverty of Philosophy*, 114; and utopianism, 162; in London, 178; and European Central Democratic Committee, 188; and Fraternal Democrats, 89; and Herzen-Herwegh conflict, 205; and the revolutionary community, 209; and sexual morality, 218; achievement of, 226; and Annenkov, 234n20
Mathé, Félix, 211
Mazzini, Giuseppe: and Sand, 15, 257n43, and Young Italy, 23; as revolutionary leader, 28; and internationalism, 62, 210; and English politics, 62–63, 210; political activity of, 63, 178–93, 222; in France, 63, 66, 68; and Herzen, 99, 113, 156, 161; and the Roman Republic, 106, 111, 258n57; publication plans of, 114; and *La Voix du Peuple*, 129, 131; and armed revolution, 188; and Herzen-Herwegh conflict, 201, 202, 204, 206, 208; and revolutionary moral code, 218
Medici, Giacomo, 113
Mervaud, Michel, 127, 129
Metternich, Klemens von, 42, 49
Meysenbug, Malwida von, 159, 193, 197, 212, 216
Michel de Bourges, 15, 184
Michelet, Jules: and Herzen, 75, 146, 154–55, 158, 160, 176; and Bakunin, 75, 155; *Le Peuple Russe et le Socialisme*, 144, 177; on Russia, 145; *Légendes démocratiques du nord*, 154–55; and Herzen-Herwegh conflict, 205, 206
Mickiewicz, Adam, 98, 102–04, 118
Mickiewicz, Ladislas, 103
Mieroslawski, Ludwik, 24, 94, 112, 130
Milan, 191
Molé, Louis Mathieu, 51
Moll, Joseph, 63, 70, 92
Monod, Gabriel, 177
Moral code, revolutionary: and court of honor, 56, 205, 206–08, 209–10; and sexual morality, 197–200, 214–19; enforcement of, 200, 202, 203–08; dishonorable conduct in, 201, 203; and duels, 202–03, 205, 214–15, 217–19, 220
Morning Advertiser, 74
Müller-Strübing, Hermann, 33, 73, 195

Nation, Le, 185, 219
National, Le, 14, 52–53, 75
Nauwerk, Karl, 154
Neue Rheinische Zeitung, 74, 92
Neue Zürcher Zeitung, 204
Nekrasov, Nikolai, 233*n13*
Nice, 139, 164, 171, 172–77, 201, 205, 207
Nicholas I, emperor of Russia, 65, 192
Nikolaevskii, Boris, 148

Ogarev, Aleksei and Elena (twin children of Herzen and Natalie Tuchkova), 214–15
Ogarev, Nikolai: in Herzen circle, 4–5, 8, 10; and Bakunin, 36; and Herwegh, 38; and Tuchkov, 46, 243*n59;* and Selivanov, 77; and Herzen, 164, 166, 168, 176, 213, 220, 224; arrest of, 171, and the revolutionary moral code, 213–17; in London, 213, 220, 224; poetry of, 227
Ogareva, Liza (daughter of Herzen and Natalie Tuchkova), 214–15
Ogareva, Mariia L'vovna, 35–36
Oppenheim, 27
Orleans, Duchesse d', 51–52
Orlov, Count Aleksei, 100
Orsini, Felice, 174, 179, 201, 202, 211
Otechestvennyia zapiski, 6, 9

Palacky, Frantisek, 74
Panaev, Ivan, 233*n13*
People's International League, 62–63, 183
People's Paper, The, 211
Perdiguer, Agricol, 14
Peuple, Le, 118
Piedmont, 154, 174, 176, 191, 202, 205, 207. *See also* Emigrés, in Piedmont
Piggott, Edward, 206
Pinto, Michelangelo, 46, 129
Pius IX, 42, 46, 49, 106
Poland, 22, 79, 91, 146, 210, 212
Polevoi, Nikolai, 104
Polish Democratic Committee, 97–98, 184

Polish Democratic Society: definition of, 23–24; in 1848 revolution, 66, 68, 72; emigration of members of to London, 178; under Worcell's leadership, 183; and Herzen, 192, 195, 220
Poludenskaia, Mariia, 35–36, 123, 232*n4*
Poncy, Charles, 14
Presse, La, 122
Proscripts, League of. *See* League of Proscripts
Proscrit, Le, 184
Proudhon, Pierre-Joseph: influence on Herzen of, 8, 11, 39, 86, 114, 119, 222; in France (1840s), 13, 15, 114; and Bakunin, 21, 37, 38, 114; as Herzen contact (1847), 37, 114; and Marx, 64, 114; and *Le Répresentant du Peuple,* 84; mentioned by Herzen, 88, 142, 170; and Chojecki, 103; and Ramon de la Sagra, 104; and *La Voix du Peuple,* 108, 122–34, 223, 225; Bamberger admiration for, 112; *Qu'est-ce que la Propriété?,* 114; *Système des Contradictions économiques,* 114; views of, 115–18; and Pyat, 115, 202; and credit, 116–17, 121–22; and the People's Bank, 117, 121; and Herzen (1849), 119–34, 151; *Carnets,* 133; Hess on, 157–58; and Mazzini, 185; and Herzen-Herwegh conflict, 200, 204, 205, 206–07, 208; and revolutionary moral code, 218
Pushkin, Aleksandr, 104, 227
Pyat, Félix, 15, 40, 113, 115

Quadruple Alliance, 61

Rasch, Gustave, 96, 100
Raspail, François, 81, 116, 119
Reasoner, The, 187
Reeve, Emily, 213
Réforme, La: founding of, 15; Bakunin's and Herwegh's contacts with, 20–21, 73; Bakunin and Polish issue, 24; and Sazonov, 36, 129; and February 1848

INDEX

revolution, 51–52, 54–55; and Proudhon, 114
Réforme, La (Verviers, Belgium), 154
Refugees. *See* Emigrés.
Reichel, Adolf, 19, 38, 74, 176
Reichel, Mariia: departure from Russia of, 30, 173, 238*n*3; and Herzen, 38, 176, 177, 192, 219–20; in Zurich with Kolia, 109, 168
Reichenbach, Oscar, 73
Répresentant du Peuple, Le, 84, 118
Revolutionary internationalism: in 1848, 61, 72; and the May 15 demonstration, 79; and emigration, 96; of *La Tribune des Peuples*, 103–04; and Proudhon, 120, 126; and *La Voix du Peuple*, 124, 128–33; and Mazzini, 179–92
Revue de Genève, La, 110
Revue indépendante, La, 14, 24
Reynolds' Newspaper, 211–12
Rheinische Zeitung, 18–19, 34, 92
Ribeyrolles, Charles, 190, 266*n*69
Romanians, 97, 179
Ronge, Johannes, 182, 190
Rothschild, James, 101, 127, 169
Rouen, 60
Rousseau, Jean-Jacques, 89
Ruge, Arnold: and Bakunin, 7; journalism and political activity of, 17–22, 227; and German radicalism, 26–27; and Müller-Strübing, 33; in the Frankfurt Parliament, 93; and the Second Democratic Congress, 94; and Herzen, 99; and the 13 June 1849 demonstration, 106; emigration of, 178; and European Central Democratic Committee, 179–80, 187; and German National Democratic Committee, 182; and the Communist League, 182; and *La Voix du Proscrit*, 184; cited in police reports, 188, 189; and Herzen-Herwegh conflict, 218–19

Saffi, Aurelio, 113
Saint-Simonism, 13, 15
Sand, George: and French radicalism, 13–15, 222; and Bakunin, 21, 73–74; and Mazzini, 28, 106, 182, 246*n*39; and Ledru-Rollin, 59, 80, 181, 182, 233*n*10; on the May 15 demonstration, 80; on the Roman Republic, 106; *La Petite Fadette*, 163; and émigré politics, 181–82; and revolutionary moral code, 194; and Herzen-Herwegh conflict, 205–06; as Paris notable, 234*n*27; on Proudhon, 257*n*43
Sanders, Jonathan, 190
Satin, Nikolai, 10, 38, 181–82
Saxony, 189
Sazonov, Nikolai: background and family of, 36; and Marx, 36; and Herzen, 37, 77, 95, 100, 240*n*34; club activity of, 66–67; conspiratorial activity of, 99, 100; and *La Tribune des Peuples*, 103–04; and Fazy, 110; and *La Voix du Peuple*, 114, 118–19, 122–24, 126–29; and peasant socialism, 148; and Herzen-Herwegh conflict, 200
Sazonova, Elizaveta, 35
Schapper, Karl, 63, 70, 92, 182
Schurz, Carl, 90, 93, 95, 161, 182, 255*n*22
Secret societies, in French history, 52, 55–56; and Herzen, 96–97
Selivanov, Ivan, 77, 78, 95, 171
Seniavin, L. G., 100
Shchepkin, Dmitrii Mikhailovich, 33
Shchepkin, Mikhail Petrovich, 33, 40, 161
Slav Congress, Prague, 73–74, 103
Slavophiles, 4–5, 8–9, 148, 152
Social Democracy, 226
Society of Seasons (Société des Saisons), 17, 52
Solger, Reinhold, 94, 99, 154, 156, 161
Sovremennik, 12, 39, 233*n*13
Spini, Leopoldo, 46–47, 113, 129
Stankevich, Nikolai, 3–5, 8
Stolzmann, Karl, 183
Struve, Gustave, 27, 71, 111, 112, 113, 130, 182
Sue, Eugène, 15
Sutherland, Mary, 216
Switzerland: history of, 65; Herzen in, 100, 105, 107–32, 138, 168, 174, 205,

216; Linton travel to, 184; revolutionaries in, 110, 189; expulsion of émigrés from, 171, 178; Herzen friends in, 193; Sasha Herzen in, 216. *See also* Emigrés, in Switzerland

Tausenau, Carl, 98–99
Tessié de Motay, Marie Edmond, 208
Thiers, Adolphe, 14, 51
Thomas, Clement, 81
Thoré, Théophile: and *La Vraie République*, 57; on French elections, 59; on May 15 demonstration, 79–80; and Herzen, 88, 120; and Mazzini, 186; on radical notables, 234n27, 257n43; on events of 1847, 241n42
Tolstoi, Lev, 280n1
Tribune des Peuples, La: expulsion of backers of, 98; and Herzen, 100; discussion of, 102–04; collaborators of, 118, 148; internationalism of, 124, 131
Tristan, Flora, 62
True Socialists, 91
Tuchkov, Aleksei: in Italy, 45–47; in Paris, 77; return to Russia of, 86, 95; arrest of, 171
Tuchkova-Ogareva, Natalie, 45, 48, 164, 168, 214–16, 242n57
Tuchkova, Elena, 48
Turgenev, Ivan: and Westernizers, 3–4; and Pauline Viardot, 14; and Bakunin, 19; Paris contacts of, 21; and Herzen, 32–33, 35, 77, 95, 170, 254n100; return to Russia of, 196
Turgenev, Nikolai, 240n33

United States: emigration to, 72; emigration of Struve to, 111; emigration of Fröbel to, 112; possible emigration of Herzen to, 144, 161, 171; emigration of Willich to, 161; utopian colonies in, 162; Kossuth fundraising in, 190; emigration of Kapp to, 252n58
Urquhart, David, 227
Utopian socialism, 162, 194

Varnhagen von Ense, Karl, 73
Vasbenter, Louis, 196

Venetia, 190
Venturi, Franco, 174
Versailles, 130
Veytaux, Switzerland, 168
Viardot, Louis, 14, 21
Viardot, Pauline, 14, 32, 77
Vienna, 73, 94, 98, 221
Vogt, Karl: and Bakunin and Herwegh, 20; in Frankfurt Parliament, 93; in Geneva, 108; and Herzen, 161, 174; police report on, 190; and Herzen-Herwegh conflict, 201, 205, 206; and *Byloe i dumy*, 208; and revolutionary moral code, 219; and Marx-Herzen hostility, 252n59
Voix du Peuple, La: and Herzen, 108, 119, 121, 122, 124, 128–29, 134, 144, 170, 172, 223; and Proudhon, 118; internationalism of, 129–32
Voix du Proscrit, La, 184, 188
Vorwärts, 21–22, 69
Vraie République, La, 57, 61

Wagner, Richard, 74, 205
Weitling, Wilhelm, 16–17, 64, 234n20
Westernizers, 4–11, 152. *See also* Herzen, intellectual background of
Willich, August: and Baden campaign, 72–73; in Cologne, 91; praise of in *La Voix du Peuple*, 130; emigration of, 161, 255n22; and Marx, 182; and Herzen-Herwegh conflict, 206, 208; views of, 250n22
Woinof, Iwan. *See* Sazonov, Ivan
Wolff, Wilhelm, 70
Worcell, Stanislas, 68, 183–84, 192, 218

Young Europe, 23, 61
Young Italy, 23, 28
Young Poland, 23

Zastenker, N. E., 123
Zurich, as German émigré center, 19; Kolia Herzen, Luisa Haag, and Mariia Ern in, 109, 168; Natalie Herzen in, 168; Emma Herwegh in, 173, 198; Herwegh in, 173, 198, 204, 218

PITT SERIES IN RUSSIAN AND EAST EUROPEAN STUDIES
Jonathan Harris, Editor

Building Socialism in Bolshevik Russia: Ideology and Industrial Organization, 1917–1921
Thomas F. Remington

The Distorted World of Soviet Type Economies
Jan Winiecki

Jan Wacław Machajski: A Radical Critic of the Russian Intelligentsia and Socialism
Marshall S. Shatz

Midpassage: Alexander Herzen and European Revolution, 1847–1852
Judith E. Zimmerman

The Moscovia of Antonio Possevino, S.J.
Hugh F. Graham, trans.

Perceptions and Behavior in Soviet Foreign Policy
Richard K. Herrmann

The Russian Empire and Grand Duchy of Muscovy: A Seventeenth-Century French Account
Jacques Margeret (Chester S. L. Dunning, trans.)

The Truth of Authority: Ideology and Communication in the Soviet Union
Thomas F. Remington